Covert Investigation

Third Edition

Clive Harfield
MSc, LLM, MPhil, PhD

and

Karen Harfield
BSc (Hons)

OXFORD
UNIVERSITY PRESS

OXFORD

UNIVERSITY PRESS

Great Clarendon Street, Oxford, OX2 6DP,
United Kingdom

Oxford University Press is a department of the University of Oxford.
It furthers the University's objective of excellence in research, scholarship,
and education by publishing worldwide. Oxford is a registered trade mark of
Oxford University Press in the UK and in certain other countries

First Edition published in 2005
Third Edition published in 2012

Impression: 1

Cover photos: © DigitalVision / Punchstock; Shutterstock; Brand X Pictures /
Punchstock; ImageState / Punchstock; Digital Vision / Punchstock; Shutterstock;
Comstock / Punchstock; Shutterstock; DigitalVision / Punchstock; Dominic Harrison
/ Alamy; Up The Resolution (uptheres) / Alamy; Photodisc / Punchstock

British Library Cataloguing in Publication Data
Data available

Library of Congress Cataloging in Publication Data
Data available

ISBN 978–0–19–964698–2

Printed in Great Britain by
CPI Group (UK) Ltd, Croydon, CR0 4YY

Foreword to the Third Edition

The value of this practical handbook, by my colleague and former colleagues Clive and Karen Harfield, is indicated by my title. This is the third edition, an unprecedented achievement in my experience of the writings for serving police officers and former police academics. Despite being on the other side of the globe their contribution to all that is best, in the application of the British Policing model in the complex shifting moral minefields of covert investigation, continues to be immense. Beyond the achievements and usage I listed in my foreword to the first and second editions I have seen this volume used on training courses, reviews of prosecutions and investigations, in arguments for more robust investigation tactics including in historic cases, in the creation of new tactics and thinking about strategy. For example their work has informed some of the thinking and concepts behind Her Majesty's Chief Inspector of Constabulary's (HMCIC) recent assessment of national policing units concerned with uncovering and preventing criminality associated with public protest (HMCIC 2012, *A review of national police units which provide intelligence on criminality associated with protest*, London, Home Office) following considerable public concern and debate. A lively public debate, which was not least, about the morality of decisions made during, and the ethics of, covert policing.

Whether the reader is a postgraduate serving officer student writing her dissertation, a Chief Officer under pressure to make a decision in a complicated investigation, or a Senior Investigating Officer in search of different investigative strategies in a serious crime case, all will benefit. As ever it is the investigative hunter-gatherers who are closest to my heart, there are many criminals who cannot prey on the vulnerable nor pursue their greed because of the advice obtained by the hunter-gatherers from this book. Good hunting to you all.

John G. D Grieve CBE QPM
Senior Research Fellow University of Portsmouth
Professor Emeritus London Metropolitan University

Acknowledgements

This third edition would not have been possible without the foundations laid in the first edition, therefore those acknowledged previously deserve continued mention. The authors wish to express their appreciation to colleagues in a number of organizations, investigations and discussions with whom informed the writing of this book, and many of whom subsequently commented on early drafts. Others have provided material for study. In particular we thank: Cara Airey, Yvonne Ball, Sue Biddle, Jackie Griffin, Glynis Hooper, Tony Hutchings, Kingsley Hyland, Mick Ives, Simon McKay, Trevor Pearce, Louise Pierpoint, Phil Swinburne, Debbie Tedds, Simon Watkin, Dave Whordley, Katie Whiting, and Tim Wright.

Organizations as well as individuals have provided practical assistance and access to information, as well as permission to reproduce copyright material: Bramshill Police Library (NPIA), the House of Commons Information Office, the National Specialist Law Enforcement Centre (NPIA), and University of Warwick Library.

At Oxford University Press, Katie Allan and Andrea Oliver brought the first edition into being; Peter Daniell, Lindsey Davis, and Jodi Towler, the second; and for their commissioning, assistance and guidance with the third edition we are grateful to Peter Daniell, Lucy Alexander, and Emma Hawes. Their support, patience, and understanding, particularly when unforseen circumstances interrupted revision and production of this third edition, is much appreciated.

Professor Emeritus John Grieve CBE QPM (former Deputy Assistant Commissioner, Metropolitan Police Service and currently Independent Monitoring Commissioner for Northern Ireland), as ever, has been a pillar of strength and support and a source of inspiration.

Contents

Table of Cases

United Kingdom

European Court of Human Rights

France

Table of Legislation

Page references in **bold** indicate that the text is reproduced in full

Regulation of Investigatory Powers Act 2000 (RIPA) Codes of Practice

Abbreviations

AC	Appeal Court
ACPO	Association of Chief Police Officers
All ER	All England law Reports
ANPR	Automatic Number Plate Recognition
CCTV	Closed Circuit Television
CDRP	Crime and Disorder Reduction Partnerships
CHIS	Covert Human Intelligence Source
CMLR	Common Market Law Reports
CPIA	Criminal Procedure and Investigations Act 1996
CPS	Crown Prosecution Service
Cr App R	Criminal Appeal Reports
Crim LR	Criminal Law Review
CSP	Communications Service Provider
ECHR	European Convention on Human Rights 1959
ECtHR	European Court of Human Rights, Strasbourg
EHRLR	European Human Rights Law Review
EHRR	European Human Rights Reports
EWHC	England and Wales High Court
GCHQ	Government Communications Headquarters
Hansard HC	Official Record of the House of Commons
Hansard HL	Official Record of the House of Lords
HMRC	Her Majesty's Revenue and Customs (formerly HMCE—Her Majesty's Customs and Excise)
HRA	Human Rights Act 1998
IOCA	Interception of Communications Act 1985 (repealed)
ISP	Internet Service Provider
JIT	Joint Investigation Team
MI5	Security Service
MI6	Secret Intelligence Service
MOD	Ministry of Defence
NCA	National Crime Authority
NCIS	National Criminal Intelligence Service
NCS	National Crime Squad
NHS	National Health Service
NIM	National Intelligence Model
NOMS	National Offender Management Service

NPIA	National Policing Improvement Agency
NSLEC	National Specialist Law Enforcement Centre
OFT	Office of Fair Trading
OSC	Office of Surveillance Commissioners
PA97	Police Act 1997
PACE	Police and Criminal Evidence Act 1984
PII	Public Interest Immunity
PSNI	Police Service of Northern Ireland
QB	Queen's Bench
RIPA	Regulation of Investigatory Powers Act 2000
SI	Statutory Instrument (secondary legislation supplementing Acts)
SOCA	Serious Organised Crime Agency
SPOC	Single Point of Contact
UKCA	UK Central Authority (department of the Home Office)
WLR	Weekly Law Reports
WTA	Wireless Telegraphy Act 2006

Special Features

This book contains several special features that it is hoped will make it more helpful to the reader. These are defined and explained below.

Case law criteria

Where case law has defined certain tests or criteria to be met in given situations or when considering certain determinations, these are highlighted in case law criteria features.

Checklists of key issues

Where appropriate, chapters conclude with a checklist of key issues that investigators and authorizing officers might usefully consider when planning or managing covert investigations.

Definitions

Definitions of specific terms are provided where this is useful.

Further information and reading

These boxes provide the reader with additional information and direct the reader towards additional reading that will elaborate upon points discussed in the text.

Hints and tips

Good-practice advice is offered where it has developed over time.

Key points

Information requiring particular emphasis is summarized in key points.

PLAN

Supporting the concluding checklists is the mnemonic PLAN, which provides a structure for investigators to use in their policy-books and for authorizing officers to use when structuring their authorizations or refusals.

Scenarios

To illustrate some of the issues discussed in the chapters, example scenarios are presented.

Tables

Some information or concepts have been tabulated for ease of illustration and presentation.

Introduction

This is the book that the authors themselves needed when, as either covert investigation managers, covert human intelligence source (CHIS) controllers, or authorizing officers, they had, in their various professional police roles at local and national levels, daily responsibilities under the Police Act 1997 (PA97) and Regulation of Investigatory Powers Act 2000 (RIPA) for managing covert investigation. As no one else had yet written it, they decided to do so themselves on the premise that others performing similar roles would probably also appreciate such a book. The continuing success of the early editions of this book would appear to support this rationale. The intention is to provide those responsible for planning, executing, and overseeing covert investigations with an introduction to covert investigation law and practical considerations that follow on from it when trying to conduct or supervise such operations. For obvious reasons discussion will stop short of disclosing specific sensitive tactics and techniques. For reasons of space, the complex arena of covert financial investigation, a specialist field in its own right, has not been addressed.

Covert investigation law in the UK is nothing if not complicated (it may come as scant consolation for British readers to learn that the Australian covert investigation statutory regime is even more complicated and fragmentary). Besides statute law, certain aspects of covert investigation, the use of informers for example, have a long history of case law. Other aspects have very little or as yet no significant case law to provide additional illumination. There are arguments to suggest that this whole body of law is incomplete and inconsistent. The implications of this for investigators will at least be highlighted even though the issues may be beyond resolution here. Interpretations of the various statutory powers vary from one expert to another and from one organization policy to another, indicating that covert investigation law is far from being the precise and unambiguous instrument that all criminal justice practitioners need it to be. Clarke LJ described RIPA as a 'very puzzling statute' (*R v W, Attorney-General's Reference (No. 5 of 2002)* [2003] EWCA Crim 1632 at para 98).

Notwithstanding that it is difficult to disagree with this analysis, the ambitious objective of this book is to provide an introduction to this arena that contributes to making these statutory powers less puzzling for investigators to understand and use.

The principal audience for this book, then, are the investigators and authorizing officers in the many hundreds of public authorities empowered to deploy some or all of the covert investigation powers provided for in both the PA97 and RIPA. The book has been structured with these readers in mind: plain English explanations cross-referenced against original texts; case law citation and interpretation; operational considerations; and extracts of the relevant legislation, both primary and secondary, together with relevant Codes of Practice, all between two covers. But it is anticipated that others will also find this work of value.

Trainee investigators and an academic audience (in the fields of law, criminology, police studies, politics, and social administration, for instance) will also find this a useful introduction to the statutory framework underpinning the use of covert investigation methods. With this audience in mind, further information references have been included to guide readers towards detailed academic arguments that practitioners may not necessarily wish to follow up. Expert commentary on covert investigation law and policy ranges from the broadly supportive to arguments that suggest the law not only fails to give sufficient effect to human rights principles, but even undermines long-established protections in procedural law governing more conventional methods of investigation (D Ormerod, 'ECHR and the exclusion of evidence: trial remedies for Article 8 breaches?' [2003] Crim LR 61, 62). Since the second edition of this volume came out, Simon McKay has published a significant addition to the available legal commentary with his forensic and insightful analysis of the construction of covert investigation law in the UK (*Covert Policing: Law and Practice*, Oxford University Press, Oxford, 2011). Amongst other discussions, McKay unpicks the confused structure of RIPA and argues that the legislation—which 'only regulates activities that are used in support of substantive investigations'—needs to be studied in a three-part framework that encompasses conceptual, substantive, and practical/operational aspects (McKay Chapter 1, particularly p. 14). McKay's audience is as much the Parliamentarian and the policy-maker as it is the legal practitioner. Law enforcement practitioners will discover between the covers comprehensive and provocative discussion that goes beyond the scope possible to achieve in the Blackstone's Practical Policing series.

The chapter structure employed in the Blackstone's Practical Policing volume is thematic. The statutory context is presented as an introduction before different aspects of covert investigation are considered in turn. Investigators are required to use the least intrusive means of investigation that will achieve their objective. Accordingly the chapters are arranged in order of increasing intrusion. The volume ends with discussions on risk assessment and covert investigation management which, based on the authors' operational supervisory experience, are areas often overlooked by investigators.

Chapters are structured around questions that have been frequently debated by colleagues. Because each chapter is intended to be a self-sufficient reference guide, readers of the entire volume will notice that repetition of some points has been preferred to cross-referencing within this volume; an approach consistent with the preference of the publishers. Various features (definition boxes, bullet point lists, key points) have been included in the chapters to render the information more readily accessible and digestible. The information is up to date as of December 2011. This arena continues to develop both through case law and statute and over ten years on since coming into force RIPA continues to ignite different and sometimes contradictory interpretations. Gradually the body of case law, which must be considered the definitive interpretation of the statute alongside the statute itself, is growing but this incremental accumulation is slow. The reality is that many issues which might be challenged have not yet been scrutinized by the courts.

Government and Parliament have striven, and continue to strive, to facilitate the more effective investigation of crime, within the context of perceived new criminal threats and trends, whilst at the same time eliminating abuses of power by investigators. The ever-increasing sophistication and scale of the criminal threat to society is argued as the justification for enacting enhanced investigation powers (Home Secretary Jack Straw MP, opening the Second Reading Debate on the Regulation of Investigatory Powers Bill, *Hansard* HC (series 6) vol 345 col 768 (6 March 2000)). The investigation methods given parliamentary authority in 1997 and 2000 were not new; what was new was their statutory foundation to ensure investigators had a legal basis for their work and regulation as a means to protect the citizen against abuse of power. Parliament enacted the powers within the British tradition of investigator autonomy. In other words, the role of the Procurator-Fiscal in Scotland aside, there is no British equivalent to the European investigating magistrate or American District Attorney overseeing criminal investigations (although in practice early consultation between investigators and the relevant prosecuting authority will benefit British investigators). British public authorities trusted and empowered with investigation and enforcement responsibilities are expected to regulate their own behaviour, only the application for search warrants and the continued detention of suspects being subject to judicial authority. Such autonomy is a privilege vulnerable to abuse, either through deliberate act or lack of awareness and competence.

Covert investigation methods often provide incontrovertible evidence because of the level of intrusion by investigators into the private lives of citizens. Such intrusion is only permitted within strict statutory and procedural frameworks and, for a defendant faced with incontrovertible evidence, the only defence strategy left available in the adversarial trial system is to attack investigation procedure and seek exclusion of the incontrovertible evidence on the basis that it was unfairly obtained and prejudicial to the defendant.

It is hoped that this volume, now in a revised third edition, will increase investigator and senior manager awareness in order to minimize the risk of unwitting abuse of these powers and to minimize the misuse of procedure leading to technical acquittals of defendants against whom the evidence is strong enough to convict. The latter will fail society by not protecting citizens from crime and the former will fail society by not protecting citizens from abuse of authority. This consequence could persuade Parliament to reconsider the powers invested in investigators.

Publisher as well practitioner needs have informed this third edition. To minimize production costs (and thus maintain an attractive retail price) it has been necessary to omit some material that featured in previous editions. The first two editions contained in appendices sizeable relevant extracts of both RIPA and the Police Act 1997, updated by the authors because at that time there were no consolidated texts of the Acts as amended. With the establishment of the government website <http://www.legislation.gov.uk>, there now exists a ready means for readers to access the latest available version of each law as amended. The website gives each law both as originally enacted and as subsequently amended. Where there are outstanding amendments still to be updated on the website, this is indicated. Thus there is no longer a need to include consolidated extracts in this volume.

At the time of the second edition a major review of RIPA was under way. This has now been completed and as a consequence the codes of practice originally published pursuant to s 71 RIPA have been revised, significantly elaborated, and additional codes have been published. At the time of writing this third edition, the Interception Code of Practice is being revised and updated (the version which is currently online is the original version). The latest available codes of practice (as published online) are reproduced here in appendices A to E because experience and anecdotal evidence suggests that the codes are not as widely accessible as they could be and so there remains an argument to retain them as appendices in this edition for the purposes of ready reference. Investigators are more likely to need daily ready reference to a code of practice than they are to need daily ready reference to statute. The chapters of this book make extensive cross-reference to the codes.

The revised and new codes of practice incorporate example scenarios. Accordingly we have omitted from this edition many of the example scenarios included in previous editions. There is clearly no need to have such scenarios in both the main text and the appendices. Those that remain in the main text have been reviewed and revised to take into account comments made by the Chief Surveillance Commissioner about the inclusion of scenarios in the codes of practice. The intention of this volume has always been to provide investigators, authorizing officers, and others with an interest in covert investigation with a structure for consideration of the issues arising. Statute and case law remain the definitive guides to what is and is not permitted. No book or code can anticipate all the permutations that will confront investigators on a daily basis but by offering frameworks for practitioner consideration based on our own observations and the documented observations of others, this volume aims to assist investigators in finding their own way through the maze of covert investigation.

Hint and tip: At the time of writing (December 2011), two further significant changes affecting the covert investigation regime are anticipated. The Protection of Freedoms Bill is being debated in Parliament and contains a proposal to change the directed surveillance authorization regime for local councils from one of self-authorization to judicial authorization (upon application to magistrates). The second change likely to occur during the shelf-life of this edition is the abolition of the Serious Organised Crime Agency (SOCA) and the coming into operation of the National Crime Authority (NCA). Whilst the future will of Parliament cannot be predicted with certainty, were precedent (the change from the National Crime Squad to SOCA) to be followed it is likely that those covert investigation powers and responsibilities currently invested in SOCA would pass to the NCA.

The Association of Chief Police Officers (ACPO), in association with the National Centre for Policing Excellence, published *Practice Advice on Core Investigative Doctrine* in 2005 (whilst the first edition of this book was being produced)—the first time that the police service has defined investigative doctrine. The principles outlined on page 103 of the doctrine, regarding covert policing, are equally applicable to non-police investigators undertaking covert investigation. They bear quotation here, providing the doctrinal context within which this book should be read and to which this book seeks to make a contribution.

Principles underpinning a covert investigation strategy which investigators should consider

- Have a good working knowledge of intelligence processes and the National Intelligence Model.
- Become fully cognizant of all current, pertinent intelligence material prior to the instigation of an operation.
- Anticipate the need for covert policing and make early and timely bids for such resources (failure to make an early request may undermine the investigation and valuable material may be lost).
- Ensure that the covert policing strategy is proportionate to the overall objectives of the investigation.
- Know how to obtain advice and guidance for covert options.
- Have a thorough understanding of RIPA and the relevant aspects of the Police Act 1997.
- Understand Public Interest Immunity procedures and legislation, and the Criminal Procedure and Investigations Act.
- Ensure that operations are run on a 'need-to-know basis' and that operational security is maintained at all times.
- Consult the Crown Prosecution Service at the earliest opportunity (in more complex cases this may be prior to the commencement of the operation).
- Establish a review mechanism if necessary. In serious or complex investigations which involve a high degree of risk, a senior officer must authorize and/or review all operations.

Covert Investigation in Context

1.1 **Introduction**

This chapter outlines the political and statutory context within which covert investigation law has developed in the UK. For the purpose of this book, 'covert investigation' is investigation of which the suspect is assumed to be unaware and which infringes upon the private life of the suspect. Primarily this means some form of active surveillance in support of a substantive investigation. Whilst this will usually be proactive investigation into crimes in progress or incomplete offences, there will be occasions when covert methods are used during a reactive investigation into reported or discovered crime. Covert investigation methods can also be deployed to acquire intelligence to inform crime management (including investigation) within the National Intelligence Model (NIM).

Further information and reading

Guidance on the NIM published by the Association of Chief Police Officers is available online at <http://www.acpo.police.uk/documents/information/2010/2 01004INFMOPI01.pdf>.

Information about NIM from the National Policing Improvement Agency is available at <http://www.npia.police.uk/en/9015.htm>.

The NIM Code of Practice is available at <http://www.npia.police.uk/en/docs/ National_Intelligence_Model_C_of_P.pdf>.

(All URLs accessed December 2011.)

The use of surveillance to gather information that may prove useful in the future is not uncontroversial. Equally of concern to some is the fact that 'covert surveillance may be used as much to prevent civil disorder and disobedience, or to effect public compliance in respect of the payment of government taxes and duties, as to deal with criminal conduct' (S Sharpe, 'Covert surveillance and the use of informants' in M McConville and G Wilson (eds), *The Handbook of the Criminal Justice Process* (Oxford University Press, Oxford, 2002) 59–73, 65).

1.2 **Why Investigate Covertly?**

Prevention is argued to be better (and cheaper) than cure. Crime prevention is, and always has been, as much if not more of a priority for UK enforcement authorities than is the investigation of offences committed (see, for instance, C Emsley, *The English Police: A Political and Social History* (2nd edn, Longman, London, 1996) 25). Overt, high-visibility policing, in its widest sense whether undertaken by police officers, community support officers, local authority wardens, customs officers or private sector security firms for instance, is premised upon the prevention of crime and reassuring the public: the deterrence and disruption of disorder by means of physical presence. Such overt activity engages the first and basic level of accountability since it takes place in the public arena, open to witness by the average citizen whose perception of reasonableness is what the law seeks to represent and what the courts seek to interpret.

By definition, a priority with such a visible objective cannot be achieved by covert means, but covert investigation has both a preventative and evidential role. It is the means by which evidence that would not otherwise be open to third-party witnesses can be gathered by investigators in order to support a prosecution. In investigations involving serious and/or organized crimes which are as yet incomplete, it can be the means by which investigators can gather sufficient evidence to prosecute for preliminary offences, whilst at the same time being able to intervene before a more serious offence is committed or at a time before the harmful consequences of an offence take effect.

For example, the trafficking or manufacture of illicit drugs are offences in which the immediate victims, drug users, are very unlikely to report the matter to enforcement authorities voluntarily because in possessing illegal drugs they are themselves committing an offence. The extent to which they can provide evidence against the organized crime syndicates supplying the drugs is limited because the street dealer who deals to the user is likely to be far removed in the criminal commercial chain from the importer profiting by trafficking. Prosecuting minor actors in the criminal chain will neither disrupt nor prevent the drug importation or manufacture nor reduce the harm to wider society. Covert investigation methods can be used to secure evidence of manufacture, importation, and distribution that would not otherwise be available to prosecuting authorities. The ideal outcome for investigators in such instances would be to intervene at the point at which they had acquired sufficient evidence to prosecute, but before the imported or manufactured narcotics had been made available to users who would suffer harm from such use, and who might themselves commit acquisitive crime (so creating more, indirect victims, thus increasing the overall harm caused) in order to fund their drug dependency. Covert investigation is considered to be the means by which such a successful outcome, evidential and preventative, can be achieved.

In this example, whereas overt policing as described above might deter or disrupt street dealing of illicit drugs, covert investigation is the only realistic means of prosecuting and preventing, through network disruption and dismantling, the manufacture or importation and distribution that precedes the street dealing and end-user harm.

Whilst not normally deployed in the reactive investigation of reported crimes, covert investigation methods can occasionally provide useful supporting evidence or intelligence that generates opportunities to secure such evidence. Because the crime has already occurred, subsequent proactive covert investigation is unlikely to produce direct evidence of the crime itself, but it can provide evidence in relation to the suspect that could support the main contention of the prosecution.

Covert investigation can be used to acquire evidence to support a prosecution in circumstances where the nature of the evidence means that it cannot be secured by conventional overt means. Covert investigation might also be required to identify or confirm the true nature of a defendant's assets for asset recovery purposes where it is suspected that criminal profits were being laundered.

Amongst non-police agencies empowered to conduct covert surveillance (the Regulation of Investigatory Powers (Directed Surveillance and Covert Human Intelligence Sources) Order 2003 (SI 2003/3171) (as amended), restricts such surveillance by most authorities to the sole purpose of preventing and detecting crime), local authority use of CCTV, if targeted at particular individuals for the purpose of an investigation, constitutes activity requiring a RIPA authority. Close liaison with police forces in connection with the use of CCTV can complicate matters, with circumstances arising in which both the police and the local authority require individual RIPA authorities for one given act of surveillance. Partnership protocols are a useful means of identifying issues of responsibility and liability in given circumstances.

Further information and reading

The Information Commissioner has published a Code of Practice on the use of CCTV systems which is available online at <http://www.ico.gov.uk/upload/documents/library/data_protection/detailed_specialist_guides/ico_cctvfinal_2301.pdf> (accessed December 2011).

On the basis of OSC inspections and reviews of the operation of RIPA, some public authorities originally empowered to conduct covert investigation have been removed from the legislation. These authorities had not made use of the available powers thus demonstrating that the powers were not really needed for the work of these particular authorities. Before Parliament at the time of writing (December 2011), the Protection of Freedoms Bill, if enacted, will remove the facility of self-authorization of directed surveillance from local authorities, replacing it with a judicial authorization regime based on the magistracy. In this eventuality two different authorization regimes for directed surveillance will co-exist. This development is a response to political concerns about the use to which local authorities have been putting their covert investigation powers.

Further information and reading

David Ormerod, Professor of Criminal Law, University of Leeds, writing on 'Recent developments in entrapment', *Covert Policing Review* (2006), 65–86, notes with some concern the increasing attraction to police of covert investigation (at 66–67):

    a) As coercive policing is subjected to ever greater regulation, there is an understandable desire from police officers to circumvent the restrictions and "red tape";

---

b) Police are under ever greater pressure to "crack" serious crime and meet targets;

c) Police protocols and policies now explicitly incorporate intelligence models;

d) Covert policing was/is less well regulated than coercive policing and there may be a perception that there will be a greater willingness from the courts to accommodate such deceptive practices;

e) Suspects have become increasingly aware of coercive police practices, and of their "rights". They also have become increasingly aware of surveillance generally;

f) Suspects have earlier and more proactive defence representation;

g) Criminals have become more sophisticated. This is a dangerous argument. Criminals have always been sophisticated. It is all too easy to rely on such unsubstantiated claims as a way of justifying the means to the ends in policing;

h) Policing in the 21st century more commonly involves detecting and investigating types of crime in which there is no "victim" who is likely, or disturbingly, willing to trigger a coercive or reactive police investigation. These are crimes in which the police have to be more proactive if they are to succeed. [...];

i) The widespread and publicly acknowledged use of covert policing methods frustrates criminal activity by deterring criminals and imposing obligations of counter-surveillance on organized criminals;

j) As the pressure to rely on such methods of policing increases, so too do the dangers. As a matter of principle it is wrong for police to be permitted to break the law to catch criminals. The rule of law is sacrosanct. It is therefore vital that the law defines the limits of police conduct, particularly in entrapment where the police must be most proactive.

For all the increasing attraction covert methods might hold for investigators, statistics published annually in the Chief Surveillance Commissioner's Annual Reports indicate a current downward trend in law enforcement recourse to covert methods; a trend mirrored amongst other public authorities following a surge in enthusiasm in the reporting year 2006–07. No detailed analysis of this apparent trend is attempted here but possible explanations that might be explored elsewhere include decreasing resources available for covert investigation (including decreasing numbers of suitably trained investigators); the growing realization based on experience that covert investigation is not a panacea that will exponentially improve detection figures; and the possibility that the historical prominence of the conventional, community policing paradigm (policing *with* the community rather than policing *of* the community) is re-emerging to counter-balance the significant securitization of policing in the immediate aftermath of the September 2001 terrorist attacks in the USA.

Table 1.1 New authorizations for covert investigation as reported in OSC Annual Reports published on the OSC website

Year	Part III PA97	Intrusive surveillance	Directed surveillance (Law enforcement)	Directed surveillance (Public authority	CHIS recruited (law enforcement)	CHIS recruited (Public authority)
2002/03	2511	479	26400		5900	
2003/04	2483	447	26986	6398	5907	273
2004/05	2210	461	25518	6110	4980	308
2005/06	2310	450	23628	6924	4559	437
2006/07	2311	350	19651	12494	4373	492
2007/08	2493	355	18767	9535	4498	204
2008/09	2681	384	16118	9894	4278	234
2009/10	2705	384[1]	15285	8477	5320	229
2010/11	2701	398	13780	8477[2]	4176	234

[1] The fact that the number of new applications in 2009–10 was the same as in the previous year is specifically commented upon in the OSC Annual Report 2009–10.
[2] Paragraph 4.8 of the 2010–2011 OSC Annual Report so closely resembles paragraph 4.7 of the 2009–2010 annual report in some of its text and key particulars that (in the absence of further explanation) the possibility cannot be excluded that a printing error has occurred and that they are in fact two versions of the same paragraph.

1.3 What Are the Issues Arising from Covert Investigation?

Further information and reading

The benefits to the police and other security and law enforcement agencies in their work to prevent and investigate serious crime and protect the public can far exceed those of surveillance for other purposes. But the consequences of decisions made on the basis of inaccurate information or wrong assumptions or of a leak of information are more serious. Moreover, where surveillance has to be carried out without the consent or knowledge of the individual, it is more intrusive.

Home Affairs Committee, *A Surveillance Society?* Fifth Report of Session 2007–08, HC58i & HC58ii (London, TSO, 2008), para 199.

The significant benefit covert investigation offers is that it produces evidence that is often considered to be incontrovertible. Although additional evidence might be necessary to prove the relevance of any given observed event or meeting, the fact that the participants were observed doing what they were doing cannot be contradicted. Investigation subjects incriminate themselves without realizing it, severely compromising their right to non-self-incrimination at trial. In regulating overt investigation, the Police and Criminal Evidence Act 1984 (PACE) ensures that subjects, even if they do not co-operate, are aware of investigative actions that are happening or have taken place. Such due process ensures that investigators do not act unlawfully, or provide protections if they do (Sharpe, 'Covert surveillance', 59–73, 65).

Within the context of due process protection, preserving the integrity of the criminal justice system is the key issue arising from the use of covert investigation. Investigators, because they are acting outside the public arena, must be capable of being held to account for their actions by other means. As much as the citizen wishes to be protected from being harmed by crime, agents within the criminal justice system must not abuse their powers and authority in providing that protection. The secrecy of covert investigation limits the ways in which investigators can be managed and held to account. Equally important in protecting the integrity of the criminal justice system is protecting investigators from malicious allegations that they have acted improperly.

Thus four principles can be said to underpin the management and regulation of covert investigation undertaken to detect and prosecute crime:

- evidence to sustain a prosecution or intelligence to facilitate criminal investigation management must be obtained in a manner that preserves the integrity of the criminal justice system and its actors;
- statutory rights of the suspect must not be breached except where there is statutory provision to do so;
- the rights and privacy of other citizens not suspected of criminal involvement must be protected and collateral harm as a consequence of covert investigation should be minimized through effective investigation management;
- the professional integrity of investigators must be demonstrated or, if necessary, its absence exposed.

Further information and reading

These four principles and the context in which they apply are considered further in C Harfield, 'The governance of covert investigation', Melbourne University Law Review, 34(3) 2010, pp. 773–804, which compares contrasting governance frameworks for covert investigation in England and Wales and New South Wales (Australia).

Covert investigation intrudes upon the private lives of individuals. Respect for private life is an obligation imposed upon UK public authorities by virtue of two legal instruments, the 1950 European Convention for the Protection of Human Rights and Fundamental Freedoms (hereafter ECHR; opened for signature at Rome, 4 November 1950; TS 71 (1953); Cmd 8969, as amended by Protocol Number 11, which entered into force on 1 November 1998) and s 6 Human Rights Act 1998 (HRA) which makes it unlawful for UK public authorities (including those who act on their behalf, s 6(3)(b)) 'to act in a way which is incompatible with a Convention right'. The right in question is outlined in Article 8(1) ECHR:

> Everyone has the right to respect for his private and family life, his home and his correspondence.

This is reinforced by Article 1 of the First Protocol to the ECHR set down in Paris, 20 November 1952:

> Every natural and legal person is entitled to the peaceful enjoyment of his possessions.

'It would be a strange reflection on our law if a man who had admitted his participation in the illegal importation of a large quantity of heroin should have his conviction set aside on the grounds that his privacy has been invaded', observed Lord Nolan (*R v Khan* [1997] AC 558); see also *Attorney-General's Reference (No. 3 of 1999)* [2001] 2 AC 91, which asserted that the interests of crime victims and the public should be taken into account).

And indeed that is not the intention of the ECHR because the right to respect for private life is qualified by Article 8(2). In certain circumstances public authorities can breach the Article 8(1) right:

> There shall be no interference by a public authority with the exercise of this right except such as is in accordance with the law and is necessary in a democratic society in the interests of national security, public safety or the economic well-being of the country, for the prevention of disorder or crime, for the protection of health and morals, or for the protection of the rights and freedoms of others.

Article 1, Protocol 1, ECHR is similarly qualified:

> No one shall be deprived of his possessions except in the public interest and subject to the conditions provided for by law and by the general principles of international law.

Further information and reading

Protocol 1 provides 'public interest' as grounds justifying deprivation of property. There is no similar justification for intrusion into private life in Article 8. A Ashworth, *Human Rights, Serious Crime and Criminal Procedure* (Sweet & Maxwell, London, 2002), particularly Chapters 2 and 3, provides a comprehensive discussion of 'public interest' in the context of covert investigation.

Thus investigators planning covert operations or managers supervising or authorizing such activity know from the outset that such investigation is likely to breach Article 8(1), given domestic effect in UK law by s 6 HRA, and that they can only proceed in certain prescribed circumstances which have come to be considered by the European Court of Human Rights at Strasbourg (hereafter ECtHR) in a framework of sequential tests:

(1) Does the investigative act fall within the scope of Article 8? (1.7.1)
(2) If yes, has the Article 8 right been interfered with by a Public Authority? (1.7.2)
(3) If it has, was this interference in accordance with the law? (1.7.3)
(4) If it was lawful, was the interference pursuant to a legitimate aim as identified in Article 8(2)? (1.7.4)
(5) Even if it was both lawful and pursuant to a legitimate aim, was it still necessary, and no more than necessary (ie proportionate), in a democratic society? (1.7.5)

Investigators must comply with these tests, which are discussed in detail later in this chapter, and defendants will seek to disrupt a prosecution by arguing that tests 1 and 2 have been met but that one or more of tests 3, 4, and 5 have not.

1.4 What Benefits and Disadvantages Arise from the UK Regulatory Regime?

The role played by continental prosecutors (usually a branch of the judiciary or else trained as judges) and investigating magistrates (where such a role exists) means that continental investigators nearly always have some form of judicial supervision, particularly for methods likely to engage ECHR rights. The advantage of judicial oversight is that it is considered to be a guarantor of the integrity of the criminal justice system and a means of ensuring that investigators do not act unfairly or unlawfully. Many have argued for judicial oversight of covert investigation within the UK, which would put covert investigation on a par with overt coercive investigation methods, such as the execution of production orders and search warrants which require judicial authority and which, so it is argued, is necessary in order to comply with ECHR. Self-regulation by investigators is as a mechanism vulnerable either to deliberate abuse or to ignorance and inadequate training.

Parliament has established a number of different supervisory regimes tailored to different aspects of covert investigation. These will be detailed in turn in subsequent chapters. It is sufficient to say here that an Office of Surveillance Commissioners (OSC), headed by a Chief Surveillance Commissioner assisted by a number of Commissioners (all of whom have held high judicial office) and Inspectors, has been set up to oversee the use of covert investigation in the UK. Oversight is managed by annual inspections, notification of authorities, and in certain types of investigation prior approval for proposed actions.

This approach has its critics. Whilst declaring a preference for judicial supervision, the ECtHR nevertheless found parliamentary oversight and independent scrutiny of investigator self-regulation, particularly if undertaken by persons with judicial experience, to be an acceptable alternative to direct judicial supervision and therefore such a regime is therefore compliant with Article 8(2). This principle, applied by the ECtHR in *Klass v Germany* (1979–80) 2 EHRR 214, 235, was reinforced in respect of the inspection and review regime for IOCA 1985, and subsequently reproduced with slight variations in the PA97 and RIPA, by *Esbester v UK* (1994) 18 EHRR CD 72 (see also *Christie v UK* (1993) 78-A DR 119; *R v Lawrence* [2002] Crim LR 584; and G Ferguson and J Wadham, 103), although elsewhere differently structured internal authorization regimes have been found to be inconsistent with the rule of law (*Kopp v Switzerland* (1999) 27 EHRR 91).

Further information and reading

- A Ashworth, *Human Rights, Serious Crime and Criminal Procedure* (Sweet & Maxwell, London, 2002) Chapter 2, for a discussion of the debate and various authorities.
- G Ferguson and J Wadham, 'Privacy and surveillance: a review of the Regulation of the Investigatory Powers Act 2000' [sic] EHRLR (2003) Special Issue 101, for a further general introductory discussion of the issues.
- S McKay, *Covert Policing: Law and Practice* (Oxford University Press, Oxford, 2011), Chapter 1 for a general introduction to covert policing law and the proposal of a specific analytical framework with which to examine the mechanics of RIPA.
- M Seneviratne, 'Policing the police in the United Kingdom', *Policing and Society* 14(4) (2004), 329–347, for discussion about the pitfalls of self-regulation and how these can be overcome.

The regulatory regime, if not judicial, should be independent from the investigating authorities and must be seen to be guarding against the abuse of powers by investigators. This has translated itself into what many investigators regard as a bureaucratic nightmare of form-filling.

The process of seeking written authority:

- helps investigators structure their operations appropriately
- enables authorizing officers to demonstrate how they have considered the issues of privacy, legitimacy, necessity, and proportionality
- records the decision-making process throughout an investigation
- is a substitute for alternative methods of due process control.

It is a means by which not only the justifications for breaching ECHR qualified rights are recorded in a transparent form, but also by which the investigator can be protected from subsequent allegations of abuse of authority and malpractice.

Self-regulation subject to scrutiny arguably is a more flexible authority regime, from the operational perspective, than one requiring investigators to go to court on a regular basis, perhaps as often as several times a day, to seek a judicial warrant for the investigative activity to be employed, which for many would provide a greater guarantee of rights protection. The current authority regime seeks to balance the need for operational flexibility and responsiveness against the obligation to protect citizens' rights. It gives investigators a flexibility they would certainly miss if it was withdrawn, and being asked to account for their actions in writing could be seen as a small price to pay for such an operational advantage.

But there are practical problems that should be acknowledged by investigators, authorizing officers, their senior executives, and by external commentators. To use a police example: authorizing officers in the Serious Organised Crime Agency deal with covert investigation daily, are very experienced in considering the human rights issues, and have become very familiar with the provisions of the PA97 and RIPA. Their opposite numbers in territorial local policing, by and large, do not have the same daily operational familiarity with covert investigation and not infrequently have additional authorizing duties under PACE as well as a wider range of managerial and community issues to deal with, all of which place competing demands on their time in addition to their RIPA obligations. It is not unknown for a Superintendent to find him- or herself in a position in which the demands of the authorizing officer role protecting human rights and ensuring the integrity of an investigation appear to conflict with the demands of their performance management role in meeting monthly targets: 'force strategic priorities and cost-effectiveness, of themselves, provide insufficient basis for authorization' (OSC *Annual Report 2009–10*, para 5.8; see also OSC *Annual Report 2008–09*, para 5.26). Authorizing officers in other public-sector organizations similarly have other duties competing with their RIPA obligations for attention and time, and the lack of adequate training and daily experience of authorizing surveillance amongst non-police authorizing officers has been commented upon in the OSC *Annual Reports 2005–06* and *2006–07*, although the Chief Commissioner also noted that lack of experience as a consequence of lack of use of covert investigation powers is also a consequence of complying with the principle that covert investigation is a matter of last resort (OSC *Annual Report 2008–09*, para 5.4 with comment on the dividend from investment in training at para 5.27).

All of this appears to reinforce the jurist argument that supervision of covert investigation should be confined to the courts. But there are a number of wider issues that militate against such a move. Leaving aside the overarching issue of how much surveillance is desirable in any given society, the amount currently being undertaken in the UK, based on the annual reports of the Office of Surveillance Commissioners, could fundamentally alter the relationship of the judiciary to the trial process. For instance, issuing a search warrant for a specific item or items of known evidence in order to render it accessible at trial tends to be a single event; however, a covert investigation operation is an entire sequence of related events intended to identify evidence, and so judicial oversight would involve a greater degree of investigation management. To some this might be desirable, but it would reduce the independence of the judiciary from the pre-trial process.

The second wider consideration concerns promotion of the rights culture and integrity of the criminal justice system. Why confine to the judiciary pre-trial consideration (as well as final determination at trial) of how the rights of an individual suspect should be balanced against the rights of the wider community and the powers of the State acting on behalf of the wider community? Investigators who daily might take actions that engage the ECHR rights of an individual should themselves be engaged in identifying how those rights ought to be protected and how any necessary breaches of qualified rights can be mini-mized. Rather than abdicating such decision-making to others, self-regulation (subject to external scrutiny) affords the opportunity to increase the profession-alism of investigators and helps to instil in state agents the very values that the ECHR seeks to protect. It forces investigators and authorizing officers to confront the ECHR daily. The concepts, which would otherwise remain remote arguments at *voir dire* become ingrained in the daily thinking of investigation practitioners and managers. Within such an approach the trial process, adjudicated by the judiciary, remains the final guarantee of individual rights, independent from the investigation process.

Confronting such issues imposes upon those empowered to resort to covert investigation the obligation to be well-versed in the appropriate legislation and the interpretation placed on the statutes by the courts. Thus the starting point for any investigator or authorizing officer is the primary and secondary legislation (the statute and any supporting statutory instruments), supplemented by case law. The latest available versions of UK statutes will be found online at <http://www.legislation.gov.uk/>, a database searchable by title and year. The website indicates where amendments have been enacted but the online version of the act has not yet been updated. Statutory instruments are to be found online at <http://www.legislation.gov.uk/uksi>. (Both sites accessed 24 November 2011.)

Further information and reading

Relevant legislation and case law can also be accessed via the following subscrip-tion websites: <http://www.westlaw.co.uk> or, <http://www.lexisnexis. co.uk>; or via the following free (at the time of writing) website: <http://www.bailii.org>.

1.5 Key Actors in the Self-authorization of Covert Investigation

In the self-authorization regime there are two key actors: the *applicant* and the *authorizing officer*. As a matter of organizational process individual agencies may insert a gatekeeping role between these two with the remit to quality-assure applications before they are considered by the authorizing officer but in terms of delivering statutory obligations, it is the applicant and the authorizing officer upon whom responsibilities fall in the self-authorization process.

It is important not to confuse the roles of applicant and authorizing officer. The roles are distinct but can become blurred, particularly if the application process is automated and computerized for the purposes of process management and creating supporting documentation as the application proceeds. It is the applicant and authorizing officer who stand to be cross-examined in court about the application and the authority (although it is the gatekeeper who is most likely to face the annual OSC inspection team).

Given their particular responsibilities, authorizing officers will wish to be wary of accepting applications on face value without careful scrutiny. An applicant may well have considered issues of legitimacy, necessity, and proportionality in the body of the application, but authorizing officers have a legal duty to consider such matters for themselves and will undoubtedly bring additional perspective to such consideration. An authorizing officer who merely rubber-stamps the application will not have discharged his or her legal obligation under the Act.

At the risk of over-simplification but for the purposes of introductory illustration, the key roles are distinguished in Table 1.2 below which identifies (for the purpose of elucidating the distinction) four sequential management stages of the overall application/authorization/review process.

1.6 Is Authorization Necessary?

There has been much police practitioner concern about the perceived bureaucracy inherent in authorizing covert investigation. This issue featured prominently in the Home Office/ACPO review of RIPA which reported in 2005. (The review has not been published but a redacted copy has been lodged in the House of Commons Library for the benefit of Parliamentarians, *Hansard* HC, 20 June 2007, col 1967W; see also Home Affairs Committee, *A Surveillance Society?* Fifth Report of Session 2007–08, HC58i & HC58ii (London, TSO, 2008), starting at para 311.) Home Office opinion, supported by the OSC and by HM Chief Inspector of Constabulary Sir Ronnie Flanagan in his 2008 *Review of Policing: Final Report* (para 5.55), was that police forces, through their desire to be thorough in their accountability, had over-complicated their own procedures and that significant duplication was involved in the police authorizing processes that had evolved. This can, perhaps, be explained in part by the police service and other public authorities coming to terms with very new and radically different legislation which even such authorities as the Law Lords have found difficult to interpret.

The use of covert investigation does not automatically require authorization. RIPA is not a law that manages covert actions; it is a law that renders lawful and compliant covert actions in circumstances where Article 8 ECHR rights are engaged. 'Where *directed* surveillance would not be likely to result in the obtaining of any private information about a person, no interference with Article 8 rights occurs and an authorization under the 2000 Act is therefore not appropriate' (*Covert Surveillance and Property Interference: Revised Code of Practice* para 1.14).

Table 1.2 The roles of applicant and authorizing officer distinguished

Applicant role	Authorizing officer role
First stage—application	**Second stage—initial authorization**
Identify intelligence/evidence gap required to be filled.	Do not rubber-stamp the application: actively consider what is being requested. Be prepared to authorize less than is being sought. Test all assumptions relied upon in the application. Read all the intelligence reports relied upon.
Document and demonstrate the gap and why the desired information is relevant and important to the ongoing investigation.	The application may look similar to others but how is it different and what individual considerations will this difference demand in considering and, if approved, phrasing the authorization?
Seek advice about and consider all possible solutions.	Have *less intrusive methods been attempted* to obtain the desired information/evidence? (What were they?)
If covert surveillance is sought, seek feasibility study from appropriate technical staff.	If not, why not?
Undertake comprehensive risk assessment of proposed action.	Is the proposed action *lawful*?
	Is the proposed action *necessary*?
Complete and submit application for consideration by authorizing officer (AO).	Is the proposed action *proportionate*? (Part of this consideration requires full understanding of the technical capabilities of any proposed equipment: can the equipment achieve more than is actually necessary or proportionate? If so, why is not less sophisticated equipment being used? If that is not possible, how will the overly sophisticated equipment be used so as not to secure more product than is proportionate?)
Where collaborative arrangements exist between police forces or other agencies, identify to which AO application should be made as per the collaboration protocol.	Where equipment is to be deployed, will its subsequent retrieval require authorization?
	Determine the schedule for reviewing the authority.
Third stage—monitoring execution (ongoing review)	**Fourth stage—review/renewal/cancellation**
Ensure that the action undertaken is that which is being authorized, which will not necessarily be that which was sought in application.	Rigorously, robustly and regularly review ongoing authorities to ensure that they remain valid, necessary and proportionate.
During conduct of the surveillance gather information to inform updated risk assessment in the event that review is necessary and renewal desired.	Do not necessarily wait until the end of the authorized period to conduct a review if changed circumstances demand earlier review.
If a previously unidentified individual is identified during the course of surveillance, seek immediate review, and if necessary, emendation or extension of the authorization from the AO, or if necessary a new authorization.	Immediately cancel authorizations on completion of surveillance or when any of the legitimacy, necessity or proportionality tests are no longer met: whichever is the sooner.
Review will generally be required wherever circumstances change.	

Fully document all the above—be prepared to be cross-examined in court

Investigators and authorizing officers will need to be aware that what constitutes private information has been broadly interpreted by various courts (see Chapter 2 at 2.8.1).

Nor is a RIPA authorization required in circumstances in which the investigating agency has 'another clear legal basis for conducting covert surveillance likely to result in the obtaining of private information about a person' (*Covert Surveillance and Property Interference: Revised Code of Practice* para 1.15; see also S McKay, *Covert Policing: Law and Practice*, Oxford University Press, Oxford, 2011, 6–9).

The nature of intrusive surveillance and property interference is such that those agencies empowered to engage in such conduct (far fewer than the number empowered to utilize directed surveillance) will always require authorization under the relevant Acts.

In a significant contribution to covert investigation case law, the Investigatory Powers Tribunal (IPT) in *C v Secretary of State for the Home Department* (IPT/03/32/H, 14 November 2006) draws a distinction between the *core functions* of an investigating, governing, or regulatory agency and the *ordinary functions* commensurate with managing a large organization. Thus it was held that whilst it was necessary for police forces to authorize surveillance conducted in the prevention and detection of crime (a core function of policing), it was not necessary to authorize under RIPA surveillance that was being conducted in relation to a former employee's disputed medical pension claim against a police force (human resource management being an ordinary function of a large organization).

If surveillance is for the purposes of preventing and detecting crime (the only purpose for which most organizations listed in Schedule 1, RIPA, as amended, can authorize surveillance), and the proposed activity engages the qualified rights protected under Article 8 ECHR, then the activity must be authorized under RIPA, and the PA97, as required.

Further information and reading

In August 2003 the ACPO Professional Standards Committee published the *Executive Authority Policy*, providing guidance on when Chief Officers might grant authorization for surveillance of police officers and staff in circumstances that did not meet the definition of crime within RIPA. The IPT decision in *C v Secretary of State for the Home Department* (IPT/03/32/H, 14 November 2006) would seem to negate the need for so-called 'Executive Authority'. For further discussion of the IPT decision in *C v Secretary of State* and for consideration of 'Executive Authority' see M Aldred, 'Does RIPA apply to disciplinary investigations by public bodies? Core functions and ordinary functions', *Covert Policing Review* (2007), 25–31. See also C Harfield, 'Issues concerning executive authority', *Covert Policing Review* (2007), 32–43.

1.7 **What Do the Article 8 Tests Mean?**

Where covert surveillance is likely to produce private information about any person—whether or not that person is the subject of the investigation—then authorization will be necessary and both applicants, but more especially authorizing officers, have to consider in detail how the proposed conduct engages with Article 8 ECHR. What do the Article 8 ECHR tests mean for investigators and authorizing officers?

1.7.1 **Does the investigative act fall within the scope of Article 8?**

If the proposed investigative activity *is intended* or *is likely* to gather information about the private life of an individual (whether or not that individual is the subject of the investigation) then such activity will fall within the scope of Article 8. If the plan is physically to watch an individual in order to observe that individual's movements or associations, or to listen to his or her conversations, or to photograph or video what he or she does, or to deploy a third party to interact with the subject in such a way as to acquire information, or to monitor his or her movements by technical tracking devices, then whether the desired product is to be used for evidential or intelligence purposes, rights protected by Article 8(1) will be infringed. This includes the rights of any third parties present in the surveillance arena regardless of whether such third parties are associated with the investigation subject or not.

A particular issue of concern to police forces and local authorities seeking to prevent crime or detect volume crime offenders is the policing of crime hotspots, particularly as the policing of such hotspots is a priority action derived from application of the NIM. Agencies working in partnerships such as the Crime and Disorder Reduction Partnerships (CDRP), established by s 97 Police Reform Act 2002 within the context of ss 5 and 6 Crime and Disorder Act 1998, will be working with police forces using the NIM (which all police forces had to implement fully by April 2004 pursuant to the statutory National Policing Plan 2004–2007) to identify and respond to crime hotspots. An oft-quoted and surprisingly controversial example is the public car park, which is vulnerable to regular thefts from unattended motor vehicles.

One traditional approach to resolving such a problem has been to deploy police officers or security staff employed by the local authority to maintain observations of such areas with the express intention of catching offenders in the act of committing crime. Since in such cases the identity of the offender is likely to be unknown, even if there are a number of likely suspects, it has been the practice to make such deployments without recourse to a surveillance authority. *Perry v UK* (2004) 39 EHRR 3, a case that actually centred on incorrect application of PACE Code D, coincidentally had implications for surveillance of hotspots because of the very broad interpretation that the ECtHR applied to the likelihood that private information might be obtained: 'the respect for private life under

Article 8 of the Convention brings with it decades of developing jurisprudence' (see N Taylor, 'Policing, privacy and proportionality', EHRLR, 2003, Special Issue, 86).

1.7.2 **If yes, has the Article 8 right been interfered with by a public authority?**

The HRA 1998 applies to public authorities. 'It is unlawful for a public authority to act in a way which is incompatible with a Convention right', prescribes s 6. A public authority is defined in HRA as a public body including 'a court or tribunal' (s 6(3)(a)) and 'any person certain of whose functions are functions of a public nature' (s 6(3)(b)), which includes not only public authorities but private contractors carrying out a public function on behalf of the authority.

Public authorities empowered to undertake directed surveillance under ss 28 and 29 RIPA are identified in Schedule 1 to that Act (see Chapter 2) whilst those authorities permitted to undertake intrusive surveillance are identified in s 32 (6) RIPA. Authorities empowered in law to interfere with property are identified in s 93 PA97 (see Chapter 4). The latest publicly available published versions of both Schedule 1 and s 32 can be accessed online via <http://www.legislation.gov.uk/ukpga/2000/23/contents> (accessed December 2011).

1.7.3 **If a public authority has so interfered with Article 8(1) rights, was this interference in accordance with the law?**

The ECHR makes reference to 'in accordance with the law', 'prescribed by law', and 'lawful'. Starmer identifies three criteria as a test to ensure compliance with the principle of legality thus established (K Starmer, *European Human Rights Law*, Legal Action Group, London, 1999, 166):

(1) domestic law must identify the legal basis for any restriction on an ECHR right;
(2) persons likely to be affected by such a restriction must be able to access the relevant domestic law; and
(3) the relevant domestic law must be clear and comprehensible so that anyone should be reasonably able to identify or foresee whether or not their behaviour is breaking or might break the law.

The principle of legality is considered to be satisfied by the following categories of law:

- statute
- delegated legislation such as Codes of Practice
- common (or case) law
- European Community law.

The extent to which these categories are truly accessible to the layperson is debatable. The potential difficulty in identifying the latest consolidated text of any given statute as amended has already been referred to. Codes of practice, held to satisfy the principle of legality (*Barthold v Germany* (1985) 7 EHRR 383) are certainly intended to make the law more comprehensible to the non-lawyer. The layperson is unlikely to be sufficiently familiar with stated cases in common law for them to be regarded as properly accessible, but through professional legal representation a layperson may be considered to have sufficient access to common law decisions. The common law was held to meet the principle of legality in *Sunday Times v UK (No. 1)* (1979–80) 2 EHRR 245, reinforced by the decision in *Huvig v France* (1990) 12 EHRR 528, that 'law' could be understood in a substantive sense rather than just in a statutory sense.

As was demonstrated in *Malone v UK* (1984) 7 EHRR 14, following *Silver v UK* (1983) 5 EHRR 347, internal or official guidelines are not sufficient to constitute being in accordance with law, even where published, particularly where the criteria for interpretation of such guidelines remains unpublished.

The PA97 and RIPA make provision for certain covert investigation tactics. Public authorities complying with such provisions will therefore be doing so in accordance with statute law supported by codes of practice. Note, however, that 'it does not follow . . . that because an act of covert surveillance is lawful it can never result in a contravention of the Convention rights' (*Re McE* UKHL [2009] 15 at para 71). Other tests have to be met.

1.7.4 If it was lawful, was the interference pursuant to a legitimate aim as identified in Article 8(2)?

If the actions of the public authority pass the legality test, they must then be considered within the context of the legitimacy test. The legitimate reasons for interfering with an Article 8(1) ECHR right are prescribed in Article 8(2).

For public officials engaged in law enforcement the legitimate reason provided by Article 8(2) is:

• the prevention of disorder or crime.

For state agents undertaking other forms of regulatory function or public protection, other legitimate reasons apply:

• the interests of national security
• the interests of public safety
• the interests of the economic well-being of the country
• the protection of health or morals
• the protection of the rights and freedoms of others.

There is no scope for adding to this list of reasons and they should be interpreted strictly within the ordinary meaning of the language. Article 18 ECHR prescribes that none of the restrictions permitted should be applied for any reason other than for the reasons prescribed (Starmer, *European Human Rights Law*, 177).

1.7.5 **Even if it was both lawful and pursuant to a legitimate aim, was it still necessary and proportionate in a democratic society?**

The final test is that of necessity in a democratic society. This test incorporates the concept of proportionality which is concerned with balancing the often conflicting interests of the individual and the wider community. Thus Sedley LJ in *B v Secretary of State for the Home Department* [2000] 2 CMLR 1086:

> a measure which interferes with a human right must not only be authorised by law but must correspond to a pressing social need and go no further than is strictly necessary in a pluralistic society to achieve its permitted purpose; or, more shortly, must be appropriate and necessary to its legitimate aim.

More recently, in *Wood v Commissioner of Police for the Metropolis* [2009] EWCA Civ 414 at 82, reliance was exclusively put upon *S and Marper v United Kingdom* (Application Nos. 30562/04 and 30566/04) at 101:

> An interference will be considered 'necessary in a democratic society' for a legitimate aim if it answers a 'pressing social need' and, in particular, if it is proportionate to the legitimate aim pursued and if the reasons adduced by the national authorities to justify it are 'relevant and sufficient'.

An action can be authorized as 'necessary' because it meets one of the grounds outlined in s 28(3) RIPA, but that should not be confused with the 'necessity' test established by the ECHR and subsequent case law. A proposed action can be RIPA-compliant but not ECHR-compliant.

Further information and reading

See Starmer, *European Human Rights Law*, 170. See also B Fitzpatrick, 'Covert human intelligence sources as offenders: the scope of immunity from the criminal law', *Covert Policing Review* (2005), 15–32, at 20.

(The authors are grateful to Kingsley Hyland, CPS, for drawing their attention to Sedley LJ's dictum quoted above.)

Section 28 RIPA imposes a specific obligation upon authorizing officers to consider proportionality in a two-fold test in relation to directed surveillance. Firstly, authorizing officers must ensure that the surveillance is necessary for the purpose of preventing or detecting crime or that it is necessary for preventing disorder. Secondly, they must believe that the proposed investigation method is proportionate to what is sought to be achieved by it, although the term 'proportionate' is not defined in either statute or the ECHR. A similar obligation is imposed in relation to s 29 RIPA and the authorizing of covert human intelligence source (CHIS) deployments.

The phrasing of the proportionality test in s 93 PA97 is slightly different but essentially amounts to providing the same protection for suspects. For property interference to be authorized the officer must believe that it is necessary because it is likely to be of substantial value in the prevention or detection of serious crime (a higher threshold than for directed surveillance) and that the desired objective cannot be reasonably achieved by other means.

The revised and new Codes of Practice published as an aid to understanding RIPA elucidate the principle of proportionality in slightly different ways. The *Covert Surveillance and Property Interference Revised Code of Practice* at paras 3.4 and 3.5 states:

> If the activities are deemed necessary on one or more of the statutory grounds, the person granting the authorization or warrant must also believe that they are proportionate to what is sought to be achieved by carrying them out. This involves balancing the seriousness of the intrusion into the privacy of the subject of the operation (or any other person who may be affected) against the need for the activity in investigative and operational terms.

> The authorization will not be proportionate if it is excessive in the overall circumstances of the case. Each action authorized should bring an expected benefit to the investigation or operation and should not be disproportionate or arbitrary. *The fact that a suspected offence may be serious will not alone render intrusive actions proportionate.*

> (Emphasis added.)

In the new *Investigation of Protected Electronic Information Code of Practice* the proportionality test is expressed slightly differently. Stipulating that the imposition of the requirement to disclose the protected electronic information 'should be proportionate to what is sought to be achieved by obtaining the disclosure' the code goes on to say (para 3.39):

> This involves balancing the extent of the intrusiveness of the interference with an individual's right to respect for their private life against the benefit to the investigation or operation being undertaken by a relevant public authority in the public interest.

The difference in the way the balancing consideration is expressed superficially seems a matter of mere semantics but actually is significant and could divert consideration: investigators and authorizing officers may be tempted to interpret 'need for the activity' broadly. It is amenable to such a reading. But 'benefit to the investigation' reminds them that the focus for consideration of proportionality is a narrow one. The seriousness of the offence being investigated does not, in and of itself, render any given investigative action proportionate.

Investigators and authorizing officers, resisting the urge to find an objective that justifies a technique, must be clear from the outset what evidence or intelligence it is that is sought and how it relates to the investigation as a whole. When reviewing existing authorities and considering applications for renewal, investigators and authorizing officers must consider whether the proportionality has changed and if so how. It may be that as a result of the evidence or intelligence gained the continued use of surveillance (in order to obtain new specific pieces of information or evidence) is proportionate. But it may equally be possible that surveillance has in fact produced the specific evidence or intelligence that was the original objective of the authorized action and that further surveillance merely to secure more of the same is disproportionate.

Consideration of proportionality for authorizing officers is a balancing act, but one in which it is easy to confuse what properly should be balanced. Taylor succinctly draws the crucial distinction: 'a balancing exercise takes place that requires a consideration of whether the interference with the right is greater than is necessary to achieve the aim . . . this is not an exercise in balancing the right against the interference, but instead *balances the nature and extent of the interference against the reasons for interfering*' (emphasis added, 2006:26). McKay elaborates in practical terms: 'an assessment of the proportionality of the resources deployed in an operation cannot be properly undertaken without knowing the nature of the offences being investigated, the evidence required to prove them and the likely dividend to society in preventing and detecting the offence or likely outcomes' (2006:49).

Although the nature of the offence may offer partial justification for the deployment of certain methods (a test purchase operation being a case in point), it is not the *seriousness* of the offence or the *extent of the harm* derived from the offence that must be balanced but *the use of coercive and intrusive methods* against the value of the evidential product derived therefrom (Ormerod 2006, 77–78).

A five-part checklist exists to help investigators and authorizing officers to assess proportionality, and will aid authorizing officers in particular to undertake their statutory obligations under ss 28 and 29 RIPA or s 93 PA97:

KEY POINTS ON PROPORTIONALITY

(1) Have relevant and sufficient reasons based on reliable information been put forward for conducting the proposed covert investigation in that particular way? *Jersild v Denmark* (1995) 19 EHRR 1.

(2) Could the same evidence or intelligence be gained by a less intrusive method? *Campbell v UK* (1993) 15 EHRR 137.

(3) Are the decision-making process by which the application is made and the authorization given demonstrably fair? *W v UK* (1988) 10 EHRR 29; *McMichael v UK* (1995) 20 EHRR 205; *Buckley v UK* (1997) 23 EHRR 101.

(4) What safeguards have been put in place to prevent abuse of the technique? *Klass v Germany* (1979–80) 2 EHRR 214. See para 59 in which it is argued safeguards represent the compromise between defending democratic society and individual rights.

(5) Does the proposed infringement in fact destroy the 'very essence' of the ECHR right engaged?

(Based on Starmer, *European Human Rights Law*, 171, 175–176)

If there is no information or evidence to support the deployment of investigation methods that will infringe Article 8(1), then an unjustifiable breach will take place.

Further information and reading

- S McKay, 'Approaching the Regulation of Investigatory Powers Act 2000', *Covert Policing Review* (2006), 46–53.
- S McKay, 'Privacy, proportionality and other human rights principles', *Covert Policing: Law and Practice* (Oxford University Press, Oxford, 2011), Chapter 2.
- D Ormerod, 'Recent developments on entrapment', *Covert Policing Review* (2006), 65–86.
- N Taylor, 'Covert policing and proportionality', *Covert Policing Review* (2006), 22–33.

The Codes of Practice accompanying RIPA and the PA97 are available online at <http://www.homeoffice.gov.uk/counter-terrorism/regulation-investigatory-powers/ripa-codes-of-practice/> (accessed December 2011). The versions of the Codes that were available in December 2011 are reproduced in the appendices to this volume.

As yet untested in the courts is the issue of cumulative 'dis-proportionality'. A single covert investigation action may not, in and of itself, be disproportionate. But a series of sequential authorizations within the context of a single investigation, it might be argued, may lead to an overall response that, cumulatively, is disproportionate. This is another issue that authorizing officers may wish to keep in mind when considering reviews, renewals, and supplementary applications.

1.8 What Issues Have Arisen from Independent Inspections of Covert Investigation?

Part III PA97 established the Office of Surveillance Commissioners (OSC) and the role of Chief Surveillance Commissioner to oversee property interference. Part IV RIPA extends the functions of the Chief Surveillance Commissioner to include oversight of directed and intrusive surveillance. (Separate Commissioners have been appointed for interception and for the intelligence services.) Part of the Chief Surveillance Commissioner's duties includes reporting annually to the Prime Minister and to Scottish Ministers. Such reports are laid before the respective Parliaments and so are publicly available.

Further information and reading

OSC *Annual Reports* published since 2002–03 are available to download from the Office of Surveillance Commissioners website at <http://surveillancecommissioners.independent.gov.uk/> (accessed November 2011).

The OSC annual reports contain an insight into how well or otherwise public authorities are handling their statutory obligations in respect of these covert investigation methods and are a source of guidance to investigators and authorizing officers alike. In the early reports the Chief Surveillance Commissioner highlighted instances of good and poor practice identified during inspections. More recently this practice has been dispensed with in favour of more general observations, partly as a response to a general improvement in covert investigation standards amongst police forces. Yet there remain perennial issues, and with the recent significant increase in directed surveillance undertaken by non-police organizations, issues encountered early on by the police service are now being encountered by other agencies.

In 2001 the Chief Surveillance Commissioner had felt it necessary to highlight the 'poor wording' in the applications for property interference submitted by police chief officers. 'There have been examples where Chief Officers have authorized the removal of property to attach surveillance equipment to it but have failed to authorize the entry on to property necessary to do so or even the return of a vehicle after the device has been fitted' (OSC *Annual Report 2000–2001*, para 15.9). 'Insufficiently specific applications and authorizations' were still an issue in 2004 (OSC *Annual Report 2003–2004*, 11). In the reporting year 2006–07, 67 unauthorized surveillance operations were reported to the OSC, most occurring because of inadequate explanation and lack of understanding between authorizing officers and staff as to what activity precisely had been authorized (OSC *Annual Report 2006–2007*, para 5.3). In 2010–11, 129 'irregularities' were reported to the Chief Commissioner (OSC *Annual Report 2010–2011*, para 3.2).

The need for comprehensive precision in both applications and authorizations cannot be overemphasized. Actions that have not been specifically authorized will not be lawful.

Deficiencies identified by the OSC have included:

- failure to authorize or authorization of the wrong type
- surveillance beyond that which was actually authorized
- confusion about the statutory definitions of directed and intrusive surveillance
- confusion about the definition of a CHIS (the OSC has strongly criticized the emerging trend of deploying 'tasked witnesses' (OSC *Annual Report 2006–2007*, para 8.9), a term of uncertain and non-statutory origin which, in the experience of the OSC, may embrace 'impropriety'; if, as the OSC supposes, there are

insufficient trained handlers and controllers, and senior investigating officers are not sufficiently trained in the deployment of CHISs, the creation of new labels will not render the tasked activity lawful)

- errors in detail such as car registration numbers and incorrect addresses leading to surveillance of subjects or property other than those actually identified in the authorization
- lateness in notification, renewal, and cancellation
- commencement of operations requiring a Commissioner's prior approval before such had been granted
- failure to explain urgency in oral authorizations
- authorizations given by staff without power to do so
- authorizing more than was sought on an application (there may, of course, be very good reasons for authorizing officers authorizing less than an applicant had applied for once proportionality and necessity had been considered)
- delegation of reviews by authorizing officers
- continuing failure on the part of authorizing officers 'properly to demonstrate that less intrusive methods have been considered and why they have been discounted in favour of the tactic selected' (OSC *Annual Report 2008–09*, para 5.8)
- codes of practice not readily available to practitioners
- persistent use of template phrases and formulaic constructions in both applications and authorizations (which indicate failure on the part of authorizing officers to execute their statutory duty to consider each case on its merits).

Overall, the OSC has repeatedly identified, from 2001 to 2007, the lack of adequate training in RIPA and covert investigation management as a theme common to all the public authorities empowered to undertake covert investigation. In 2007–08 an apparent improvement in the training of authorizing officers was evident on inspection (OSC *Annual Report 2007–08*, para 8.3) but a lack of specialist training concerning the authorization and deployment of CHIS was recorded (para 9.5). Criticism was to the fore once more in the OSC *Annual Report 2008–09* in which the Chief Commissioner lamented the fact that 'too many ACPO officers and senior executives have yet to receive formal training in this legislation' (para 5.22). The Chief Commissioner felt it necessary to observe that (para 5.27):

> Public authorities which invest in training usually achieve a higher standard of compliance. The quality of training is variable.

Subsequently the Chief Commissioner has observed that the failure of authorizing officers to describe 'the particulars of each case in a manner that is bespoke to the particular investigation' (ie the reliance of both applicants and authorizing officers on the use of formulaic phrases) is 'probably the consequence of poor training' (OSC *Annual Report 2009–10*, para 5.1).

The Chief Commissioner has advertised a continuing focus on training provision in future inspections (OSC *Annual Report, 2010–11*, para 3.8), with particular attention being paid to the use of authorizing officers of temporarily promoted staff or staff acting up a rank/grade as these individuals, by definition, are less likely to have had adequate training for the role of authorizing officers (para 5.18).

Such deficiencies heighten the risks of improperly authorized or unauthorized investigations taking place. Such investigations will, by definition, be non-compliant, thus undermining the integrity of the criminal justice and other public regulatory systems.

On the frequent complaint about the bureaucracy of self-regulation under RIPA and PA97, the OSC originally offered this palliative: '[c]onscientious completion of the application form will incline the judge, if the authorization is called into question, to uphold it, if he can' (OSC *Annual Report 2003–2004*, 8); a maxim supported indirectly by the decision in *R v Kennedy and others* (unreported, 2001), in which proceedings were stayed due to inadequate police records and documentation, and by the upholding of the conviction in *R v Paulssen* [2003] EWCA Crim 3109. Despite *minor* infringements of RIPA leading to a technical failure of authorization continuity, the judge in *Paulssen* held that police had acted in good faith even if the authorization process had been incorrectly applied. More recently, however, the Chief Surveillance Commissioner has taken a rather different stance, observing that much of the perceived bureaucratic burden surrounding RIPA and the PA97 'does not result from the legislation or the Codes. It is largely the making of law enforcement agencies who often repeat the same statements in different sections of the forms' (OSC *Annual Report 2006–2007*, para 12.1): 'unnecessary repetition and verbosity produce self-inflicted bureaucracy' (OSC *Annual Report 2006–2007*, para 8.6). Such bureaucracy is symptomatic of poor training (OSC *Annual Report 2007–08*, para 8.7).

Unnecessary repetition and verbosity, together with reliance upon formulaic constructions, is regarded as evidencing a lack of clear and concise preparation in application and in authorization consideration. The use of tick boxes and template phrasing gives rise to the suspicion that authorizing officers, for instance, have failed in their statutory duty to consider proportionality properly. Criticism of the use of templates and formulaic language has been a perennial theme in recent OSC *Annual Reports* (*2008–09*, para 5.1; *2009–10*, para 5.13; *2010–11*, para 5.7).

A key vulnerability in the employment of stock phrases or the use of imprecise language and broad constructions is that specific conduct will not be found to have been authorized even if both applicant and authorizing officer think that it is covered by the deliberately vague and generalized nature of an authorization that seeks to be all-encompassing. There are no short cuts in the application and authorization process. Precision does not have to be bureaucratic. Granted, investigations can often develop dynamically in unexpected directions: in such circumstances review and, if necessary, the seeking and granting of new authorizations is the appropriate approach to ensure that the surveillance product is not subsequently vulnerable to being ruled inadmissible as evidence.

> It is fundamental to a proper authorization process that covert activity has been specifically authorized. It is incompatible with this principle that

25

authorizations be so loosely framed as to permit activity not anticipated at the time of authorization.

(OSC *Annual Report 2009–10*, para 5.13)

Linked to this is the issue of organization guidance and the use of hypothetical scenarios. Scenarios can be equally useful or vulnerable to misinterpretation if regarded as a 'one-size-fits-all' solution. There is also the temptation to word an authorization so that it fits an apparently relevant scenario rather than the circumstances of the actual matter at hand. 'Examples given in handbooks tend to be inflexibility applied leading to a wrong conclusion which consideration of the specific facts of the case would have avoided' (OSC *Annual Report 2008–09*, para 3.15). The Chief Commissioner expressed concern at plans to include scenarios in the draft revised codes of practice (OSC *Annual Report 2008–09*, para 3.15), and subsequently criticized their actual inclusion in the published versions (OSC *Annual Report 2009–10*, para 5.3).

Statute does not require the OSC to train or to provide guidance (OSC *Annual Report 2008–09*, para 3.13; OSC *Annual Report 2009–10*, para 3.7). Nevertheless the OSC website does include web pages dedicated to advice and guidance—accessible at <http://surveillancecommissioners.independent.gov.uk/advice_guidance.html> (accessed December 2011)—and in December 2008 the OSC also circulated to relevant law enforcement agencies and public authorities specific guidance (OSC *Annual Report 2008–09*, para 3.13) which is updated from time to time. Of concern to the Chief Commissioner in 2011 was the fact that this restricted access guidance seems not to be widely available to practitioners and such additional guidance may yet be published on the OSC website also (OSC *Annual Report 2010–2011*, para 3.4).

The Chief Commissioner has made plain that OSC 'inspections are and will continue to be based on the most authoritative and current judicial interpretation of the legislation' (OSC *Annual Report 2009–10*, para 3.6), and that such interpretation will be accorded precedence over any organization guidance or Ministerial policy statement that is at odds with the OSC view (para 3.7; see also OSC *Annual Report 2008–09*, para 5.1). 'There is good reason' the Chief Commissioner goes on to observe (a little testily some readers might think) 'why my Commissioners are required to have held high judicial office' (para 3.8; see also OSC *Annual Report 2008–09*, para 3.16). Commissioners may be required to have held high judicial office for the purpose of post facto inspection of the use of covert surveillance powers but those charged with authorizing the use of such powers will have no such experience despite the burden placed upon them. (Nor is there any prospect that there will ever be sufficient numbers of individuals with experience of high judicial office to be available 24 hours a day, seven days a week, 365 days a year to manage the authorization workload evident in the statistics published in the OSC annual reports.) To ensure compliance with RIPA, PA97 and the Article 8 tests, authorizing officers and the organizations for which they work will wish to have access to the best training available, and just as importantly the time available free from other operational demands to undertake the authorizing and review functions properly pursuant to the statutory obligations imposed upon them. If, in a period of severe public sector economic stringency, the necessary resources are not made available to resolve the multiple issues raised by OSC inspections, then the stark political choice is that recourse to covert investigation as a tactic will have to be abandoned until such time as remedy can be achieved.

1.9 **What Are the Consequences of Investigator Malpractice?**

There are four possible adverse consequences for investigators who have not acted properly during a covert investigation: a stay of proceedings (where investigators are considered to have unfairly entrapped an offender or enticed an offence that would not otherwise have been committed); exclusion of evidence from trial; becoming the subject of a complaint (and possibly associated civil litigation); or being subject to adverse comment from the Chief Surveillance Commissioner. RIPA Part 1 provides that unauthorized interception specifically is unlawful. Breaches of RIPA Parts 2 and 3 result in surveillance that will be unauthorized and so non-compliant but which will not, of itself, be unlawful. Nevertheless, acting in a way which is incompatible with a Convention right is unlawful under s 6 HRA 1998.

Proceedings were stayed in *R v Sutherland* (unreported, Nottingham Crown Court, 29 January 2002), in *R v Sentence* (unreported, Lincoln Crown Court, 1 April 2004) and, so the Court of Appeal adjudged, should have been stayed in *R v Grant* [2005] EWCA Crim 1089. In each case, Lincolnshire Police, acting in what was held to be bad faith, covertly recorded in the exercise yard at police stations legally privileged conversations between suspects and their solicitors (3.7.2 below). (See also *Archbold* 2005, para 15-532 and *R v Mason* [2002] 2 Cr App R 38.)

Section 78 PACE provides for the exclusion from trial of unfair evidence as follows:

> A court may refuse to allow evidence on which the prosecution proposes to rely to be given if it appears to the court that, having regard to all the circumstances, including the circumstances in which the evidence was obtained, the admission of the evidence would have such an adverse effect on the fairness of the proceedings that the court ought not to admit it.

PACE does not impose an absolute duty upon courts to exclude unfairly obtained evidence. The power to do so is discretionary. Section 78 PACE ensures that a court is competent to consider whether or not, in the interest of ensuring fair trial, evidence obtained by unlawful covert investigation should be adduced. If the court decides that it would be unfair to admit evidence that had been unlawfully obtained, for instance through improperly authorized or unauthorized surveillance, then such evidence should be excluded. Since PACE came into force 'there have been many such cases under section 78' (M Zander, *The Police and Criminal Evidence Act 1984* (3rd edn, Sweet & Maxwell, London, 1996), 171).

Neither Europe nor the UK has followed New Zealand's example in automatically excluding any evidence that has been secured in breach of the New Zealand Bill of Rights Act (Starmer, *European Human Rights Law*, 298–299). When considering whether to not to admit evidence that has been unfairly obtained, both UK and Strasbourg courts have taken a broad view when having regard to all the circumstances and apply a standard test: what would be the effect on the fairness of the trial if evidence that had been obtained unlawfully is admitted?

The European Court of Human Rights has held that rules of evidence regarding admissibility are primarily the preserve of domestic courts, Strasbourg's role being to determine the fairness of a trial as a whole (*Schenk v Switzerland* (1991) 13 EHRR 242). It would appear that the requirements of a fair trial do not necessarily demand the exclusion of evidence unlawfully obtained. But as *Schenk v Switzerland* illustrates, careful consideration will be given to the probative weight of the evidence, and the opportunities available to the defence to challenge the evidence and any other relevant factors in a given case before unlawfully obtained evidence will be admitted by the court. In both *Khan v UK* (2000) 31 EHRR 1016 and *PG v UK* [2002] Crim LR 308, the ECtHR found unanimous breaches of Article 8 yet no unfairness arising from the evidence adduced therefrom. 'Technical breaches especially of qualified rights might not impact on fairness' (Ormerod, 'ECHR and the exclusion of evidence', 61, 66). Unattractive though the unlawful or non-compliant activities of investigators might be, the courts have held that there are circumstances in which evidence improperly obtained should nevertheless be put before the jury. The Court of Appeal has held that exclusionary rules cannot be employed merely to express disapproval of the manner in which investigators have secured relevant evidence (*R v Chalkley and Jeffries* [1998] 2 All ER 155). Critics have argued that 'the courts routinely admit covert surveillance evidence owing to its reliability, despite acknowledged breaches of Article 8' (Ormerod, 'ECHR and the exclusion of evidence', 66 and 67). 'A problem with this approach is that it does nothing to encourage or exhort police officers to uphold the law and to conduct ethical investigations' (Sharpe, 'Covert surveillance', 70). The same could be said in relation to other investigators.

The unlawful or non-compliant conduct of investigators, whether deliberate or unwitting, can never be condoned. The fact that courts have not always excluded evidence unlawfully or improperly obtained as a result of covert investigation does not excuse investigators from always complying with procedural law. Admission of the evidence notwithstanding, such judgments are damning indictments of the investigators concerned for acting unlawfully or improperly, thereby compromising their integrity, that of the organization for which they work, and the integrity of the criminal justice and public regulatory systems as a whole.

Up until October 2000 the OSC investigated complaints from the public relating to the exercise of investigation powers to interfere with property. From that date such complaints, together with complaints arising against any public authority empowered under RIPA, have been investigated by the independent Investigatory Powers Tribunal established pursuant to s 65 RIPA for that purpose. The tribunal shall determine its findings according to the same principles that are applied in judicial review, ss 67(2) and 67(3)(c) RIPA.

The tribunal shall first determine whether or not the individual against whom the complaint has been made has, in relation to the complaint made, engaged in:

(1) conduct by or on behalf of any of the intelligence services
(2) conduct for or in connection with the interception of communications in the course of their transmission by means of a postal service or telecommunications system
(3) conduct to which RIPA Part I Chapter II applies (access to communications data)
(4) conduct to which RIPA Part II applies (directed and intrusive surveillance or CHISs)
(5) the giving of a notice under s 49 or any disclosure or use of an encryption key to protect information
(6) any entry on or interference with property or any interference with wireless telegraphy.

The tribunal shall then investigate the authority under which the individual concerned acted, pursuant to s 67(3)(b) RIPA. No frivolous or vexatious complaint will be entertained. Complaints will not normally be investigated if they are made more than a year after the date of the alleged incident. The tribunal has the power to award compensation or make such other order as they see fit and their decisions are final, not being subject to appeal. By virtue of s 68(6) and (7) anyone working for an organization empowered with covert investigation powers under RIPA shall provide the tribunal with such documents or other information as is required.

For complaints arising out of conduct relating to covert investigation which does not fall within the specific remit outlined and (1) to (6) above, the normal complaints procedures relating to the investigator's organization apply.

Complainants also have recourse to civil suit against investigators who are alleged to have breached Article 8 rights, pursuant to ss 7 and 8 HRA.

1.10 **Scotland**

The jurisdiction focus of this book is England and Wales. RIPA also applies to Northern Ireland. The use of covert investigation in the separate jurisdiction of Scotland is provided for by the Regulation of Investigatory Powers (Scotland)

Act 2000 (RIP(S)A). Where all proposed covert investigation conduct is likely to take place in Scotland then authorizations should be sought and granted pursuant to RIP(S)A, to which a separate code of practice applies. There are limited exceptions and these are explained in para 1.18 of the *Covert Surveillance and Property Interference Revised Code of Practice* issued pursuant to s 71 RIPA and included in the appendices at the end of this volume.

1.11 **Conclusion**

This chapter has sought to outline, by way of basic introduction, the background and general principles underpinning covert investigation law in England and Wales and so set a context for the more detailed consideration of individual statutory powers that follow. Attempting to achieve such an objective in the space of one chapter is not unambitious and the reader is encouraged to explore further discussion of these issues in the additional literature cited above. This chapter should also be read in conjunction with Chapter 12, which considers the management of covert investigation. Authorizing officers in particular have to be aware of management principles as well as the statutory principles considered briefly here. In both areas of consideration, just because it *can* be done does not mean it *should* or *has* to be done.

Checklist of key issues when considering whether or not to deploy covert investigation techniques

- What evidence or intelligence is being sought?

- How is it relevant to the operation under consideration?

- What is the least intrusive means of securing such evidence or information?

- Has the least intrusive means of securing the evidence or information been attempted? If not, why not?

- What is the likelihood of collateral intrusion against the privacy of persons not being investigated? How will collateral intrusion be prevented (or if not, minimized) and how will the product of collateral intrusion be managed?

- What are the risks to the organization of such tactics? (Chapter 11)

- What are the risks to the organization's staff of such tactics? (Chapter 11)

- What are the risks to the public or specific third parties when such tactics are deployed? (Chapter 11)

- What are the risks to the subject of the investigation? (Chapter 11)

- Will the proposed methods breach Article 8(1)? (1.7.1)

- Is there justification for doing so provided by Article 8(2)? (1.7.4)

- How is the legality test met? (1.7.3)

- How is the legitimacy test met? (1.7.4)

- How is the necessity test met? (1.7.5)

- How is the proportionality test met? (1.7.5)

- Are the arguments justifying the application to use covert investigation based on reliable information/intelligence, or has the applicant adopted a 'tick-the-box' approach to completing the application without giving full consideration to the facts of the case and the issues arising?

- Have the arguments justifying the granting of authorization to use covert investigation been fully articulated, or has the authorizing officer merely paid lip service to the pro forma authorization template via which authority is granted?

- When should this authority be reviewed? What circumstances will or may arise that will necessitate review before then?

- How are the methods by which the evidence/intelligence will be obtained to be protected at trial? (Chapter 12)

- How will the product of the surveillance be managed? (Chapter 12)

Directed Surveillance

2.1 **Introduction**

Surveillance is defined at s 48(2) RIPA.

Definition of surveillance

Surveillance 'includes

(a) monitoring, observing or listening to persons, their movements, their conversations or their other activities or communications

(b) recording anything monitored, observed or listened to in the course of surveillance; and

(c) surveillance by or with the assistance of a surveillance device.'

Because they are subject to their own specific authority regimes (as will be discussed in later chapters), the conduct of covert human intelligence sources and interference with property under either Part III PA97 or s 5 Intelligence Services Act 1994 are not included in this definition (s 48(3) RIPA), notwithstanding that these tactics are deployed for exactly the same purposes.

A two-part hierarchy of surveillance is prescribed by law: directed and intrusive. Chapters 2 and 3 consider directed and intrusive surveillance separately because:

- not all public authorities empowered to conduct directed surveillance may also conduct intrusive surveillance, and
- the circumstances in which intrusive surveillance may be conducted are more restricted than those in which directed surveillance may take place.

A revised Code of Practice for Covert Surveillance and Property Interference has been published. It is reproduced in Appendix A below and is available online for download from <http://www.homeoffice.gov.uk/publications/counter-terrorism/ripa-forms/code-of-practice-covert?view=Binary> (accessed December 2011) . In this volume 'CSPI Code' refers to this Code.

2.2 **Which Public Authorities May Deploy Directed Surveillance?**

Public authorities empowered to utilize directed surveillance are defined in Schedule 1 RIPA as amended. This is accessible online via <http://www.legislation. gov.uk/ukpga/2000/23/contents> (accessed December 2011). Readers should be aware that although the online statutory database will have the latest available updated version of the Schedule (which has changed numerous times since original enactment), the online version may not have been amended to take account of all recent changes. The website will provide information about which amendments have yet to be updated in the published version of the Schedule.

Some public authorities are empowered to use directed surveillance under s 28 RIPA but not to deploy CHIS under s 29 RIPA. Other public authorities are empowered to do both. Authorizing officers will need to understand clearly what it is that their organization is empowered to do, and what conduct falls within and outside the definition of directed surveillance.

2.3 What Powers Does the Law Provide in Relation to Directed Surveillance?

Directed surveillance, subject to it being authorized, can be conducted for the purpose of *preventing or detecting crime* or of *preventing disorder*. This means establishing by whom, for what purpose, by what means and generally in what circumstances any criminal offence was committed. It may also be conducted in order to apprehend the suspected offender (ss 28(3), 81(2), and 81(5) RIPA).

In limited circumstances certain specified agencies may conduct surveillance for other purposes (s 28(3) RIPA), namely:

- in the interests of national security
- in the interests of the economic well-being of the UK
- in the interests of public safety
- for the purpose of protecting public health
- for the purpose of assessing or collecting certain fiscal levies.

It should be noted, however, that although these additional statutory purposes have been enacted they are not generally available. The Regulation of Investigatory Powers (Directed Surveillance and Covert Human Intelligence Sources) Order 2003 (SI 2003/3171) (as amended) defines not only which staff can authorize directed surveillance but also the purposes for which such authorization can be given. Many organizations have only a restricted number of statutory purposes for which directed surveillance authority can be given. Whereas the former National Crime Squad and former National Criminal Intelligence Service could authorize directed surveillance for any of the statutory purposes for instance, their successor, the Serious Organised Crime Agency, can only conduct directed surveillance for the purpose of preventing or detecting crime or of preventing disorder (Serious Organised Crime and Police Act 2005 (Consequential and Supplementary Amendments to Secondary Legislation) Order 2006 (SI 2006/594), Schedule, para 40, amending SI 2003/3171). The Chief Surveillance Commissioner noted with disappointment in the OSC *Annual Report 2006–2007* (paras 10.2 and 10.3) that a number of local authorities had failed to take notice of the fact that SI 2003/3171 restricts them to authorizing directed surveillance and CHIS operations *only for the purposes of preventing or detecting crime or of preventing disorder.*

Organizations and investigators intending to use directed surveillance and senior staff considering an application to authorize such activity will need to ensure that the intended activity is for a statutory purpose authorization for which they are entitled to give.

Definition of directed surveillance

Perhaps a little confusingly, directed surveillance is defined (s 26(2) RIPA) both by what it is not as well as what it is. Surveillance will require a directed surveillance authority if:

- it comprises covert observation or monitoring by whatever means;
- it is for the purpose of a specific investigation or specific operation (any crime or any other offence);
- it will or is likely to obtain private information about *any* person, not just the subject of the operation (this is the key element that engages Article 8 ECHR); but
- it does not include observations conducted in an immediate response to spontaneous events.

Directed surveillance scenario

On patrol, investigators see a person acting suspiciously near a house. In order to maintain a view of the individual without raising their suspicions, the investigators conceal themselves behind a nearby wall.

Such a reactive intervention triggered by spontaneous events does not require an authority for directed surveillance as it is conduct consistent with normal patrol duties.

Directed surveillance can take place anywhere *except*:

- inside any premises at the time being used as a residence, no matter how temporary, including hotel accommodation, tents, caravans, a prison cell, or even railway arches
- in any vehicle which is primarily used as a private vehicle either by the owner or the person having the right to use it (taxis are specifically excluded from this definition, s 48(7)(a) RIPA)
- outside such premises or vehicles if conducted by remote technical means (for instance a long-range microphone) which enables events and conversations inside residential premises and private vehicles to be monitored from outside, producing a surveillance product of the same quality as would be obtained by devices or persons inside such premises or vehicles.

In these three circumstances such surveillance is considered to be intrusive and may be carried out only by certain public authorities (see Chapter 3).

> ## Scenario illustrating action that goes beyond directed surveillance
>
> Investigators wish to confirm whether a benefit claimant lives at a particular address identified to the social security department. At the address investigators are unable to get an answer to a knock at the door. They consider whether it would be appropriate to push open a window that is slightly ajar at the front of the house in order to look inside.
>
> By opening the window investigators would be engaged in surveillance that is carried out on private premises, ie a dwelling house. This would constitute intrusive surveillance and property interference and therefore would not be lawful in these circumstances unless it was carried out by an investigating authority with such powers in circumstances that met the criteria for conducting intrusive surveillance and property interference.
>
> (OSC *Annual Report 2005*, 4.18)

Surveillance conducted in offices or in business vehicles (including taxis) requires a directed surveillance authority, not an intrusive surveillance authority.

Definition of private information

Private information is defined (s 26(10) RIPA) as being:

- any information relating to a person's private or family life or personal relationships with others.

See also CSPI Code, paras 2.4–2.7.

The fact that an individual happens to be located in a public space, for instance a car park, does not negate the obligation on public authorities to respect that individual's right to privacy and conduct surveillance only if duly authorized. It is not only the rights of the investigation subject that have to be respected. There will be collateral intrusion into the privacy of third parties present in the surveillance arena and so investigators and authorizing officers must be able to demonstrate why it is proportionate and necessary to violate their Article 8 rights and what steps are to be taken to minimize the intrusion and the consequences thereof.

2.4 What Authority Regime is Required for Directed Surveillance?

Individuals empowered within each public authority to grant authorities for directed surveillance have been defined in the Regulation of Investigatory Powers (Prescription of Offices, Ranks and Positions) Order 2000 (SI 2000/2417)

37

and the Regulation of Investigatory Powers (Prescription of Offices, Ranks and Positions) (Amendment) Order 2002 (SI 2002/1298) as amended and consolidated by 2003/3171, 2005/1084, 2006/594, and 2006/1874.

Thus authorizing officers include, amongst others, police superintendents, military Provosts Marshal, Lieutenant Colonels, Wing Commanders, or Commanders (Royal Navy), Band 9 customs officers, assistant directors of the SFO, prison service area managers, and local authority assistant chief officers.

Authorizing officers can only authorize an application for directed surveillance made by members of their own organization. An exception to this principle exists when two or more *police forces* have entered into a collaborative working agreement pursuant to s 23 of the Police Act 1996, (for English and Welsh forces; s 12 of the Police (Scotland) Act 1967 for Scottish forces), *and* the collaboration agreement permits applicants and authorizing officers to be from different forces. Where a collaborative working agreement is established for the purpose (*inter alia*) of facilitating covert investigation for the signatory parties such agreements must document specific arrangements for the management of covert investigation between the partners. 'Mere agreement to share resources is insufficient' (OSC *Annual Report 2010–11*, para 5.12; see also CSPI Code paras 3.19–3.21).

Further information and reading

CSPI Code Chapter 3 discusses general rules on authorizations (see below Appendix A).

At the time of writing (December 2011), Parliament is debating the Protection of Freedoms Bill which if enacted will alter the authority regime for local authorities wishing to undertake directed surveillance. The measures being debated include the proposal that local authorities would have to seek authorization for directed surveillance from a magistrate.

2.5 What Information is Required in an Application for Directed Surveillance?

Written applications for directed surveillance authority should describe both the purpose of the operation/investigation and the conduct for which authorization is sought. CSPI Code para 5.8 details further information that should be included in applications.

2.6 Review and Renewal of Authorities

The CSPI Code (para 3.22) stresses the need for regular reviews of directed surveillance authorities, the frequency of which should be set by the authorizing officer when first authorizing the application. Where directed surveillance is likely to obtain confidential information or there is a high degree of ether direct or collateral intrusion it will be necessary to review relevant authorities more regularly. Reviews are the responsibility of the authorizing officer; they should be documented and retained for three years (see CSPI Code, Chapter 8).

Further information and reading

CSPI Code paras 3.22–3.26 discuss the reviewing of covert investigation authorities.

CSPI Code paras 5.12–5.15 discuss the renewing of directed surveillance authorities.

Written authorities for directed surveillance can be made for periods of up to three months. Applications for renewal of an authority would not normally be made until shortly before the current authorization period is due to end. CSPI Code para 5.15 details the information to be recorded when seeking renewal of an authorization for directed surveillance.

2.7 **Cancellation of Authorities**

Authorizations must be cancelled as soon as the desired product is achieved or if circumstances change that require the application for and granting of a new authorization. The authorizing officer who granted or last renewed the authorization (or, if no longer available, the person who has succeeded him in that role) must cancel it if he is satisfied that the directed surveillance no longer meets the criteria upon which it was authorized (CSPI Code, paras 5.17–5.18). The time and date of cancellation must be recorded and instructions to cease surveillance issued immediately. Whether the surveillance had produced the planned objective should also be recorded.

Definition of urgent circumstances

Urgent circumstances are defined as instances in which to wait for an authorizing officer to become available to consider a written application would either

- endanger life, or
- jeopardize the investigation concerned (CSPI Code, para 5.6).

Hint and tip: *Negligence on the part of an applicant or conduct of the authorizing officer's own making does not constitute urgency.*

Thus where an investigator forgets to apply for authorization until just before the operation is due to begin or where the authorizing officer does not or cannot attend to the application before the operation is due to start, the operation will have to be postponed until the full written application procedure is carried out.

There are two types of urgent authority procedure: one where an authorizing officer is available, and one where such an officer is unavailable.

In genuinely urgent cases an available authorizing officer may issue an *oral authority* (CSPI Code, para 5.9), recording the fact that this has been done as soon as practicable. In the police service it is almost unheard of now for there not to be a duty on-call superintendent to deal with urgent PACE and RIPA authorities.

In urgent cases in which there is no authorizing officer immediately available, specified individuals entitled to act in urgent cases (SI 2003/3171, SI 2005/1084, SI 2006/594, SI 2006/1874) may give a *written authorization* for directed surveillance for a period of 72 hours (CSPI Code, para 5.11). Such individuals cannot issue oral authorities.

Scenario illustrating issues around urgent authorization for directed surveillance

Intelligence came to light at 0300 one night about a burglary being planned for immediate execution. Police desired to maintain surveillance on the offender's house. Having tried unsuccessfully several times to contact the duty superintendent, officers thought it expedient to seek an urgent authority from the night duty inspector on the basis of an oral application. The inspector gave verbal authority for the surveillance to be conducted. However, the OSC confirmed that, absent an authorizing officer, an inspector could only consider a full written application upon which to base an authorization. In this particular instance circumstances were such that there would not have been time to complete and submit such an application to the inspector before the burglary had been committed and the burglar had returned home. Thus alternative intervention strategies not involving surveillance, including perhaps disruption such as the presence of a marked police vehicle patrolling in the immediate vicinity, should have been considered.

Authorizing officers should not authorize covert surveillance in investigations in which they have direct involvement, although this may sometimes be unavoidable (CSPI Code, para 5.7).

Authorizing officers must apply two tests when considering whether to grant an authorization. These are set out in s 28(2) RIPA and are explained in the OSC *Annual Report 2000–2001*, para 4.13: 'When giving an authorization for directed surveillance... the authorizing officer must *believe* that the authorized surveillance is *proportionate* to what is sought to be achieved by carrying it out, and that the action is *necessary* for' one of the purposes defined in s 28(3) RIPA (emphasis added). The seriousness of the crime under investigation will not, in and of itself, provide a basis for meeting the proportionality test. Authorizing officers must articulate and document why the proposed method is proportionate to the product it is intended to produce (see Chapter 1, 1.7.5).

Section 28(4) makes it clear that only conduct and circumstances specified in the authority will be authorized and therefore lawful. This important sub-section obliges investigators and authorizing officers to be very precise in the wording of their applications and authorities.

For example, investigators conducting surveillance decide to secure photographic and video evidence. If the use of still photography and video cameras is not specified in the authority, then any evidence so secured will have been obtained in an unauthorized way and therefore vulnerable to exclusion under s 78 PACE. Lack of precision in the wording of authorities, resulting in unlawful or unauthorized activity by investigators, is a recurring deficiency identified by the OSC (*Annual Report 2003–2004*, 12).

Thus investigators must seek detailed authority for all the conduct they wish to engage in, and authorizing officers must ensure that their authorities specify in detail all conduct that they are content to authorize. Where authorizing officers authorize more than has been applied for they must state their reasons for doing so (OSC *Annual Report* 2005, 3.5). Similarly they must record their reasons for not authorizing all or any of the conduct detailed in an application.

In relation to town centre CCTV systems, the CSPI Code (paras 2.27–2.28) provides that, *except when used for preplanned surveillance operations*, the use of such systems does not require a directed surveillance authority.

Further information and reading

The Information Commissioner has published a Code of Practice on the use of CCTV systems which is available online at <http://www.ico.gov.uk/upload/documents/library/data_protection/detailed_specialist_guides/ico_cctvfinal_2301.pdf > (accessed December 2011).

2.8 What Significant Case Law Has Been Decided in Relation to Directed Surveillance?

Key principles have been established or confirmed in case law both pre-RIPA and post-RIPA and from case law nor directly concerning criminal investigations.

2.8.1 Private life

An initial issue for investigators and authorizing officers is the determination of whether surveillance will or is likely to obtain information about anyone's private life. Strasbourg has interpreted 'private life' and what might constitute information about private life very broadly.

In *Peck v UK* (2003) 36 EHRR 41, in which CCTV footage of the aftermath of Peck's suicide attempt in a town centre was released to TV broadcasters by the local council whose CCTV system had captured the images, the court held that 'Private life is a broad term not susceptible to exhaustive definition... There is a zone of interaction of a person with others, even in a public context, which may fall within the scope of "private life"' (at 730, para H5).

In *Von Hannover v Germany* [2006] 43 EHRR 7, the court held that private life can take place in the public domain; just because something happens in the public domain does not mean it is not private. Reinforcement for the notion that privacy still exists within a public environment is also found in UK case law. In *Campbell v MGN* [2004] 2 AC 457 at 458, the court held that 'although the photographs of the claimant were taken in a public place, the context in which they were used ... added to the overall intrusion into the claimant's life'.

Collateral intrusion of third party privacy must also be considered and addressed. In *XXX & YYY v ZZZ* [2004] EWCA Civ 231, an au pair set up covert cameras in the home where she worked to record sexual advances from her male employer. The cameras also recorded the children, which was considered a breach of their privacy.

Further information and reading

For a further discussion around the case law enforcement interpreting private life, see K Starmer, *European Human Rights Law* (Legal Action Group, London, 1999) paras 3.109–3.111 (a little dated now in terms of case law but still a very useful guide to rights jurisprudence); *Niemitz v Germany* (1993) 16 EHRR 97; *Costello-Roberts v UK* (1995) 19 EHRR 112; *Friedl v Austria* (1996) 21 EHRR 83; *Halford v UK* (1997) 24 EHRR 523; *Perry v UK* (2004) 39 EHRR 3 (although a case involving a breach of PACE, it has been applied by OSC inspectors when interpreting private life). See also OSC *Annual Report 2003–2004*, 8. S McKay, *Covert Policing: Law and Practice* (Oxford University Press, Oxford, 2011) devotes Chapter 2 to the issues of privacy, proportionality and other human rights issues.

2.8.2 Protection of observation posts

Recognizing that failure to secure observation posts from which to conduct surveillance could seriously impede legitimate investigations, the Appeal Court applied, in *R v Rankine* [1986] 1 QB 861, the same presumption of protection applied to human sources of information, namely that the identity of locations used should be protected unless doing so would lead to a miscarriage of justice. Minimum evidential standards were applied to this principle in *R v Johnson* [1988] 1 WLR 1377, confirmed by *R v Hewitt and Davis* [1992] 95 Cr App R 81, and *R v Grimes* [1994] Crim LR 213.

Case law criteria: *R v Johnson* [1988] 1 WLR 1377

The criteria set out in *R v Johnson* are reproduced in the ACPO *Practice Advice on Core Investigative Doctrine* (2005) 104:

The police officer in charge of observations of a rank not lower than sergeant must be able to testify that beforehand he or she visited all the observation places to be used and ascertained the attitude of the occupiers of the premises:

- as to the use of the premises;
- to the disclosure of the use of the premises;
- to the possible identification of the premises or the occupiers.

The difficulties, if any are encountered, in obtaining observation posts in the area.

In addition, immediately prior to the trial, an officer of a rank not lower than chief inspector must be able to testify that he or she visited the premises used for observations and ascertained if the occupiers are the same as when the observations were conducted and, whether they are or not, what their attitude is to:

- the possible disclosure of the use made of the premises;
- the disclosure of facts which would lead to the identification of those premises and their occupiers.

This evidence will be given in the absence of the jury when the application to exclude the material evidence is made. The judge should explain to the jury the effect of his or her ruling regarding the disclosure of the premises.

Because exposure of unmarked police vehicles would not necessarily involve the same threat of harassment or fear of violence for members of the public (*Blake and Austin v DPP* (1993) 97 Cr App R 169), the presumption of protection for private premises used as observation points would not, as a matter of policy, be applied to police vehicles from which observations were conducted (*R v Brown and Daley* (1988) 87 Cr App R 52).

2.8.3 Disclosure of surveillance authorizations

The statutory presumption of disclosure is founded in the Criminal Procedure and Investigations Act 1996 (CPIA). Because surveillance authorities may contain sensitive detail, exposure of which would be against the public interest, such authorities may be scheduled as sensitive unused material. If the prosecutor recognizes contentious issues regarding the authorization process, a redacted version of the authority should be disclosed and an unedited version supplied to the judge for determination that the defendant is not vulnerable to a miscarriage arising from non-disclosure (*R v Hardy and Hardy* [2002] EWCA Crim 3012). Where the defence declare specific issues with the authorization process, as in *R v Grant* [2005] EWCA Crim 1089, full disclosure of all documentation related to a covert investigation authorization may be ordered. In *R v Harmes* [2006] EWCA

Crim 928 the court considered the authorization documentation in detail, noting (at para 22) that renewals of the authorization had failed to detail either changes in circumstances or changes in planned police activity, and concluding (at para 42) that 'there were serious breaches of the Act and the Code in the process of authorization'.

2.8.4 Surveillance of legal consultations

The case of *McE* [2009] UKHL 15 considered the issue of directed surveillance that captured *legal consultations*. Consequently the Regulation of Investigatory Powers (Extension of Authorization Provisions: Legal Consultations) Order 2010 (SI 2010/461) was issued.

'Legal consultation is a narrower concept than legal privilege, so a matter that is likely to cause confusion to an already confused area of the law . . .' (S McKay, *Covert Policing: Law and Practice* (Oxford University Press, Oxford, 2011, para 6.68). Legal consultation material falls within the scope of legally privileged material.

The 2010 Order requires (s 3 (1)) that where directed surveillance on specified premises is likely to result in acquisition of legal consultation material, the surveillance must be regraded, treated and accordingly authorized as intrusive surveillance.

Legal consultation is defined in the Order (s 2 (a)) as:

   (i) a consultation between a professional legal adviser and his client or any person representing his client, or

  (ii) a consultation between a professional legal adviser or his client or any such representative and a medical practitioner made in connection with or in contemplation of legal proceedings and for the purposes of such proceedings.

The specified premises are detailed in s 3 (2) of the Order as follows:

  (a) any place in which persons who are serving sentences of imprisonment or detention, remanded in custody or committed in custody for trial or sentence may be detained;

  (b) any place in which persons may be detained under paragraph 16(1), (1A) or (2) of Schedule 2 or paragraph 2(2) or (3) of Schedule 3 to the Immigration Act 1971 or section 36(1) of the UK Border Act 2007;

  (c) police stations;

  (d) hospitals where high security psychiatric services are provided;

  (e) the place of business of any professional legal adviser; and

  (f) any place used for the sittings and business of any court, tribunal, inquest or inquiry.

The revised CSPI Code now devotes an entire chapter (Chapter 4) to discussion of issues concerning legally privileged and confidential information.

2.9 **Considerations in Respect of Authorizing Directed Surveillance**

Concern exists that example scenarios may tempt authorizing officers to construct an authorization better suited to the example scenario than to the facts of the application before them (see OSC *Annual Report 2008–09,* para 3.15; OSC *Annual Report 2009–2010*, paras 3.8 and 5.3). Accordingly, whereas previous editions of this book have used scenarios to suggest courses of action, this approach has been modified in this edition to highlight certain practicalities to which applicants and authorizing officers should give consideration. The decision whether or not to authorize a specific application for covert investigation remains the responsibility of the authorizing officer: 'the law obliges an Authorizing Officer to satisfy his [or her] own mind he [or she] is not to be dictated to or obliged to follow any particular interpretation' (OSC *Annual Report 2009–10*, para 3.8). Authorizing officers may be required to account for any decision made either to the OSC or in cross-examination at trial. The following considerations are neither exclusive nor exhaustive. They are intended to illustrate issues that applicant investigators and authorizing officers might wish to consider when being asked to authorize directed surveillance.

Example 1

A uniformed police officer wishes to record covertly a conversation with a member of the public in order to have an accurate record of the meeting which is due to take place at the police station.

A directed surveillance authority may be considered even though the officer is in uniform, as a member of the public would not be aware of the recording. This might be considered a higher level of intrusion than would normally be expected in such an encounter. An investigator may still be capable of executing some actions covertly even if those with whom the investigator is interacting are aware of who and what the investigator is. In some jurisdictions, New South Wales (Australia) for instance, police officers are equipped routinely to record conversations with the public and announce this fact to the member of the public when first introducing themselves. Were this practice to be adopted in England and Wales, would a directed surveillance authority be required?

Example 2

A local authority has installed CCTV in an area subject to frequent crime and disorder. Investigators intend to carry out an operation where CCTV operators identify those responsible for committing offences so that officers can attend and make arrests.

When CCTV is monitored in order to trigger immediate reactive intervention to a spontaneous crime observed this would seem to amount to routine observations as part of the normal duty of the CCTV operator. Where the use of CCTV is planned as part of a targeted covert investigation based on specific intelligence about ongoing criminality, the investigation being conducted in a manner which is likely to produce private information about persons observed (either subject of the investigation or unassociated third parties), then consideration must be given to authorizing such use as directed surveillance.

Note: The Information Commissioner has published a Code of Practice in relation to the use of CCTV systems that monitor public spaces. It is accessible online at <http://www.ico.gov.uk/upload/documents/library/data_protection/detailed_specialist_guides/ico_cctvfinal_2301.pdf> (accessed December 2011).

Example 3

A commercial catering premises has been the subject of early morning thefts of its milk supply. The thefts occur in the early hours after the milk delivery but before the premises open. An officer wishes to set up an observation point in premises opposite those where the thefts occur. If it is likely that this operation will capture private information about persons frequenting or passing through the area, whether suspects or innocent third parties, then an authority for directed surveillance should be considered. Investigators operating an observation post must comply with *R v Johnson*. Successful observations may trigger a successful prosecution for the single occasion of theft observed. Absent a corroborated confession, no prosecution of the previous offences is likely. Is covert investigation justified in this context? Is the object to secure a prosecution for one instance of theft or to prevent future thefts? Would enhanced visible patrolling of the area (with perhaps recourse to PACE stop and search powers) achieve the same purpose?

Example 4

Local residents are complaining about young people drinking alcohol in the park in the evenings. Residents believe that those drinking in the park are under 18 years of age and are obtaining their alcohol from a local shop which has previously been visited by officers outlining the problems in the local area. The shop owner denies selling alcohol to anyone under age. Investigators wish to set up surveillance to establish a pattern of business in the store and identify anyone under age being sold alcohol.

Whether these observations are conducted by police or other licensing/regulatory bodies, if it is likely that private information will be obtained as a consequence of the planned observations then consideration must be given to authorizing the operation as directed surveillance. Such an operation may obtain evidence to support a prosecution against the shop owner but will such intervention resolve the underlying problem? Is the real problem one of unlawful retailing (arguably a symptom) or underage drinking (arguably a symptom or the cause)? Will prosecution of the shopkeeper resolve the problem of underage misuse of alcohol in this local authority area? Can covert investigation of a shopkeeper, with its concomitant collateral intrusion against the privacy of lawful customers, be justified if social and educational intervention alternatives (which may not engage Article 8 rights) could also be applied? In the context of alternative interventions, can covert investigation be justified by the authorizing officer as necessary?

Example 5

As part of an operational order in which a search warrant is to be executed on a premises, investigators wish to set up observations in order to establish who is on the premises prior to the execution of the warrant. Intelligence suggests a number of potentially violent individuals use and stay at the address and the intention is to execute the warrant when such persons are away from the premises in order to minimize risk.

A directed surveillance authority should be considered if covert observation of the premises is likely to capture private information of persons on or near the premises. The fact that such observations are to facilitate the safe execution of a subsequent overt intervention does not of itself automatically absolve investigators from considering whether an authority for directed surveillance is required for this part of the overall process. Where such an authority is deemed not necessary, those responsible for taking the decision may wish to document the reasons upon which it is based. If visual equipment planned to be used by the officers for the purposes of such observations from outside the premises were capable of providing information on activities inside the dwelling of the same quality as if the surveillance devices were inside the dwelling, then an intrusive surveillance authority should be considered.

It is not suggested that any of these example considerations is typical. Indeed, that is the point. No matter how similar individual investigations may be in terms of *circumstance*, the *facts* of each investigation will differ. It is upon the particular facts of each case that authorizing officers must determine whether or not to authorize directed surveillance.

Checklist of key issues when considering whether or not to deploy covert investigation techniques

- What evidence or intelligence is being sought?

- How is it relevant to the operation under consideration?

- What is the least intrusive means of securing such evidence or information?

- Has the least intrusive means of securing the evidence or information been attempted? If not, why not?

- What is the likelihood of collateral intrusion against the privacy of persons not being investigated? How will collateral intrusion be prevented (or if not, minimized) and how will the product of collateral intrusion be managed?

- What are the risks to the organization of such tactics? (Chapter 11)

- What are the risks to the organization's staff of such tactics? (Chapter 11)

- What are the risks to the public or specific third parties when such tactics are deployed? (Chapter 11)

- What are the risks to the subject of the investigation? (Chapter 11)

- Will the proposed methods breach Article 8(1)? (1.7.1)

- Is there justification for doing so provided by Article 8(2)? (1.7.4)

- How is the legality test met? (1.7.3)

- How is the legitimacy test met? (1.7.4)

- How is the necessity test met? (1.7.5)

- How is the proportionality test met? (1.7.5)

- Are the arguments justifying the application to use covert investigation based on reliable information/intelligence, or has the applicant adopted a 'tick-the-box' approach to completing the application without giving full consideration to the facts of the case and the issues arising?

- Have the arguments justifying the granting of authorization to use covert investigation been fully articulated, or has the authorizing officer merely paid lip service to the pro forma authorization template via which authority is granted?

- When should this authority be reviewed? What circumstances will or may arise that will necessitate review before then?

- How are the methods by which the evidence/intelligence will be obtained to be protected at trial? (Chapter 12)

- How will the product of the surveillance be managed? (Chapter 12)

Planning covert investigation actions

Remember to include the PLAN for covert investigation tactics in all investigation policy-book entries relating to covert investigation considerations and decisions.

P   PROPORTIONALITY

Why is it proportionate to obtain the intended product of this surveillance in the manner proposed? (1.7.5)

L   LEGITIMACY

What is the legitimate purpose of the proposed action: the prevention of disorder or crime; the interests of national security; the interests of public safety; the interests of the economic wellbeing of the country; the protection of health or morals; the protection of the rights and freedoms of others? (1.7.4)

A   AUTHORITY TO UNDERTAKE PROPOSED ACTION

What is the lawful foundation and authority for the proposed action? From whom must authorization be sought? (1.7.3)

N   NECESSITY OF PROPOSED ACTION

Why is the proposed action necessary? (1.7.5)

Flowchart for Authorizing a Directed Surveillance Operation

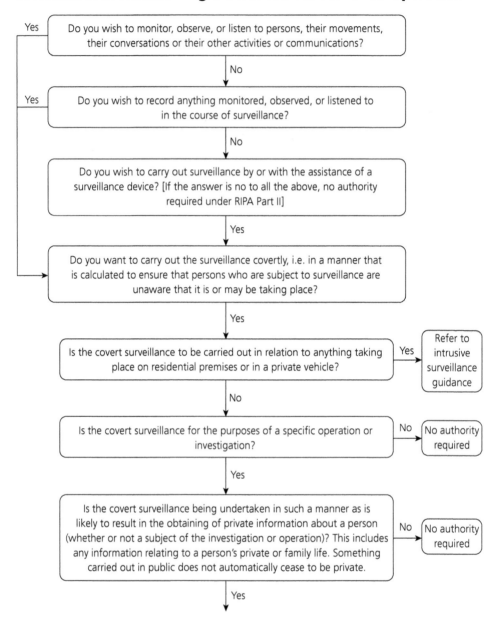

Flowchart for Authorizing a Directed Surveillance Operation continued

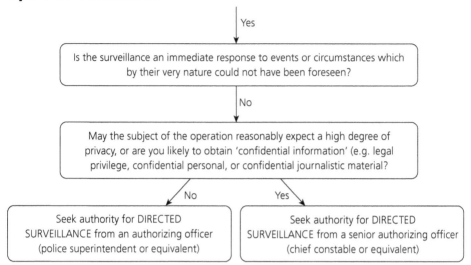

3

Intrusive Surveillance

3.1 **Introduction**

Surveillance is defined at s 48(2) RIPA.

Definition of surveillance

Surveillance 'includes:

(a) monitoring, observing or listening to persons, their movements, their conversations or their other activities or communications;

(b) recording anything monitored, observed or listened to in the course of surveillance; and

(c) surveillance by or with the assistance of a surveillance device.'

Because they are subject to their own specific authority regimes (as will be discussed in later chapters), the conduct of CHISs and interference with property under either Part III PA97 or s 5 Intelligence Services Act 1994 are not included in this definition (s 48(3) RIPA), notwithstanding that these tactics are deployed for exactly the same purposes.

A two-part hierarchy of surveillance is prescribed by law: directed and intrusive. Chapters 2 and 3 consider directed and intrusive surveillance separately because:

- not all public authorities empowered to conduct directed surveillance may also conduct intrusive surveillance, and
- the circumstances in which intrusive surveillance may be conducted are more restricted than those in which directed surveillance may take place.

A revised Code of Practice for Covert Surveillance and Property Interference has been published. It is reproduced in Appendix A below and is available online for download from <http://www.homeoffice.gov.uk/publications/counter-terrorism/ripa-forms/code-of-practice-covert?view=Binary> (accessed December 2011). In this volume 'CSPI Code' refers to this Code.

3.2 **Which Public Authorities May Deploy Intrusive Surveillance?**

Public authorities empowered to utilize intrusive surveillance are defined by reference to senior authorizing officers within each organization able to grant an intrusive surveillance authority (s 32(6) and s 41(1) RIPA). Fewer organizations may conduct intrusive surveillance than those empowered to conduct directed surveillance. Those organizations are:

- Any police force maintained under s 2 Police Act 1996
- Any police force maintained under s 1 Police (Scotland) Act 1967

- The Metropolitan Police Service
- The City of London Police
- The Police Service of Northern Ireland
- The Ministry of Defence Police
- The British Transport Police
- The Serious Organised Crime Agency
- The Army, Royal Navy, and Royal Air Force
- HM Revenue and Customs
- Office of Fair Trading
- MI5, MI6, and GCHQ.

3.3 **What Powers Does the Law Provide in Relation to Intrusive Surveillance?**

Definition of intrusive surveillance

Intrusive surveillance is (s 26(3) RIPA):

- covert surveillance
- carried out on any residential premises or in any private vehicle and which involves
- the presence of an individual on the premises or in the vehicle or
- the use of a surveillance device (ie audio or visual probe).

Hint and tip: *A stolen vehicle is not a private vehicle for the purposes of RIPA authorization as the necessity for authorization relates to the rightful owner or user of the vehicle.*

If a technical device deployed outside the premises or the vehicle nevertheless produces a product of the same quality as would have been obtained by a device inside the premises or vehicle, then this also requires authority for intrusive surveillance; for instance, a long-range microphone capable of hearing conversations inside a building.

The meaning of residential premises is discussed in the CSPI Code, paras 2.13–2.16. Outside locations in public space where homeless persons sleep can be included in the protections provided by the concept of residential premises.

A device attached to a vehicle merely to reveal its location does not constitute intrusive surveillance (s 26(4)(a) RIPA), but will comprise directed surveillance and interference with property (s 26(2) RIPA in conjunction with s 93 PA97). Where both a surveillance authority and a property interference authority is required, a combined authority may be issued (s 33(5) RIPA). The relevant provisions of each Act apply in a combined authority and so in practice the different authority levels mean that whoever is the senior appropriate authorizing officer under the two regimes will consider combined applications.

Surveillance conducted in offices or in business vehicles (including taxis) requires a directed surveillance authority, not an intrusive surveillance authority.

Intrusive surveillance, subject to it being authorized, may be conducted for the purpose of *preventing or detecting serious crime*. Which means establishing by whom, for what purpose, by what means and generally in what circumstances any *serious crime* was committed and apprehending the suspected offender (ss 32(3) and 81(5) RIPA). Note that there is a higher threshold for intrusive surveillance—serious crime—than for directed surveillance (any crime or offence).

Other purposes for which intrusive surveillance is permitted are (s 32(3) RIPA):

- in the interests of national security, and
- in the interests of the economic well-being of the UK.

The Regulation of Investigatory Powers (Extension of Authorization Provisions: Legal Consultations) Order 2010 (SI 2010/461) requires (s 3(1)) that where directed surveillance on specified premises is likely to result in acquisition of legal consultation material, the surveillance must be regarded, treated and accordingly authorized as intrusive surveillance (see Chapter 2, 2.8.4).

Definition of serious crime

Serious crime is defined as (ss 81(2)(b) and 81(3) RIPA, following s 93(4) PA97):

(a) An offence for which, on first conviction, a person aged 21 years or over with no previous convictions might receive three years imprisonment, or
(b) The conduct
  - involves the use of violence;
  - results in substantial financial gain; or
  - is engaged in by a large number of persons for a common purpose.

(Section 81 RIPA does not reproduce that part of s 93(4) PA97 which refers to matters assigned under s 1(1) Customs and Excise Management Act 1979.)

3.4 What Authority Regime is Required for Intrusive Surveillance?

Authorizations for intrusive surveillance may be given by:

- Chief Constable or Commissioner of a police force as defined at 3.2 above, including the Ministry of Defence Police and British Transport Police
- Director General of the Serious Organised Crime Agency
- The Chief Constable and Deputy Chief Constable, Police Service of Northern Ireland

- Any Assistant Commissioner of the Metropolitan Police Service
- A designated senior officer of HM Revenue and Customs
- A Provost Marshal in the Army, Royal Air Force, or Royal Navy
- The Secretary of State in relation to the intelligence agencies.

Authorizations last for three months and can be renewed. They should be reviewed at monthly intervals or whenever there is a material change in circumstances affecting the validity of the authority.

Applications to conduct intrusive surveillance may only be made to, and considered by, investigators and authorizing officers working in the same organization. Thus a police officer may only seek authority from, or grant authority to, a member of the same force. An exception to this general principle is made when two or more *police forces* have entered into a collaborative working agreement pursuant to s 23 of the Police Act 1996, (for English and Welsh forces: s 12 of the Police (Scotland) Act 1967 for Scottish forces), _and_ the collaboration agreement permits applicants and authorizing officers to be from different forces. Where a collaborative working agreement is established for the purpose (*inter alia*) of facilitating intrusive surveillance or other forms of covert investigation such agreements must document specific arrangements for the management of covert investigation between the partners.

KEY POINT ON PROPORTIONALITY

The seriousness of the crime under investigation will not, in and of itself, provide a basis for meeting the proportionality test. Authorizing officers must articulate and document why the proposed method is proportionate to the product it is intended to produce (see Chapter 1.7.5).

KEY POINTS FOR AUTHORIZATIONS

- When considering combined authorities (s 33(5) RIPA) first identify whether this will lead to complications as a result of disclosure requirements.
- To ensure precision of applications (and therefore lawful authority), be careful to use words that are not ambiguous (for instance 'monitor' is open to varied interpretation, 'listen' and 'watch' are more precise; use both if both are required).
- Do not use the term 'subject' without identifying the person.
- If an authorization is no longer necessary it must be cancelled and notice given to the OSC within four hours of signing the cancellation.
- Rank or position of the authorizing officer must be indicated on the authority and if the authorizing officer is a designated deputy, this must also be indicated on the authority, as must the reason why the deputy has given the authority.

> - Designated deputies can only authorize if the authorizing officer is too ill, on annual leave, or absent from their office or home and so not able to access a secure telephone or fax machine within a reasonable time. The reason for the absence of the authorizing officer must be included in the application.
> - The scope of an authority may not be expanded on renewal but it may be reduced. A new authority is required if the scope of the surveillance is to increase.
>
> Authorizing officers must review and renew the authorities they gave.
>
> OSC *Annual Report 2005*, section 4

3.5 The Need for Prior Approval from the Office of Surveillance Commissioners

Before any investigative action pursuant to the authority can be carried out, the authorizing officer must notify the OSC in writing (s 35 RIPA). To make the authorization effective *prior approval* is required from the OSC *and* written notice of the OSC approval has to be given to the person who granted the authorization (s 36(2) RIPA).

Surveillance cannot commence until the authorizing officer has received written approval from the OSC.

If the authorizing officer considers the matter to be so urgent that prior approval cannot be sought, the authority will be effective upon written notification to the OSC (s 36(3) RIPA), subject to the OSC confirming or quashing the authority, having considered both whether it is an authority that would have received prior approval in normal circumstances *and* whether the circumstances in this case were really urgent.

Where the OSC decides not to approve an authority or to quash an authority, the decision will be conveyed to the most senior relevant person in the organization concerned.

Prior approval has been withheld in cases where:

- the matter under investigation failed to meet the serious crime criteria;
- where the proposed action was not necessary; or
- where the proposed action would not have been of substantial value to the investigation (OSC *Annual Report 2001–2002*, 8–9).

3.6 What Information is Required in an Application for Intrusive Surveillance?

Written applications for intrusive surveillance authority should describe both the purpose of the operation/investigation and the conduct for which authorization is sought. CSPI Code para 6.19 details further information that should be included in applications.

Further information and reading

Applications should be in writing and describe the conduct to be authorized and the purpose of the investigation or operation. The following matters must be covered in an application:

- an explanation of the *information or evidence* which it is desired to obtain as a result of the surveillance;
- the reasons why the authorization is *necessary* in the particular case and on the grounds listed in s 32(3) RIPA;
- the reasons why the surveillance is considered *proportionate* to what it seeks to achieve;
- an explanation as to why the information sought cannot reasonably be acquired by other means;
- the nature of the surveillance (ie precisely what actions investigators intend to take);
- precise details of the residential premises or private vehicle in relation to which the surveillance will take place;
- details of any potential *collateral intrusion* and why the intrusion is justified;
- details of any *confidential information* that is likely to be obtained as a consequence of the surveillance.

A subsequent record should be made of whether authority was given or refused, by whom and the time and date.

CSPI Code Chapter 6 deals with authorization procedures for intrusive surveillance. It should be read in conjunction with Chapter 2 (definitions) and Chapter 3 (general rules on authorizations).

Hint and tip: In relation to confidential information (communications subject to legal privilege; confidential personal information; or confidential journalistic material), special rules of authorization exist when such material is likely to be gathered by a CHIS or as a consequence of property interference (including variously the need for authorization by more senior staff and OSC prior approval). These rules are not reproduced for intrusive surveillance because such actions must have OSC prior approval, regardless of whether confidential information is likely to be acquired. Nevertheless the likelihood of doing so must be brought to the attention of the OSC in the application and authority.

3.7 Review and Renewal of Authorities

The CSPI Code (para 3.22) stresses the need for regular reviews of intrusive surveillance authorities, the frequency of which should be set by the authorizing officer when first authorizing the application. Where intrusive surveillance is likely to obtain confidential information or there is a high degree of either direct or collateral intrusion it will be necessary to review relevant authorities more regularly. Reviews are the responsibility of the authorizing officer; they should be documented and retained for three years (see CSPI Code, Chapter 8).

Further information and reading

CSPI Code paras 3.22–3.26 discuss the reviewing of covert investigation authorities.

CSPI Code paras 6.25–6.31 discuss the renewing of intrusive surveillance authorities.

3.8 Cancellation of Authorities

'The senior authorizing officer who granted or last renewed the authorization must cancel it, or the person who made the application to the Secretary of State must apply for its cancellation, if he is satisfied that the authorization no longer meets the criteria upon which it was authorized'. If this individual is no longer available, this statutory duty will fall to the person who has succeeded them in the relevant role (s 45 RIPA; CSPI Code paras 6.32–6.34; Regulation of Investigatory Powers (Cancellation of Authorisations) Regulations 2000 (SI 2000/2794)).

The OSC must be notified where authorities are cancelled.

KEY POINTS ON PROPORTIONALITY

Authorities and renewals last for a period of *three months* from when authorization is given. For *prior approval* this means authority from the Commissioner; thus if an authority was given at 0900 hours on 10 May, it expires at 2359 hours on 9 August.

Authorities given under the urgency provisions last only *seventy-two hours*.

3.9 What Significant Case Law Has Been Decided in Relation to Intrusive Surveillance?

Key principles have been established or confirmed in case law both pre-RIPA and post-RIPA and from case law not directly concerning criminal investigations.

3.9.1 Private life

An initial issue for investigators and authorizing officers is the determination of whether surveillance will or is likely to obtain information about anyone's private life. Strasbourg has interpreted 'private life' and what might constitute information about private life very broadly. It is difficult to envisage any circumstances in which intrusive surveillance will not involve acquiring private information.

In *Peck v UK* (2003) 36 EHRR 41, in which CCTV footage of the aftermath of Peck's suicide attempt in a town centre was released to TV broadcasters by the local council whose CCTV system had captured the images, the court held that 'Private life is a broad term not susceptible to exhaustive definition . . . There is a zone of interaction of a person with others, even in a public context, which may fall within the scope of "private life"'(at 730, para H5).

In *Von Hannover v Germany* [2006] 43 EHRR 7, the court held that private life can take place in the public domain; just because something happens in the public domain does not mean it is not private. Reinforcement for the notion that privacy still exists within a public environment is also found in UK case law. In *Campbell v MGN* [2004] 2 AC 457 at 458, the court held that 'although the photographs of the claimant were taken in a public place, the context in which they were used... added to the overall intrusion into the claimant's life'.

Collateral intrusion of third party privacy must also be considered and addressed. In *XXX & YYY v ZZZ* [2004] EWCA Civ 231, an *au pair* set up covert cameras in the home where she worked to record sexual advances from her male employer. The cameras also recorded the children, which was considered a breach of privacy.

Further information and reading

For a fuller discussion around the case law enforcement interpreting private life, see Starmer, *European Human Rights Law* (Legal Action Group, London) paras 3.109–3.111; *Niemitz v Germany* (1993) 16 EHRR 97; *Costello-Roberts v UK* (1995) 19 EHRR 112; *Friedl v Austria* (1996) 21 EHRR 83; *Halford v UK* (1997) 24 EHRR 523; *Perry v UK* (2004) 39 EHRR 3 (although a case involving a breach of PACE, it has been applied by OSC inspectors when interpreting private life). See also OSC *Annual Report 2003–2004*, 8; S McKay, *Covert Policing: Law and Practice* (Oxford University Press, Oxford, 2011) devotes Chapter 2 to the issues of privacy, proportionality and other human rights issues.

3.9.2 Audio devices in police cells and exercise yards

Several cases provide guidance about this intrusive surveillance tactic, two of which pre-date RIPA. Covert recording of suspects in custody for serious offences was held not to be contrary to PACE in *R v Mason and others* [2002] 2 Cr App R 38 at 648, para 77, in which Woolf LCJ determined:

> The police did no more than arrange a situation which was likely to result in the appellants volunteering confessions. The appellants were not tricked into saying what they did even though they were placed in a position where they were likely to do so. If evidence of a satisfactory nature could be obtained by

other means, it is preferable that it is obtained by those means rather than covertly. Here, it was not unreasonably considered by the Chief Constable that the evidence would not be obtained by more conventional means.

R v Bailey and Smith [1993] 3 All ER 513 established the principle that conversations between co-defendants placed in the same cell after charge, which were recorded by police, could be admitted in evidence. Such admissibility was reconsidered in *R v Roberts (Stephen Paul)* [1997] 1 Cr App R 217, in which the Appeal Court held that it was for the trial judge to determine admissibility on the merits of each case. The crucial test would be the conduct of the investigators and whether such conduct would result in an unfair trial.

The conduct of investigators was a key determining factor in three cases—*Sutherland, Sentence*, and *Grant*—arising from the deployment of audio surveillance devices in police station exercise yards by Lincolnshire Police. In each case the surveillance devices recorded conversations between suspects and their legal representatives; conversations that were legally privileged. In each case Lincolnshire police asserted that the capture of such conversations had been inadvertent.

In *R v Sutherland* the judge stayed proceedings to prevent abuse of process because he concluded that the police had acted in bad faith and that the recording of privileged conversations had been deliberate, not inadvertent (unreported, Nottingham Crown Court, 29 January 2002; discussed in *Archbold's Criminal Pleading, Evidence and Practice* (revd edn, Sweet & Maxwell, London, 2005) para 15–532, at 1626; cited in *R v Mason and others* [2002] 2 Cr App R 38 at 643, para 60).

In *R v Sentence* a defence application to stay proceedings due to a breach of process was also successful, the judge determining that the circumstances were identical to those in *Sutherland* and concluding:

> It is plain that I have not been told the whole truth by several police officers, namely . . . I am driven by all the evidence in this case to the clear conclusion on the balance of probabilities that there was a planned and deliberate capture of privileged conversation between a solicitor and his client [. . .]. This is not a case of a chapter of accidents or a comedy of errors.

> (Transcript 64E–65A, 1 April 2004, HH Judge Heath, Lincoln Crown Court).

In quashing Grant's conviction the Court of Appeal, *R v Grant* [2005] EWCA Crim 1089, rejected the trial judge's acceptance of such police tactics and doubted his acceptance from police officers at the *voir dire, Sutherland* and *Sentence* notwithstanding, that the possibility of privileged conversations being recorded in such circumstances had not crossed their minds. The Court of Appeal found that police investigators had deliberately interfered with the appellant's rights so acting in bad faith.

3.9.3 Surveillance of legal consultations

Following on from the above, the case of *McE* [2009] UKHL 15 considered the issue of directed surveillance that captured *legal consultations*. Consequently the

Regulation of Investigatory Powers (Extension of Authorization Provisions: Legal Consultations) Order 2010 (SI 2010/461) was issued.

'Legal consultation is a narrower concept than legal privilege, so a matter that is likely to cause confusion to an already confused area of the law . . .' (McKay 2011, para 6.68). Legal consultation material falls within the scope of legally privileged material.

The 2010 Order requires (s 3 (1)) that where directed surveillance on specified premises is likely to result in acquisition of legal consultation material, the surveillance must be regarded, treated and accordingly authorized as intrusive surveillance.

Legal consultation is defined in the Order (s 2 (a)) as:

(i) a consultation between a professional legal adviser and his client or any person representing his client, or

(ii) a consultation between a professional legal adviser or his client or any such representative and a medical practitioner made in connection with or in contemplation of legal proceedings and for the purposes of such proceedings.

The specified premises are detailed in s 3 (2) of the Order as follows:

(a) any place in which persons who are serving sentences of imprisonment or detention, remanded in custody or committed in custody for trial or sentence may be detained;

(b) any place in which persons may be detained under para 16(1), (1A) or (2) of schedule 2 or para 2(2) or (3) of schedule 3 to the Immigration Act 1971 or section 36(1) of the UK Border Act 2007;

(c) police stations;

(d) hospitals where high security psychiatric services are provided;

(e) the place of business of any professional legal adviser; and

(f) any place used for the sittings and business of any court, tribunal, inquest or inquiry.

The revised CSPI Code now devotes an entire chapter (Chapter 4) to discussion of issues concerning legally privileged and confidential information.

Further information and reading

Sutherland, Sentence and *Grant* are more fully discussed in D Ormerod & A Waterman, 'Abusing a stay for Grant?' *Covert Policing Review* (2005), 5–14, in which the authors draw attention to Lord Taylor CJ's assertion regarding legal privilege:

Legal professional privilege is… much more than an ordinary rule of evidence, limited in its application to the facts of the particular case. It is a fundamental condition on which the administration of justice as a whole rests.

(*R v Derby Magistrates' Court ex p B* [1996] AC 487 at 507)

3.9.4 **Protection of observation posts**

Recognizing that failure to secure observation posts from which to conduct surveillance could seriously impede legitimate investigations, the Appeal Court applied, in *R v Rankine* [1986] 1 QB 861, the same presumption of protection applied to human sources of information, namely that the identity of locations used should be protected unless doing so would lead to a miscarriage of justice. Minimum evidential standards were applied to this principle in *R v Johnson* [1988] 1 WLR 1377, confirmed by *R v Hewitt and Davis* (1992) 95 Cr App R 81 and *R v Grimes* [1994] Crim LR 213.

Case law criteria: *R v Johnson* [1988] 1 WLR 1377

The criteria set out in *R v Johnson* are reproduced in the ACPO *Practice Advice on Core Investigative Doctrine* (2005) 104:

The police officer in charge of observations of a rank not lower than sergeant must be able to testify that beforehand he or she visited all the observation places to be used and ascertained the attitude of the occupiers of the premises:

- as to the use of the premises;
- to the disclosure of the use of the premises;
- to the possible identification of the premises or the occupiers.

The difficulties, if any are encountered, in obtaining observation posts in the area.

In addition, immediately prior to the trial, an officer of a rank not lower than chief inspector must be able to testify that he visited the premises used for observations and ascertained if the occupiers are the same as when the observations were conducted and, whether they are or not, what their attitude is to:

- the possible disclosure of the use made of the premises;
- the disclosure of facts which would lead to the identification of those premises and their occupiers.

This evidence will be given in the absence of the jury when the application to exclude the material evidence is made. The judge should explain to the jury the effect of his or her ruling regarding the disclosure of the premises.

Because exposure of unmarked police vehicles would not necessarily involve the same threat of harassment or fear of violence that members of the public who make premises available for observation posts might face (*Blake and Austin v DPP* (1993) 97 Cr App R 169), the same presumption of protection would not, as a matter of policy, be applied to police vehicles from which observations were conducted (*R v Brown and Daley* (1988) 87 Cr App R 52).

3.9.5 **Disclosure of surveillance authorizations**

The statutory presumption of disclosure is founded in the CPIA. Because surveillance authorities may contain sensitive detail exposure of which would be against the public interest, such authorities may be scheduled as sensitive unused material. If the prosecutor recognizes contentious issues regarding the authorization process, a redacted version of the authority should be disclosed and an unedited version supplied to the judge for determination that the defendant is not vulnerable to a miscarriage arising from non-disclosure (*R v Hardy and Hardy* [2002] EWCA Crim 3012). Where the defence declare specific issues with the authorization process, as in *R v Grant* [2005] EWCA Crim 1089, full disclosure of all documentation related to a covert investigation authorization may be ordered. In *R v Harmes* [2006] EWCA Crim 928 the court considered the authorization documentation in detail, noting (at para 22) that renewals of the authorization had failed to detail either changes in circumstances or changes in planned police activity, and concluding (at para 42) that 'there were serious breaches of the Act and the Code in the process of authorization'.

Checklist of key issues when considering whether or not to deploy covert investigation techniques

- What evidence or intelligence is being sought?

- How is it relevant to the operation under consideration?

- What is the least intrusive means of securing such evidence or information?

- Has the least intrusive means of securing the evidence or information been attempted? If not, why not?

- What is the likelihood of collateral intrusion against the privacy of persons not being investigated? How will collateral intrusion be prevented (or if not, minimized) and how will the product of collateral intrusion be managed?

- What are the risks to the organization of such tactics? (Chapter 11)

- What are the risks to the organization's staff of such tactics? (Chapter 11)

- What are the risks to the public or specific third parties when such tactics are deployed? (Chapter 11)

- What are the risks to the subject of the investigation? (Chapter 11)

- Will the proposed methods breach Article 8(1)? (1.7.1)

- Is there justification for doing so provided by Article 8(2)? (1.7.4)

- How is the legality test met? (1.7.3)

- How is the legitimacy test met? (1.7.4)

- How is the necessity test met? (1.7.5)

- How is the proportionality test met? (1.7.5)

- Are the arguments justifying the application to use covert investigation based on reliable information/intelligence, or has the applicant adopted a 'tick-the-box' approach to completing the application without giving full consideration to the facts of the case and the issues arising?

- Have the arguments justifying the granting of authorization to use covert investigation been fully articulated, or has the authorizing officer merely paid lip service to the pro forma authorization template via which authority is granted?

- When should this authority be reviewed? What circumstances will or may arise that will necessitate review before then?

- How are the methods by which the evidence/intelligence will be obtained to be protected at trial? (Chapter 12)

- How will the product of the surveillance be managed? (Chapter 12)

Planning covert investigation actions

Remember to include the PLAN for covert investigation tactics in all investigation policy-book entries relating to covert investigation considerations and decisions.

P   PROPORTIONALITY
Why is it proportionate to obtain the intended product of this surveillance in the manner proposed? (1.7.5)

L   LEGITIMACY
What is the legitimate purpose of the proposed action: the prevention of disorder or crime; the interests of national security; the interests of public safety; the interests of the economic wellbeing of the country; the protection of health or morals; the protection of the rights and freedoms of others? (1.7.4)

A   AUTHORITY TO UNDERTAKE PROPOSED ACTION
What is the lawful foundation and authority for the proposed action? From whom must authorization be sought? (1.7.3)

N   NECESSITY OF PROPOSED ACTION
Why is the proposed action necessary? (1.7.5)

Flowchart for Authorizing an Intrusive Surveillance Operation

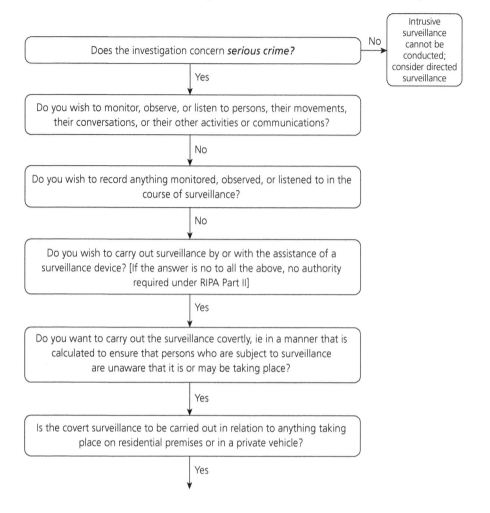

Does the investigation concern *serious crime?*

No → Intrusive surveillance cannot be conducted; consider directed surveillance

Yes

Do you wish to monitor, observe, or listen to persons, their movements, their conversations, or their other activities or communications?

No

Do you wish to record anything monitored, observed, or listened to in the course of surveillance?

No

Do you wish to carry out surveillance by or with the assistance of a surveillance device? [If the answer is no to all the above, no authority required under RIPA Part II]

Yes

Do you want to carry out the surveillance covertly, ie in a manner that is calculated to ensure that persons who are subject to surveillance are unaware that it is or may be taking place?

Yes

Is the covert surveillance to be carried out in relation to anything taking place on residential premises or in a private vehicle?

Yes

Flowchart for Authorizing an Intrusive Surveillance Operation continued

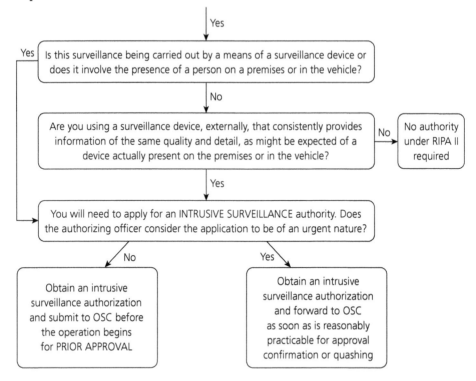

Yes

Yes — Is this surveillance being carried out by a means of a surveillance device or does it involve the presence of a person on a premises or in the vehicle?

No

Are you using a surveillance device, externally, that consistently provides information of the same quality and detail, as might be expected of a device actually present on the premises or in the vehicle? — No → No authority under RIPA II required

Yes

You will need to apply for an INTRUSIVE SURVEILLANCE authority. Does the authorizing officer consider the application to be of an urgent nature?

No

Obtain an intrusive surveillance authorization and submit to OSC before the operation begins for PRIOR APPROVAL

Yes

Obtain an intrusive surveillance authorization and forward to OSC as soon as is reasonably practicable for approval confirmation or quashing

4

Interference with Property or Wireless Telegraphy and Entry onto Land

4.1 **Introduction**

Certain tactics that facilitate covert investigation involve actions that constitute crimes or torts. The deployment of a listening device at private residential premises or the attachment of a location-tracking device to a vehicle, for instance, will certainly involve trespass and could involve criminal damage being caused. Part III PA97 provides the statutory regime under which such actions may be authorized and so rendered lawful within the context of the authorized action. In other circumstances, such as a siege situation, the authorities may regard it as necessary and proportionate to jam or otherwise interfere with radio signals. Authorizations should be sought wherever members of the empowered organizations 'or persons acting on their behalf, conduct entry on, or interference with, property or wireless telegraphy that would be otherwise unlawful' (CSPI Code, para 7.1).

Such activity was originally subject to Home Office Guidelines issued in 1984 but guidelines, as discussed in Chapter 1, fail the legality test (in accordance with law) under Article 8(2) ECHR. Concerning property interference, the leading UK case confirming this principle is *Khan*. In filling this particular legislative lacuna, the 1997 Act did not make provision for surveillance itself, hence the need to provide an additional statutory regime for surveillance in the RIPA. Because property interference will often be a prerequisite for intrusive surveillance under RIPA, provision is made for joint authorizations to be made where authority is required for property interference and intrusive surveillance in order to complete a single operation within an investigation.

Further information and reading

R v Khan [1997] AC 558; *Khan v UK* (2001) 31 EHRR 45; see also K Starmer, M Strange, and Q Whitaker, *Criminal Justice, Police Powers and Human Rights* (Blackstone Press, London, 2001), 37.

B Emmerson and D Friedman, *A Guide to the Police Act 1997* (Butterworths, London, 1998), 4.

A revised Code of Practice for Covert Surveillance and Property Interference has been published. It is reproduced in Appendix A below and is available online at <http://www.homeoffice.gov.uk/publications/counter-terrorism/ripa-forms/code-of-practice-covert?view=Binary> (accessed December 2011). In this volume 'CSPI Code' refers to this Code.

Applicants and authorizing officers, when considering property interference and the need for an authorization, should consider:

- whether anyone is in a position to consent to the interference, and whether such consent can be obtained without compromising the operation;
- whether the proposed action can be reconfigured so as to avoid property interference; and

- whether the interference is so minor as to be insignificant and is rendered lawful by virtue of s 27(2) RIPA.

Section 27(2) RIPA states that a person shall not be subject to civil liability in respect of any conduct that is incidental to the authorized conduct and which cannot be otherwise authorized and might reasonably not have been anticipated when seeking the original authorization.

4.2 Which Public Authorities May Interfere with Property or Wireless Telegraphy and Enter onto Land?

The following organizations may carry out these aspects of covert investigation:

- Police forces in England and Wales maintained under s 2 Police Act 1996
- The Metropolitan Police
- The City of London Police
- Police forces maintained under s 1 Police (Scotland) Act 1967
- The Police Service of Northern Ireland
- HM Revenue and Customs
- The Serious Organised Crime Agency
- MI5, MI6, GCHQ.

The organizations are defined by reference to who may authorize such interference and entry (s 93(5) PA97) and, in the case of the intelligence agencies, by virtue of s 5 Intelligence Services Act 1994.

4.3 What Powers Does the Law Provide in Relation to Interference with Property or Wireless Telegraphy and Entry onto Land?

Investigators can take such action, in respect of property or wireless telegraphy in the relevant area, as is specified in the authorization (s 93(1) PA97). Authorizing officers are advised to 'state explicitly what is being authorized' (OSC *Guidance and Procedures*, para 3.4). Thus in relation to the placing of an audio device inside residential premises, for example, every action required to achieve this objective must be specifically authorized, including separate reconnoitering operations to determine feasibility prior to the actual deployment and subsequent operations to retrieve the device.

Certain criteria must be present for the power to be applied.

> **KEY POINT FOR AUTHORIZING OFFICERS**
>
> Before authorizing such action as may be required the authorizing officer must believe:
>
> (a) that the taking of the action specified is *necessary* for the purpose of preventing or detecting *serious crime*; and
>
> (b) that the taking of such action is proportionate to what the action seeks to achieve (s 93(2) PA97).
>
> When considering proportionality, applicants and authorizing officers will have to take into account that increasingly sophisticated surveillance technology may negate the need for property interference: for instance, external monitoring of conversations within a premises rather than internal monitoring.

Definition of serious crime

Conduct will constitute serious crime if:

(a) it involves the use of violence, or it results in substantial financial gain, or it is conducted by a large number of persons in pursuit of a common purpose; or

(b) the offence, or one of the offences, is an offence for which a person who has attained the age of twenty-one and has no previous convictions could reasonably be expected to be sentenced to imprisonment for a term of three years or more (s 93(4) PA97).

Note: This statutory definition is worded slightly differently from, but appears to have influenced, the definition of serious crime in ss 81(2)(b) and 81(3) RIPA which sets the threshold for recourse to intrusive surveillance.

4.4 What Authority Regime is Required for Interference with Property or Wireless Telegraphy and Entry onto Land?

Where the above criteria are met the following may authorize such interference (s 93(5) PA97), in some circumstances (described below 4.5) subject to the prior approval of the OSC:

- Chief Constable (police forces in England, Wales, and Scotland)
- Commissioner or Assistant Commissioner (Metropolitan Police)
- Commissioner (City of London Police)
- Chief Constable and Deputy Chief Constable Police Service of Northern Ireland
- A designated authorizing officer within the Serious Organised Crime Agency

- Chief Constable British Transport Police
- Chief Constable Ministry of Defence Police
- Provost Marshals in the Army, Royal Navy, and Royal Air Force
- Any customs officer designated by the Commissioners of Revenue and Customs for this purpose.

Where it is not reasonably practicable to obtain the authority of the authorizing officer identified above, the Act specifies that designated deputies may make such authorizations (s 94 PA97).

Authorizations may only be given to applicants from the same organization as the authorizing officer. An exception to this general principle is made when two or more *police forces* have entered into a collaborative working agreement pursuant to s 23 of the Police Act 1996, (for English and Welsh forces: s 12 of the Police (Scotland) Act 1967 for Scottish forces), _and_ the collaboration agreement permits applicants and authorizing officers to be from different forces. Where a collaborative working agreement is established for the purpose (*inter alia*) of facilitating directed surveillance or other forms of covert investigation, such agreements must document specific arrangements for the management of covert investigation between the partners.

KEY POINTS ON PROPERTY INTERFERENCE AUTHORIZATION TIMESCALES

Property interference authorities are effective from the time of signing, but authorizations are notified to the Commissioner for scrutiny. Property interference authorities requiring prior approval are only effective from the time the authorizing officer receives written approval from the OSC (OSC *Annual Report 2005*, 3.16). Authorizations, renewals, and cancellations should be notified to the OSC within *four working hours* of being given. In the case of *prior approval* authorizations, notifications should be sent to the OSC *at least sixteen working hours* before surveillance is due to start. Decisions on *prior approval* applications from Commissioners should be received within eight working hours.

KEY POINTS ON DRAFTING APPLICATIONS AND AUTHORITIES

- When considering combined authorities (s 33(5) RIPA), first identify whether this will lead to complications as a result of disclosure requirements.
- To ensure precision of applications (and therefore lawful authority), be careful to use words that are not ambiguous (for instance 'monitor' is open to varied interpretation, while 'listen' and 'watch' are more precise; use both if both are required).

KEY POINTS FOR AUTHORIZING OFFICERS

- Do not use the term 'subject' without identifying the person.
- If an authorization is no longer necessary it must be cancelled and notice given to the OSC within four hours of signing the cancellation.
- Rank or position of the authorizing officer must be indicated on the authority and if the authorizing officer is a designated deputy, this must also be indicated on the authority, as must the reason why the deputy has given the authority.
- Designated deputies can only authorize if the authorizing officer is too ill, on annual leave, or absent from their office or home and so not able to access a secure telephone or fax machine within a reasonable time. The reason for the absence of the authorizing officer must be included in the application.
- The scope of an authority may not be expanded on renewal but it may be reduced. A new authority is required if the scope of the surveillance is to increase.

Authorizing officers must review and renew the authorities they gave.

(OSC *Annual Report 2005*, section 4)

The seriousness of the crime under investigation will not, in and of itself, provide a basis for meeting the proportionality test. Authorizing officers must articulate and document why the proposed method is proportionate to the product it is intended to produce (see Chapter 1.7.5).

Excepting property warrants issued to the intelligence services by the Secretary of State (s 5 Intelligence Services Act 1994), authorizations for such interference or entry onto property must be in writing and will last for three months (s 95 PA97). Authorities issued orally in matters of urgency have effect for seventy-two hours only.

Authorizing officers may only authorize applications made by members of their organization (s 93(3)) and may only authorize activity with the relevant area over which they have jurisdiction (s 93(6)). In each case this includes, where appropriate, the twelve nautical miles of territorial waters adjacent to the relevant area.

Section 96 imposes on authorizing officers the obligation to notify the OSC as soon as reasonably practicable when granting, renewing, or cancelling any authority.

It is accepted that occasionally incidental property interference will occur. No civil liability arises where such conduct is 'incidental to correctly authorized, directed or intrusive surveillance activity and for which an authorization or warrant is not capable of being granted or might not reasonably have been expected to be sought under any existing legislation' (CSPI Code, para 7.6). Authorization should be sought whenever it might be reasonably expected to do so and the public authority concerned is capable of doing so (CSPI Code, para 7.7).

The acquisition of samples (DNA, fingerprints, footwear impressions) is not itself unlawful interference with property if no damage is caused in the acquisition. Authorization will be required where it is necessary to interfere with property in order 'to access and obtain the samples' (CSPI Code, para 7.8).

4.5 The Need for Prior Approval from the Office of Surveillance Commissioners

Prior approval must be sought from the OSC before the authorized activity can take place when the property specified in the authority is (s 97(2) PA97):

- wholly or mainly used as a dwelling
- a hotel bedroom
- constitutes office premises

or when the action authorized is likely to result in the acquisition of knowledge about:

- matters subject to legal privilege (defined in s 98)
- confidential personal information (defined in s 99)
- confidential journalistic material (defined in s 100).

In such circumstances the authorized action can only commence once the authorizing officer has received written approval from the OSC (Covert Surveillance Code, para 6.30), which will only be given if the Commissioner holds the beliefs specified at s 93(2) (see 'Key points for authorizing officers' box above). Where prior approval is refused, the authorizing officer shall be given a report explaining why. Appeals against a refusal may be made to the Chief Commissioner in the manner prescribed in s 104.

The interference may not take place until the approval has been communicated by the OSC to the authorizing officer.

An authority to interfere with property that is not a dwelling, a hotel bedroom or office premises does not require prior approval.

A combined property interference and intrusive surveillance authority will always require prior approval because of the intrusive element.

4.6 What Information is Required in an Application for Interference with Property?

Written applications for authority to interfere with property should describe both the purpose of the operation/investigation and the conduct for which authorization is sought. CSPI Code, para 7.18 details further information that should be included in applications.

Further information and reading

Applications should be in writing and describe the conduct to be authorized and the purpose of the investigation or operation. The following matters must be covered in an application:

- property that is to be subject to the interference;
- sufficient information to identify the property which the entry or interference will affect;
- the nature and extent of the proposed interference; the details of any collateral intrusion, including the identity of individuals and/or categories of people, where known, who are likely to be affected, and why the intrusion is justified;
- details of the offence suspected or committed;
- how the *authorization* criteria (as set out above) have been met;
- any action which may be necessary to maintain any equipment, including replacing it;
- any action which may be necessary to retrieve any equipment;
- in case of a renewal, the results obtained so far, or a full explanation of the failure to obtain any results; and
- whether an *authorization* was given or refused, by whom and the time and date on which this happened.

See CSPI Code, paras 7.18–7.19.

4.7 Review and Renewal of Authorities

The CSPI Code (para 3.22) stresses the need for regular reviews of intrusive surveillance authorities, the frequency of which should be set by the authorizing officer when first authorizing the application. Where intrusive surveillance is likely to obtain confidential information or there is a high degree of ether direct or collateral intrusion it will be necessary to review relevant authorities more regularly. Reviews are the responsibility of the authorizing officer; they should be documented and retained for three years (see CSPI Code, Chapter 8).

Further information and reading

CSPI Code, paras 3.22–3.26 discuss the reviewing of covert investigation authorities.

CSPI Code, paras 7.27–7.29 discuss the renewing of property interference authorities.

4.8 **Cancellation of Authorities**

'The senior authorizing officer who granted or last renewed the authorization must cancel it, or the person who made the application to the Secretary of State must apply for its cancellation, if he is satisfied that the authorization no longer meets the criteria upon which it was authorized.' If this individual is no longer available, this statutory duty will fall to the person who has succeeded them in the relevant role (s 95(5) PA97; CSPI Code, paras 7.30–7.32; the Police Act 1997 (Notification of Authorisations etc) Order 1998 (SI 1998/3241)).

4.9 **What Significant Case Law Has Been Decided in Relation to Property or Wireless Telegraphy Interference and Entry onto Land?**

In September 1992 Khan, together with his cousin N, entered the UK at Manchester airport. They were detained by HMCE. N was found to be in possession of heroin with a street value of £100,000 and was prosecuted. In interview Khan made no admissions and, in the absence of other evidence, was not proceeded against.

In January 1993 police deployed a listening device at the house of B in Sheffield who was under separate suspicion of heroin dealing. Deployment of the device involved trespass and minor criminal damage. Unknown to police at the time, B was an associate of Khan. Khan visited B whilst the listening device was deployed and recording. The listening device recorded a casual conversation between B and Khan, in which the latter described his involvement in the heroin shipment the previous September for which N had been convicted. This recording was relied upon in evidence in the prosecution of Khan for importation.

Khan sought exclusion of the recording in a *voir dire* arguing that the Home Office Guidelines (deposited in the library of the House of Commons and available on application from the Home Office) under which the surveillance had been conducted did not constitute law and so breached Article 8(2). The judge admitted the evidence as being relevant regardless of any ECHR breach. The Appeal Court subsequently held he was right to do so (*R v Khan* [1997] AC 558).

The ECtHR subsequently held that the deployment of the device in the absence of a statutory regime constituted a violation of Article 8(2), but the use of the evidence obtained thereby did not constitute a violation of Article 6, nor had the investigators acted in bad faith because they had complied with the prevailing regime even though it subsequently was held to be unlawful (*Khan v UK* (2001) 31 EHRR 45). This decision followed the principles previously asserted in *Govell v UK* (1997) 23 EHRR CD101 and was reasserted in *Lewis v UK* (2004) 39 EHRR 9.

This finding highlighted the need for the statutory regime subsequently established in Part III PA97 and reaffirmed the principle that relevant evidence unlawfully obtained may yet be admitted by the court.

Interference with property scenario

Mr Leonard is believed to be a money-launderer from a group involved in people trafficking. His refuse is collected weekly from the front drive of his house. It is desired to examine the contents of the refuse to ascertain details of any bank accounts he may have. In order to do this investigators will need to enter the front drive of Mr Leonard's house and remove the refuse bags.

In order to enter the driveway of the house (a private property), a property interference authority will be required. The refuse bags, although abandoned by the owner, still remain property because they have only been abandoned in favour of the refuse collector. Therefore, investigators will also require an authority to interfere with the refuse bags. This would also be true if the refuse bags were left outside the perimeter of the premises on the public highway.

(OSC *Annual Report 2005*, 4.7)

Checklist of key issues when considering whether or not to deploy covert investigation techniques

- What evidence or intelligence is being sought?

- How is it relevant to the operation under consideration?

- What is the least intrusive means of securing such evidence or information?

- Has the least intrusive means of securing the evidence or information been attempted? If not, why not?

- What is the likelihood of collateral intrusion against the privacy of persons not being investigated? How will collateral intrusion be prevented (or if not, minimized) and how will the product of collateral intrusion be managed?

- What are the risks to the organization of such tactics? (Chapter 11)

- What are the risks to the organization's staff of such tactics? (Chapter 11)

- What are the risks to the public or specific third parties when such tactics are deployed? (Chapter 11)

- What are the risks to the subject of the investigation? (Chapter 11)

- Will the proposed methods breach Article 8(1)? (1.7.1)

- Is there justification for doing so provided by Article 8(2)? (1.7.4)

- How is the legality test met? (1.7.3)

- How is the legitimacy test met? (1.7.4)

- How is the necessity test met? (1.7.5)

- How is the proportionality test met? (1.7.5)

- Are the arguments justifying the application to use covert investigation based on reliable information/intelligence, or has the applicant adopted a 'tick-the-box' approach to completing the application without giving full consideration to the facts of the case and the issues arising?

- Have the arguments justifying the granting of authorization to use covert investigation been fully articulated, or has the authorizing officer merely paid lip service to the pro forma authorization template via which authority is granted?

- When should this authority be reviewed? What circumstances will or may arise that will necessitate review before then?

- How are the methods by which the evidence/intelligence will be obtained to be protected at trial? (Chapter 12)

- How will the product of the surveillance be managed? (Chapter 12)

Planning covert investigation actions

Remember to include the PLAN for covert investigation tactics in all investigation policy-book entries relating to covert investigation considerations and decisions.

P   PROPORTIONALITY
Why is it proportionate to obtain the intended product of this surveillance in the manner proposed? (1.7.5)

L   LEGITIMACY
What is the legitimate purpose of the proposed action: the prevention of disorder or crime; the interests of national security; the interests of public safety; the interests of the economic well-being of the country; the protection of health or morals; the protection of the rights and freedoms of others? (1.7.4)

A   AUTHORITY TO UNDERTAKE PROPOSED ACTION
What is the lawful foundation and authority for the proposed action? From whom must authorization be sought? (1.7.3)

N   NECESSITY OF PROPOSED ACTION
Why is the proposed action necessary? (1.7.5)

Flowchart for Authorizing Interference with, or Entry onto, Premises or Private Land

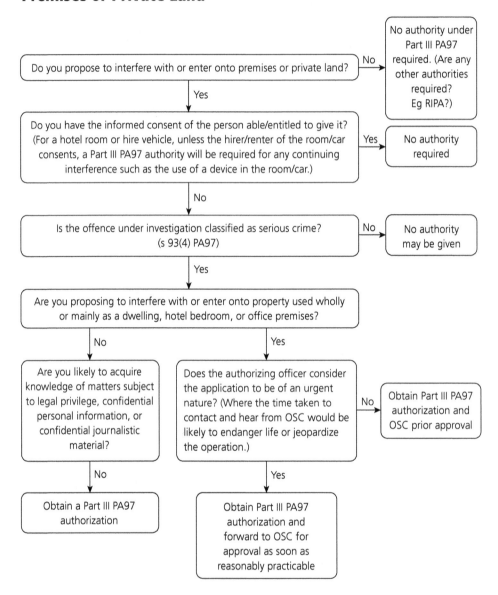

Flowchart for Authorizing Interference with Property

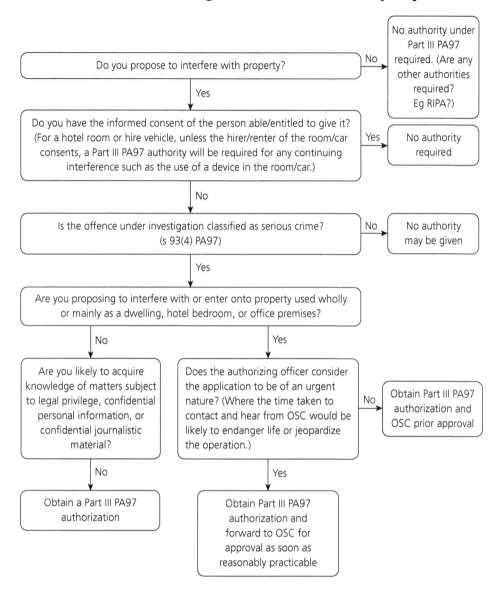

Flowchart for Authorizing Interference with Wireless Telegraphy

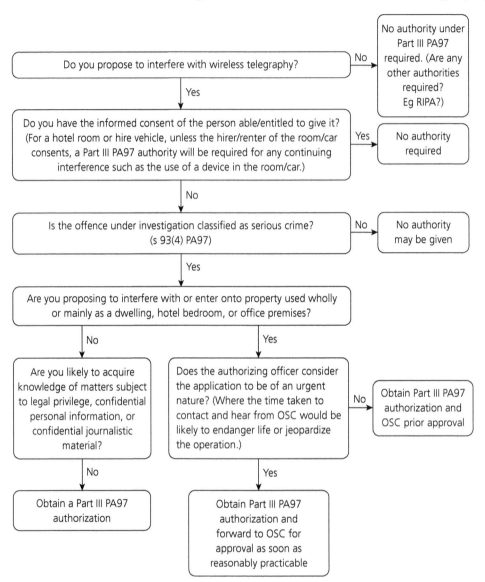

5

Covert Investigation and Computers

5.1 **Introduction**

Computers can be the scene of a crime (victim evidence), the means by which a crime is planned or committed (offender evidence; intelligence), a means of communication when facilitating a conspiracy (offence and offender evidence; intelligence), and a means of (covertly) investigating crime. Once again, precision in the drafting of applications and authorities is important, especially so given the multiple roles of the computer within covert investigation.

This is an area of developing law. It is also an area in which investigators without expertise in hi-tech crime investigation would be well advised to seek up-to-date advice from computer crime investigators when planning covert operations. This chapter should be seen as a general introduction to a rapidly evolving arena.

This is also an area in which particular attention must be made to collateral intrusion since the surveillance can be focused on the use made of a computer rather than direct surveillance of a person. Since in any given household more than one person might use any given computer, the potential for collateral intrusion when monitoring computer use is particularly high and careful consideration to the potential for and management of such intrusion will be required in both applications and authorities. No intrusion can be authorized that is disproportionate to the crime under investigation and the information that is expected to be obtained as a result of this particular investigation tactic.

5.2 **Which Public Authorities Can Investigate Computers Covertly and Which Legal Authorities Are Required?**

Computers are property and so covert investigation of computers will constitute *interference with property* if it is necessary to access, either physically or through the deployment of software, the target computer in order to effect the investigation or surveillance.

Additionally, surveillance of the use of a computer will often take place in circumstances that comprise *intrusive surveillance*. And since live-time email (as opposed to stored emails) is a communication in progress, should that be the subject of investigation, then an *interception* warrant will be required.

The authority regimes for intrusive surveillance, property interference, and interception of communications therefore dictate which public authorities can conduct such covert investigation of computers (see Chapters 2, 3, and 7). Those agencies empowered to *interfere with property* are:

- Police forces in England and Wales maintained under s 2 Police Act 1996
- Police forces maintained under s 1 Police (Scotland) Act 1967
- The Metropolitan Police
- The City of London Police

- The Police Service of Northern Ireland
- HM Revenue and Customs
- The Serious Organised Crime Agency
- MI5, MI6, and GCHQ (s 5 Intelligence Services Act 1994).

The organizations are defined by reference to who may authorize such interference and entry (s 93(5) PA97 and s 5 Intelligence Services Act 1994). Those agencies able to conduct *intrusive surveillance* are:

- Any police force maintained under s 2 Police Act 1996
- Any police force maintained under s 1 Police (Scotland) Act 1967
- The Metropolitan Police Service
- The City of London Police
- The Police Service of Northern Ireland
- The Ministry of Defence Police
- The British Transport Police
- The Serious Organised Crime Agency
- The Army, Navy, Royal Marines, and Air Force
- HM Revenue and Customs
- MI5, MI6, and GCHQ (by virtue of s 42 RIPA).

There are circumstances in which computers can be the subject of *directed surveillance*, in which case a greater number of public authorities may lawfully conduct such investigations (see Chapter 2).

Regarding which authorities are required under what circumstances, the simplest approach to answering this question is to distinguish the answers according to investigation technique typology.

5.3 What Action Requires a Directed Surveillance Authority in Relation to the Investigation of Computers?

In circumstances where a kidnapper or blackmailer is communicating with the victim via email, as with the monitoring of phone calls in such circumstances, with the written consent of one of the parties to the communication, the communication may be lawfully monitored under a directed surveillance authority (ss 3(2), 26(2), and 28 RIPA).

A directed surveillance *may* also be appropriate where the surveillance is to be carried out in an internet café, but the exact tactics to be employed and the desired product would dictate the exact authority regime required. For instance, if the investigator's intention was to intercept emails being sent from a terminal in the café, then an interception warrant would be required. A directed surveillance authority would be appropriate in circumstances where the intention was to monitor a suspect's use of the computer by camera or by the deployment of surveillance officers in the café, *but* where the use of a camera meant that both sides of chatroom conversation could be seen and this was the purpose of the surveillance then an interception warrant would be required.

5.4 What Action Requires an Intrusive Surveillance Authority in Relation to the Investigation of Computers?

Where surveillance is to be conducted on use made of a computer in private residential dwellings, hotel rooms, office premises or in a private vehicle, an intrusive surveillance authority with OSC *prior approval* will be required. If the surveillance also requires entry into and trespass onto property, and or interference with the computer that is to be monitored, then a property interference authority will also be required (see Chapters 2, 3, and 4).

For example, the deployment of devices onto a home computer, either by physical attachment or remotely via software, will necessitate interference with property prior to the surveillance being carried out. Because the surveillance is being carried out in a dwelling, it will be intrusive. Similarly, remote activation of a home computer will constitute both an interference with property (the remote activation of the computer) and intrusive surveillance (the conduct of surveillance in a private dwelling).

5.5 What Action Requires a Property Interference Authority in Relation to the Investigation of Computers?

Any action that interferes with the hardware of a computer or alters the software profile of a particular computer will require authority under Part III PA97.

This would include, for instance, the covert deployment of a physical device, the loading of software onto a computer without the computer owner's knowledge, or the remote covert activation of a computer. (The latter would additionally require intrusive surveillance authority.)

Where it is proposed to deploy a physical device onto a keyboard or covertly to copy the contents of a hard drive, and the computer is on private premises, then the authorization will have to cover all preparatory acts required to facilitate such a deployment or action, as well as the deployment or action itself. Recovery of equipment will also have to be properly authorized.

Investigators should be aware that certain software remotely deployed will enable alteration of data, an action which might render the computer and any data stored therein unreliable and inadmissible as evidence. The advice of the relevant Computer Crime Unit should be sought.

5.6 What Action Requires an Interception Authority in Relation to the Investigation of Computers?

The interception of communications whilst in the course of their transmission made via computers constitutes interception for which a Secretary of State's warrant is required (see Chapter 7).

Important case law exists in relation to emails. It has been held (and at the time of writing, May 2008, this has not been appealed) that s 1(5) RIPA must be read as providing implicit lawful authority within the context of s 9 PACE, even where the net effect amounts to an interception of email outside the warranted regime provided for under s 5 RIPA (*NTL Group Ltd v Ipswich Crown Court* [2002] EWHC 1585). In this case a service provider had to divert (thus intercept) emails to an alternative server pending judicial consideration of an application for a production order. The production order was granted and investigators were allowed to access the emails that had been stored in this manner. The product from such interception could be used in evidence (s 18(4) and (5) RIPA).

5.7 What Action Requires a CHIS Authority in Relation to the Investigation of Computers or Using Computers?

Where it is proposed to deploy investigators or victims acting on behalf of investigators, to interact with suspects via a computer either by email, webcam or in chatrooms, a CHIS authority will be required if it is proposed to use, for the purpose of the investigation, any information obtained by the investigator as a result of the on-line relationship in circumstances in which the other party will not be aware of the investigator's true purpose in acquiring such information.

Covert on-line investigation to identify internet offenders creates the potential for 'blue-on-blue' situations to arise: circumstances in which two undercover, on-line investigators interact on-line and begin to investigate each other. Proper procedures through SOCA or the relevant department within NCA which will replace SOCA are in place to avoid this.

It is good practice to video the interaction of undercover investigators on-line for evidential integrity purposes. The use of webcams should be avoided unless the investigator is an undercover investigator also trained to engage in, and for the purpose of the investigation intending to conduct, face-to-face meetings.

Deployment of a conventional CHIS (formerly known as an informer) to obtain information via an online interactive relationship also requires a CHIS authority. Where a CHIS coincidentally is requested to obtain information from a database to which he or she has lawful access, if this does *not* involve the CHIS maintaining a relationship that facilitates the accessing or obtaining of the information it would not appear to require an authorization.

5.8 What is the Appropriate Authority for Accessing Data Stored on a Computer?

Covert investigation of data stored on a computer hard drive constitutes interference with property and so requires the necessary authority under Part III PA97. An alternative, but overt, coercive means of accessing such stored data would be via a PACE warrant or production order.

One of the most frequently asked questions from investigators involves accessing the email account of a suspect when the password to that account has come into the possession of investigators. 'I have X's password: can I access his email account?' Without the informed (and preferably written) consent of the suspect, *no*: such action constitutes a criminal offence under the Computer Misuse Act 1990.

5.9 Accessing Protected Electronic Information

Within the context of a covert investigation, accessing protected electronic information presents particular challenges. It may not always be possible to maintain secrecy in these circumstances and investigations which, to avoid compromise, must necessarily remain secret from those under investigation will have to be managed accordingly.

The exercise of covert investigation powers under either Part I or Part II RIPA, or Part III Police Act 1997, may result in investigators acquiring *possession* of protected electronic information. Protected electronic information is defined in para 3.12 of the new Investigation of Protected Electronic Information Code of Practice (hereafter the PEI Code; reproduced in Appendix B) and includes encrypted or password-protected digital data. (PEI can also come into the possession of investigators through the exercise of overt investigation powers or through voluntary surrender of such material: see PEI Code, para 3.13.)

Having acquired *possession* of PEI, investigators then need to obtain *access* to the protected information in an intelligible form.

Investigator access to PEI is legislated for under Part III RIPA, specifically s 49, which came into force in October 2007. Part III RIPA is supplemented by an extensive Code of Practice on *Investigation of Protected Electronic Information*. Public authorities can only seek access to PEI using the RIPA Part III statutory provisions if the authority has received prior written approval to seek such statutory access from the National Technical Advisory Centre (NTAC) (para 3.10 PEI Code; also para 9.3). Such prior written approval can be provided on a case by case basis. Alternatively NTAC can provide a general written approval for any public authority deemed competent by NTAC to make applications for permission to issue a requirement notice under s 49.

Obtaining *access* to PEI is an overt action because necessarily it will involve assistance from third parties: an individual or individuals who hold the passwords needed to access, or encryption key(s) needed to decrypt—and so render intelligible—the protected information. The third party may, of course, be the suspect under investigation or an associate.

The statutory provisions (see also PEI Code, Chapter 3) enable investigators:

- to require *disclosure of PEI* in an intelligible form (s 49 RIPA); or
- to require disclosure of the *means to access* PEI (s 50(3)(c) and s 51 RIPA); or
- to require disclosure of the *means of putting* PEI in an intelligible form (s 50(3)(c) and s 51 RIPA).

Information security is paramount and the statutory framework is designed to minimize possible collateral disclosure of or access to additional information beyond that which is specifically sought. It is, after all, the specific protected information that is of relevance to the investigation, not (necessarily) the means by which the information is protected. Of the three possible courses of action identified above it is the first which is to be used at all times unless investigators reasonably believe that the required assistance to render the PEI intelligible or compliance with such a requirement are unlikely to be forthcoming or effective. The second and third powers listed above are 'more likely to be exercised in relation to individuals who are the subject of investigation and are responsible for protecting information which is believed to be evidence of unlawful conduct or relevant material to the investigation' (Code PEI, para 3.8; see also Chapter 6 of the Code).

A s 49 notice requiring disclosure of PEI in an intelligible form, or disclosure of the means to access PEI, or of the means of putting PEI in an intelligible form, can only be served by an investigator who has received prior permission. (Note that Part III prefers the arguably weaker 'permission' rather than the more forceful 'authorization').

Who may give permission for the issuing of a s 49 notice?

Appropriate written permission for the giving of a s 49 notice may be granted by persons identified in Schedule 2 RIPA (see also PEI Code, Chapter 9). In summary:

- a person holding a specified judicial office—this is the default option to which the options below are exceptions available only in specified circumstances;
- the Secretary of State;
- in relation to PEI (likely to be) obtained as a consequence of action under Part III Police Act 1997, an authorizing officer as defined in that Act; or
- a person exercising a statutory function, subject to specified general requirements.

Appropriate additional permission is required where disclosure of a key is required rather than merely disclosure of the PEI in intelligible form (PEI Code, para 9.26). The duration of the permission will be set out in the written permission and PEI cannot be obtained once the written permission expires (s 7, Schedule 2, RIPA).

Applications for permission must contain such information as is specified in PEI Code, para 4.13, and must be in a format prescribed in PEI Code, paras 4.17–4.21.

The protected information to which investigators desire access must be described 'as precisely as possible' in the application so that the recipient of the s 49 notice is able to identify and render legible only the specific information subject of the notice (PEI Code, paras 4.27–4.30).

General information to be provided to those receiving such a notice at the time it is served is set out in PEI Code, para 4.35.

A s 49 notice may be issued where the following criteria are met:

- once the applicant has appropriate permission; *and*
- the applicant reasonably believes that:
    a. a key to PEI is in the possession of a person (s 49(2) RIPA); *and*
    b. a disclosure requirement is necessary:
        i.   in the interests of national security (s 49(3) RIPA); or
        ii. for the purpose of preventing or detecting crime (need not be serious crime) (s 49(3) RIPA); or
        iii. in the interests of the economic well-being of the United Kingdom (s 49(3) RIPA); or
        iv. for the purpose of securing the effective exercise or proper performance by any public authority of any statutory power or statutory duty (s 49(2)(b)(ii) RIPA); and
    c. the imposition of the requirement is proportionate to what is sought to be achieved by its imposition (s 49(2)(c) RIPA); *and*
    d. that it is not reasonable to obtain access to the PEI in an intelligible form other than by service of a notice (s 49(2)(d) RIPA; see also PEI Code, para 3.15).

The obligations imposed on the person on whom a s 49 notice is served are set out in s 50 RIPA and elaborated in PEI Code, Chapter 5. The recipient of such a notice:

- may use any key or keys in his or her possession to access the PEI and then put it in an intelligible form; *and*
- is required to disclose the PEI in an intelligible form; *and*
- is required to make the disclosure in accordance with the s 49 notice (PEI Code, para 5.1).

The recipient of a s 49 notice, or their legal advisor, may contact NTAC to verify the authenticity of the notice (PEI Code, para 4.22).

Nothing prevents the recipient of a s 49 notice voluntarily disclosing the key or password so that investigators can access the protected information, and in doing so the recipient will satisfy the obligation under the notice. A s 49 notice should usually only be served on a corporate body following prior consultation with that body as to the feasibility and cost of executing the request (PEI Code, para 4.7). A notice can only be served on a corporate body without prior consultation where the investigator has 'reasonable grounds for believing' that prior consultation would 'prejudice an investigation or operation and this includes where the corporate body or firm is suspected of complicity in unlawful conduct' (PEI Code, para 4.6). At issue here is the likely disruption to legitimate business activity arising from the service of a s 49 notice.

To preserve the integrity of an ongoing covert investigation, in specified circumstances *certain public authorities may impose a requirement for secrecy* upon those who are required to provide the PEI in an intelligible form (s 54 RIPA).

The purpose of the secrecy requirement is to prohibit those providing access to the PEI from 'tipping off' persons subject to the investigation. Tipping off is made a criminal offence under s 54 RIPA (note that the section also establishes numerous statutory defences to this offence).

Which public authorities can require secrecy under s 54?

- Those police forces listed in s 56 RIPA (as amended)
- The Serious Organised Crime Agency
- The Scottish Crime and Drug Enforcement Agency
- Any of the intelligence services.

In what circumstances may secrecy be required?

The secrecy requirement 'is designed to preserve—but only where necessary—the covert nature of an investigation and to deter deliberate and intentional behaviour designed to frustrate statutory procedures and assist others to evade detection' (PEI Code, para 10.9). Secrecy may be required of the person on whom a s 49 notice is served and on every other person who becomes aware of the notice and its contents (s 54(1) RIPA).

Three preconditions that must be met before secrecy can be imposed as part of a s 49 requirement to disclose:

1. the person giving permission for the s 49 notice to be issued must consent to the inclusion of a secrecy requirement (s 54(2) RIPA); *and*
2. PEI must have come into the possession of, or be likely to come into the possession of, one of the public authorities listed above (s 54(3) RIPA); *and*
3. secrecy is needed 'to maintain the effectiveness of any investigation or operation or of investigatory techniques generally, or in the interests of the safety or wellbeing of any person' (s 54(3) RIPA; see also PEI Code, para 10.10).

The requirement for secrecy must be clearly stated on the notice and those upon whom it is imposed must be made explicitly aware of the requirement (PEI Code, para 10.13).

Investigators must be aware that some software systems have the function of automatically alerting persons to the fact that PEI has been accessed.

Such 'automatic tipping off' can 'conflict with a secrecy requirement' (PEI Code, para 10.16). It will be for investigators to establish, if possible, whether the intended recipient of the notice uses such software and if so what, if any, steps can be taken to preserve the integrity of the covert investigation.

Little in the way of case law has been decided so far concerning PEI. In *R v S and A* [2008] EWCA Crim 2177, the court considered whether requiring a suspect to comply with a s 49 notice infringed the principle against self-incrimination. The Court of Appeal held that any engagement of the privilege against self-incrimination was 'very limited'.

Further information and reading

Although the appellants' knowledge of the means of access to the data may engage the privilege against self-incrimination, it would only do so if the data itself—which undoubtedly exists independently of the will of the appellants and to which the privilege against self-incrimination does not apply—contains incriminating material. If that data was neutral or innocent, the knowledge of the means of access to it would similarly be either neutral or innocent. On the other hand, if the material were, as we have assumed, incriminatory, it would be open to the trial judge to exclude evidence of the means by which the prosecution gained access to it. Accordingly the extent to which the privilege against self-incrimination may be engaged is indeed very limited.

R v S and A [2008] EWCA Crim 2177, para 24

5.10 Good Practice for the Covert Investigation of Computers

It will always be good practice to consult expert advice (both legal and technical) in relation to computers. Prior to the establishment of computer or hi-tech crime units within the police service, it was not unheard of for colleagues 'who knew a bit about computers' to volunteer to investigate computers and the digital evidence such devices contained. This is no longer advisable. Under the ACPO hi-tech crime strategy all ACPO police forces have both network and digital forensic investigation capability. There is similar expert provision for police in Scotland. Other organizations also have hi-tech investigation units. These experts should be approached for advice and guidance and will probably be the only persons trained to conduct covert computer investigation tactics.

Only trained staff should undertake computer investigation. This applies not only to the deployment of surveillance devices or software, but also to interaction with suspects via computers.

> **Further information and reading**
>
> ACPO has produced, in conjunction with 7Safe Information Security, an updated Good Practice Guide for Computer-Based Electronic Evidence, which is available online from <http://www.7safe.com/electronic_evidence/ACPO_guidelines_computer_evidence.pdf> (accessed December 2011).

5.11 Issues for Consideration Regarding the Investigation of Computers

As has been seen, there is much from the armoury of investigation techniques and tactics that can be employed in relation to computers. Nevertheless, there are a number of issues that complicate such investigation and, in some cases, await clarification.

For instance, where it is proposed to access a computer remotely how will investigators ascertain the geographical location of the computer in order to identify the appropriate chief officer to whom to apply for authority under Part III PA97? Designated authorizing officers under Part III PA97 may only authorize activity within their 'force' area (s 93(1)(b) in conjunction with s 93(6)). Preliminary enquiries may be necessary to locate a computer before the appropriate authorizing officer can be identified. If the computer is located abroad, mutual legal assistance procedures will apply to actions that would otherwise constitute interference with property in England and Wales.

Jurisdiction is similarly an issue for the serving of Data Protection Act notices on internet service providers (ISPs). Usually the municipal law of the location of the ISP's servers applies. Web addresses or an email account ending '—.com' may indicate that the address-owner or ISP is US-based, and so application for data will have to be made either via formal mutual legal assistance mechanisms or via other recognized routes such as requests to the FBI legal attaché at the US Embassy, who will be able to issue a notice under US federal law as part of police-to-police informal mutual assistance. A US-based ISP which also runs '—.co.uk' email accounts may, depending on the company, recognize UK Data Protection Act notices in respect of such accounts because they purport to be UK-based, regardless of where the server actually is. At least one US-based ISP with offices in the UK will accept UK Data Protection Act notices served at its UK offices for any of the email accounts it services. Practice will vary from ISP to ISP and computer investigation units will be best placed to advise on such issues.

The legal debate about what constitutes private information on the internet is too vast to consider here in depth. Clearly where an individual has posted information about themselves in a chatroom, or on a website, the privacy of that information has, to some degree, been surrendered depending on the level of public access to the chatroom or website. But if the information has been maliciously or unwittingly posted by a third party, it will clearly remain private information. How is the investigator to know? The best that an investigator can hope to achieve is to act in good faith, recording meticulously every thought process and reasoning as to why a piece of information on the internet is not private, or why it is private and its covert acquisition through surveillance is lawful, necessary, legitimate, and proportionate. It will be for the courts to decide whether to admit or refuse the evidence.

Computer covert investigation scenario

A concerned parent has reported that her thirteen-year-old daughter has struck up a relationship with an individual in a chatroom on the internet using a home-based computer. The individual purports to be a fourteen-year-old male and has suggested to the daughter that they meet. The parent is suspicious because the fourteen-year-old male insists that the daughter keeps the meeting a secret from her parents. After further investigation, information suggests that this is not a fourteen-year-old but a thirty-two-year-old male. Investigators wish to continue communicating in the chatroom with the male using a decoy officer, in order to set up a meeting where the intention is to arrest the male.

Trained specialist *covert computer investigators* or *undercover operatives* must be deployed in order to continue the communication, and therefore a CHIS authority is required. A directed surveillance authority will also be required for the one-sided consensual interception of the communications data.

Checklist of key issues when considering whether or not to deploy covert investigation techniques

- What evidence or intelligence is being sought?

- How is it relevant to the operation under consideration?

- What is the least intrusive means of securing such evidence or information?

- Has the least intrusive means of securing the evidence or information been attempted? If not, why not?

- What is the likelihood of collateral intrusion against the privacy of persons not being investigated? How will collateral intrusion be prevented (or if not, minimized) and how will the product of collateral intrusion be managed?

- What are the risks to the organization of such tactics? (Chapter 11)

- What are the risks to the organization's staff of such tactics? (Chapter 11)

- What are the risks to the public or specific third parties when such tactics are deployed? (Chapter 11)

- What are the risks to the subject of the investigation? (Chapter 11)

- Will the proposed methods breach Article 8(1)? (1.7.1)

- Is there justification for doing so provided by Article 8(2)? (1.7.4)

- How is the legality test met? (1.7.3)

- How is the legitimacy test met? (1.7.4)

- How is the necessity test met? (1.7.5)

- How is the proportionality test met? (1.7.5)

- Are the arguments justifying the application to use covert investigation based on reliable information/intelligence, or has the applicant adopted a 'tick-the-box' approach to completing the application without giving full consideration to the facts of the case and the issues arising?

- Have the arguments justifying the granting of authorization to use covert investigation been fully articulated, or has the authorizing officer merely paid lip service to the pro forma authorization template via which authority is granted?

- When should this authority be reviewed? What circumstances will or may arise that will necessitate review before then?

- How are the methods by which the evidence/intelligence will be obtained to be protected at trial? (Chapter 12)

- How will the product of the surveillance be managed? (Chapter 12)

Planning covert investigation actions

Remember to include the PLAN for covert investigation tactics in all investigation policy-book entries relating to covert investigation considerations and decisions.

P   PROPORTIONALITY
   Why is it proportionate to obtain the intended product of this surveillance in the manner proposed? (1.7.5)

L   LEGITIMACY
   What is the legitimate purpose of the proposed action: the prevention of disorder or crime; the interests of national security; the interests of public safety; the interests of the economic well-being of the country; the

protection of health or morals; the protection of the rights and freedoms of others? (1.7.4)

A   AUTHORITY TO UNDERTAKE PROPOSED ACTION
What is the lawful foundation and authority for the proposed action? From whom must authorization be sought? (1.7.3)

N   NECESSITY OF PROPOSED ACTION
Why is the proposed action necessary? (1.7.5)

6

Examining Mobile Phones

6.1 **Introduction**

Mobile phones, taken here to include any hand-held electronic device capable of voice telecommunication, are potentially a rich source of intelligence and evidence which often come into the possession of investigators. But mere lawful possession or detention of a suspect's mobile phone, for instance when a detained person's property is seized upon taking the individual into custody, does not entitle investigators to access the data contained within the device or accessible via it. Investigators will need the appropriate authorities under RIPA and PA97 to access such data covertly or under PACE if an overt examination with the knowledge of the suspect is proposed.

This is a new and developing area of law and technology and there is as yet almost no case law to provide clarity of interpretation. Here the current 'rules of thumb' are presented as a basis of interpretation subject to confirmation by the courts.

6.2 **Which Public Authorities Can Examine Mobile Phones?**

Public authorities can examine mobile phones to the extent that they have powers to conduct covert investigation under either RIPA or the PA97. Overt examination of mobile phones can be achieved through PACE powers. Not infrequently, those investigators wishing to access covertly data held within or accessible by the mobile phone will require a property interference authority.

Those agencies empowered to *interfere with property* are:

- Police forces in England and Wales maintained under s 2 Police Act 1996
- Police forces maintained under s 1 Police (Scotland) Act 1967
- The Metropolitan Police
- The City of London Police
- The Police Service of Northern Ireland
- HM Revenue and Customs
- The Serious Organised Crime Agency
- MI5, MI6, and GCHQ.

The organizations are defined by reference to who may authorize such interference and entry (s 93(5) PA97 and s 5 Intelligence Services Act 1994).

6.3 **What Powers Does the Law Provide in Relation to the Examination of Mobile Phones?**

Mobile telephony stores data in three different ways. Some data, voicemails for instance, are stored on network servers which can be accessed via the handset.

The handset itself contains a SIM card on which data can be stored and also has its own internal memory. The majority of data stored on the handset is likely to be located in the internal memory.

Investigators can use interception powers under Part I RIPA and property interference powers under Part III PA97 to access this data and any communications in the course of transmission.

6.4 What Authority Regime is Required for the Examination of Mobile Phones?

For the latest current advice investigators should always consult the relevant single point of contact (SPOC) within their organization.

The appropriate authority regime depends upon where the data to be examined is held. These different technical solutions dictate different statutory regimes for investigators to use when examining mobile phones. In the absence of case law the prevailing consensus is that accessing data stored on the communication service provider (CSP) network server constitutes interception, subject to this being lawful either through a warrant issued by the Secretary of State or because the circumstances constitute lawful interception within the meaning of the judgment in *NTL Group Ltd v Ipswich Crown Court* [2002] EWHC 1585 (see 6.5). Data stored by either method on the handset is currently considered (subject to any future judgment to the contrary) to be analogous to the data stored on a personal computer hard drive. Therefore a property interference authority combined with a directed surveillance authority will probably be required. (In circumstances where both the PA97 regime and the RIPA regime apply, it is the senior authorizing officer who authorizes the combined authority, which will almost invariably be the authorizing officer designated by PA97.)

Some of the data stored on the handset constitutes communications data (see Chapter 7) in that it records the contact identity of calls made and received. These are data that would normally only be accessible by service of a Part I Chapter II RIPA authorization or notice which would not apply in the case of seized mobile phones. Accessing these data can either be achieved through PACE search powers or, for the purposes of covert investigation, with a Part III PA97 authority to interfere with property in conjunction with a directed surveillance authority to view the data (which will be private information) (OSC *Annual Report 2005*, 4.5).

The location of a mobile phone can also be examined. Again different technologies and different investigation purposes dictate different approaches and the permutations are so varied that they cannot be comprehensively covered in a work of this nature. SPOCs will be able to advise what is feasible with any given CSP and therefore what the appropriate authority regime will be.

6.5 What Significant Case Law Has Been Decided in Relation to the Examination of Mobile Phones?

There is almost no case law yet available specifically in relation to the covert physical investigation of mobile phones. There is, however, relevant case law in relation to interception that would appear to apply to mobile phone emails and voicemail.

In relation to accessing email data intended to be accessed by the recipient via his or her mobile phone and stored on a CSP's network server, case law (not appealed) has held that s 1(5) RIPA must be read as providing implicit lawful authority within the context of s 9 PACE, even where the net effect amounts to an interception of email outside the warranted regime provided for under s 5 RIPA (*NTL Group Ltd v Ipswich Crown Court* [2002] EWHC 1585). In this case a CSP had to divert (thus intercept) emails to an alternative server pending judicial consideration of an application for a production order.

The product from such interception may be used in evidence (s 18(4) and (5) RIPA).

Checklist of key issues when considering whether or not to deploy covert investigation techniques

- What evidence or intelligence is being sought?

- How is it relevant to the operation under consideration?

- What is the least intrusive means of securing such evidence or information?

- Has the least intrusive means of securing the evidence or information been attempted? If not, why not?

- What is the likelihood of collateral intrusion against the privacy of persons not being investigated? How will collateral intrusion be prevented (or if not, minimized) and how will the product of collateral intrusion be managed?

- What are the risks to the organization of such tactics? (Chapter 11)

- What are the risks to the organization's staff of such tactics? (Chapter 11)

- What are the risks to the public or specific third parties when such tactics are deployed? (Chapter 11)

- What are the risks to the subject of the investigation? (Chapter 11)

- Will the proposed methods breach Article 8(1)? (1.7.1)

- Is there justification for doing so provided by Article 8(2)? (1.7.4)

- How is the legality test met? (1.7.3)

- How is the legitimacy test met? (1.7.4)

- How is the necessity test met? (1.7.5)

- How is the proportionality test met? (1.7.5)

- Are the arguments justifying the application to use covert investigation based on reliable information/intelligence, or has the applicant adopted a 'tick-the-box' approach to completing the application without giving full consideration to the facts of the case and the issues arising?

- Have the arguments justifying the granting of authorization to use covert investigation been fully articulated, or has the authorizing officer merely paid lip service to the pro forma authorization template via which authority is granted?

- When should this authority be reviewed? What circumstances will or may arise that will necessitate review before then?

- How are the methods by which the evidence/intelligence will be obtained to be protected at trial? (Chapter 12)

- How will the product of the surveillance be managed? (Chapter 12)

Planning covert investigation actions

Remember to include the PLAN for covert investigation tactics in all investigation policy-book entries relating to covert investigation considerations and decisions.

P   PROPORTIONALITY
Why is it proportionate to obtain the intended product of this surveillance in the manner proposed? (1.7.5)

L   LEGITIMACY
What is the legitimate purpose of the proposed action: the prevention of disorder or crime; the interests of national security; the interests of public safety; the interests of the economic well-being of the country; the protection of health or morals; the protection of the rights and freedoms of others? (1.7.4)

A   AUTHORITY TO UNDERTAKE PROPOSED ACTION
What is the lawful foundation and authority for the proposed action? From whom must authorization be sought? (1.7.3)

N   NECESSITY OF PROPOSED ACTION
Why is the proposed action necessary? (1.7.5)

7

Communications Data

7.1 **Introduction**

Acquisition of communications data provides intelligence of criminal associations and behaviour patterns that can either inform an application for the deployment of more intrusive surveillance or provide evidence to support a prosecution. In the words of the Explanatory Memorandum to the Data Retention (EC Directive) Regulations 2007:

> this valuable data has allowed investigators to identify suspects, examine their contacts, establish relationships between conspirators and place them in a specific location. Communications data is used in numerous other ways, including assisting investigation of suspects' interaction with victims and in support of suspects' alibi.

The Regulations, given domestic effect in the Data Retention (EC Directive) Regulations 2007 (SI 2007/2199), require communication service providers (CSPs) based in the UK to retain communications data from fixed line and mobile telephony for twelve months for the purposes set out in s 102(3) Anti-terrorism, Crime and Security Act 2001. Namely for:

(a) the purposes of safeguarding national security; and
(b) the purposes of prevention or detection of crime or the prosecution of offenders which may relate directly or indirectly to national security.

A new Acquisition and Disclosure of Communications Data Code of Practice has been published pursuant to s 71 RIPA and applies both to investigating authorities and communications service providers (CSP). Referred to here as the Communications Data Code, the Code is reproduced in Appendix C below.

Communications data acquired pursuant to Chapter II Part I RIPA may be adduced in evidence. Communications data acquired as a coincidental result of the execution of an interception warrant issued under Chapter I Part I RIPA is referred to as 'related communications data' (Communications Data Code, para 1.9) and is considered an interception product. Therefore related communications data may not be used in evidence by virtue of s 17 RIPA. Investigation managers wishing to use communications data in evidence will have to ensure that it has been acquired using the Chapter II powers (which allow for communications data to be adduced in evidence) and not as a by-product of interception (in which case the data will be subject to the s 17 RIPA prohibition on adducing any references that indicate interception has taken place) (see Chapter 8).

The Communications Data Code, para 3.1, identifies four roles relevant to the acquisition of communications data: applicant (paras 3.3–3.6), designated person (equivalent to authorizing officer for other covert investigation functions: paras 3.7–3.14); the single point of contact (paras 3.15–3.21); and the senior responsible officer (para 3.22). The key role in the acquisition of communications data is that of the *single point of contact* (SPOC) (either an accredited individual or a group of accredited individuals) representing the investigating authority in all data acquisition from CSPs.

No SPOC—no communications data.

7.2 **What is Communications Data?**

Communications data is defined in s 21(4) RIPA (see also Communications Data Code, paras 2.12–2.29). It may be described as data identifying:

- *who made* a communication;
- *who received* a communication;
- *where* the communication was made;
- *what communication services* were accessed by a user; and
- *how* the services were accessed.

Communications data *does not include content* of communications.

Communications data exists in three types: traffic data; service use data; and subscriber information data.

Definition of traffic data

Traffic data means those data, attached to a communication, for the purpose of transmission which identify the addressee and the means of transmission and can include the identity of a computer file or program to which access has been obtained.

Examples include information identifying:

- the origin or destination of a communication
- the location of equipment used to make or receive a communication
- the sender or recipient of the communication
- the equipment through which the communication has passed
- web browsing to the extent that only the host machine, server, or domain is disclosed.

(See s 21(4)(a) and 21(6) RIPA; also Communications Data Code, paras 2.19–2.22.)

Definition of service use data

Service use data means data identifying the use made by a person of a postal or telecommunication service.

Examples include:

- itemized telephone call records (all numbers called)
- itemized internet connections
- timing and duration of service used
- information about the amount of data uploaded or downloaded

- whether or not forward/redirection services have been used
- records of special services such as recorded deliveries or conference calling.

  (See s 21(4)(b) RIPA; also Communications Data Code, paras 2.23–2.24.)

Definition of subscriber information data

Subscriber information data is that information held by the CSP about the customers to whom communication services have been provided.

Examples include:

- where a suspect's phone bill is in the possession of investigators, the identities of persons whose number the suspect has phoned
- the identity of email account holders
- the identity of persons with posting access to a website
- information about how accounts are paid
- billing and installation addresses
- any demographic data supplied to the CSP by the subscriber when signing up to the communication service.

  (See s 21(4)(c) RIPA; also Communications Data Code, paras 2.25–2.29.)

Hint and tip: Investigators sometimes refer to 'billing data'. It is a term that may mean different things to different CSPs and can be interpreted literally. Some telephone service contracts provide free calls within certain networks, or up to a certain usage (after which calls will be charged), or at certain times of the day. For such CSPs, billing data is often interpreted as merely those data relating to the incurring of a charge. Therefore an investigator who requests billing data without further qualification may find that he or she receives only data in relation to calls that have been charged and not data in relation to all calls made because some calls may have been free. Itemized call data incorporate all calls made, both charged and free. Here the expertise of the trained and accredited SPOC is vital in avoiding such errors that may seriously impede the investigation.

7.3 Which Public Authorities Can Acquire Communications Data?

Those authorities that may acquire communications data are listed in s 25(1) RIPA:

- A police force, including armed services police forces
- The Serious Organised Crime Agency
- The Scottish Crime and Drug Enforcement Agency

- The Commissioners of HM Revenue and Customs
- MI5, MI6, and GCHQ.

In addition to these authorities described on the face of the Act, the Home Secretary may by order specify other authorities that may acquire communications data.

The current lists of specified other authorities are scheduled in *The Regulation of Investigatory Powers (Communications Data) Order* 2010 (SI 2010/480) available online at <http://www.legislation.gov.uk/uksi/2010/480/contents/made> (accessed December 2011). The Schedules are divided into those authorities empowered to access all three types of communications data (SI 2010/480 Schedule 1 and Schedule 2 Part I), and those which may access only service use data and subscriber information: communications data falling within s 21(4) (b) and (c) RIPA (SI 2010/480 Schedule 2 Part II). Schedule 2 Part III identifies agencies that may acquire communications data only in respect of postal communications.

7.4 What Powers Does the Law Provide in Relation to Communications Data?

Section 21 RIPA provides lawful authority without civil liability for any conduct in relation to a postal service or telecommunication system for obtaining or disclosing communications data, other than conduct consisting in the interception of communications during the course of their transmission.

Acquisition of traffic data, service use data, and subscriber information must be *necessary* for one or more of the purposes detailed in s 22(2) RIPA and added to by SI 2006/1878 (see also Communications Data Code, para 2.2) (note that these purposes are more extensive than the purposes for which communications data must be retained):

- in the interests of national security;
- for the purpose of preventing or detecting crime (as defined in s 81(5) RIPA) or of preventing disorder;
- in the interests of the economic well-being of the UK (subject to this being directly related to state/national security as defined in Directive 97/66/EC: see Communications Data Code, para 2.11);
- for the purpose, in an emergency, of preventing death or injury or any damage to a person's physical or mental health, or of mitigating any injury or damage to a person's physical or mental health;
- to assist investigations into alleged miscarriages of justice;
- for the purpose of assisting in identifying any person who has died otherwise than as a result of crime or who is unable to identify themselves because of a physical or mental condition, other than one resulting from crime (eg natural disaster, accident: see Communications Data Code, Chapter 5);

- in relation to a person who has died or is unable to identify themselves, for the purpose of obtaining information about the next of kin or other connected persons of such a person or about the reason for the death or condition (see Communications Data Code, Chapter 5).

The following necessity criteria are also identified in s 22(2) RIPA, but art 7 SI 2003/3172 restricts the application of these criteria to the acquisition of *subscriber information* only:

- in the interests of public safety;
- for the purpose of protecting public health;
- for the purpose of assessing or collecting any tax, duty, levy, or other imposition, contribution, or charge payable to a government department.

The above criteria do not constitute grounds upon which to acquire traffic data and service data.

Even when legitimacy and necessity criteria are met, data acquisition may only proceed if, and to the extent that, such action is proportionate to what is sought to be achieved by acquiring such data (s 22(5) RIPA).

Any errors made when granting an authority or issuing a notice have to be reported by the investigating authority to the Interception of Communications Commissioner, who, experience has shown, will then require a detailed action plan of how such errors will be avoided in future.

7.5 What Authority Regime is Prescribed for the Acquisition of Communications Data?

Communications data can be obtained in either of two ways: an *authorization* under s 22(3) RIPA entitling the investigators to gather the data themselves, or a *notice* under s 22(4) RIPA requiring a CSP to supply the data to the investigators. Designated persons (in effect authorizing officers) specified to grant authorities or issue notices are identified in the Schedules to *The Regulation of Investigatory Powers (Communications Data) Order* 2010 (SI 2010/480).

Examples of when it will be appropriate to grant an authorization rather than issue a notice include the following circumstances:

- Where a CSP has no capability to obtain or disclose the required data, but where investigators might have such a capability.
- Where the designated person (authorizing officer) believes an investigation or operation may be compromised if the CSP were to obtain or disclose the data.
- Where an agreement regarding appropriate disclosure mechanisms exists between the investigating authority and a CSP.
- Where there is a need to conduct a telephone subscriber check, but a CSP has yet to be conclusively identified as the holder of the appropriate data.

Definition of a s 22(3) authorization

A *s 22(3) authorization* lasts for one month and may be renewed (s 23(4) and (5)). It:

- must be granted in writing or (if not in writing) in a manner that produces a record of its having been made;
- must describe the conduct (s 21(1)) authorized and the communications data for the acquisition of which authority has been granted;
- must specify the reason the authority is necessary (s 22(2));
- must specify the office, rank, or position held by the person granting the authority.

(See Communications Data Code, paras 3.23–3.32; also 3.42–3.48.)

Definition of a s 22(4) notice

A *s 22(4) notice* lasts for one month and may be renewed (s 23(4) and (5)). It:

- must be granted in writing or (if not in writing) in a manner that produces a record of its having been made;
- must describe the communications data to be obtained or disclosed under the notice;
- must specify the reason the authority is necessary (s 22(2));
- must specify the office, rank, or position held by the person granting the authority;
- must specify the manner in which any disclosure required by the notice is to be made.

(See Communications Data Code, paras 3.33–3.48.)

When responding to a notice, a CSP may disclose the required data only to the person issuing the notice or the SPOC (s 23(3)).

The relevant ranks or roles for the purposes of granting an authority or issuing notices are listed in the Schedules to SI 2010/480. A police inspector or above can issue an authority or notice in relation to *subscriber information* (s 21(4)(c)), whilst a superintendent or above can issue an authorization or notice for *traffic data* and *service use data* (s 21(4)(a) and (b)).

Any designated person may only authorize persons working in the same relevant public authority for the purposes of acquiring communications data. There appears to be no provision of arrangements for collaborative working as has been made for other forms of covert investigation (Communications Data Code, para 3.24).

In contrast to para 3.8 of the CSPI Code (which imposes a responsibility for documenting a collateral intrusion risk assessment firmly on the authorizing officer), para 2.6 of the Communications Data Code requires merely that an application for authorization to acquire communications data 'should draw attention to any circumstances that give rise to a meaningful degree of collateral intrusion'. Whilst such a construction, which does not elaborate on what degree of collateral intrusion actually constitutes 'meaningful', appears to impose this requirement on the applicant, designated persons will wish to document their own considerations of collateral intrusion at the time of authorization.

Authorizations or notices remain valid for one month from the date of authorization or the date on which a notice was given. Authorizations and notices must specify the exact period for which communications data is sought. Authorizations and notices may be renewed by the granting of further authorization or the issuing of a new notice (Communications Data Code, paras 3.42–3.48).

A notice must be cancelled as soon as it is no longer necessary for the CSP to comply with the notice (s 22(4) RIPA). Where a designated person considers that an authorization is no longer required, it will cease to be necessary and proportionate and so must be withdrawn (Communications Data Code, paras 3.49–3.55).

Provision for urgent oral authorizations or giving of notices is made for 'exceptionally urgent circumstances' where there is an immediate threat to life (Communications Data Code, para 3.56).

7.6 What is the Role of the Senior Responsible Officer?

Whereas the CSPI Code (para 3.28) only recommends that a senior responsible officer be identified for the purposes of coordinating and leading an organization's policy, procedure and practice in relation to covert investigation, para 3.22 of the Communications Data Code makes such a role *mandatory* in relation to the acquisition of communications data.

> Within every relevant public authority a senior responsible officer must be responsible for:
>
> - the integrity of the process in place within the public authority to acquire communications data;
> - compliance with Chapter II of Part I of the Act and with this code;
> - oversight of the reporting of errors to the Interception of Communications Commissioner's Office (IOCCO) and the identification of both the cause(s) of errors and the implementation of processes to minimise repetition of errors;
> - engagement with the IOCCO inspectors when they conduct their inspections, and where necessary, oversee the implementation of post-inspection action plans approved by the Commissioner.

The senior responsible officer must hold a position or rank within the relevant public authority which would entitle the officer to be a designated officer for the purposes of s 21(4)(a) or (b) RIPA.

7.7 **The Keeping of Records and Data Protection Subject Access**

The keeping of records is discussed in all the new and revised codes of practice (see Communications Data Code, Chapter 6; also Chapter 12 of this volume). In relation to communications data acquisition, recordkeeping obligations are imposed upon both the investigating public authority seeking to acquire the data and the communication service provider asked to disclose such data. The latter is also bound by the Data Protection Act 1998 and is neither necessarily nor automatically exempted from its requirements in the same way as a law enforcement organization (see Communications Data Code, Chapter 7). Accordingly, investigation managers would be advised to take these circumstances into account when planning the acquisition of communications data as part of the overall strategy for any given investigation.

Table 7.1 Recordkeeping requirements for communications data acquisition

Communications data category	Duties of relevant public authority	Duties of communication service provider
Acquired under Part II RIPA by way of authorization or Notice	Copies of applications, authorizations, notices together with records of withdrawal and/or cancellation, in either written or electronic form, cross-referenced as required (or else physically attached): retained centrally by SPOC for inspection by Information Commissioner. Also, number of applications made to a designated person that were rejected; number of notices given; number of authorizations made; number of urgent notices or authorizations: retained in a manner stipulated by the Information Commissioner.	Records of disclosures made or required to be made, including the public authority concerned, the date of authorization or notice; any disclosure of the authorization by the public authority to the CSP; date the relevant public authority acquired the communications data: retained for inspection by Information Commissioner.
Acquired as related communications data by way of Part I RIPA warranted interception	Records to be kept in accordance with the non-disclosure regime under Part I RIPA and the related Interception Code.	(Not applicable)

There is no provision in RIPA that prevents a CSP providing information to individuals about the fact that the CSP has disclosed communication data to a relevant public authority in compliance with either an acquisition notice or authority. Individuals may apply under s 7 Data Protection Act 1998 (DPA) for the disclosure of information held about them by organizations. This would include whether or not communications data has been disclosed to a relevant public authority.

Depending on the facts of each case, a CSP may apply certain exemptions to the principle of subject access. Section 28 DPA provides that an exemption will always apply where data is held relating to the safeguarding of national security (Communications Data Code, para 7.5). The exemption upon which law enforcement generally relies, s 29 DPA, does not automatically apply to a CSP. Where a CSP receives a subject access request under s 7 DPA, the response to which will disclose that a communications data authorization or notice has been complied with, the CSP is required to consider carefully whether disclosure of the fact of the data acquisition would itself prejudice the prevention or detection of crime (Communications Data Code, para 7.7). Each case has to be decided on its merits and no blanket exemption applies. CSPs are required to document and retain records of their considerations (para 7.10). In cases of uncertainty a CSP may consult the SPOC who in turn will seek the view of the relevant applicant/investigation manager (Communications Data Code, para 7.8).

7.8 What Significant Case Law Has Been Decided in Relation to Communications Data?

At the time of writing other than in relation to general principles regarding legality, necessity, and proportionality (see Chapter 1), there has been relatively little case law decided specifically in relation to communications data, not least because Part I Chapter II RIPA only came into force in January 2004 and regulations regarding retention did not come into force until late 2007. Some of the key cases discussed in relation to interception touch upon communications data (see Chapter 8).

Proportionality is of particular relevance in the acquisition of communications data because so much data is generated and potentially can be acquired. A blanket request for all available communications data over a given period at the outset of an investigation will fail the proportionality test because it will result in a significant amount of data about an individual's communications much of which will be irrelevant and therefore an unjustifiable intrusion into both that individual's privacy and that of those persons with whom communication has been made. Requests made later in the course of an investigation, which are more targeted and focused as a result of more precise lines of enquiry emerging during the developing investigation, will be more likely to satisfy the proportionality requirements.

Further information and reading

- SI 2010/480 The Regulation of Investigatory Powers (Communications Data) Order 2010.

See also:

R Jones, 'UK data retention regulations', Computer Law & Security Report 24(2) (2008), 147–150.

V Russell, 'Data retention requirements for communication service providers', *Privacy and Data Protection* 8(4) (2008), 13–15.

S McKay, *Covert Policing: Law and Practice* (Oxford University Press, Oxford, 2011) Chapter 4.

Checklist of key issues when considering whether or not to deploy covert investigation techniques

- What evidence or intelligence is being sought?

- How is it relevant to the operation under consideration?

- What is the least intrusive means of securing such evidence or information?

- Has the least intrusive means of securing the evidence or information been attempted? If not, why not?

- What is the likelihood of collateral intrusion against the privacy of persons not being investigated? How will collateral intrusion be prevented (or if not, minimized) and how will the product of collateral intrusion be managed?

- What are the risks to the organization of such tactics? (Chapter 11)

- What are the risks to the organization's staff of such tactics? (Chapter 11)

- What are the risks to the public or specific third parties when such tactics are deployed? (Chapter 11)

- What are the risks to the subject of the investigation? (Chapter 11)

- Will the proposed methods breach Article 8(1)? (1.7.1)

- Is there justification for doing so provided by Article 8(2)? (1.7.4)

- How is the legality test met? (1.7.3)

- How is the legitimacy test met? (1.7.4)

- How is the necessity test met? (1.7.5)

- How is the proportionality test met? (1.7.5)

- Are the arguments justifying the application to use covert investigation based on reliable information/intelligence, or has the applicant adopted a 'tick-the-box' approach to completing the application without giving full consideration to the facts of the case and the issues arising?

- Have the arguments justifying the granting of authorization to use covert investigation been fully articulated, or has the authorizing officer merely paid lip service to the pro forma authorization template via which authority is granted?

- When should this authority be reviewed? What circumstances will or may arise that will necessitate review before then?

- How are the methods by which the evidence/intelligence will be obtained to be protected at trial? (Chapter 12)

- How will the product of the surveillance be managed? (Chapter 12)

Planning covert investigation actions

Remember to include the PLAN for covert investigation tactics in all investigation policy-book entries relating to covert investigation considerations and decisions.

P   PROPORTIONALITY

Why is it proportionate to obtain the intended product of this surveillance in the manner proposed? (1.7.5)

L   LEGITIMACY

What is the legitimate purpose of the proposed action: the prevention of disorder or crime; the interests of national security; the interests of public safety; the interests of the economic well-being of the country; the protection of health or morals; the protection of the rights and freedoms of others? (1.7.4)

A   AUTHORITY TO UNDERTAKE PROPOSED ACTION

What is the lawful foundation and authority for the proposed action? From whom must authorization be sought? (1.7.3)

N   NECESSITY FOR PROPOSED ACTION

Why is the proposed action necessary? (1.7.5)

8

Interception of Communications

8.1 **Introduction**

The interception of communications made between criminal conspirators, particularly telephone calls, is potentially a significant source of intelligence. Conventional and electronic mail can also be intercepted. The interception of internet-based communication is complicated by the fact that that which is technically possible may go further than an interception warrant issued by the Home Secretary can lawfully permit. An interception warrant will permit interception of communication between persons but the technology will also intercept communication between an individual computer user and the remote server on which the computer user might archive personal documents and information never intended for communication with another: such material, arguably, can only lawfully be accessed using a search warrant. Investigators should be aware that the FBI, in testimony to Congressional hearings, have made explicit in the public domain the extent to which it is possible, with available technology, to filter Internet-based communications in order to intercept only those which are of interest to investigators.

Further information and reading

V Benjamin, 'Interception of Internet communications and the Right to Privacy: an Evaluation of Some Provisions of the Regulation of Investigatory Powers Act against the Jurisprudence of the European Court of Human Rights' EHRLR 6 (2007), 637–648.

The main principle regarding interception of communications in the UK is that the product of such interception cannot be adduced in evidence. In other words, interception is for intelligence purposes only. There are limited exceptions to this general principle, as will be seen below (at 8.4).

Whether all intercept products should be used evidentially has been much debated since the 1950s. The background to the British debate prior to interception being placed on a statutory footing, with the Interception of Communications Act 1985, is summarized in the ECtHR judgment on *Malone v UK* [1984] 7 EHRR 14; see also D Ormerod and S McKay, 'Telephone intercepts and their admissibility' Crim LR 15 (2004), 18.

More recently the issue has been revisited at length during the Committee stages of RIPA (*Hansard* HL (series 6) vol 614, cols 107–117 (19 June 2000)) and during the Committee and Report stages of the Serious Organised Crime and Police Act 2005 (*Hansard* HC Standing Committee D, cols 205–224 (18 January 2005); *Hansard* HC (series 6) vol 430, cols 1231–1241 (7 February 2005)). Despite finding itself in a position in which it appeared to be arguing that (for terrorist suspects) imprisonment without charge was preferable to allowing intercept evidence at trial, the government remained resolute.

In June 2007 the Government announced a review of the issue (Home Office Oral Statement on Counter Terrorism, 7 June 2007). The review was undertaken by a team of four Privy Counsellors led by Sir John Chilcot GCB which reported to Parliament in January 2008. Their qualified recommendation was for the acceptance of the principle of intercept product as evidence subject to certain safeguards being developed; a recommendation that the government was willing to consider further. Consideration of suitable safeguards, involving consultation across Whitehall and with all relevant agencies has been conducted at length but a solution which accommodates both the political desire of the intercepting agencies to retain control and discretion over how much intercept product might be made available in evidence and the legal necessity of operating UK laws of criminal procedure and evidence in a manner compatible with the principle of fair trial within the context of UK statutory construction and trial procedure has to date (December 2011) proved elusive. The Coalition government announced its intention to continue seeking a 'practical way to allow the use of intercept evidence in court' (Cabinet Office, *The Coalition: Our Programme for Government*, May 2010 p 24) and reaffirmed this in a Green Paper entitled *Justice and Security* (Cm 8194, 19 October 2011). For the time being, the general prohibition on the evidential use of intercept product remains.

Further information and reading

Privy Council, 2008, *Review of Intercept as Evidence: Report to the Prime Minister and Home Secretary*, Cm 7324.
The Prime Minister's response to the Chilcot Report was made in a Parliamentary Statement, *Hansard* HC, col 959 (6 February 2008).
Home Secretary statement to Parliament, *Hansard* HC, col 31-32WS (10 December 2009).
Home Secretary statement to Parliament, *Hansard* HC, col 61-62WS (25 March 2010).
Joint Committee on Human Rights, *Counter-Terrorism Policy and Human Rights (Seventeeth Report)* HC 111 (25 March 2010).
Home Office, *Justice and Security*, Cm 8194 (19 October 2011).
House of Commons Library, *The Use of Intercept Evidence in Terrorism Cases*, SN/HA/5249 (24 November 2011).
Civil liberties non-governmental organizations (NGOs) are in favour of the evidential use of intercept product arguing that it is a due process alternative preferable to the administrative solutions that have been attempted to restrict the movements of suspected terrorists. See for instance:
Justice press release, *JUSTICE criticizes government delays over intercept evidence* (10 December 2009).
Justice, *Response to the Coalition Programme for Government* (May 2010) para 54.
Liberty, *Liberty's Analysis of the Coalition Programme for Government* (20 May 2010) p 6.

Part I RIPA has repealed and updated provisions enacted in the Interception of Communications Act 1985. Pursuant to s 71 RIPA, a Code of Practice for the interception of communications has been issued. The latest available version (unrevised at the time of writing this edition) is reproduced in the Appendices below and online at <http://www.homeoffice.gov.uk/publications/counter-terrorism/ripa-forms/interception-comms-code-practice?view=Standard&pubID=832093> (accessed 1 December 2011). References to 'Interception Code' in this chapter refer to this Code.

Definition of interception and transmission

Interception means (s 2(2) and (4) RIPA) the

- modification of or interference with a telecommunications system;
- monitoring of transmissions made by such a system by means of the system itself or through wireless telegraphy or other apparatus;
- the interception of a postal item

so that some or all of the communication content is made available during the course of transmission to a third party other than the sender or intended recipient.

The interception, interference, modification, or monitoring must take place within the UK. Investigation conduct in relation only to traffic data (the means by which the communication is addressed to its intended recipient) connected with the communication does not constitute interception if none of the contents are made known to the investigator (s 2(5) RIPA).

In the course of transmission includes the time in which a communication is stored in order to enable the intended recipient to collect, download, or otherwise have access to it. This includes a pager message waiting to be collected or an email waiting to be downloaded (s 2(7) RIPA; Interception Code, para 2.14).

8.2 **Which Public Authorities Can Intercept Communications?**

Distinction is drawn between private telephone systems and public telephone systems.

Any organization, including public authorities, can intercept telephone calls made on or to its own *private* telephone system for the purposes of business monitoring (s 4(2) RIPA and the Telecommunications (Lawful Business Practice) (Interception of Communications) Regulations 2000 (SI 2000/2699)). A person with the right to control the operation or use of a private telephone system may intercept or monitor calls in which users have given express or implied consent for such interception (usually in the form of an employment contract or a notice outlining their terms and conditions of employment; hence it will not, strictly speaking, be covert) (s 1(6) RIPA). The National Offender Management Service (formerly HM Prison Service) can monitor communications of prisoners under existing prison legislation (s 4(4) RIPA).

Only certain organizations can apply for a warrant to intercept *public* postal or telecommunications under s 5 RIPA. These are listed in s 6 RIPA (Interception Code, para 2.1):

- MI5
- MI6
- GCHQ
- The Metropolitan Police
- The Police Service of Northern Ireland
- The Serious Organised Crime Agency
- Any Scottish police force
- HM Revenue and Customs
- Defence intelligence
- A competent foreign authority seeking mutual legal assistance from the UK concerning the interception of communications.

8.3 What Powers Does the Law Provide in Relation to Interception of Communications?

Types of communication capable of being intercepted are telephone calls, conventional mail, email, voicemail, and answerphone messages. The statutory framework comprises two general offences of unlawful interception, followed by exceptions in which interception will be lawful.

The two general offences are intercepting a public postal or telecommunication without lawful authority (s 1(1) RIPA—a crime) and unauthorized interception on a private telephone system (s 1(2) and (3) RIPA—a tort).

8.4 What Authority Regime is Required for Interception of Communications?

There are a number of ways in which communications may be intercepted lawfully. These vary according to circumstance.

8.4.1 Business purposes

Communications by which business transactions are entered into or communications relating to such a business or conducted during the course of such business may be monitored. This is to ensure a record of such transactions; to facilitate regulatory and self-regulatory practices; to protect the interests of national security; to prevent or detect crime; to investigate or detect unauthorized use of such systems; and to ensure effective system operation (s 4(2) RIPA; SI 2000/2699; Interception Code, para 10.6; relevant regulations are at <http://www.opsi.gov.uk/si/si2000/20002699.htm> (accessed 15 August 2008)).

In connection with the business of providing postal or telecommunication services, providers may lawfully intercept communications pursuant to the provision of their service or to any enforcement, in relation to that service, of any laws regarding the use of such services (s 3(3) RIPA; Interception Code, para 10.5). See also s 83 Postal Services Act 2000.

The product from such interception may be used in evidence (s 18(4) and (5) RIPA).

8.4.2 Two-party consent

Where both the sender and recipient so consent, a communication may be lawfully intercepted without further authority (s 3(1) RIPA; Interception Code, para 10.3).

The product from such interception may be used in evidence (s 18(4) and (5) RIPA).

8.4.3 One-sided consent

Where one party (either sender or recipient) to the communication consents *and* there is a surveillance authority under Part II RIPA in respect of the communication and either the recipient or sender, then the communication may be lawfully intercepted without further authority (s 3(2) RIPA; Interception Code, para 10.4).

This makes it lawful to monitor the communications of undercover officers with persons subject of investigation, or to monitor communications between kidnappers or blackmailers and the persons of whom they are making their demands. Such actions should be specifically authorized in the text of the CHIS or surveillance authority.

The product from such interception may be used in evidence (s 18(4) and (5) RIPA). However, where police used this technique to acquire evidence by asking a rape victim to phone her attacker (who had denied the offence in interview) and instigate discussion of the offence, this was held to constitute entrapment and the evidence was excluded as unfair under s 78 PACE (*R v H* [1987] Crim LR 47).

8.4.4 In connection with wireless telegraphy

With the authority of a person designated under s 48 Wireless Telegraphy Act 2006 (WTA), interception will be lawful for purposes connected with the issuing of WTA licences; with the prevention and detection of interference with wireless telegraphy (s 3(4) and (5) RIPA).

The product from such interception may be used in evidence (s 18(4) and (5) RIPA).

8.4.5 Existing statutory power to acquire stored communications

Search warrants or production orders issued pursuant to s 9 PACE, together with Schedule 1 PACE, provide statutory authority in prescribed circumstances to access stored communications (*Archbold's Criminal Pleading, Evidence and Practice* (revd edn, Sweet & Maxwell, London, 2005, paras 15–74 to 15–89a, together with 25–368 to 25–385; see also Interception Code, paras 2.14–2.15)). An example would be where investigators come into possession of a pager and wish to access messages stored on it. The same procedure could be used to access messages stored on the SIM card or internal memory of a mobile phone, although this is slightly more ambiguous as there is a school of thought that argues such messages are still in the course of transmission. The issue has yet to be determined by case law.

Case law (not appealed) has held that s 1(5) RIPA must be read as providing implicit lawful authority within the context of s 9 PACE, even where the net effect amounts to an interception of email outside the warranted regime provided for under s 5 RIPA (*NTL Group Ltd v Ipswich Crown Court* [2002] EWHC 1585). In this case a service provider had to divert (thus intercept) emails to an alternative server pending judicial consideration of an application for a production order.

The product from such interception may be used in evidence (s 18(4) and (5) RIPA).

8.4.6 Interception by warrant

The final lawful means of interception provides products that *cannot* be used in evidence: interception of public telecommunications and postal systems under the authority of a Secretary of State's warrant (s 5 RIPA) upon application by those public authorities listed in s 6 RIPA.

The Secretary of State shall not issue a warrant permitting interception, unless he believes that it is necessary for the grounds laid out in s 5(3) RIPA (which include national security and *serious* crime) and that such conduct is proportionate to what is sought to be achieved (s 5(2) RIPA; Interception Code, para 2.4). There are two types of interception warrant: s 8(1) warrants refer to interception as defined in s 2(1) RIPA (Interception Code, para 4.1), whilst s 8(4) warrants permit the interception of external communications defined as communications sent or received from outside the British Isles (Interception Code, para 5.1).

Definition of serious crime

Serious crime is defined in s 81(3) RIPA as:

- an offence for which a person aged twenty-one or over with no previous convictions could reasonably expect to be sentenced to three years imprisonment or more; or
- an offence where violence is involved; or
- in which there is substantial financial gain; or
- in which a large number of persons are in pursuit of a common purpose.

By excluding reference to serious financial loss, RIPA departs from the formula for a serious arrestable offence prescribed in PACE, which it otherwise follows.

The Serious Organised Crime Agency will advise on the application process and the proper content of an application. Guidance will also be found in paras 4.2 and 5.2 of the Interception Code. Arranging and executing interception is not a quick process and whilst there are urgency provisions even these take time (Interception Code, paras 4.6 and 5.7). There is also a limited capacity. Investigators should not therefore regard interception as the immediate and primary option for investigation.

The warrant is issued in respect of a specific person or premises, together with a schedule that lists the communications to be intercepted (s 8 RIPA). This affords some flexibility for investigators where the subject of an investigation uses multiple phones. Amending the schedule of phone numbers is a simpler process than applying for the warrant (s 10 RIPA). The Secretary of State must certify the material s/he considers it necessary and proportionate to examine. No other material may be examined notwithstanding that it has been intercepted under warrant.

Thus two elements constitute lawful interception of public systems:

(a) the interception must be warranted (s 5 RIPA), and
(b) in the case of external communications, the examination must be certified (s 8(4) and (5) RIPA).

Warrants have a duration of six months and may be renewed. Warrants issued under the urgency procedure last for five days (s 9 RIPA as amended by s 32 Terrorism Act 2006).

The heavy strictures imposed by s 17(1) RIPA dictate careful handling of intercept products. The product must be destroyed once it has been examined. The procedure for doing this is outlined in 8.9 below.

8.4.7 Interception in prisons

Section 4(4) RIPA provides that prisoner's communications can be intercepted under Prison Rules. The Prison Rules 1999 (SI 1999/728) rr 35A to 35D, inserted by the Prison (Amendment) (No. 2) Rules 2000 (SI 2000/2641), apply. Similar provisions exist for Young Offender Institutions. A protocol originally drawn up between NCIS and the National Offender Management Service (NOMS) details the regime within which prison governors will afford assistance in this matter. Investigators are advised to contact their Prison Liaison Officer who will assess the feasibility of any planned operation. Written application must be made via the Police Advisors Section at NOMS HQ. Upon approval, investigators will be given access to intercept products obtained under Prison Rules.

KEY POINTS REGARDING INTERCEPTION IN PRISONS

- Any intercept product will usually be for intelligence purposes only.
- The subject of the interception *must* be the principal subject of the investigation, the 'pivotal player'. Police cannot use Prison Rules as a means of by-passing RIPA to intercept communications where the subject of interest is outside the prison communicating with an inmate.
- The Police Advisors Section will quality assure applications for interception to ensure that they comply both with RIPA and with the Protocol.

The action must be proportionate to what is sought to be achieved by the interception and it must be:

(a) in the interests of national security;
(b) for the prevention, detection, investigation, or prosecution of serious crime (as defined in s 81(3) RIPA);
(c) in the interests of public safety;
(d) for securing or maintaining prison security or good order and discipline in prison.

If investigators wish to intercept the communications of a prisoner who is not the principal subject of the investigation, it will be necessary to seek a warrant for interception under s 5 RIPA as with a subject who was not in prison.

Nothing prevents a prison governor from disclosing on an ad hoc basis information that has come to the attention of prison staff. This is not a means of circumventing prison rules or s 5 RIPA.

Where telephone calls previously made by a prisoner are stored in a prison (eg in a high-security prison), investigators can apply for production orders under PACE for the stored communications to be produced. This mechanism is available only where interception is not feasible and is not a means of avoiding a warrant under s 5 RIPA.

Subject always to the authority of the prison governor, given that material intercepted under Prison Rules is normally provided on an intelligence-only basis, such a product would be admissible as evidence at trial under s 18(4) RIPA because interception in prisons is lawful under s 4(4) RIPA.

> **Further information and reading**
>
> A Hopkins, 'Testing lawfulness: the authorisation of interception of communications and covert surveillance under the Regulation of Investigatory Powers Act 2000', *Covert Policing Review* (2005), 35–51.

8.5 What Are the Procedures for Intercepting Legal Privilege Communications?

Matters subject to legal privilege are defined in s 98 PA97 and art 12 Police and Criminal Evidence (Northern Ireland) Order 1989 (SI 1989/1341 (NI 12)). Legal privilege is attached to the provision of professional legal advice by persons or organizations qualified to do so. Communications made with the intent of furthering a criminal purpose are not protected by privilege.

RIPA does not prohibit the interception of communications likely to contain legally privileged material, but it does provide additional criteria to be met when applying for a warrant to intercept such communications. Paragraph 3.6 of the Interception Code outlines the procedures to be adopted in such circumstances (the Interception Code is reproduced in Appendix D). At the time of writing (December 2011), the Interception Code published online and reproduced below is the latest available although a revised and updated Code is being prepared (Home Office letter to authors dated 5 December 2011). Pending publication of the revised Interception Code investigators have Chapter 4 of the revised CSPI Code to guide them concerning matters involving legal privilege material.

8.6 What Are the Procedures for Intercepting Communications Containing Confidential Personal Information?

Confidential personal information is defined in s 99 PA97. It comprises personal information (from which an individual can be identified and which concerns the physical or mental health of the individual concerned, or spiritual counselling and guidance afforded to that person) acquired or created in the course of any trade, business, profession, or other occupation or for the purposes of any paid or unpaid office, which is held in confidence.

RIPA does not prohibit the interception of communications likely to contain confidential personal information, but it does provide additional criteria to be met when applying for a warrant to intercept such communications. Paragraph 3.9 of the Interception Code outlines the procedures to be adopted in such circumstances (the Interception Code is reproduced in Appendix D).

8.7 **What Are the Procedures for Intercepting Communications Containing Confidential Journalistic Material?**

Confidential journalistic material is defined in s 100 PA97. It is essentially material acquired for or created for the purposes of journalism which is held in confidence.

RIPA does not prohibit the interception of communications likely to contain confidential journalistic material, but it does provide additional criteria to be met when applying for a warrant to intercept such communications. Again, para 3.9 of the Interception Code outlines the procedures to be adopted in such circumstances (the Interception Code is reproduced in Appendix D).

8.8 **What Are the Interception Provisions of s 83 Postal Services Act 2000?**

Postal items are considered Crown property. There are only certain circumstances in which they can be interfered with during the course of posting and delivery:

- when a lawful interception warrant is in existence;
- at points of entry and exit to the UK for the purposes of HM Revenue and Customs;
- where the mailed item is likely to cause injury to postal staff;
- where an item is likely to contain obscene material.

Investigators cannot seek a PACE warrant to search an item whilst it is in the course of delivery (transmission). Section 125(3)(a) Postal Services Act 2000 clarifies that a letter in a post box or in Post Office premises is still considered to be in the course of transmission.

8.9 **What Are the Procedures for Handling Intercept Products?**

The Home Secretary has statutory obligations under s 15 and 16 RIPA to ensure safeguards for the handling of intercept products. These are dealt with in detail in Chapter 6 of the Interception Code.

As soon as it is no longer required for the purpose of preventing or detecting crime (which for RIPA Part I specifically excludes gathering evidence for legal proceedings: s 81(5)), or for any of the other purposes for which an interception may be issued under s 5(3) or listed at s 15(4) (Interception Code, para 6.2), intercept material (including copies, extracts, or summaries which can be identified as the product of interception) *must be destroyed* (s 15(3) RIPA; Interception Code, para 6.8).

'The number of persons to whom any of the material is disclosed, and the extent of disclosure, must be limited to the minimum that is necessary for the authorized purposes set out in section 15(4) of the Act' (Interception Code, para 6.4). Dissemination of an intercept product is limited to the minimum number of persons necessary to execute any of the functions listed at s 15(4).

8.10 How is Disclosure of an Intercept Product Addressed?

Given that s 17 RIPA prohibits any reference to interception in criminal proceedings, and that s 15(3) requires the prompt destruction of an intercept product, the general principle of disclosure is set aside in respect of an intercept product. Sections 3(7), 8(6), and 23(6) CPIA (as amended by RIPA) confirm this by prescribing that material must not be disclosed if it has been intercepted under s 5 RIPA or its disclosure is prohibited under s 17.

Nevertheless there is, under s 18(7), provision for limited disclosure by investigators to either the prosecutor or a judge of any material that has not yet been destroyed pursuant to s 15(3), because it has been retained for an authorized purpose under s 15(4). This is so that the prosecutor can satisfy the continuing duty under CPIA in the interests of fairness to review the obligation to disclose up to the moment of determination in a trial. Under exceptional circumstances, which are not defined, a judge can order disclosure to himself if he is satisfied that the exceptional circumstances demand this in the interests of justice.

The prosecutor cannot use material of which he is aware under s 18(7) other than to determine what needs to be done to ensure a fair trial. As the defendant will not know of the interception, none of its product must be used against him in evidence. However, where material still exists, the prosecutor must determine whether it constitutes information that will be of benefit to the defence.

Intercept material can never be disclosed to the defence (Interception Code, para 7.14).

8.11 What is a 'Preston' Briefing?

Section 18(7) follows pre-RIPA case law in which the contradictory obligations of secrecy and disclosure were considered (*R v Preston* [1994] 2 AC 130, 166–168) giving rise to the so-called 'Preston' Briefing given by investigators to the prosecutor. Where the intercept product has been destroyed and so no longer exists to be revealed to the prosecutor under s 18(7), and where a person relevant to a trial has been arrested as a result of intelligence derived from warranted interception, this must be revealed to the prosecutor together with the declarations that all the material has been destroyed in accordance with s 15(3); that no one has an accurate recollection of exactly what was said in the intercepted conversations;

and that a copy of the warrant is available at SOCA to prove the lawfulness of the interception.

8.12 **What Significant Case Law Has Been Decided in Relation to Interception of Communications?**

Malone v UK was the catalyst for the IOCA (*Malone v UK* (1984) 7 EHRR 14). *Halford v UK* ensured that RIPA would extend provision for lawful interception to private telephone systems (*Halford v UK* (1997) 24 EHRR 523).

In an era of mobile communications it is probable that covert listening devices deployed in premises or vehicles will record persons within operational range of the device talking on mobile phones. This will not amount to an interception (s 2(2) RIPA) if the speech of the other party to such a communication is not recorded. In other words, it is not an interception if only one end of the conversation is monitored in such circumstances because the Law Lords distinguished between interception of the telephone transmission technology and the collateral, separate recording of spontaneous sound (*R v E* [2004] EWCA Crim 1243). The Law Lords were invited to consider the proposition that the requirement to use 'hands-free' telephone in vehicles meant that an audio surveillance device placed in a vehicle would necessarily 'intercept' any 'hands-free' telephone communication within the vehicle and that such interception must require a Home Secretary's warrant in order to be lawful and that no part of any such communication could be adduced in evidence. It was held that this would still not amount to an interception because of the narrow and technology-based construction of interception applied by the court in this case.

Further information and reading

For a critical analysis of the Law Lords' decision in *R v E* see S McKay, '*R v E*: surveillance and the interception of communications: walking the tightrope between Part I and Part II of the Regulation of Investigatory Powers Act 2000', *Covert Policing Review* (2005), 52–61. McKay argues that the court's analysis and decision is problematic and that such a narrow interpretation of interception may tempt investigators to try to use such circumstances as a means of circumventing RIPA Part I—an outcome likely to invite further case law.

For further detailed consideration of court interpretations of RIPA Part I see D Ormerod & S McKay, 'Telephone intercepts and their admissibility', Crim LR (2004), 15–38.

Because the restrictions under s 17 RIPA apply only to interception conducted in the UK, communications lawfully intercepted by foreign authorities in their own jurisdictions may be adduced in evidence in the UK assuming they are relevant (*R v Aujla* [1998] 2 Cr App R 16; approved in *R v P (Telephone Intercepts: Admissibility of Evidence)* [2001] 2 WLR 463). Where the prosecution proposes to do this, all of the material must be considered with a view to disclosure.

R v Preston [1994] 2 AC 130, 166–168 is the key case in determining how the prosecution should discharge its duties of disclosure within the context of interception secrecy. The practical implications of *Preston* have already been considered above (8.11).

In *R v Hardy and Hardy* [2002] EWCA Crim 3012, the Appeal Court held that the taping by undercover officers of telephone conversations they had with the suspects (subsequently defendants) did not amount to interception because these were conversations about which the officers could testify as witnesses and for which the recordings merely provided corroboration. The undercover activity had been properly authorized, and there was no requirement for an interception authority to be in place.

Further information and reading

- SI 2000/2699
  The Telecommunications (Lawful Business Practice) (Interception of Communications) Order 2000

- SI 2004/157
  The Regulation of Investigatory Powers (Conditions for Lawful Interception of Persons outside the United Kingdom) Regulations 2004

See also the Annual Reports of the Interception of Communications Commissioner.

Checklist of key considerations when planning to apply for an interception warrant

Before an application for interception can be made to the Home Office, investigators will have to identify the following for inclusion in their application:

- The specific phones (or correspondence) being used by the subject(s)

- How the phones (or correspondence) are being used for a criminal purpose (sequential event analysis using phone billing data could demonstrate this, for instance)

- Why interception is relevant, necessary, and proportionate within the context of the specific investigation and what other investigation methods have been considered, deployed, or rejected

- How compliance with the statutory safeguards is to be achieved

- What collateral intrusion will occur

- The likelihood of legally privileged material, confidential personal information, or confidential journalistic material being intercepted

- The feasibility of undertaking this interception.

Besides these specific criteria that will form part of the application for interception, the general considerations include:

- Is the interception necessary under s 5(3) RIPA?

- Is the criminality involved serious as defined in s 81(3) RIPA?

- What evidence or intelligence is being sought?

- Whose communications are to be intercepted? (Are they in prison?)

- What communications are to be intercepted?

- Which are the relevant communication service providers?

- How is it relevant to the operation under consideration?

- Is interception proportionate to what is sought to be achieved?

- What will be the extent of collateral intrusion arising from this interception?

- What are the risks to the organization of such tactics? (Chapter 11)

- What are the risks to the organization's staff of such tactics? (Chapter 11)

- What are the risks to the public or specific third parties when such tactics are deployed? (Chapter 11)

- What are the risks to the subject of the investigation? (Chapter 11)

- Will such methods breach Article 8(1)? (1.7.1)

- Is there justification for doing so provided by Article 8(2)? (1.7.4)

- How is the legality test met? (1.7.3)

- How is the legitimacy test met? (1.7.4)

- How is the necessity test met? (1.7.5)

- How is the proportionality test met? (1.7.5)

- Are the statutory safeguards in place concerning the handling of the intercept material?

- Who needs to know that the application is being sought? Why?

- Who will have access to the product, an extract, or a summary of it? Why?

129

Planning covert investigation actions

Remember to include the PLAN for covert investigation tactics in all investigation policy-book entries relating to covert investigation considerations and decisions.

P   PROPORTIONALITY

Why is it proportionate to obtain the intended product of this surveillance in the manner proposed? (1.7.5)

L   LEGITIMACY

What is the legitimate purpose of the proposed action: the prevention of disorder or crime; the interests of national security; the interests of public safety; the interests of the economic well-being of the country; the protection of health or morals; the protection of the rights and freedoms of others? (1.7.4)

A   AUTHORITY TO UNDERTAKE PROPOSED ACTION

What is the lawful foundation and authority for the proposed action? From whom must authorization be sought? (1.7.3)

N   NECESSITY OF PROPOSED ACTION

Why is the proposed action necessary? (1.7.5)

Covert Human Intelligence Sources

9.1 **Introduction**

Informers, paid or unpaid, and staff working undercover or as test purchase operatives are all covert human intelligence sources (CHIS), as defined in s 26(8) RIPA: the first time such activity has been placed on a statutory footing in the UK. Their use and deployment requires authorization. The manner in which they should be managed is also prescribed and specified individuals have statutory obligations in respect of source management.

A Code of Practice has been issued in respect of CHISs. It is reproduced in Appendix E and is available for download from <http://www.homeoffice. gov.uk/publications/counter-terrorism/ripa-forms/code-practice-human-intel?view=Binary> (accessed December 2011). In this volume references to the CHIS Code refer to this Code.

This is an area in which there has been a considerable amount of relevant case law, which is summarized below. This chapter represents an introduction and general guide to an area of law enforcement that could easily occupy an entire book. (For the purpose of this chapter an 'informer' is taken to mean a person who covertly provides information to the police about criminal activity; an 'informant' is taken to mean someone who volunteers or otherwise provides information to the police, not for reward nor necessarily expecting anonymity. A caller reporting a matter to a police control room would be an informant.)

9.2 **Which Public Authorities May Deploy CHISs?**

Public authorities empowered to utilize covert human intelligence sources are defined in Schedule 1 RIPA as amended. This is accessible online via <http://www. legislation.gov.uk/ukpga/2000/23/contents> (accessed December 2011). Readers should be aware that although the online statutory database will have the latest available updated version of the Schedule (which has changed numerous times since original enactment) the online version may not have been amended to take account of all recent changes. The website will provide information about which amendments have yet to be updated in the published version of the Schedule.

Some public authorities are empowered to use directed surveillance under s 28 RIPA but not to deploy CHIS under s 29 RIPA. Other public authorities are empowered to do both. Authorizing officers will need to understand clearly what it is that their organization is empowered to do, and what conduct and relationships fall within and outside the definition of a covert human intelligence source.

9.3 **What is a CHIS?**

The following are sequential tests derived from the statutory definition at s 26(8).

Definition of a CHIS

---

(1) Does the potential source establish or maintain a relationship (personal or otherwise)?

(2) Is the relationship conducted in a manner calculated to ensure that one party is unaware of its real purpose? (See s 28(9) RIPA for a definition of covert purpose.)

If the answer to these preliminary tests is *yes*, three further tests are applied:

(3) Is the purpose of the relationship to facilitate the obtaining of information?

(4) Is the purpose of the relationship to facilitate access to information?

(5) Is the purpose of the relationship to facilitate the disclosure of information obtained during (or as a consequence of) the relationship without the knowledge of one of the parties?

If the answer to any one of these three tests is *yes*, then taken in conjunction with tests 1 and 2, the source is a CHIS whose conduct must be properly authorized and managed.

CHIS authorization is necessary in all circumstances where the CHIS uses and exploits a personal relationship to acquire information from another person that the other person would regard as being private information. The issue is not who the CHIS is nor what he or she produces, but the new relationships that are established or the existing relationships that are maintained and the covert use that is made of these relationships (see also CHIS Code, para 2.12).

9.4 What Are 'Confidential Sources', 'Confidential Contacts', and 'Tasked Witnesses'?

There has been considerable confusion in a number of organizations over what have been termed 'confidential sources', 'confidential contacts', 'confidential source (or contact) register', and 'tasked witnesses'. With the exception of the more recent 'tasked witness' these terms appear to have come into use well before the enacting of RIPA as a means of managing informants (rather than informers) from a variety of backgrounds whose true identity had to be protected. They are not terms that have any statutory basis under RIPA. Indeed, in his Annual Report for 2006–07, the Chief Surveillance Commissioner observes that he has been:

> disturbed by the introduction, in some forces, of the term 'tasked witness' as an apparent alternative to the correct, legally-recognised, term 'covert human intelligence source'. These individuals have been engaged in a manner that establishes or maintains a covert relationship and I have not been satisfied that the arrangements for their welfare, security and management have been of the standard required by law. The reasons for the introduction of this term are not clear, but it appears to me that the explanation may be a lack of trained handlers or the ignorance of senior investigating officers. I will continue to criticise

the term and, when appropriate, the impropriety of the activity which it may embrace. (para.8.9)

Any person providing information to investigating authorities under circumstances outlined in the definition box above will be a CHIS and must be managed according to the statutory provisions of RIPA and the relevant Code.

Where organizations have categories of confidential sources or contacts, tasked witnesses, and a register of such, these should be reviewed to ascertain whether or not they should be registered as CHISs.

The CHIS Code, paras 2.13–2.19 elaborate upon conduct that falls outside the definition of a CHIS.

9.5 What Powers Does the Law Provide in Relation to CHISs?

Three general types of conduct may be authorized for a CHIS (s 29(4) RIPA; Code, para 4.6).

- Any such activities involving conduct by a CHIS or the use of a CHIS as are specified in the authorization. This gives considerable latitude to authorizing officers and is very flexible. By the same token, if a particular conduct is not mentioned on the authority, it will not be authorized. This reaffirms the importance of precision when drafting applications and authorizations.
- Conduct by or in relation to a specified subject to whose actions the CHIS authorization relates.
- Conduct carried out for the purposes of or in connection with a specific investigation or operation, as described in the authorization.

Organizational use *of* a CHIS and conduct *by* a CHIS are two different things. Most authorizations will need to cover both use and conduct (CHIS Code, paras 2.5–2.7).

In terms of participation, either by an informer or by an undercover operative, RIPA is silent, leaving much room for interpretation.

One interpretation holds that, since RIPA does not specifically permit infiltration and participation (in other words there is no specific statutory provision for participation), no CHIS may be authorized to engage in such conduct. This would severely inhibit the use of CHISs, particularly when investigating serious organized crime, and such an interpretation is inconsistent with a case law tradition that unambiguously authorizes such conduct within strict parameters.

Parliament's intentions about how far infiltration should go were further outlined in debate about one of the many statutory instruments:

It was always the intention that the Act would not provide immunity from prosecution. The intention was that it would provide ECHR cover for the use of a CHIS. However, we have since reconsidered, taken further advice and concluded that, in a very limited range of circumstances, it may be possible that participation in a criminal offence might be rendered lawful by virtue of a *correctly authorised CHIS authorisation*. Ultimately, it still remains a matter for the prosecution authorities and the courts to decide whether an authorisation would render conduct that would usually be considered unlawful as lawful.

(Bob Ainsworth MP, *Hansard* Fifth Standing Committee on Delegated Legislation, col 004 (3 July 2002); emphasis added.)

The revised CHIS Code provides little in the way of elucidation merely stating (para 1.9) that neither RIPA Part II nor the CHIS Code 'is intended to affect the existing practices and procedures surrounding criminal participation of CHIS'. For existing practices see the case law discussed below at 9.12.

9.6 **What Authority Regime is Required for a CHIS?**

Before authorizing the deployment of a CHIS, the authorizing officer must believe (s 29(2) and (3)) that:

(1) It is *necessary* to so deploy for one of the following reasons:

- in the interests of national security;
- for the purpose of preventing or detecting any crime or preventing disorder;
- in the interests of the economic well-being of the UK;
- in the interests of public safety;
- for the purpose of protecting public health;
- for the purpose of assessing or collecting any tax, duty, levy, or other imposition, contribution, or charge payable to a government department; or
- for other purposes which may be specified by order of the Secretary of State.

(2) The authorized conduct is *proportionate* to what is sought to be achieved by the conduct or use.
(3) That arrangements are in place for the management of the CHIS that meet the criteria prescribed in s 29(5) RIPA.

Appropriate authorization of a CHIS is discussed in the CHIS Code, paras 2.9–2.11. The authorizing officer is required by paras 3.8–3.9 CHIS Code to take into account the risk of collateral intrusion and to ensure that measures have been taken to minimize such intrusion. Authorizing officers should document such considerations and action taken.

The majority of organizations empowered under RIPA are only able to deploy CHISs for the purpose of preventing or detecting any crime or preventing disorder (Regulation of Investigatory Powers (Directed Surveillance and Covert Human Intelligence Sources) Order 2003 (SI 2003/3171)).

Persons who can act as authorizing officers are prescribed in the Regulation of Investigatory Powers (Prescription of Offices, Ranks and Positions) Order 2000 (SI 2000/2417) as amended by SI 2003/3171, SI 2005/1084, SI 2006/594, and SI 2006/1874. They include, amongst others: a police superintendent; Royal Navy Provost Marshal or Commander; RAF Wing Commander; an Army Lieutenant Colonel; and an Assistant Director of the SFO.

Where a combined authorization is sought for the deployment of a CHIS and from the Secretary of State for the carrying out of intrusive surveillance, the Secretary of State is the authorizing officer (CHIS Code, paras 3.19–3.21).

Written authorities last for twelve months and may be renewed. An authorization issued under the urgency provisions (CHIS Code, paras 5.5–5.7) lasts for seventy-two hours. Authorizations must be cancelled by the authorizing officer as soon as there is no further need for the registered individual to act as a CHIS. There is no need to wait until the end of the twelve-month period to cancel an authorization.

9.7 What Information is Required in an Application for a CHIS?

Written applications for a CHIS authority should describe *both* the purpose of the operation/investigation *and* the conduct for which authorization is sought. CHIS Code, para 5.10 details further information that should be included in applications.

9.8 Review and Renewal of Authorities

The CHIS Code stresses the need (para 3.14) to keep CHIS use and conduct authorizations under regular review and to review immediately where it becomes apparent that the extent of direct or collateral intrusion is greater than originally anticipated. Reviews are the responsibility of the authorizing officer; they should be documented and retained for three years (see CHIS Code, Chapter 7).

Further information and reading

CHIS Code, paras 3.12–3.16 and 5.15–5.22 discuss the reviewing and renewal of CHIS authorities.

9.9 Juveniles and Vulnerable Persons as CHISs

Special safeguards apply when investigators contemplate the deployment of a CHIS who is under the age of eighteen years. A more senior authorizing officer is required than for an adult CHIS: in the case of the police service the authorizing officer must be at least an assistant chief constable. The relevant customs officer will be band 11 or above and in other organizations the designated individual is often the chief executive or director. The relevant ranks and positions and special conditions are defined in the Regulation of Investigatory Powers (Juveniles) Order 2000 (SI 2000/2793) as amended.

The authorization of a juvenile CHIS lasts for one month instead of the twelve-month authorization for adult CHISs. No CHIS under sixteen can be authorized to provide information about any person with parental responsibility for the juvenile (CHIS Code, para 4.23).

CHIS Code, para 4.22 describes a vulnerable individual as a 'person who is or may be in need of community care services by reason of mental or other disability, age or illness and who is or may be unable to take care of himself, or unable to protect himself against specific harm or exploitation'. Such individuals should only be deployed as CHISs in the most exceptional circumstances and, as with juveniles, a higher level of authorizing officer is specified in Annex A of the Code (CHIS Code, para 4.22).

Further information and reading

The Regulation of Investigatory Powers (Juveniles) Order 2000, SI 2000/2793, made 10 October 2000, in force 6 November 2000, provides additional regulation regarding juvenile CHISs. The following paragraphs are extracts from that Order. ('Guardian', in relation to a source, has the same meaning as is given to 'guardian of a child' by s 105 Children Act 1989.)

Sources under 16: prohibition

3.—No authorisation may be granted for the conduct or use of a source if—

    (a) the source is under the age of sixteen; and

    (b) the relationship to which the conduct or use would relate is between the source and his parent or any person who has parental responsibility for him.

Sources under 16: arrangements for meetings

4.—

    (1) Where a source is under the age of sixteen, the arrangements referred to in section 29(2)(c) of the 2000 Act must be such that there is at all times a person holding an office, rank or position with a relevant investigating authority who has responsibility for ensuring that an appropriate adult is present at meetings to which this article applies.

    (2) This article applies to all meetings between the source and a person representing any relevant investigating authority that take place while the source remains under the age of sixteen.

(3) In paragraph (1), 'appropriate adult' means—

    (a) the parent or guardian of the source;

    (b) any other person who has for the time being assumed responsibility for his welfare; or

    (c) where no person falling within paragraph (a) or (b) is available, any responsible person aged eighteen or over who is neither a member of nor employed by any relevant investigating authority.

Sources under 18: risk assessments etc.

5.—An authorisation for the conduct or use of a source may not be granted or renewed in any case where the source is under the age of eighteen at the time of the grant or renewal, unless—

    (a) a person holding an office, rank or position with a relevant investigating authority has made and, in the case of a renewal, updated a risk assessment sufficient to demonstrate that:

        (i) the nature and magnitude of any risk of physical injury to the source arising in the course of, or as a result of, carrying out the conduct described in the authorisation have been identified and evaluated; and

        (ii) the nature and magnitude of any risk of psychological distress to the source arising in the course of, or as a result of, carrying out the conduct described in the authorisation have been identified and evaluated;

    (b) the person granting or renewing the authorisation has considered the risk assessment and has satisfied himself that any risks identified in it are justified and, if they are, that they have been properly explained to and understood by the source; and

    (c) the person granting or renewing the authorisation knows whether the relationship to which the conduct or use would relate is between the source and a relative, guardian or person who has for the time being assumed responsibility for the source's welfare, and, if it is, has given particular consideration to whether the authorisation is justified in the light of that fact.

Sources under 18: duration of authorisations

6.—In relation to an authorisation for the conduct or the use of a source who is under the age of eighteen at the time the authorisation is granted or renewed, section 43(3) of the 2000 Act shall have effect as if the period specified in paragraph (b) of that subsection were one month instead of twelve months.

9.10 **Acquisition of Confidential Information by a CHIS**

Where a CHIS is likely to acquire communications subject to legal privilege, confidential personal information of confidential journalistic material, special rules for authorizations are outlined in Chapter 4 and Annexe A of the Code (see Appendix E). These include the fact that a more senior authorizing officer is required to authorize such operations than is required for normal deployment of a CHIS. Legally privileged material obtained by a source is unlikely ever to be admissible at trial and deployment of a source in circumstances in which such material is likely to be acquired can only be authorized in exceptional and compelling circumstances (CHIS Code, para 4.6).

Where any confidential information is acquired, the OSC Commissioner or Inspector must be informed at the next inspection of that organization.

9.11 **What Management Regime is Required for a CHIS?**

The management regime is defined in s 29(5) RIPA. It is essentially a statutory requirement for CHIS risk management.

It includes specific arrangements to ensure that the source is independently managed and supervised via a three-tier hierarchy of supervision, that records are kept of the use made of the source, and that the source's identity is protected from those who do not need to know it. (The Secretary of State can amend these arrangements by order.) The responsibility for the management and supervision of a source falls to specified individuals within the organization benefiting from the use of the source. As there may be cases where a source carries out activities for more than one organization, it is provided that only one organization will be identified as having responsibility for each requirement in relation to such arrangements and recordkeeping.

There must be a person within the organization using the CHIS who is responsible for day-to-day dealings with the CHIS (usually called the handler). Handlers will be supervised by controllers who must have general oversight of the use of the source.

The highest tier comprises an individual of suitable rank whose function it is to maintain records of how CHISs are used. These records are scrutinized annually by the OSC.

The CHIS Code, para 9.1 requires that every relevant public authority must have a senior responsible officer responsible for:

- the integrity of the process in place within the public authority for the management of CHIS;
- compliance with Part II of the Act and with this Code;

- oversight of the reporting of errors to the relevant oversight Commissioner and the identification of both the cause(s) of errors and the implementation of processes to minimise repetition of errors;
- engagement with the OSC inspectors when they conduct their inspections, where applicable; and
- where necessary, oversight of the implementation of post inspection action plans approved by the relevant oversight Commissioner.

Risk assessment (see Chapter 11) is a vital ingredient of successful CHIS management whether the CHIS be an informer or an undercover investigator. It is an ongoing dynamic process which should be documented as thoroughly as possible.

Thorough documentation in the form of precisely worded authorizations and terms of reference, comprehensive contact sheets, and comprehensively documented instructions to CHISs, is also good practice that will assist in subsequent public interest immunity (PII) applications as well as recording the integrity of the CHIS deployment for external scrutiny.

Further information and reading

The Regulation of Investigatory Powers (Source Records) Regulations 2000, SI 2000/2725, specify the particulars to be documented in the records for each CHIS, pursuant to s 29(5)(d) RIPA (made 4 October 2000, in force 1 November 2000).

(a) the identity of the source;

(b) the identity, where known, used by the source;

(c) any relevant investigating authority other than the authority maintaining the records;

(d) the means by which the source is referred to within each relevant investigating authority;

(e) any other significant information connected with the security and welfare of the source;

(f) any confirmation made by a person granting or renewing an authorisation for the conduct or use of a source that the information in paragraph (d) has been considered and that any identified risks to the security and welfare of the source have where appropriate been properly explained to and understood by the source;

(g) the date when, and the circumstances in which, the source was recruited;

(h) the identities of the persons who, in relation to the source, are discharging or have discharged the functions mentioned in section 29(5)(a) to (c) of the 2000 Act or in any order made by the Secretary of State under section 29(2)(c);

(i) the periods during which those persons have discharged those responsibilities;

(j) the tasks given to the source and the demands made of him in relation to his activities as a source;

(k) all contacts or communications between the source and a person acting on behalf of any relevant investigating authority;

(l) the information obtained by each relevant investigating authority by the conduct or use of the source;

(m) any dissemination by that authority of information obtained in that way; and

(n) in the case of a source who is not an undercover operative, every payment, benefit or reward and every offer of a payment, benefit or reward that is made or provided by or on behalf of any relevant investigating authority in respect of the source's activities for the benefit of that or any other relevant investigating authority.

9.12 **What Significant Case Law Applies to CHISs?**

In the absence of precise statute prior to RIPA, the lawful parameters around informers, infiltration, and the use of test purchase as an evidence-gathering mechanism were determined by case law. RIPA is largely silent on CHISs other than to provide the framework for authorization and the risk management regime.

General endorsement for the deployment of informers and undercover investigators was approved in *R v Birtles*: 'whilst the police are entitled to make use of information concerning an offence already laid on and while... it may be proper for the police to encourage the informer to take part in the offence... the police must never use an informer to encourage another to commit an offence which he would not otherwise commit' ([1969] 1 WLR 1047; and confirmed in *R v Horseferry Road Magistrates Court ex p Bennett (No. 1)* [1994] 1 AC 42).

The value of informers to the authorities recognized in *Birtles* has continued to be acknowledged. In *R v King* (1998) 7 Cr App R (S) 227, Lane LCJ opined:

One of the most effective weapons in the hands of the detective is the informer. Once the identity of a suspect can be established, even if he does not confess, it will often be possible to obtain scientific or other evidence to connect the suspect with a crime and so corroborate the informer. It is to the advantage of law abiding citizens that criminals should be encouraged to inform upon their criminal colleagues.

The wider benefit to society of this form of covert investigation was also remarked upon by Woolf LCJ in *R v J* [2001] 1 Cr App R (S) 79:

In the battle against drugs it is absolutely essential that the prosecuting authorities are given information which can help to lead to the detection of others who are engaged in this trade. The courts must do what they can to assist those who are involved in trying to combat the ever growing trade in drugs by giving incentives to those who are convicted and come to be sentenced to provide information.

In *R v Clarke* (1985) 80 Cr App R 344 the court accepted that motive was irrelevant to the liability of an accessory to the fact, but held that it was 'quite another thing to conclude... that conduct which is overall calculated and intended not to further but to frustrate the ultimate result of the crime is always immaterial and irrelevant'. In essence this provides a mechanism outside RIPA for rendering lawful behaviour that would otherwise be unlawful, which should be viewed within the context of para 2.10 of the Code.

Further information and reading

The issues raised by *R v Clarke* are considered in a wider context in B Fitzpatrick, 'Covert human intelligence sources as offenders: the scope of immunity from the criminal law', *Covert Policing Review* (2005), 15–32.

It is helpful to consider the numerous key cases thematically. They draw some very fine lines between what is acceptable and what is not.

9.12.1 Agents provocateurs

It is a fundamental principle that CHISs, be they (participating) informers or undercover investigators, should never incite the commission of a crime. Participating informers, as seen in the general authority of *R v Birtles*, may only participate in offences which are already laid on, ie are already planned. Their role should only be minor.

An *agent provocateur* is defined in *R v Mealey and Sheridan* [1974] 60 Cr App R 59 at 61, quoting the 1928 Royal Commission on Police Powers (Cmd 3297): 'a person who entices another to commit an express breach of the law which he would not otherwise have committed and then proceeds or informs against him in respect of such offence'. This sets the boundary of unacceptable behaviour.

But in also defining what was acceptable, the same judgment held that a person infiltrating a criminal organization, either as an undercover investigator or as a participating informer, must show a 'certain amount of interest and enthusiasm' for the proposed criminality in order to maintain their cover and render the infiltration tactic effective.

Teixeira de Castro v Portugal (1999) 28 EHRR 101 provides a clear example of investigators who went too far. Two undercover investigators posed as drug addicts and asked Teixeira to supply them with heroin. He had no heroin in his house, being a dealer in cannabis, but the investigators took him to another house and persuaded him to buy heroin there in order to sell it to the investigators. The Strasbourg court held that the investigators had incited the commission of an offence that would not otherwise have been committed.

Likewise in *R v Moon* [2004] EWCA Crim 2872, investigators were held to have encouraged Moon, a mere drug user, to become a supplier and so commit more serious offences that she would not otherwise have committed. Her conviction was quashed on appeal. *Moon* took a contradictory view to an earlier judgment, *R v Coutts-Jarman* [2001] EWCA Crim 2376, in which the Court of Appeal upheld the conviction for supplying drugs in circumstances where investigators had made six increasingly pressurized demands for Coutts-Jarman to sell them drugs, the last demand 'reinforced' with the claim that the partner of the intending purchaser was in serious withdrawal.

The investigators in *R v Edwards* [1991] Crim LR 45 adopted a more passive role, making a test purchase which, far from being the isolated instigation argued by the defence, was demonstrably within the context of a wider pattern of drug dealing by the suspect.

Behaviour that similarly fell short of constituting incitement was confirmed in *R v Pattemore* [1994] Crim LR 836, in which the defendant had acquiesced with the requests of an informer. The court held there had been no pressure applied to the defendant and that fairness to the defence had to be balanced in this case by fairness to the public.

Specifically in relation to test purchase operations, *DPP v Marshall and Downes* [1988] 3 All ER 683 established that the tactic itself was not deception just because investigators did not reveal their true identities. The tactic itself was reaffirmed as legitimate in *Borough of Ealing v Woolworths Plc* [1995] Crim LR 58, which also held that deploying an eleven-year-old boy to try to purchase products restricted to persons over eighteen years old was legitimate where the test purchaser had passively sought a purchase rather than actively tried to persuade the retailer.

Courts have taken notice of test purchase operative behaviour in determining investigators have incited an offence. Acting like an ordinary customer was taken to include the use of aggressive language in *R v Chandler* [2001] EWCA Crim 3167. In *R v Byrne* [2003] EWCA Crim 1073, the court noted that investigators had done nothing to tempt Byrne 'to move outside her usual way of life' (at para 12). Similarly in *R v Jones* [2010] EWCA Crim 925 the court held that an undercover officer had not overstepped the boundary of incitement when engaged in asking questions of a cannabis paraphernalia retailer (who provided advice about growing tomatoes in a context when no reasonable person could have concluded that the conversation was not really about growing cannabis).

Whether the deployment of a test purchase operative requires authorization as a CHIS will depend on the full facts of the investigation. The CHIS Code, para 9.12 offers contrasting examples of circumstances in which CHIS authorization may or may not be considered for test purchase operations. Use of recording equipment by test purchase operatives will amount to directed surveillance.

....

Case law criteria establishing whether an informer has acted as an agent provocateur

(1) Was a crime of the same kind as that charged already afoot at the time of the intervention of the CHIS?

(2) Had the defendant committed an offence of a class which he would not have committed but for the encouragement of the CHIS?

(3) Had the defendants a propensity to engage in the crime charged?

(4) Did the CHIS play a major part in the criminal activity?

(5) Is the Court certain, in retrospect, of the CHIS's reliability?

(6) Was the CHIS's participation approved in accordance with the statutory regime?

(7) Is the offence so grave that the public interest could justify the use of such tactics?

Based on *R v Ameer and Lucas* Crim LR (1977) 104. The judgment in *R v Ameer and Lucas* was disapproved by *R v Sang* [1980] AC 402, at 430, but this seven-part test applied in the case still has relevance.

....

9.12.2 Entrapment

Closely connected to the problem of investigators acting as *agents provocateurs* is the issue of entrapment: investigators creating situations in which suspects commit offences that they would not otherwise have committed. 'It is simply not acceptable that the state through its agents should lure its citizens into committing acts forbidden by the law and then seek to prosecute them for doing so': thus Lord Nicholls in *R v Loosley* [2001] UKHL 53, para 1. This defining principle having been set, there are investigative actions that fall short of entrapment and the boundaries are defined in case law.

It is well established in English law that entrapment is no defence (*R v Sang* [1980] AC 402; *R v Smurthwaite and Gill* [1994] 1 All ER 898), but that does not release investigators from the obligation to act lawfully. If offenders take advantage of an opportunity to commit a crime and in doing so play a trick on themselves, then this is considered a lawful means of securing evidence. Hence *R v Christou and another* [1992] 4 All ER 559, in which the defendants sold stolen property to undercover police officers masquerading as second-hand property dealers in a shop. Police had established the shop for the very purpose of recovering stolen property from those willing to sell it. Another example is *Williams and another v DPP* [1993] 3 All ER 365, in which an insecure lorry containing dummy packets of cigarettes was parked unattended in a street, thus constituting a tethered-goat-type lure. Once again, those who took the opportunity to steal from the lorry were held to have played a trick on themselves.

In *Nottingham City Council v Amin* [2000] 1 WLR 1071, a taxi driver had agreed to take two special constables on duty in plain clothes to a specified area in the city for which they paid a fare. The taxi driver had no licence to ply for hire in that area. It was held that the police had a duty to enforce the law and that it was not offensive to provide an individual with an opportunity to commit a crime which had then been taken up. The defendant did not have to take advantage of the opportunity.

These should be viewed within the context of *R v Loosley* [2001] UKHL 53, which reaffirmed that where the involvement of an accused was a direct result of incitement by an investigator, then the evidence should rightfully be excluded under s 78 PACE. But where the investigator had done no more than provide an opportunity for the accused to commit a crime, in exactly the same circumstances as another person might have provided such an opportunity (ie a test purchase investigator purporting to be a drug addict when trying to secure evidence of the accused's dealing), there was no reason why the evidence should be excluded, particularly if it was part of a properly authorized operation in which every effort had been made to secure corroboration through tape-recording.

Ormerod, in essence, summarizes a test for entrapment in his paper in *Covert Policing Review* 2006.

KEY POINTS IN DETERMINING WHETHER INVESTIGATORS HAVE ENGAGED IN ENTRAPMENT

- What was the trigger for the operation? Was there reasonable suspicion that the person subject to the operation was already engaged in the suspected criminality?
- Was the operation properly authorized and supervised?
- Was the operation a proportionate response to the offence?
- Was the investigator's conduct no more than to offer the suspect an opportunity to commit the crime—was the investigator acting in an unexceptional way given the type of crime in question? Did the investigator cause the crime?
- Was the conduct with the suspect contemporaneously recorded?

Based on Ormerod 2006, 72 and 75.

Further information and reading

For wider discussion of the issue of entrapment see:

- D Ormerod, 'Recent developments in entrapment', *Covert Policing Review* (2006), 65–86;
- S McKay, 'Entrapment: competing views on the effect of the Human Rights Act 1998 on the English criminal law', European Human Rights Law Review (2002), 764; and
- A Ashworth, 'Redrawing the boundaries of entrapment', Criminal Law Review (2002), 161–179.

9.12.3 **Securing evidence**

The extent to which undercover investigators can secure evidence by questioning those with whom they interact is constrained by the PACE Codes of Practice in relation to interviews. The Codes have been held to apply to interviews outside a police station or other custody centre (*R v Christou and another* [1992] 4 All ER 559).

In *R v Bryce* [1992] 4 All ER 567, investigators asked questions that were essentially evidential in nature and so constituted an unlawful interview because the

PACE regime had not been complied with. In *R v Christou and another* [1992] 4 All ER 559, the undercover officers had asked only such questions as were necessary to maintain their cover as second-hand property dealers.

In *Bryce* the conversations had not been tape-recorded whereas in *Christou* they had been. Tape-recording such interactions ensures that there is an accurate and unassailable record of conversations between CHISs and suspects or investigators. Tape-recordings will demonstrate, for instance, that a conversation is an offence in the commission rather than a conversation about past events that constitutes an admission. The value of this was established in *R v Smurthwaite and Gill* [1994] 1 All ER 898, which also identified good-practice criteria for such recordings, reaffirmed in *R v Mann and Dixon* [1995] Crim LR 647, and in *R v Horseferry Road Magistrates Court ex p Bennett (No. 1)* [1994] 1 AC 42. More recently, *R v Kennedy, Palmer and Warburton* (unreported, 2001) reaffirmed the value of tape-recording and the expectation of courts that this represented 'best evidence': proceedings were stayed due to inadequate police recording and documentation of the alleged offending and interaction with investigators. In *R v Hardy and Hardy* [2002] EWCA Crim 3012, the Appeal Court held that the tape-recording by undercover officers of telephone conversations which they had with the suspects (subsequently defendants) did not amount to interception because these were conversations about which the officers could testify as witnesses and for which the recordings merely provided corroboration.

Case law criteria for assessing fairness at trial where it is sought to exclude evidence from undercover operations

The Court will consider:

(1) Whether the CHIS acted as an *agent provocateur*
(2) The nature of any entrapment
(3) Whether the recorded evidence constitutes an offence in progress or an admission of an historical offence
(4) Whether the investigator's role in securing the evidence was active or passive
(5) Whether there is an unassailable record or robust corroboration of what occurred
(6) Whether the CHIS abused his role to ask questions that should have been put only under the PACE Codes.

> Based on *R v Smurthwaite and Gill* [1994] 1 All ER 898.

9.12.4 Protecting informers

Case law going back as far as 1794 has established the principle that it is in the public interest to protect the identities of CHISs, unless to do so would deny a defendant the chance to establish innocence and thus lead to a miscarriage. As was seen in 2.8.2, the same principle was extended to the protection of observation points.

Further information and reading

The protection of informers: the historical precedent for the protection of the identity of police informers is to be found in: *Hardy's case* (1794) 24 St Tr 199; *AG v Briant* (1846) 15 M&W 169; *Marks v Beyfus* [1890] 25 QBD 494; *D v NSPCC* [1978] AC 171; *R v Hennessy* (1979) 68 Cr App R 419; *R v Hallett and others* [1986] Crim LR 462; *R v Turner (Paul)* [1995] 1 WLR 264; *R v Pattemore* [1994] Crim LR 836.

Through the statutory CHIS management regime and the relevant Code of Practice, RIPA establishes that public authorities have a duty of care towards informers (Billingsley 2005, 210–211).

Case law criteria—test for duty of care

Caparo Industries Plc v Dickman & others [1990] 2 AC 605 establishes a three-point test to identify whether a duty of care exists.

(1) Damage/harm must have been done.
(2) There must be proximity in the relationship between the person alleging damage/harm and the party alleged to be negligent.
(3) It must be reasonable, in the circumstances, for a duty of care to exist.

In *Donnelly v CC of Lincolnshire & Others* [2001] Po LR 313; [2001] All ER (D)) the *Caparo* test was applied in circumstances where a CHIS claimed his anonymity had been assured by police who subsequently revealed his identity during suspect interviews. The CHIS suffered damage/harm (his life was imperilled); his relationship to Lincolnshire Police was proximate (he was an informer providing information covertly to the police); and it was reasonable in these particular circumstances for the informer to expect a duty of care from police.

These and other cases are considered at length in R Billingsley, 'Duty of care for informers', *The Police Journal*, 78 (2005), 209–221.

Swinney and another v Chief Constable of Northumbria [1996] 3 All ER 449 affirmed that there was a general duty of care to take reasonable steps to avoid public disclosure of information provided by a CHIS. Documented information provided by an informer was stolen from an unattended police car. The person about whom the information had been provided subsequently subjected the informer and her family to threats and arson attacks, having been told who had provided information to the police.

There have been case law exceptions: *R v Agar* [1990] 2 All ER 442 established that where there were *specific, detailed* allegations of a set-up, the defence could ask investigators about their sources. This did not establish a disclosure precedent nor did it provide a vehicle for defence fishing-trips. *Savage v Chief Constable of Hampshire* [1997] 2 All ER 631 held that an informer who chose to disclose his role could not be prevented from doing so on public policy grounds.

In relation to protecting CHISs through a Public Interest Immunity application, *R v H and C* [2004] 2 AC 134 confirms that neutral material or material
damaging to the defendant need not be disclosed and should not, therefore, be
brought to the attention of the court. Where a CHIS testifies at court, it is legitimate for the defence to seek to ascertain the circumstances in which the CHIS
was recruited, details of the assistance provided and the rewards made, and the
motivation of the CHIS.

9.13 **Good Practice in Light of the Above Case Law**

The importance of precise and detailed documentation in relation to CHIS
conduct cannot be overemphasized, particularly given the absence of specific
statutory reference concerning infiltration and participation.

Where it is necessary to conduct directed surveillance of an individual to evalu-
ate the potential benefit and risks involved in their deployment as a CHIS, it may
be necessary to authorize such conduct if the circumstances of the case coincide
with the statutory grounds for which authorization is required. Regardless of
whether authorization is required in the circumstances or not, the surveillance
will be an infringement of Article 8(1) ECHR and must therefore be capable of
justification under Article 8(2) (see CHIS Code, para 3.23).

The lawfulness of a CHIS's conduct will be contingent upon the extent to
which the CHIS complies with the authorization (s 27(1) RIPA). It follows that
the authority itself must be precise and detailed with reasons given for each decision and direction. Conduct not specified in the authorization will not be lawful.
The briefing of CHISs should be fully documented so as to demonstrate not only
that the individual has been properly briefed but that the terms of reference
are fully understood, particularly where infiltration or participation are being
authorized. 'If an authorization covers participation in a criminal offence, and
the authorization itself is valid (that is to say, it meets the statutory tests), then it
would appear that the behaviour of the CHIS is not criminal' (Fitzpatrick 2005,
29). An example developed by Fitzpatrick is where a CHIS infiltrates a terrorist
organization, as a consequence of which the operative has to wear insignia associated with the organization which would be an offence under the Terrorism Act
2000 but would nevertheless be necessary to maintain cover.

Further information and reading

B Fitzpatrick, 'Covert human intelligence sources as offenders', *Covert Policing
Review* (2005), 15–32.

Corroboration of information provided by a CHIS is crucial. For undercover or test
purchase investigators this can be achieved through technical means (where it is
safe for the investigator to wear a tape-recorder) or through other surveillance as

appropriate. In relation to informants reporting on their encounters with criminal associates there will rarely be the opportunity to corroborate conversations during such interaction, and so their intelligence must be assessed accordingly and actions arising therefrom suitably risk-managed.

Similarly the debriefing of CHISs should be fully documented and adjustments made to their risk assessment or conduct authorization as required.

9.14 **International Deployment of CHIS**

Paras 4.26–4.30 of the CHIS Code deal briefly with circumstances in which a UK CHIS might be deployed in a foreign jurisdiction and in which a foreign CHIS might be deployed in the UK. With increasing reliance upon biometric border security controls, management of such deployments is increasingly complex and advice from the international expertise within SOCA should be sought.

KEY POINTS ON PROPORTIONALITY

(1) A test purchase investigator must not act as an *agent provocateur*. This means they must not incite or procure a person, or through that person anybody else, to commit an offence or an offence of a more serious character, which that person would not otherwise have committed.

(2) However, a test purchase officer is entitled to join a conspiracy which is already in being or an offence which is already laid on or, for example, where a person has made an offer to supply goods, including drugs, which involves the commission of a criminal offence.

(3) If, during the course of an investigation into an offence or series of offences, a person involved suggests the commission of, or offers to commit, a further-similar offence, a test purchase officer is entitled to participate in the proposed offence. The investigator must not incite such an offence.

(4) It is proper for the test purchase investigator to show interest in, and enthusiasm for, proposals made even though they are unlawful, but in doing so they must try to tread the difficult line between showing the necessary interest and enthusiasm to keep their cover (and pursue their investigation) and actually becoming an *agent provocateur*. Invariably this means the investigator will enter a criminal conspiracy or become part of a pre-arranged criminal offence.

(5) Test purchase investigators must obtain confirmation that the information they are acting on is accurate and reliable before becoming involved in operations.

(6) Test purchase investigators must bear in mind that, by virtue of s 78 PACE, a judge may take into account the circumstances in which evidence was obtained in considering its adverse effect on the fairness of proceedings in court.

(7) Police officers must be fully conversant with Article 6 ECHR (right to fair trial) and Article 8 (right to respect for private and family life).

Further information and reading

The Regulation of Investigatory Powers (British Broadcasting Corporation) Order 2001, SI 2001/1057, made 15 March 2001, in force 16 March 2001, prescribes the new s 27A RIPA empowering the authorization of detection of television receivers.

Checklist of key issues when considering whether or not to deploy a CHIS

- What evidence or intelligence is being sought?

- How is it relevant to the operation under consideration?

- What is the least intrusive means of securing such evidence or information?

- Has the least intrusive means of securing the evidence or information been attempted? If not, why not?

- What is the likelihood of collateral intrusion against the privacy of persons not being investigated? How will collateral intrusion be prevented (or if not, minimized) and how will the product of collateral intrusion be managed?

- What are the risks to the organization of such tactics? (Chapter 11)

- What are the risks to the organization's staff, especially the CHIS, of such tactics? (Chapter 11)

- What are the risks of the CHIS being compromised by another person? (Chapter 11)

- What are the risks of the CHIS compromising him or herself? (Chapter 11)

- If the CHIS has compromised him or herself, how are the additional risks going to be managed? (Chapter 11)

- What are the risks to the public or specific third parties, including the family and friends of the CHIS, when such tactics are deployed? (Chapter 11)

- What are the risks to the subject of the investigation? (Chapter 11)

- Will such methods breach Article 8(1)? (1.7.1)

- Is there justification for doing so provided by Article 8(2)? (1.7.4)

- How is the legality test met? (1.7.3)

- How is the legitimacy test met? (1.7.4)

- How is the necessity test met? (1.7.5)

- How is the proportionality test met? (1.7.5)

- Is the proposed CHIS a juvenile? If so, have the appropriate safeguards been put in place? (CHIS Code, para 4.23)

- Is the proposed CHIS a vulnerable person? If so, have the appropriate safeguards been put in place? (CHIS Code, para 4.22)

- Has the CHIS been properly trained as an undercover investigator?

- Has the CHIS been properly assessed, evaluated, briefed, and debriefed as a (paid) informer?

- Is the CHIS prepared to enter into the witness protection scheme if necessary?

- Is the organization prepared to provide the resources necessary to place the CHIS on the witness protection scheme?

- Are the arguments justifying the application to use covert investigation based on reliable information/intelligence, or has the applicant adopted a 'tick-the-box' approach to completing the application without giving full consideration to the facts of the case and the issues arising?

- Have the arguments justifying the granting of authorization to use covert investiga-tion been fully articulated, or has the authorizing officer merely paid lip service to the pro forma authorization template via which authority is granted?

- How will the product of the surveillance be managed? (Chapter 12)

- When should this authority be reviewed? What circumstances will or may arise that will necessitate review before then?

- How are the methods by which the evidence/intelligence will be obtained to be protected at trial?

Planning covert investigation actions

Remember to include the PLAN for covert investigation tactics in all investi-gation policy-book entries relating to covert investigation considerations and decisions.

P **PROPORTIONALITY**
   Why is it proportionate to obtain the intended product of this surveillance in the manner proposed? (1.7.5)

L **LEGITIMACY**
   What is the legitimate purpose of the proposed action: the prevention of disorder or crime; the interests of national security; the interests of public safety; the interests of the economic well-being of the country; the

protection of health or morals; the protection of the rights and freedoms of others? (1.7.4)

A   AUTHORITY TO UNDERTAKE PROPOSED ACTION
What is the lawful foundation and authority for the proposed action? From whom must authorization be sought? (1.7.3)

N   NECESSITY OF PROPOSED ACTION
Why is the proposed action necessary? (1.7.5)

Flowchart for Authorizing CHIS Operations

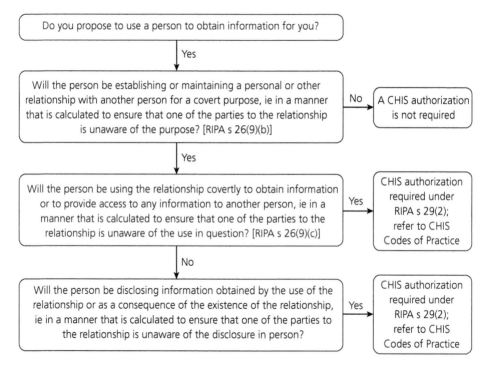

10

Covert Investigation Abroad

10.1 **Introduction**

Criminals have always utilized jurisdiction borders as a means of evading prosecution or disrupting investigation. In the final quarter of the twentieth century, as global communications and transport networks became accessible to ever more people, it became easier to escape from a jurisdiction and easier to commit crime on a transnational scale, for instance the trafficking of illicit commodities from source countries to criminal markets overseas. With local community policing in the UK increasingly incorporating transnational communities with links in the UK and overseas, for instance in the EU or the Indian sub-continent, it is possible that a covert investigation otherwise contained within a single local English police force may nevertheless have transnational actions associated with it. A surveillance team from anywhere in the UK could quite conceivably find that their subject travels through the Channel Tunnel in the space of twenty-five minutes to meet criminal associates in France or Belgium, before returning to the UK the same day.

To counter transnational criminality and aid its investigation a corpus of instruments and conventions has been created to facilitate mutual legal assistance and international law enforcement co-operation: these are the means by which domestic investigators can secure help as required in their own investigations where evidence or the suspect is located outside their own jurisdiction.

Further information and reading

This is an area of increasing activity for investigators and lawyers alike. For legal commentary (together with the reproduction of some key legal instruments) see D McClean, *International Judicial Assistance* (Clarendon Press, Oxford, 1992); C Murray and L Harris, *Mutual Assistance in Criminal Matters* (Sweet & Maxwell, London, 2000); A Jones and A Doobay, *Jones and Doobay on Extradition and Mutual Assistance* (Sweet & Maxwell, London, 2005), 362–377. For a collection of key legal instruments, C Van den Wyngaert (ed), *International Criminal Law: A Collection of International and European Instruments* (3rd revd edn, Martinus Nijhoff, Leiden, 2005).

The term *transnational* (cross-border) is preferred here to *international* (between states) because the latter term is used to qualify specific behaviours, instruments, and institutions in relation to international law that do not apply to the cross-border investigation of crimes proscribed in domestic jurisdictions. The International Criminal Court has permissive jurisdiction only over genocide, crimes against humanity, war crimes, and international aggression, not domestic crimes committed on a transnational scale (Statute of the International Court, Article 5 (Rome, 17 July 1998, UN Doc A/CONF 183/9) *International Legal Materials* 1998, 999; alternatively, Van den Wyngaert, *International Criminal Law*, 139, 140).

In the absence of an international or supranational criminal code, different domestic jurisdictions have to be able to work alongside each other in co-operation when criminality crosses their mutual border. This is the *raison d'être* of mutual legal assistance treaty law and the premise underpinning the new philosophy of mutual recognition now being promoted within the EU by the UK (*Hansard* HL (series 6) vol 411, col 973 (2 December 2003)).

10.2 Which Public Authorities May Conduct Covert Investigation Abroad?

Section 27(3) RIPA prescribes that surveillance authorized under s 26 can include 'conduct outside the United Kingdom'. In respect of directed or intrusive surveillance and the deployment of CHISs, those authorities empowered to conduct such investigations within the UK can also conduct such authorized activity abroad without offending UK law.

Part III PA97 limits the area of lawful authorization in relation to property interference to the relevant area overseen by the authorizing officer and, as appropriate, adjacent UK territorial waters (s 93).

Therefore relevant empowered investigators are as described in Chapters 2 and 9.

10.3 What Powers Does the Law Provide in Relation to Covert Investigation Abroad?

Section 27(3) RIPA prescribes that surveillance authorized under s 26 can include 'conduct outside the United Kingdom'. In respect of directed or intrusive surveillance and the deployment of CHISs, conduct that can be authorized within the UK can also be authorized to take place in a foreign jurisdiction without offending UK law. However, such activity may breach the domestic law of the foreign jurisdiction in which it is proposed to conduct surveillance.

Part III PA97 limits the area of lawful authorization in relation to property interference to the relevant area overseen by the authorizing officer and, as appropriate, adjacent UK territorial waters (s 93).

Therefore relevant investigation powers are as described in Chapters 2 and 9, taking into account the provisions of the foreign jurisdiction in which it is proposed to conduct the covert investigation.

Two international instruments make provision for international law enforcement covert investigation co-operation within the EU: the Schengen Convention 1990 (International Legal Materials 1991, 84) and the EU Convention on Mutual Assistance in Criminal Matters 2000, done 29 May 2000 Brussels, OJ 2000/C 197/1. The latter supplements the 1959 Convention on Mutual Assistance in Criminal Matters, which is open to Member States of the Council of Europe and not just EU members but which contains no specific provisions for covert investigation (European Treaty Series 30, done Strasbourg 20 April 1959).

Article 40 of the Schengen Convention provides for 'cross-border surveillance', where a person under surveillance and presumed to have taken part in a criminal offence to which extradition may apply (Article 40(7)) crosses the mutual border of two contracting parties to the Convention. If investigators in the requesting state have prior authorization to do so from the requested state which the suspect enters during the course of the surveillance, Article 40(1) permits the original investigators to continue their surveillance in the territory of the requested state, subject to any request to the requested state to assume responsibility for the surveillance. In spontaneous circumstances where it was not possible to seek prior authorization, surveillance may be continued for up to five hours in the territory of the requested state whilst authorization to continue the surveillance is sought from the requested state. Article 40(3)(f) expressly prohibits the domestic surveillance team operating in a foreign territory pursuant to this article from challenging or arresting the subject under surveillance whilst in the jurisdiction of another state. The UK entered into this Article of the Schengen Convention on 22 December 2004 (*Mutual Legal Assistance Newsletter 19*, UK Central Authority, February 2005), the obligations being given domestic effect in s 83 Crime (International Co-operation) Act 2003 which creates new s 76A RIPA.

Article 40 can only be applied by police and customs investigators engaged on a criminal investigation. Although the government has repeatedly asserted that SOCA is not a police force (*Hansard* HC Standing Committee D, cols 9 and 34 (11 January 2005); see also cols 32, 33, 35, 38 and 43), the Serious Organised Crime Agency has been designated as such to enable its staff to utilize Article 40. (Authorities designated for the purposes of Article 40 are listed in the *Schengen Handbook on Cross-Border Police Co-Operation*, OJL 239, 408, 22 September 2000.)

This provision is not to be confused with 'hot pursuit' permitted by Article 41 Schengen Convention, which is restricted to uniformed officers (or plain-clothes officers clearly displaying visible insignia identifying them as police officers) pursuing a suspect fleeing the scene of a crime or escaping from custody across a land border. As the UK and Eire have not entered into this part of the Schengen Convention, hot pursuit is not permitted across the UK's only EU land border. Contracting parties and the law enforcement agencies permitted to use Articles 40 and 41 are listed in the Schengen Handbook.

Other covert investigation tactics may be permitted under Article 14 of the EU Mutual Legal Assistance Convention subject to the agreement of the requesting and requested states. Under this provision it is for the requested state to decide whether or not to implement the request for covert investigation put to it, having 'due regard to its national law and procedures'. The domestic law of the state in which the covert investigation takes place shall apply to the activities undertaken.

Article 13 EU Mutual Legal Assistance Convention makes provision for the establishment of multi-national joint investigation teams (JITs), members of which could apply for any such domestic covert or coercive measures within their own jurisdictions without recourse to mutual legal assistance procedures. Diplomatic negotiation is required to establish a JIT and advice should be sought from the Home Office Judicial Co-Operation Unit (Home Office Circulars 53/2002 and 26/2004 refer).

Further information and reading

Joint investigation teams are given a liability framework by ss 103 and 104 Police Reform Act 2002 and a statutory powers framework by ss 16(2)(b), 16(4)(b), 18(2), and 27(1) Crime (International Co-operation) Act 2003. See also the EU Council Framework Decision of 13 June 2002 on Joint Investigation Teams (2002/465/JHA) OJ 2002/L 162/1 and the EU Commission Recommendation for a Model Agreement for setting up Joint Investigation Teams, 7 April 2003, CRIMORG 17, 7061/0. For UK government guidance on JITs, see Home Office Circulars 53/2002 and 26/2004.

There are an increasing number of studies into the effectiveness and practicalities of joint investigation teams. See, for instance, L Block, *From Politics to Policing: The Rationality Gap in EU Council Policy-Making* (Chapter 7 'Case study: joint investigation teams'; also C Rijken, (2006) 2(2) *Utrecht Law Review*, 99.

In relation to non-EU states, the capability to request covert investigation assistance abroad will depend upon the nature of any mutual legal assistance treaty in force between the UK and the other state in question. On existing mutual legal assistance treaties and their provisions, advice should be sought from the UK Central Authority.

Further information and reading

The UK Central Authority is the single point of contact in England and Wales by which international letters of request (also known as *Commissions Rogatoires*) are transmitted and received. Information about the UK Central Authority and mutual legal assistance is contained on <http://www.homeoffice.gov.uk/police/mutual-legal-assistance/> (accessed December 2011).

UK accession to the EU Mutual Legal Assistance Convention meant that provision had to be made for providing assistance in respect of communication interception notwithstanding the general prohibition on the use of intercepted communications as evidence in UK criminal trials (s 17 RIPA).

Section 1(4) RIPA permits UK investigators to request foreign interception of communications when three conditions are met: (1) where the UK is party to a designated international agreement which has come into force; (2) where the interception is being carried out for the purposes of a criminal investigation; and (3) where the investigation is being carried out in the territory of a state party to the designated agreement. The EU Mutual Legal Assistance Convention is the only such designated agreement at the time of writing. (See Regulation of Investigatory Powers (Conditions for the Lawful Interception of Persons outside the UK) Regulations 2004 (SI 2004/157); Regulation of Investigatory Powers (Designation of an International Agreement) Order 2004 (SI 2004/158).)

Such requested intercepted communications could not be used in evidence in the UK by virtue of the prohibition in s 17 RIPA.

The reciprocal arrangement is provided under s 5(1)(c). The Secretary of State is able to stipulate that any communications intercepted in the UK and provided to foreign authorities should not be used in evidence abroad.

Further information and reading

It is useful to read the official record of parliamentary debates on these issues to understand the Government's position. See Caroline Flint, Parliamentary Under-Secretary of State for the Home Department (*Hansard* HC, Standing Committee D, col 219 (18 January 2005)). The whole issue of interception evidence was debated during consideration of the Serious Organised Crime Bill (*Hansard* HC, Standing Committee D, cols 205–224 (18 January 2005)). It was previously debated at length during the RIP Bill debates (*Hansard* HL (series 5) vol 613, cols 1407–1444 (12 June 2000)).

10.4 What Authority Regime is Required for Covert Investigation Abroad?

The authority provided by s 27(3) RIPA is constrained by mutual legal assistance treaty law. An investigator cannot simply operate abroad on the basis of this RIPA sub-section alone.

Thus *in addition* to the authority regimes for directed and intrusive surveillance and the deployment of CHISs described in Chapters 2 and 9, *permission must be sought* from the foreign authorities in whose jurisdiction the surveillance is going to take place.

With the exception of circumstances provided for by Article 40 Schengen Convention, covert investigation abroad will normally be conducted on behalf of English investigators by the authorities in the requested state. This fact does not negate the need for a RIPA authority to be in place authorizing the covert investigation to take place.

Where the evidence required and to be obtained by English covert investigation teams operating overseas is to be relied upon by the prosecution, in any cases of doubt about the need for a surveillance authority it is good practice to have a surveillance authority in place (OSC *Procedures and Guidance* 2005, para 4.39). Evidence derived from unauthorized covert investigation is vulnerable to exclusion from trial under s 78 PACE (arguments for which could be based on Articles 6 or 8 ECHR, as well as English case law).

Where a vehicle-tracking device is deployed and it is anticipated that the vehicle will travel through multiple national jurisdictions, a single authorization naming the different jurisdictions will suffice rather than a different authorization for each jurisdiction (OSC *Procedures and Guidance* 2005, para 3.33).

Where the work of a JIT will lead to trial in the UK and reliance therein on evidence from covert investigations undertaken by the JIT, the appropriate surveillance authority for the covert investigation will be required no matter where it took place. The establishment of a JIT may offer a mutual legal assistance short cut but it does not negate the necessity of obtaining the appropriate surveillance authorities.

Where the subject of the covert investigation is neither a UK national nor likely to be the subject of criminal proceedings in the UK, and the conduct under investigation would neither affect a UK national nor give rise to material likely to be used in evidence before a UK court, it would appear in these specific circumstances (which might arise from a JIT investigation) that a RIPA authority would not be required (OSC *Procedures and Guidance* 2005, para 3.9; see also CSPI Code, paras 1.20–1.23 and CHIS Code, paras 4.26–4.30).

In respect of interception of communications, the powers and authority regime (Secretary of State's warrant) are stipulated in s 1(4) RIPA.

10.5 What Significant Case Law Has Been Decided in Relation to Covert Investigation Abroad?

Further information and reading

For illuminating discussions of the various issues that can arise from gathering evidence abroad, including by means of covert investigation, see C Gane and M Mackarel 'The admissibility of evidence obtained from abroad into criminal proceedings: the interpretation of mutual legal assistance treaties and use of evidence irregularly obtained', *European Journal of Crime, Criminal Law and Criminal Justice*, 4 (1996), 98–119.

Although it pre-dates RIPA, it nevertheless contains much pertinent consideration and comparative study of covert investigation principles within the context of mutual legal assistance.

Where foreign agencies undertake covert investigation in their own jurisdiction, either on behalf of UK authorities or pursuant to their own investigations being prepared to share the product with UK authorities, consideration must be given to whether the foreign product has been obtained in a manner that might lead to it being excluded from trial in England because foreign agencies may lawfully act in ways that UK authorities cannot. See, for example, C Harfield, 'The governance of covert investigation', Melbourne University Law Review, 34(3), pp 773–804, specifically p 803; also C Harfield, 'Managing human rights and covert methods in transnational criminal investigations',

---

> in S Hufnagel, C Harfield and S Bronitt (eds), *Cross-Border Law Enforcement: Regional Law Enforcement Cooperation—European, Australian and Asia-Pacific Perspectives* (Routledge, London, 2011) pp 231–242.

The fact that evidence for use in an English trial has been obtained from abroad with the aid of a mutual legal assistance treaty does not guarantee its admissibility nor preclude any procedural challenge by the defence. The evidence may be subject to restrictions placed on its use by the requested state and cannot be used for any other purpose than was specified in the original request for assistance (s 9 Crime (International Co-operation) Act 2003). Where evidence is relied upon both to secure a conviction and subsequently confiscate assets, both purposes should be articulated in the international letter of request (*R v Gooch (No. 1)* [1999] 1 Cr App R (S) 283).

Investigators must also beware of how evidence is perceived and used abroad when supplying covert investigation material gathered within the UK to requesting foreign jurisdictions. Criminal intelligence material supplied to foreign jurisdictions on an 'intelligence only' basis has, nevertheless and within the context of foreign evidential laws, legitimately been disclosed to the defendant (and in some cases also the press) before trial. Hence, for instance, 'evidence is unlimited in French law, when acts discovered by foreign judicial or police authorities are used in a French case, they are considered as information and are therefore subject to discussion during the arguments in the trial as to the facts of the case' (*Kamal Jain*, Appeal Court of Aix en Provence 4 May 1992, confirmed by the Cour de Cassation, Paris, 7 October 1993, case no. M92-83.707 D). Information that might normally and successfully be protected from disclosure at trial through PII applications in the UK may not be so protected abroad. In some jurisdictions, if it exists, it must be used at trial.

Further information and reading

For comparative studies on criminal procedure, including rules of evidence, in Belgium, England, France, Germany and Italy, see M Delmas-Marty and J Spencer (eds), *European Criminal Procedures* (Cambridge, Cambridge University Press, 2002).

Whether or not the contents of an international letter of request are disclosable is debatable. Confidentiality cannot be relied upon in mutual legal assistance. See Jones and Doobay, *Jones and Doobay on Extradition and Mutual Assistance*, 402. See also Murray and Harris, *Mutual Assistance in Criminal Matters*, 47.

Similarly CPIA disclosure issues can be complicated further when evidence from a foreign jurisdiction is relied upon. With careful investigation planning and prior consultation with the appropriate prosecutor, such issues need not be prohibitively problematic.

Other case law guidance suggests that the discretion permitted the court under s 78 PACE extends to evidence sought to be adduced from abroad. Indeed, some authorities argue such discretion affords investigators the opportunity to engage in 'forum shopping' or 'process laundering'. Certainly the courts have held that violation of Article 8 ECHR will not automatically result in exclusion of the evidence obtained as a result, but investigators and the prosecution cannot rely upon that discretion as a means of by-passing prescribed procedure (*R v Governor of Pentonville Prison, ex p Chinoy* [1992] 1 All ER 317, following *R v Sang* [1979] 2 All ER 1222; *Khan v UK* (2001) 31 EHRR 45 supporting *R v Khan* [1997] AC 558). 'Fishing expeditions' have been criticized by courts and requests for covert investigation should be specific and closely founded upon the chain of evidence, although it is accepted that not all evidence obtained through mutual legal assistance will necessarily be relied on in court (*R v Secretary of State ex p Fininvest SpA* [1997] 1 WLR 743).

R v Aujla [1998] 2 Cr App R 16 highlights an anomaly in respect of intercepted communications evidence and mutual legal assistance. It was held that intercept products by a foreign jurisdiction that had already been adduced at trial in the Netherlands was admissible in an English trial because the prohibition on the use of intercept products as evidence in the UK (at the time prohibited under s 9 Interception of Communications Act 1985; a restriction subsequently preserved under s 17 RIPA) applied only to intercept products obtained in the UK. The prohibition on evidential use thus does not apply to intercept products obtained abroad by foreign authorities for their own purposes. This reasoning was affirmed by the House of Lords in *R v P (Telephone intercepts: Admissibility of Evidence)* [2001] 2 WLR 463.

10.6 **Sources of Advice**

Once it is clear that an investigation is likely to necessitate evidence or intelligence-gathering abroad and that such needs are likely to require the use of covert investigation methods, investigators will need to engage with a number of different agencies in order to achieve a successful outcome.

Failure to follow protocols in transnational investigation can lead to any or all of the following consequences: loss of or inability to access evidence; abandonment of investigation or prosecution; or, where investigators have operated unilaterally and without permission overseas, the arrest, conviction, and imprisonment abroad of the investigators concerned.

The numerous sources of specialist advice are listed in Table 10.1.

> ### Further information and reading
>
> The UK Central Authority is based in the Home Office and is the single point of contact in England and Wales by which international letters of request (also known as *Commissions Rogatoires*) are transmitted and received. There is limited scope for direct transmission of requests with the EU. The latest list of states allowing direct transmission is held by the UK Central Authority. Home Office advice on mutual legal assistance (both for UK authorities seeking assistance from abroad and for foreign authorities seeking assistance from the UK) is available online at <http://www.homeoffice.gov.uk/police/mutual-legal-assistance/> (accessed December 2011).
>
> The UK National Central Bureau of Interpol is co-located with the UK Europol Bureau within the Serious Organised Crime Agency.
>
> International considerations are also discussed in the CSPI Code, paras 1.20–1.23; the CHIS Code, paras 4.26–4.30; the Interception Code, para 2.1; and the Communications Data Code, paras 7.11–7.21.

Table 10.1 Sources of guidance for investigators planning (covert) investigations abroad

Mutual legal assistance law	A Jones and A Doobay, *Jones and Doobay on Extradition and Mutual Assistance* (Sweet & Maxwell, London, 2005), ch 20
	Crown Prosecution Service (or equivalent prosecution authority)
	UK Central Authority, Home Office
Non-evidential foreign assistance	Europol (EU only)
	Interpol
Planning an international request	Crown Prosecution Service
	Eurojust
	European Judicial Network
	UK Central Authority
Drafting an international request	Crown Prosecution Service
	Eurojust
	UK Central Authority
Request transmission procedures	Crown Prosecution Service
	UK Central Authority
Joint investigation teams	Judicial Co-Operation Unit, Home Office
	Eurojust

The first source of advice should be the prosecutor: is covert investigation abroad vital in achieving a successful conviction? The question is as much practical as legal.

For instance, some foreign jurisdictions do not permit their surveillance personnel to testify in court. Their evidence is adduced in the inquisitorial trial system by way of third-party report, a method prohibited by the hearsay rules in the adversarial court process. How foreign surveillance evidence might be adduced in an English court must inform the operational planning of the surveillance as such practicalities may limit the surveillance options available, although with UK adoption of Article 40 Schengen Convention this has become less of a problem for English investigators within the EU. Prosecutors (supported by Eurojust) will be able to resolve such practicalities.

There are other factors for consideration. Is there a realistic prospect of conviction without the foreign evidence? Would a conviction for a different charge (which did not require foreign surveillance evidence) achieve the same reduction in harm? As the person whose role it is to present the evidence and case at court, the prosecutor is often as well positioned as an investigator, if not better positioned, to make such a determination.

Once the decision has been made in conjunction with a prosecutor to proceed with a request for covert surveillance to be conducted abroad, the advice of the other authorities listed in Table 10.1 should be sought. Because the prosecutor is pivotal in the management of investigations in many foreign jurisdictions, British investigators may find that foreign authorities will expect to deal with a British prosecutor rather than a British investigator.

Further information and reading

On foreign investigators conducting covert investigation in the UK see CSPI Code, paras 5.19–5.21 and CHIS Code, paras 4.26–4.30.

Checklist of key considerations when planning covert investigation abroad

- What evidence or intelligence is being sought?

- How is it relevant to the operation under consideration?

- Is it absolutely necessary, in order to secure a conviction, to conduct covert investigation abroad?

- Would an alternative charge, not dependent upon foreign evidence, secure the same reduction in harm upon conviction (eg the same length of prison sentence as a conviction that relied upon the foreign evidence)?

- What is the advice of the prosecutor?

- What is the advice, if applicable, of Eurojust?

- What is the advice, if applicable, of Europol or Interpol?

- What is the least intrusive means of securing such evidence or information?

- What are the risks to the organization of such tactics? (Chapter 11)

- What are the risks to the organization's staff of such tactics? (Chapter 11)

- What are the risks to the British public, the foreign public, or specific third parties when such tactics are deployed? (Chapter 11)

- What are the political/diplomatic risks arising from this operation? (Chapter 11)

- What are the risks to the subject of the investigation? (Chapter 11)

- Will such methods breach Article 8(1)? (1.7.1)

- Is there justification for doing so provided by Article 8(2)? (1.7.4)

- How is the legality test met? (1.7.3)

- How is the legitimacy test met? (1.7.4)

- How is the necessity test met? (1.7.5)

- How is the proportionality test met? (1.7.5)

- Are the arguments justifying the application to use covert investigation based on reliable information/intelligence, or has the applicant adopted a 'tick-the-box' approach to completing the application without giving full consideration to the facts of the case and the issues arising?

- Have the arguments justifying the granting of authorization to use covert investigation been fully articulated, or has the authorizing officer merely paid lip service to the pro forma authorization template via which authority is granted?

- How are the methods by which the evidence/intelligence will be obtained to be protected at trial in the UK?

- If covert investigation product from the UK is to be used in a trial abroad how are the methods by which the evidence/intelligence will be obtained to be protected at trial overseas?

- What are the consequences of foreign authorities disclosing confidential intelligence or unused material supplied by British authorities?

- What risk management plan is in place to address these consequences?

Planning covert investigation actions

Remember to include the PLAN for covert investigation tactics in all investigation policy-book entries relating to covert investigation considerations and decisions.

P   PROPORTIONALITY
Why is it proportionate to obtain the intended product of this surveillance in the manner proposed? (1.7.5)

L   LEGITIMACY
What is the legitimate purpose of the proposed action: the prevention of disorder or crime; the interests of national security; the interests of public safety; the interests of the economic well-being of the country; the protection of health or morals; the protection of the rights and freedoms of others? (1.7.4)

A   AUTHORITY TO UNDERTAKE PROPOSED ACTION
What is the lawful foundation and authority for the proposed action? From whom must authorization be sought? (1.7.3)

N   NECESSITY OF PROPOSED ACTION
Why is the proposed action necessary? (1.7.5)

11

Risk Management

11.1 **Introduction**

Society today tends to be risk-averse. The fear of compensation litigation looms large. But risks are everywhere and cannot be avoided. They exist on parallel continuums from low probability/high impact to high probability/low impact. They are inherent in every covert investigation and are multi-faceted. There is a growing literature on risk and policing risk, particularly in relation to the dangerousness of serious or serial offenders released on completion of sentence. From an ethical perspective it can be argued that no matter how attractive the desired end product, the risks posed in achieving it may not justify the means (see J Kleinig, *Ethics and Criminal Justice: An Introduction* (Cambridge University Press, Cambridge, 2008) p.104).

The key message is NOT that covert investigation is too risky to undertake but rather that with proper risk management covert investigations can be successfully concluded, with every operation contributing to accumulated operational and organizational learning. The risks of intervention have always to be balanced against the risks of non-intervention.

Managing risk is a complex and developing subject and it is one that investigators and their managers conducting and supervising covert investigations have to consider when planning, authorizing, executing, and reviewing such operations. There may be no right answer and any given decision may have to be based on a professional judgment taking into account any number of factors (eg what is known, what is unknown and what can reasonably be surmised). It is helpful to have a framework within which to make such considerations, and with which to identify appropriate risk control measures and so determine a risk management strategy. This chapter presents some models to use as such a framework.

Risk in relation to covert investigation can be viewed from three perspectives. Firstly, risk analysis constitutes one of the analytical tools and techniques within the National Intelligence Model (NIM): if an issue is assessed through the NIM business management process as warranting attention at, and action derived from, a tasking and co-ordinating meeting, then the determination of an appropriate intervention constitutes the first step in the proportionality rationale. Spontaneous serious incidents aside, should covert investigation be used in operations not sanctioned under the NIM process?

Secondly, there is the issue of identifying risks associated with tactical options in the planning stage of an operation and then managing the risks throughout the operation before reviewing operational risk management at the conclusion of individual interventions and completed investigations. In an era in which partnership is promoted assiduously the various perceptions of risk and priorities complicate risk management in multi-agency investigations. In partnership and collaborative working risk (itself arguably an area of risk) analysis either has to be undertaken jointly from the outset, or else should be a two-stage process in which organizations individually assess risks and then collaborate in finding the most appropriate intervention or management strategy once the matter requiring intervention is raised in a multi-agency forum.

Covert investigation operations generating either intelligence or evidence then create a third arena of risk in relation to the storing, utilization, and dissemination of the covert investigation product.

11.2 What Positive Obligations Are Imposed on Investigators?

The failure to consider risks and apply an appropriate risk management strategy constitutes, at best, poor working practice, at worst, negligence. In certain circumstances such omission goes beyond mere negligence. Court interpretations of Article 2 ECHR place upon public authorities the positive obligation to protect life. *Osman v UK* [1999] 1 FLR 193 illustrates this point (see also K Starmer, *European Human Rights Law* (Legal Action Group, London, 1999) 89–90, 199–200 for general discussion). A positive obligation was held to exist where 'the authorities knew or ought to have known at the time of the existence of a real and immediate risk to the life of an identified individual or individuals from the criminal acts of a third party and that they failed to take measures within the scope of their powers which, judged reasonably, might have been expected to avoid that risk' (*Osman v UK* [1999] 1 FLR 193, note 19 at para 116).

This general principle can be held to apply elsewhere even where positive obligations under ECHR do not apply: investigators and investigation managers should take reasonable measures to manage foreseeable risks. Application forms for covert investigation authority, both in paper form and in the various software versions commercially available, usually include pages or boxes that have to be completed to demonstrate that the applicant has identified the risks involved with the application and determined an appropriate risk management strategy. The risks anticipated and how they are managed might have a bearing on the necessity and proportionality arguments supporting the application. Experience has shown that risk assessments for covert investigation applications are not infrequently omitted altogether on initial submission. Those that are submitted are often inadequate. And even where a risk assessment is included on first submission, for subsequent reviews and renewals the assessment is almost never revised and is very often dispensed with a perfunctory 'no change'.

Surveillance conducted for covert investigation may not produce the intelligence anticipated nor the evidence sought, but the one guaranteed product of covert surveillance will be vital information with which to review the risk assessment.

At initial application risk assessments will be estimations. Investigators will identify what they think the risks of the operation might be and how these anticipated risks should be managed. Managers and authorizing officers will review such assessments from their own perspectives, considering any additional risks posed by the operation to the organization as a whole. Once a period of surveillance has been conducted information about risks will have been updated by default in one or more of three ways: new risks may have been identified; previously anticipated risks may now be discounted; or previously anticipated risks will have been confirmed. It is important that this information is captured and included in subsequent risk assessments on submission of investigation authority reviews and renewal applications.

Where initial surveillance has demonstrated that there are no additional risks to take into consideration, and none that can now be dismissed, and where there has been no compromise of staff or equipment, then this should be incorporated in the risk assessment attached to the review consideration or renewal application. It is not simply a case of stating 'no change'. What was previously an initial estimation is now supported by empirical and observational information. An initial estimation has become an informed evaluation. At the very least such a revised risk assessment might say: 'Following x hours/days of surveillance, no new risks associated with this operation have been identified. None of the previously identified risks can be discounted. There is no intelligence to indicate that staff or surveillance techniques deployed in this operation have been compromised. Therefore the current risk management plan remains valid.'

Risk management or reduction is as dynamic a process as is the manifestation of the risks themselves. It must be held under constant review. In some operations it will be so dynamic that the commanding officer will have undertaken several revised risk assessments during the course of any given phase of the operation, possibly within a very short space of time and with little or no opportunity to record the rationale at the time, in which case documenting the variation as soon as practicable after the event must suffice.

Further information and reading

The revised CSPI and CHIS codes of practice specifically draw attention (para 3.8 in both codes) to the fact that *authorizing officers* should take into account the risk of obtaining private information about persons who are not subject to the surveillance or property interference activity (collateral intrusion). The codes of practice are admissible as evidence in criminal or civil proceedings and code provisions must be taken into account by any court or tribunal if considered relevant to the matter before them.
(CSPI Code, para 1.6; CHIS Code, para 1.5.)

11.3 The Benefits of Good Risk Assessment

Some definitions at this stage will be helpful.

Definition

Risk can be defined as the likelihood of an adverse harm occurring. This is not to be confused with a *threat*, which is the source of that harm. *Vulnerability* is the measurement of probability against impact. (The probability of a given outcome occurring may be very low but the adverse impact may be very significant.) A *risk assessment* is the means by which the risks involved in an operation can be balanced against the benefits.

The relevance to covert investigation is to be found at a number of levels. Some operations involve physical danger to staff. All covert investigations run the risk of investigators acting unlawfully in the absence of effective management or in cases where enthusiasm exceeds knowledge and competence. Depending on particular community sensitivities, a clumsily managed operation might result in public disorder.

Particularly where an operation engages Article 8 rights, risk assessment helps validate the thinking of applicant and authorizing officer alike, producing the following benefits:

- professional, credible risk management/reduction processes
- reviews of working assumptions, taking into account changing risk circumstances
- a process for real-time decision-making amenable to subsequent review (either in an operational debrief or a subsequent public enquiry)
- reduction in the number of perverse decisions
- reduction in corporate/personal liability.

The demonstrable dangers in covert investigation include the death of surveillance staff; the compromised safety of CHISs; compromised investigations, tactics, techniques, and technology; corruption within investigation teams; organizational and individual reputational damage; and loss of public confidence in agencies investigating criminality. The risk of all these adverse outcomes can be mitigated and minimized through appropriate risk management.

11.4 Identifying Risks and How to Manage Them: The Model Approach

Structuring thinking around established conceptual models aids precise consideration of risk issues. From the police service, created by former Deputy Assistant Commissioner John Grieve whilst serving with the Metropolitan Police Service, comes a useful model that helps an investigator and the manager to begin to identify risks associated with any given operation, often referred to as the '3 Ps L E M' model because of its acronym (PPPLEM) (see 11.5 below).

It is helpful to apply the PPPLEM model to all the different facets of risk, otherwise regarded as the different 'at risk' groups: risk to the organization, risk to staff and other resources engaged in the operation (including for this purpose technical equipment, remotely deployed CHISs, and members of the public who allow their premises to be used as observation points), risk to the subject of the operation, and risk to third parties such as members of the public unconnected with the investigation but likely to be present in the surveillance arena.

As will be seen below, PPPLEM is not the only such model: the PLAICE model of risk assessment (see 11.5 below) has been designed specifically for covert investigation by Metropolitan Police staff who were concerned that the PPPLEM model was too generic to capture all possible risks involved in covert investigation. It is suggested here that either model is a useful tool to aid risk identification. Investigators will find that much of the available covert investigation authorization management software structures risk assessment around PPPLEM.

Once risks have been identified, a determination has to be made on how to manage them. For this there are the RARA and TTTT models (see 11.6 below), which can be used in conjunction with the vulnerability assessment.

The culmination of this consideration should be a structured risk management plan or risk reduction strategy for those risks, amongst the many identified, which are likely to cause the most harm. The use of models aids thinking for both applicants and authorizing officers and should thus facilitate a more succinct written assessment, ensuring that it does not become a bureaucratic nightmare that actually adds nothing of value to the investigation or its management.

Overarching the risk management plan or reduction strategy must be the assessment of how the identified risk control measures themselves might engage the ECHR rights of staff, investigation subject, and general public.

Although the investigator and manager have primary responsibility for risk assessment and management, on occasions they will need to draw upon expert advice when encountering specialist fields and techniques. For instance, experts from computer crime units will be best placed to advise on what sort of electronic footprints will be created when computers are used to conduct e-surveillance. Non-experts will not necessarily appreciate the full range of risks to be managed in specialist arenas.

11.5 **Models of Risk Identification**

The PPPLEM model (the acronym translates as shown in Table 11.1), applied to the four risk groups, will help identify the risks inherent in any given operation. A matrix is a useful aid to complete the assessment, with the 'at risk' groups placed on the vertical axis and the PPPLEM elements placed along the horizontal axis (Table 11.2).

It may well be the case that not all the elements of the model apply to all the 'at risk' groups. Indeed, if there was something significant to say in each of the

Table 11.1 The PPPLEM model for risk assessment

P—Police and community risks	Alternatively, public and organizational risks. In general terms: what are the risks to the organization within the community of engaging in this operation? Is there any general risk to/from the community at large? Adverse publicity? Public disorder possible? What are the risks to the organization from the investigation subject/staff/public at large? What are the risks to the community from the organization engaging in this operation? What are the risks to the community from the investigation subject? What are the risks to the community from the organization staff? What are the risks of not doing anything?
P—Physical risks	What are the physical risks to staff/subject/third parties? Organization premises or premises borrowed for the purpose?
P—Psychological risks	What are the psychological risks to staff/subject/third parties?
L—Legal risks	What are the legal risks to the organization? Its staff? The subject? Third parties?
E—Economic risks	What are the economic risks to the organization? Its staff? The subject? Third parties? The community? Cost of operation? Possible litigation claims?
M—Moral risks	What are the moral risks to the organization? Its staff? The subject? Third parties? Can the operation be justified morally as well as legally? Is there a danger that the very essence of the ECHR will be breached as well as the Article 8 rights in question? What are the risks of not doing anything?

Table 11.2 PPPLEM matrix

PPPLEM matrix	Police/ community	Physical	Psychological	Legal	Economic	Moral
Organization						
Staff						
Subject						
Third parties						

matrix boxes the proposed operation should probably be considered too risky! The advantage of using this model lies not only in helping structured consideration: it demonstrates and records the thought processes of investigators and managers alike and in this way saves the trouble involved in composing lengthy prose to make the same point. More detailed discussion can thus be saved for those risks identified through the vulnerability and RARA models as requiring particular management (see 11.6 below).

The PLAICE model of risk assessment, advocated by Roger Billingsley of the Metropolitan Police Service, is summarized in Table 11.3. Once again, specific risks within each of the above categories are to be identified and documented, together with the proposed control measures. The importance of documenting and continually reviewing risks and reasoning is emphasized, particularly in relation to defending the service and staff against subsequent litigation. For the purpose of using this model, Billingsley suggests that 'information technology' should include sensitive data gathered using technology and the systems used to process, analyse, and document such data. The environment, readers are reminded, should include possibly hostile environments overseas when deploying staff abroad on covert investigations.

The issue here is not which model is used (and besides these two currently being used in the police service there are other models) but that some model of structured consideration and reasoning should be used to identify risks and appropriate control measures. The PPPLEM and PLAICE models are not mutually exclusive—and both rely on good intelligence for any meaningful consideration of risk to be undertaken.

Further information and reading

See R Billingsley, 'Risk management: is there a model for covert policing?', *Covert Policing Review* (2006), 98–109.

Table 11.3 The PLAICE model for risk assessment

P	Physical risks
L	Legal risks
A	Risks to organizational assets
I	Information and information technology risks
C	Risk of compromise to staff, tactics and techniques
E	Environmental risks

11.6 **Vulnerability and Risk Strategy Models: RARA and TTTT**

Vulnerability, *probability versus impact*, can be measured as two scales of 1 to 10, one for each of probability and impact. Alternatively it can more simply be expressed in terms of 'high', 'medium', or 'low' set in a matrix, with one axis representing probability and the other impact (Table 11.4).

Greatest vulnerability, and therefore risk, will be inherent where the probability and impact are both high or where one is high and the other medium. These are the risks that require management or a reduction strategy (see Table 11.4).

Risks that are both low in impact and low in probability need not concern the investigator, investigation manager, or authorizing officer too greatly.

Once the vulnerability factor has been identified risk management and reduction prioritization can be undertaken. For this the RARA model can be applied.

There are four strategies that can be adopted in relation to any given risk: *remove* it, *avoid* it, *reduce* it, *accept* it—hence RARA. This is a sliding scale of strategies. Preferably operations should be planned so as to remove all risks. This ideal world is rarely achievable, however. Changing tactics to achieve the same objective may afford a means of avoiding a risk. If the risk cannot be removed or avoided, then there may be measures that can be put in place to reduce the risk. There will be a number of risks that investigators will wish simply to accept. This might be because the risks have a low vulnerability factor: low probability/low impact.

Table 11.4 Impact/probability matrix

High impact	Contingency plan required	ACTION REQUIRED	ACTION REQUIRED
Medium impact		ACTION REQUIRED	ACTION REQUIRED
Low impact			
Impact/Probability matrix	Low probability	Medium probability	High probability

As with the PPPLEM model, Billingsley offers an alternative to RARA—the TTTT model: **terminate, treat, transfer,** or **tolerate**. In essence, albeit with the second and third elements reversed, the TTTT model is intended to achieve exactly the same outcome in the same way as the RARA model.

Potential control measures aimed at reducing the likelihood or adverse consequences of any given risk may themselves have risks attached. It may not be possible, for instance, to deploy a full surveillance team to provide protective cover for the deployment of an undercover operative because the surveillance team itself would show out in the deployment arena. In such a case alternative means of providing protection and rescue for such operatives must be devised, or else the desired evidence or intelligence must be acquired by other means—a way of avoiding identified risks.

As with the PPPLEM and PLAICE models, the application of the RARA or the TTTT model in determining a risk management strategy and appropriate control measures illustrates and records the thought processes of the decision-takers based on available information at the time, and herein lies its value to investigators, managers, and authorizing officers.

11.7 **Conclusion**

Risk assessment depends upon having information that is as accurate as possible and as up to date as possible. Such information is to be found, in part, as a by-product of surveillance. If such information has not been recorded and assessments consequently reviewed, then individuals and organizations are vulnerable not only to the risks inherent in the investigation, but to the risk of—and consequences from—being negligent.

There is always scope for the unforeseen to occur. Use of these models to aid risk management will not alter that truism. These models cannot accurately predict the future. They will help identify those risks that can reasonably be foreseen. They will help prioritize a risk management strategy according to whether any given risk can be removed, avoided, reduced, or accepted. The models must be utilized in conjunction with the latest available information and intelligence. In the event of something unforeseen occurring that leads to particularly adverse consequences, the documented use of these models may well determine whether the investigators and the organizations concerned can be shown to have done everything that was reasonable in the circumstances or whether they are vulnerable to a civil claim based on negligence.

Besides the models for structured consideration of risk discussed above, force crime managers have three strategic approaches to managing risk: through training; through process; and through physical security. Staff engaged in covert investigation must be appropriately trained and skilled. CHISs, for instance, should be managed through dedicated source units with handlers and controllers appropriately qualified to national standards. Foot and vehicle surveillance require different skills and different levels of training. Those intending to use specialist technical equipment must understand its operation, capability, and limitations.

Risk management through procedure does not seek to stifle innovation and creativity but it does seek to protect staff through adherence to established processes and statutory provision, such as surveillance authorization, that provide structure and frameworks tested through experience. Incorporated in this should be consideration of the necessity to conduct security-vetting of key staff involved in covert investigation. Security-vetting of key roles reduces the vulnerability of organizations and of their staff to cultivation and compromise by hostile elements keen to acquire access to information held by organizations or to compromise on-going investigations. In connection with this, in 2001 ACPO adopted the Government Protective Marking Scheme.

Further information and reading

There are four levels of protective marking: 'TOP SECRET', 'SECRET', 'CONFIDENTIAL', and 'RESTRICTED'. Documents falling outside all of these areas of sensitivity are UNCLASSIFIED.

TOP SECRET

Compromise would:

- Threaten directly the internal stability of the UK or friendly countries
- Lead directly to widespread loss of life
- Cause exceptionally grave damage to the effectiveness or security of UK or allied forces or to the continuing effectiveness of extremely valuable security or intelligence operations
- Cause exceptionally grave damage to relations with friendly governments
- Cause severe long-term damage to the UK economy.

SECRET

Compromise would:

- Raise international tension
- Seriously damage relations with friendly governments
- Threaten life directly or seriously prejudice public order or individual security or liberty
- Cause serious damage to operational effectiveness or security of UK or allied forces or the continuing effectiveness of highly valuable security or intelligence operations
- Cause substantial material damage to national finances or economic and commercial interests.

CONFIDENTIAL

Compromise would:

- Materially damage diplomatic relations, that is, cause formal protest or sanctions
- Prejudice individual security or liberty

- Cause damage to operational effectiveness or security of UK or allied forces or the effectiveness of valuable security or intelligence operations
- Work substantially against national finances or economic and commercial interests
- Substantially undermine the financial viability of major organizations
- Impede the investigation or facilitate the commission of serious crime
- Seriously impeded the development or operation of major government policies
- Shut down or otherwise substantially disrupt significant national operations.

RESTRICTED
Compromise would:

- Adversely affect diplomatic relations
- Cause substantial distress to individuals
- Make it more difficult to maintain the operational effectiveness or security of UK or allied forces
- Cause financial loss or loss of earning potential to, or facilitate improper gain or advantage for, individuals or companies
- Prejudice the investigation or facilitate the commission of crime
- Breach proper undertakings to maintain the confidence of information provided by third parties
- Impede the effective development or operation of government policies
- Breach statutory restrictions on disclosure of information.

For further information and access to supporting papers regarding ACPO's rationale for adopting the GPMS, see <http://www.acpo.police.uk/asp/policies/Data/covering_letter_prot_marking_scheme_16feb01.doc> (accessed 26 February 2007).

See also Harfield and Harfield, *Intelligence: Investigation, Community, and Partnership* (Oxford, OUP, 2008) 155–158 on maintaining a professional intelligence environment, the principles of which apply also to managing covert investigation and the product thereof.

For police-specific guidance which is RESTRICTED and so not within the public domain, police officers and staff can refer to *Guidance on the Lawful and Effective Use of Covert Techniques* (Wyboston, NPIA, 2007).

Alongside procedural security, physical security is an additional means of risk management. Unauthorized disclosure takes place either when hostile elements access directly intelligence and sensitive evidence acquired through covert investigation (from which tactics and techniques may be deduced and so compromised) or when such elements through corruption or blackmail secure complicity from a member of the intelligence or covert investigation staff in passing on the acquired product. Assuming that the measures above have been implemented, the risk of the latter scenario, whilst not eradicated, is reduced. Removing the opportunities for self-initiated unauthorized access is a means to reducing the former risk.

Physical security means quality locks on doors (for instance a combination of monitored personal key card and digital lock access would be an example of good security); a clear desk policy; regular password-changing on computers; security filing cabinets in locked offices for classified hard-copy documents; and locked offices for those computer terminals networked to sensitive databases. It also means regular review by the organization's security officer.

Every deployment of covert investigation risks the exposure and compromise both of techniques and methods and the identity of individuals performing the various CHIS roles. It is too easy for the documentation of risk assessment and management strategies to be perceived, erroneously, as bureaucratic box-ticking. Documentation is necessary in order to ensure colleagues and partners are aware of the issues and the strategies for dealing with them. But that is just a supporting function for the main principle: ongoing, perpetual, dynamic risk assessment underpins the successful deployment of covert investigation. Without it, the chances of a successful operation (ie acquisition of the desired objective, lawfully, without compromising methods, techniques, or personal safety; the adducing of evidence secure from procedural challenge at trial) are significantly reduced.

Managing Covert Investigation

12.1 **Introduction**

At the risk of inducing apoplexy in die-hard detectives, the key to successful covert investigation management is to think like managers, not investigation practitioners. The reflective reader will have discerned from the previous chapters that managing covert investigation is more than just ensuring the quality and accuracy of authorization applications: it involves skilled investigation management together with complex resource management in an environment in which there are frequently many competing priorities for scarce skills and capacity. Securing a covert investigation authority may be easier than securing the resources needed to execute the covert investigation activity. Investigators planning the use of covert techniques will need to plan for circumstances in which the resources are not available: and if an alternative means of obtaining the intelligence/evidence is available, that immediately begs questions about the proportionality of the proposed action. Alternatively there may be occasions on which covert investigation methods offer a less resource-intensive means of acquiring information that could also be obtained by non-intrusive means: the issue for managers in these circumstances is whether authorization can be given lawfully in circumstances where desired information could be obtained in a way that engages Article 8 rights at lesser cost than a method that would produce the same information for greater expense but without engaging Article 8 rights. At trial judges will be concerned with compliance with the law rather than management theory. McKay observes:

> It is likely that in the future, legal challenges will be mounted based on the central question of whether covert policing resources were justified at all having regard to the circumstances of the case as well as scrutinizing the human rights issues increasingly assiduously.

(S McKay, *Covert Policing*, Oxford University Press, Oxford, 2011, para 2.01)

In the event resources are available, the proportionality test is met, and an authorization is granted, management of the covert investigation does not stop when the specific activity is completed and the authorization cancelled. There then exists the covert investigation product that has to be managed, and the organizational learning from each operation to be captured and, as appropriate, disseminated.

In functional terms governance of covert investigation can be viewed as a three-tier hierarchy:

- Statute and case law—mechanisms defining what investigators can and cannot do with the case law remedy providing a form of indirect governance through adverse consequences, such as the (discretionary) exclusion of evidence, and establishing external scrutiny mechanisms.
- External inspection—auditable governance in which proper records demonstrate compliant/lawful and appropriate deployment.

- Internal management—procedures to prioritize appropriate operations in which covert investigation may be necessary to guard against overuse and unnecessary deployment.

(C Harfield, 'The governance of covert investigation', Melbourne University Law Review, 34(3) (2010) 801.)

Professional management is thus the first layer of covert investigation governance and accountability: from the outset, empowered organizations have the opportunity to demonstrate that covert investigation has been used only when lawful, compliant and appropriate and not extravagantly.

KEY POINTS

- How does the proposed investigation/operation relate to NIM tasking and co-ordinating?
- What evidence/information is being sought? Is it essential or desirable?
- Is it already known (by another agency perhaps?) Can it be obtained by non-covert means?
- What are the resource implications of the proposed action?
- If used, what is the risk of covert investigation methods being exposed in the surveillance arena or at court?

Further information and reading

The revised CSPI Code recommends that within each organization undertaking covert investigation a *senior responsible officer* (of at least the rank of an authorizing officer as identified in RIPA and the PA97) should have executive responsibility for:

- the integrity of the process in place within the *public authority* to authorize directed and intrusive surveillance and interference with property or wireless telegraphy;
- compliance with Part II of the 2000 Act, Part III of the 1997 Act and with this code;
- engagement with the Commissioners and inspectors when they conduct their inspections, and
- where necessary, overseeing the implementation of any post-inspection action plans recommended or approved by a Commissioner (para 3.28).

It is suggested here that such a role could usefully have responsibility for ensuring not just the proper application for and granting of covert investigation authorities but the whole process of covert investigation management within an organization which includes the preparatory tasks of prioritizing and selecting investigations to be supported by covert investigation and the post investigation tasks of product and evidence management. Such an executive role provides strategic leadership of covert investigation as a function within the overall work of the organization. It is not suggested here that such a role should in any way erode or obscure the statutory responsibilities imposed on authorizing officers under the act. In some jurisdictions, albeit operating a different governance paradigm for covert investigation, support mechanisms for senior investigators and authorizing officers have appeared to have absolved, or have created the vulnerability of absolving, such individuals of their statutory responsibilities (C Harfield, 'The governance of covert investigation', Melbourne University Law Review, 34(3) (2010) 797). The recommended role of *senior responsible officer* is understood here to be one of over-arching organization leadership in matters relating to covert investigation and not an operational role, notwithstanding that the recommendation is that the *senior responsible officer* have practical authorizing officer experience. The two roles are separate and should not be confused.

Nor should the senior responsible officer role recommended in the CSPI Code be confused with the senior responsible officer role mandatorily required pursuant to the Communications Data Code, para 3.22 (see Chapter 7.6 of this volume) or the senior responsible officer role mandatorily required pursuant to the CHIS Code, para 9.1 (see Chapter 9.11 of this volume). But there is no reason why the same individual should not undertake all three of these strategic roles and a case can be made for investing a single senior executive officer with these roles to achieve strategic cohesion in the overall management of covert investigation within any given organization.

12.2 Do You Really Need To?

The statutory requirement for necessity has already been considered (Chapter 1 above). There is, arguably, also a managerial necessity test. It is presumably only a matter of time (if the issue has not already been raised) before an operation that does not meet managerial necessity is challenged on the basis that the statutory necessity test is consequently undermined. The basic managerial test is simply expressed: how does the proposed investigation, or operation in support of an investigation, relate to organizational tasking and co-ordination?

Tasking and co-ordination procedures and policies will vary from organization to organization. Within the police service, the business processes within the framework of the National Intelligence Model (NIM) specifically provide for tasking and co-ordination and it is suggested here that any covert investigation within the police service will be undertaken pursuant to an appropriate tasking and co-ordination direction given either at Basic Command Unit (NIM Level 1) or at Force/Regional level (NIM Level 2).

There are two generic circumstances that provide exceptions to this principle. The first is the distinction drawn between 'core' and 'ordinary' functions in the case of *C v Police & Secretary of State* IPT/03/32/H (14 November 2006). Where covert investigation is deployed in the management of staff for disciplinary and professional standards purposes, such action will not feature in fortnightly task-ing and co-ordination meetings. The second circumstance is that of the sponta-neous investigation, such as a crime in action (a kidnapping for example), which will not reasonably have been foreseen in a planning meeting. The net practical effect would seem to be the confining of covert investigation to identified prior-ity crimes and spontaneous serious crimes.

Definition: how are crimes prioritized?

Crimes can be prioritized for intervention in a number of ways.

- In response to a specific assessment of risk and threat.
- Through community consultation within the philosophical context of a police service and other agencies responsive to community needs.
- In order to meet (politically-imposed) performance measures.

The weighting applied to these three approaches is a matter of judgement and influences the determination of necessity when considering applications for the use of covert investigation. Inevitably there will be variations between organizations, communities and individuals in making such judgements and identifying priorities.

The deployment of covert investigation by other empowered organizations equally will be determined by the relevance of the proposed investigation to the core functions of the organization and whether or not the proposed investiga-tion is compliant with the statutory purpose(s) for which the organization in question can undertake covert investigation.

The relationship between covert investigation powers and organization per-formance management is potentially fraught. In the absence of specific intel-ligence about ongoing criminality it is unlikely that covert investigation can be justified to meet performance targets such as types of offence investigated or types of operation undertaken. (For the Chief Surveillance Commissioner's concerns about performance target culture see OSC *Annual Report 2008–09*, para 5.26 and OSC *Annual Report 2010–11*, para 5.6.)

Case study—local authorities and covert investigation

Sir Simon Milton, Chair of the Local Government Association, has responded to public concerns about the growth of a surveillance society (for example 'Council uses criminal law to spy on school place applicants', *The Guardian* (11 April 2008)) with a word of caution to LGA members to use RIPA powers appropriately in an open letter dated 23 June 2008 to local authorities (published on the Local Government Association website <http://www.lga.gov.uk/lga/core/page.do?pageId=740231> (accessed 24 June 2008). Extended extracts are reproduced here:

> Parliament clearly intended that councils should use the new powers, and generally they are being used to respond to residents' complaints about fly tippers, rogue traders and those

defrauding the council tax or housing benefit system. Time and again, these are just the type of crimes that residents tell us that they want to see tackled. Without these powers, councils would not be able to provide the level of reassurance and protection local people demand and deserve.

. . .

The Act also requires that the powers should only be used when 'necessary and proportionate to prevent or detect a criminal offence' and you will all know of the examples where councils have been criticized for using the powers in relation to issues that can be portrayed as trivial or not considered a crime by the public.

. . .

My purpose in writing is to ask that you satisfy yourself that the use of these powers is only being authorized after the most careful consideration at the appropriate senior political and managerial level. It would also be helpful if you could review existing permissions to ensure that their continuance meets the 'necessary and proportionate' test. Perhaps you might consider reviewing these powers annually by an appropriate scrutiny committee or panel of your council which could invite evidence from the public. Whilst it is a matter for each council to determine for its area, our advice is that, save in the most unusual and extreme of circumstances, it is inappropriate to use these powers for trivial matters.

. . .

. . . specifically, we do not consider dog fouling or littering as matters which fall within the test of necessary and proportionate.

. . .

The LGA and LACORS are working with the Government, police chiefs and the Chief Surveillance Commissioners to clarify some of the details of the legislation and make sure it is clear when and how surveillance should be used. By their nature, surveillance powers are never to be used lightly but it is important that councils don't lose the power to use them when appropriate. . . .

This letter illustrates a number of key issues confronting those managing the use of covert investigation in all agencies and organizations, not just local authorities.

- Is public perception a reliable source of legitimacy? (The public, at the time of writing in mid-2008, persists in maintaining a heightened fear of crime despite the overall fall, sustained over a period of time, in the number of crimes reported to the police and the fall in victim self-identification in the British Crime Survey. Public perceptions are not necessarily based on hard data.)
- What is perceived as serious, trivial or perennial anti-social nuisance to be addressed will vary from community to community; from organization to organization.
- The importance of not confusing necessity in relation to preventing a harm to society with the proportionality of the method in relation to the specific product of the covert investigation.
- The importance of reviewing and monitoring use of covert investigation in order to ensure it is not being used inappropriately.
- In what circumstances, for which organizations, and by whom undertaken (eg elected or non-elected persons), consideration at a senior level about the politics of using covert investigation is appropriate? The 'necessity' test clearly could be a political issue and the political will of Parliament as expressed in statute should be the guiding principle; the proportionality test of methods used theoretically is apolitical but such determination could be vulnerable to political perception.

Further information and reading

For official consideration of the wider issues of surveillance see:
Home Affairs Committee, *A Surveillance Society?*, Fifth Report of Session 2007–08, HC58i & HC58ii (London, TSO, 2008);
Home Affairs Committee, *A Surveillance Society?*: *Information Commissioner's Response to the Committee's Fifth Report of Session 2007–08*, HC1124 (London, TSO, 2008);
House of Lords Select Committee on the Constitution, *Surveillance: Citizens and the State,* Second Report of Session 2008–09, HL 18-I and HL 18-II (London, TSO, 2009).

Where multi-agency partnership working is envisaged, partner organizations will wish to ensure that powers are applied for and utilized appropriately in order to avoid becoming vulnerable to challenges about whether one agency's powers have been used to achieve another agency's objectives when the latter would not normally have access to such powers: circumstances sometimes referred to as 'process-laundering'. In such circumstances it would seem prudent to ensure that tasking, co-ordination, objectives and responsibility for subsequent action based on covert investigation product were clearly identified at the outset in the planning documentation and joint-investigation policy book.

Covert investigation is intended to secure either specific intelligence to inform planned future intervention or evidence for use at trial. The intended final objective determines whether the information or evidence being sought is desirable or essential. Prosecutor advice may be helpful at this planning stage, particularly in more serious cases. There will be instances when no prosecution is possible without the covert investigation product. But there will be other instances when prosecution of a different (lesser) charge may be an option, which may not entail the need for covert investigation product to be acquired and adduced. It is not for investigators to second-guess sentencing in the event of a conviction but if covert investigation product is going to make no difference to the possible sentence on conviction, then for investigation managers and covert capability resource managers such considerations may help prioritize the allocation of scarce skilled resources between investigations where covert product is essential and those where it is desirable.

Managers and investigators need to consider whether the information sought is already directly available and known to, or easily ascertainable, by other agencies, or whether it may be deduced or inferred from information already available elsewhere. Once again, at issue are partnerships and the impetus for better information sharing between agencies and organizations: the beneficial obverse of the process-laundering vulnerability identified above. Authorizing officers, in discharging their duty to consider the proportionality of the proposed technique in relation to the information or evidence to be gained, will wish to be confident that the information is not already in the possession of a public authority in a position to share it. If another organization does have access to the information then it should be obtained from that organization in the first instance subject to information-sharing protocols, unless making such a request to another organization poses a risk of compromise: differences between organizations in vetting standards and other corruption prevention measures may be an issue here.

Both police and local authorities find themselves confronted with incident hot-spots (for example thefts from unattended vehicles in public car parks or fly-tipping) in which the first issue of any investigation is to identify possible suspects (as opposed to trying to obtain identity details of a confirmed offender, such as a street drug dealer regularly operating in an area, whose identity is as yet unknown to investigators). If an operation is targeted at an area or location rather than a named or described suspect, what issues arise in considering whether an authorization for covert investigation (by definition this applies only to directed surveillance) is required? How can collateral intrusion be recognized and managed in circumstances where the parameters are imprecise? How can distinctions be made between capturing private and public information? If it is impossible to tell, is there an issue at all—or alternatively is everything an issue because it is impossible to tell?

This is an issue in which case law would benefit those contemplating such operations: the jurisprudence on private information already discussed above provides some guidance. Courts have accepted that those actively engaged in criminality must expect to be investigated and therefore voluntarily assume the risk of interference with their right to have their private life respected (*Ludi v Switzerland* (1993) 15 EHRR 173). But collateral intrusion of third parties uninvolved in the suspected criminality will, in the case of a public car park or the remote country lane where fly-tipping takes place in addition to lawful passage, occur whether the offenders are known, described but unnamed, or the purpose of the operation is to identify possible suspects. As ever, the precise circumstances of each operation will dictate the need for authorization. The fact that the purpose of an operation is to identify possible suspects rather than gather evidence or intelligence about named or described offenders, does not absolve applicants or authorizing officers from considering whether the proposed covert investigation engages human rights.

One discriminator that could inform such consideration is the nature of the intended intervention. Where general observations are kept with the intention of triggering an immediate reactive intervention to any crime witnessed by the observing investigators then this might be considered to be within the general duties of an organization's statutory function, as opposed to a recourse to specific and exceptional powers. Where the observations are kept with the intention of securing information in order to inform subsequent intervention then private information will probably be gathered about both individuals whose conduct reveals them to be suspects and third parties whose conduct engages no prohibition at all. The gathering of such private information (recalling the broad construction courts have applied to this concept) will probably require surveillance authorization. (See also CSPI Code, para 2.24 and OSC *Annual Report 2008–09*, para 5.26.)

12.3 **What Are the Resource Implications?**

If there is a need for covert investigation, then the operation to execute the covert method will need to be resourced properly and adequately. Covert investigation is often time-consuming and expensive (both in terms of actual and opportunity costs). Managers need to challenge themselves and investigators with the following questions:

- What is the required objective of the whole operation?
- What is the objective of the covert element (within the context of the whole operation)?
- How might it be achieved?
- Can it be afforded?
- Even it can be afforded, is the proposed action cost effective?
- What is the organization going to have to sacrifice, abandon or postpone in terms of other work in order to resource and support a covert investigation? (What are the opportunity costs of a covert investigation?)

The first three questions provide the contextual framework within which the remaining three questions must be considered.

Case study—the expense of technical support

An investigator wanted covert photographic surveillance of the rear of a house set in rural farmland. Avoiding the all-too common professional discourtesy of telling the Technical Support Unit how to do their job by specifying the equipment they should use, the investigator instead, and quite properly, asked simply for the desired product: photographic evidence, suitable for use at court if necessary, of persons entering and leaving the premises via the rear door.

A feasibility study highlighted a significant consequence. There was a need to deploy the camera in an elevated position in order to obtain the desired product. There being no suitable natural features in which to disguise such a deployment, a man-made solution would have to be constructed. This solution, on its own would have appeared out of place and so would attract undue attention. Therefore it would have to be disguised within the context of property improvement work, if the owners of the neighbouring property could be persuaded to accept such unsolicited enhancements. These were going to be very expensive photographs.

For managers, consideration of such circumstances must focus on whether the evidential value of the product obtained is proportionate to the cost of its acquisition. In this respect managers have their own proportionality considerations alongside those required by law of authorizing officers. That which is possible is not necessarily feasible.

There are four general resource areas for consideration:

- Skills capability and capacity—how many appropriately-skilled staff needed and available?
- Technical capability and capacity—feasibility study needed prior to authorization
- CHIS requirement, if any—a specialism defined by interactive rather than remote surveillance
- Sustainability of operation—once started can it be continued, and for how long?

These considerations, it is suggested, should be contemplated prior to detailed planning and authorization application. An established covert investigative method may exist, but can it be adequately and safely executed by available staff? Safety in this consideration is as much about not compromising the method as it is about ensuring the personal safety of staff. The case study above illustrates the value of undertaking technical feasibility studies at the early contemplation stage. The deployment of CHISs (be they informers, undercover officers, or test purchase officers) may require significant advance planning, especially if trained staff have to be borrowed from other organizations for the purpose. The sustainability of operation can, of course, be adversely affected by unforeseen events occurring after the commencement of the operation, either within the context of the operation itself or as a result of events elsewhere to which the organization has to respond by diverting effort from existing operations. There is little that can be done to avoid such spontaneous developments. But how might that which can be foreseen or reasonably anticipated (eg annual leave, requirements to attend court, planned events to which the organization has to respond) influence the sustainability of the action being contemplated? What will be the cut-off point if the desired product is not achieved in the anticipated timescale?

Protection of resources is also at issue. Consultation with the organizational security officer and with professional standards staff will identify opportunities to reduce the risk of compromising resources and investigations through proactive measures. This needs to be considered not only at the systemic level but also in relation to individual operations at the pre-planning stage. Planning following a compromise is too late.

These are the considerations that senior investigators and intending authorization applicants need to resolve prior to the detailed planning phase of a covert operation.

12.4 **Planning and Preparation**

It is increasingly common for investigators and applicants to be required to give a presentation to authorizing officers in order to enable the latter properly and fully to undertake their role. This is especially necessary for complex operations.

A lot is required of authorizing officers in terms of their statutory responsibilities and it can be argued that if the individual concerned is not familiar with the investigation or the geographical area in which the operation is intended to take place, it will be difficult to make an informed judgement on many of the issues that will fall to be considered. A paper-based, or electronic authorization system, cannot provide answers to questions that may arise in the authorizing officer's mind while reflecting upon the legality, necessity and proportionality of the proposed action: for example, what other tactics were considered? Why were they dismissed? How was the threat level arrived at?

A possible framework for approaching such presentations is suggested below. It may also serve to inform general operational planning, tasking and coordination meetings, and resource allocation meetings.

Checklist—Framework for authorization/planning presentations

- This operation is a priority because…

- The objectives and outcomes of the operation are…

- The objectives of the proposed covert investigation, within the context of the wider operation, are…

- What sort of covert investigation is being contemplated? Will prior approval be necessary? Does it involve multi-phase action (ie reconnoitre, deployment, recovery; each of which will have to be specifically authorized) in order to achieve a single objective?

- It meets the legal framework compliance because…

- The associated risks and threats are… [refer to Chapter 11 for risk management]

- The impact on the community will be…

- The impact on the organization (and/or partnership) will be…

12.5 Managing Deployment and Authorization

Covert investigation activity will be undertaken alongside other forms of investigation. The degree to which this takes place will vary from operation to operation. The relationship between the use of covert investigation and other investigation and intervention methods will need to be understood in order to achieve planned objectives and outcomes. In some cases covert investigation will be used in a simple role to corroborate intelligence and inform a search warrant application: depending on the physical evidence, witness testimony and interview evidence that follows on from the execution of the search warrant, it may or may not be necessary to adduce the covert investigation product at trial. In more complex operations the interrelationship between different methods and constituent objectives will be more intricate. In other cases covert investigation will identify suspects against whom more conventional evidential opportunities can then be planned which may avoid the need to have to adduce the covertly obtained evidence at trial. Covert investigation may inform decisions about the point in the investigation plan that forensic evidence will be required; it might inform a parallel stream of financial investigation with a view to providing evidence at trial or information upon which to base asset freezing and recovery; it will always provide, collaterally, information about the nature of risks and threats involved in the investigation. Investigation and intelligence managers will be looking for new opportunities or lines of enquiry emerging from the intelligence picture developing as a result of the use of covert investigation.

Management of the investigation strategy runs in parallel with management of the investigation logistics. Basic command unit covert investigations may require logistical support from level 2 resources, for which bids will have to be made to force managers. Such bids will have to be in conjunction with appropriate tasking and co-ordination direction and may be in competition with similar bids from other BCUs. Non-police agencies intending to undertake covert investigation may wish to buy in surveillance skills from other public sector organizations or from the private sector—the latter option does not avoid the need for RIPA authorization because s 6 HRA is interpreted as including actions taken on behalf of a public authority by a third party.

Ongoing logistical management includes management of the authorization application, renewals, and cancellations. For those agencies empowered to undertake intrusive surveillance, prior approval must be received in writing from the Office of the Surveillance Commissioners before the covert activity can commence. Failure to comply fully with the prescribed schedules will render investigations vulnerable to being unauthorized and so subject, together with any evidence derived therefrom, to challenge in subsequent trial proceedings. One such challenge was made in *R v Paulssen* [2003] EWCA Crim 3109; however, the Court of Appeal upheld the conviction despite the failure of authorization continuity, which the Court viewed as only a minor technical infringement of RIPA. It is certainly not suggested here that investigators should rely on this case to avoid rigorous authorization management. Successful challenges may result in covert investigation product being excluded from evidence.

Larger organizations regularly engaging in covert investigation may wish to establish, if they do not already exist, central bureaux to assist in the management of the authority regime. Such bureaux can become centres of excellence and expertise which can greatly facilitate the appropriate and secure use of covert methods, manage the authorization process, ensure secure procedures for the handling and preservation of covert investigation product, and undertake operational reviews in order to capture organizational learning.

A consequential temptation of the central bureau concept is to have full-time or rota-based authorizing officers. The extent to which such individuals can meaningfully undertake the statutory considerations of legality, necessity, and proportionality, within the context of wider organization management issues, depends upon their familiarity with the investigation in question and the communities in which covert activity is to take place. The balance to be struck is between the authorizing officers being sufficiently independent of the investigation as to be able to be objective when considering and reviewing applications whilst not being so independent that they are not sufficiently aware of the circumstances and so cannot arrive at an informed decision. (This is where presentations in support of an application can be of particular benefit.)

Further information and reading

The revised codes of practice now detail specific requirements in relation to the keeping of records about covert investigation applications and authorizations. See:

- CSPI Code, Chapter 8
- CHIS Code, Chapter 7
- PEI Code, Chapter 7
- Communications Data Code, Chapter 6: see also Chapter 7 for the implications of the Data Protection Act 1998 concerning subject access to information from communication service providers about investigator acquisition of communications data.

There is no equivalent chapter in the Interception Code as published on the Home Office website, December 2011, but that Code does contain a chapter on disclosure.

Ensuring that these requirements are met would seem to fall to the *senior responsible officer* within each organization: a role recommended in the CSPI Code, para 3.28 and mandatorily required under the Communications Data Code, para 3.22.

12.6 Managing the Product: Dissemination, Disclosure, Debrief

Managing the product of covert investigation divides into three generic areas: dissemination of intelligence derived; the use of such product as evidence at trial; and organizational reflection on lessons learnt.

12.6.1 Dissemination of intelligence acquired

Covert investigation will generate intelligence tangential to the primary investigation objective. For example, as a result of surveillance, associations between criminals may be newly identified or those hypothesized corroborated; use of identified vehicles may be confirmed; links between criminals and businesses through which criminal profits might be laundered may be identified; all related to the primary investigation objective by virtue of being discovered in the authorized surveillance arena but not destined to be part of a prosecution case. Such intelligence, building up a picture of criminal networks and markets, because it has both investigative tactical value and policy strategic value, has to be documented and disseminated appropriately. Which means not only to the correct colleagues, both within and outwith the originating agency, but also in the correct fashion that takes measures necessary to ensure that covert techniques are not compromised.

Further information and reading

C Harfield and K Harfield, *Intelligence: Investigation, Community, and Partnership* (Oxford University Press, Oxford, 2008), particularly Chapters 7–10.

It is equally possible, of course, that something is observed within the surveillance arena that has no direct or indirect relevance to the authorized investigation but which nevertheless warrants documentation and dissemination in timely and appropriate fashion.

Occasionally dilemmas will arise in which prompt dissemination of such intelligence, no matter how well sanitized, will disclose the existence of ongoing covert investigation simply because the information could not have been obtained in any other way. Investigation and intelligence managers and, if necessary, senior organization managers will have to confer in such circumstances and decide how best to proceed. It would be difficult to justify *not* acting on a piece of intelligence, particularly if harm could be prevented, just because of a reluctance to compromise an ongoing covert investigation through the dissemination of collateral intelligence: given the primary function of the police to preserve life and prevent crime, the latter will always be more important than not disrupting an operation. This is similar to a dilemma frequently faced by CHIS controllers when a CHIS has acquired intelligence that could only have come from the CHIS and so acting on it (before the intelligence can be corroborated and its acquisition sanitized so as to disguise the involvement of a CHIS) would expose, compromise, and potentially endanger the CHIS.

Trying to balance intelligence value against investment costs (in terms of the investigation already underway and through support of which covert methods have produced the collateral intelligence) is not a straightforward equation.

12.6.2 Disclosure

Disclosure occurs in one of two ways: through revelation to the prosecutor pursuant to statutory obligations under CPIA; or through unauthorized means such as careless information management or purposeful corruption.

The latter risk can be guarded against through the creation and maintenance of an appropriate professional and secure environment for the handling of sensitive intelligence or, as required, evidence acquired through covert investigation. Appropriate measures will include security vetting (a five-yearly process), interim review and management of vetting in between vetting processes, and proactive measures to prevent compromise and corruption.

Covert investigation methods will only remain effective to the extent that criminals remain ignorant of them, yet every trial represents an opportunity for those accused (and by extension the general public) to learn about the methods that brought them before the court. Revelation to the prosecutor, a statutory requirement enabling the prosecutor to fulfil his or her duty under s 3 CPIA, does not automatically mean disclosure to the defence. Circumstances exist under which sensitive information (such as covert investigation methods, the identity of a CHIS, or information that might facilitate future offences or aid future suspects to evade arrest) can be protected from exposure at court. The management of this issue is therefore of crucial importance and may warrant the appointment of a specialist covert investigation disclosure officer alongside the general disclosure officer on complex cases.

Potentially all information and material acquired through covert investigation, *and* the documentation relating to the authorization of covert investigation, is liable to disclosure at trial. Just because evidence or other material has been obtained by covert means, does not mean that either the information or the methods used are automatically exempt from statutory disclosure. (The one exception to this is the product of intercepted communications, currently prohibited from use at trial by s 17 RIPA—see Chapter 8 for further discussion of this and the relevance of 'Preston' briefings.) Investigators will need to liaise closely and fully with their prosecuting authorities in respect of information that they wish judges to withhold subject to a PII order. Prosecutors have a continuing duty to review all material, both pre-trial and during the trial, to ascertain whether it undermines the prosecution case or assists the defence case. 'If no duty to disclose arises, then no issue of public interest immunity arises' (McKay, 'Public interest immunity after *Edwards and Lewis v United Kingdom* and *R v C* and *R v H* and the role of special advocates', *Covert Policing Review* (2006), 110–124).

R v H and C [2004] 2 AC 134 provides the defining test that interprets CPIA (as amended by the Criminal Justice Act 2003) and its associated Code of Practice.

Case law criteria: *R v H* and *C* [2004] 2 AC 134—public interest immunity (PII)

Full disclosure should be made of all material held by the Crown that weakens its own case or assists the defence. An exception from this rule may be justified if an important public interest has to be protected. If material does not undermine the Crown case or assist the defence, there is no requirement to disclose it or apply for PII. Sensitive/unused neutral material or sensitive/unused material damaging to the defence need not be disclosed and should not be brought to the attention of the court. PII should be sought only where absolutely necessary.

For further discussion see S McKay, 'Public interest immunity after *Edwards and Lewis v United Kingdom* and *R v C* and *R v H* and the role of Special Advocates', *Covert Policing Review* (2006), 110–124, particularly 119–124.

Investigators seeking to protect information through PII have the option of having their application heard openly (defence present), privately (defence aware of the application but not present), or secretly (defence unaware of the application). The guiding regulations are to be found in the following:

- Magistrates' Courts (Criminal Procedure and Investigations Act 1996) (Disclosure) Rules 1997 (SI 1997/703)
- Crown Court (Criminal Procedure and Investigations Act 1996) (Disclosure) Rules 1997 (SI 1997/698)
- Criminal Procedure Rules 2005 (SI 2005/384).

There has been mixed case law on the issue of whether documentation from the authorization application process should be subject to disclosure. In *R v GS* [2005] EWCA Crim 887, the appellants sought disclosure of all documentation relating to the granting of OSC approval for intrusive surveillance, including the applications. Since only one of the defence counsel in the case expressed any concern about the lawfulness of the application procedure, the Court of Appeal regarded the remaining defence applications for disclosure as a 'fishing expedition' (at para 16 of the judgment).

Dismissing the appeal the Court held (at para 32):

> it is not open to the criminal court to embark upon an examination of material underlying an approved authorization, to determine whether the correct statutory criteria have been correctly taken into account and so on, all of which go to the issue of lawfulness.

The Court went on to assert that production of the OSC signed approval forms or alternatively the testimony of a Chief Officer supported by the approval forms, should be sufficient to establish lawfulness (para 35), and that evidence unlawfully obtained is not automatically rendered unfair and subject to exclusion under s 78 PACE.

In *R v Sutherland, R v Sentence*, and *R v Grant* (see 3.7.2 above) the Court took a significantly different view. The authorization processes in these cases were subject to full scrutiny: notebook entries, deployment feasibility studies, and testimony from officers involved in making the applications and staff deploying technical equipment were all disclosed and admitted in submissions, to establish that there had been an intention on the part of investigators from the outset to use audio surveillance to capture privileged conversations between suspects and their legal advisors, and that such capture had not been an unforeseen collateral occurrence.

Further information and reading

For further detailed discussion of the cases considered above, see A Hopkins, 'Testing lawfulness: the authorization of interception of communications and covert surveillance under the regulation of Investigatory Powers Act 2000', *Covert Policing Review* (2005), 33–51, particularly 45–48.

The use of covert investigation by State agents against individual citizens is an illustration of the asymmetrical power relationship between State and citizen that the principles of due process at trial seek to rebalance in the interests of fairness. There may be justifiable arguments to protect methodology and identities through PII applications, but in the context of self-authorization or non-judicial prior approval, investigators cannot be surprised that transparency and accountability of decision-making will be subject to court scrutiny through disclosure.

12.6.3 **Debriefing**

Whilst it is true that every deployment of covert investigation risks compromising methods or personnel, it is equally true that each deployment offers opportunities for organizational learning. Such practice-based learning must be captured. Operational debriefing and investigation review are two structured ways of identifying useful lessons. Potentially there is an additional role here for a central bureau that facilitates the management of covert investigation within the organization. Such a bureau would thus become the centre of expertise within the organization. The police service already operates a structured murder investigation peer review system. It is worth considering whether regular internal or peer review of covert investigation deployment would help capture learning and identify areas for improvement—before such opportunities were identified through external audit and inspection by the OSC. Regular review also reinforces and demonstrates organizational responsibility and professional attitudes towards covert investigation. It can be used to demonstrate that covert investigation is not being used extravagantly.

In the police service the national capture of learning and good practice falls to the National Policing Improvement Agency (NPIA). Good practice is promulgated through the various guidance manuals published by NPIA.

The OSC inspection programme (which is not confined to the police service but includes all bodies empowered to undertake covert investigation) informs the annual report that the Chief Surveillance Commissioner must make to the Prime Minister and Scottish Ministers. Whilst the OSC role is not primarily to capture and disseminate good practice, the annual reports are a valuable source of information and insight into wider management issues concerning covert investigation.

In whatever form it takes, practice-based debriefing and organizational learning must inform both future strategic use of covert investigation and also the training of surveillance operatives and those who facilitate covert investigation. Failure to train staff adequately (which includes training delivery by 'well-meaning but inadequately-informed providers'), and failure to identify and adopt lessons to be learnt, both contribute to the diminution of the overall covert investigation skills base which the Chief Surveillance Commissioner has observed (*Annual Report 2006–2007*, para 7.2; quote taken from para 10.5).

Further information and reading

- The OSC annual reports are available on the OSC website: <http://www.surveillancecommissioners.gov.uk>
- The Home Office also operates a RIPA news service on: <http://security.homeoffice.gov.uk/ripa/about-ripa/news>
- The NPIA, in conjunction with ACPO, has published *Guidance on The Lawful and Effective Use of Covert Techniques* (Wyboston, NPIA, 2007).

12.7 Contracting Out, Joint Operations, and Collaborative Working

Provisions exist for public authorities to engage in joint operations, collaborate with other public authorities in the purchase or services or undertaking of functions or to contract out some of their functions to private enterprise. The management rationale for these initiatives is to save money. In relation to covert investigation such money-saving strategies give rise to additional considerations for senior responsible officers and for authorizing officers.

Any private enterprise undertaking public functions on behalf of a public authority will engage s 6 HRA 1998. When acting on behalf of a public authority, it will be unlawful for the private enterprise to act in a way which is incompatible with an ECHR right. Those sub-contracted will be restricted in what they can do lawfully by what the contracting authority is empowered to do. Thus there will be occasions when private investigators in possession of the technical capability to undertake certain methods on behalf of private customers will not be able to employ such methods on behalf of public authorities because the latter are not empowered to use them. For example, the deployment of vehicle tracking devices constitutes property interference which, in the public authority arena, can only be utilized and authorized by a limited number of law enforcement and intelligence agencies under s 93(5) PA97 or s 5 Intelligence Services Act 1994. A local authority could not, therefore, ask a private investigator to undertake this method of surveillance even though the private investigator might have the technical capability (see OSC *Annual Report 2010–11*, para 5.14).

Authorities investigating together in a joint operation may be in a position to pursue their own individual prosecutions or regulatory interventions arising from that operation. For example, arising from a joint operation a police force might pursue criminal charges against some of the suspects identified whilst a local authority partner in the investigation might pursue regulatory matters within their own remit against other suspects identified. In such a joint operation it will be necessary to plan the investigation and prosecutions in such a way as to ensure that evidence obtained during covert surveillance is used appropriately and for a proper purpose. Where it is anticipated that evidence obtained using restricted covert surveillance powers might be relied upon for the prosecution of matters for which no covert power of investigation exists (simply because such evidence was secured during a collaborative or joint investigation), legal advice should be sought as to the likely admissibility of such evidence in the planned proceedings. It does not seem to have been the intention of Parliament, in making provision for joint operations and collaborative working, that collaboration should be used as a means to circumvent restrictions on the use of certain powers established in RIPA and the PA97.

A third area of new complexity concerns the making of covert investigation applications for and the granting of authorities for such conduct within the context of collaborative working. The default position in both RIPA and PA97 is that applicants and authorizing officers must be members of the same organization. The exception to this principle exists when two or more *police forces* have entered into a collaborative working agreement pursuant to s 23 of the Police Act 1996, (for English and Welsh forces: s 12 of the Police (Scotland) Act 1967 for Scottish forces), *and* the collaboration agreement permits applicants and authorizing officers to be from different forces. Where a collaborative working agreement is established for the purpose (*inter alia*) of facilitating covert investigation for the signatory parties such agreements must document specific arrangements for the management of covert investigation between the partners. 'Mere agreement to share resources is insufficient' (OSC *Annual Report 2010–11*, para 5.12; see also CSPI Code, paras 3.19–3.21).

The need to document the entire covert investigation process, from initial planning to subsequent evidential or intelligence product management, is an intrinsic part of covert investigation management and is imposed as a statutory duty on each public authority availing itself of covert investigation powers. Neither joint operations nor collaborative working agreements absolve individual partner agencies from maintaining their own records for each operation. 'Primary legislation requires each designated public authority to maintain its own central record of authorizations and to be responsible for the covert surveillance conducted on its behalf' (OSC *Annual Report 2010–11*, para 5.13). As the Chief Surveillance Commissioner observes, such duplication creates consequential duplication for the inspection regime: at the time of writing this edition the OSC is consulting with the Home Office on this and other issues arising from the fact that the original covert investigation legislation was not enacted with collaborative working in mind.

Further information and reading

On joint operations and collaborative working see CSPI Code, paras 3.15–3.21; 6.9–6.10; 7.12–7.14; and CHIS Code, paras 5.9 and 6.13. See also OSC *Annual Report 2010–11*, paras 3.9 and 5.12–5.14.

Contracting out, joint operations, and collaborative working may complicate the management of covert investigation and reinforce the need for public authorities to consider seriously the good practice recommendation in CSPI Code, para 3.28 that an executive level senior responsible officer (with authorizing officer experience) be designated for the strategic management of covert investigation within the organization. These three strategic initiatives for making best use of scarce resources each give rise to separate issues. (The examples raised here are neither exclusive nor exhaustive and the growing body of operational experience in these areas will generate new issues as yet unidentified.) It would be easy, and is equally important not to, conflate and confuse such issues. Sharing services is not necessarily the same thing as undertaking joint investigations. Any given joint investigation may be a one-off, ad hoc operation: collaborative working cannot be established on an ad hoc basis and must be pursuant to documented agreements between the collaborating authorities. Contracting out a function is not necessarily the same thing as delegating a power, nor is it likely ever to absolve organizational or individual statutory responsibility.

12.8 **Conclusion**

Failings and frustrations apparent within the undertaking of covert investigation are often proving to be management rather than legislative issues. The operationally advantageous, statutory self-authorization regime (with non-judicial prior approval as required) will withstand legal challenge only so long as it is demonstrably well-managed, transparent in its accountability, and robust in review and self-reflection. Surveillance operatives have to be skilled and sophisticated; authorizing officers have defined and significant statutory obligations; those involved in the management of covert investigation (which will include individuals from the first two groups here identified), equally have a crucial role in successful covert investigation: an arena in which not only do the powers of the State have to be balanced against the rights of the individual, but in which also a plethora of (sometimes conflicting) organizational management issues have to be balanced against each other. That which the Law Lords have found to be a puzzling statute in reflective interpretation can be just as challenging in its frontline operational implementation and management.

Appendix A

Covert Surveillance and Property Interference

Revised Code of Practice
Pursuant to section 71 of the Regulation of
Investigatory Powers Act 2000

Chapter 1

Introduction

<small>DEFINITIONS</small>

1.1 In this code:

- "1989 Act" means the Security Service Act 1989;
- "1994 Act" means the Intelligence Services Act 1994;
- "1997 Act" means the Police Act 1997;
- "2000 Act" means the Regulation of Investigatory Powers Act 2000;
- "RIP(S)A" means the Regulation of Investigatory Powers (Scotland) Act 2000;
- "2010 Order" means the Regulation of Investigatory Powers (Extension of Authorisation Provisions: Legal Consultations) Order 2010;
- terms in *italics* are defined in the Glossary at the end of this code.

<small>BACKGROUND</small>

1.2 This code of practice provides guidance on the use by *public authorities* of Part II of the 2000 Act to authorise covert surveillance that is likely to result in the obtaining of *private information* about a person. The code also provides guidance on entry on, or interference with, property or with wireless telegraphy by *public authorities* under section 5 of the Intelligence Services Act 1994 or Part III of the Police Act 1997.

1.3 This code is issued pursuant to Section 71 of the 2000 Act, which stipulates that the *Secretary of State* shall issue one or more codes of practice in relation to the powers and duties in Parts I to III of the 2000 Act, section 5 of the 1994 Act and Part III of the 1997 Act. This code replaces the previous code of practice issued in 2002.

1.4 This code is publicly available and should be readily accessible by *members* of any relevant *public authority*[1] seeking to use the 2000 Act to authorise covert surveillance that is likely to result in the obtaining of *private information* about a person or section 5 of the 1994 Act or Part III of the 1997 Act to authorise entry on, or interference with, property or with wireless telegraphy.[2]

1.5 Where covert surveillance activities are unlikely to result in the obtaining of *private information* about a person, or where there is a separate legal basis for such activities, neither the 2000 Act nor this code need apply.[3]

<small>EFFECT OF CODE</small>

1.6 The 2000 Act provides that all codes of practice relating to the 2000 Act are admissible as evidence in criminal and civil proceedings. If any provision of this code appears relevant to any court or tribunal considering any such proceedings, or to the Investigatory Powers Tribunal established under the 2000 Act, or to one of the Commissioners responsible for overseeing the powers conferred by the 2000 Act,

---

[1] Being those listed under section 30 of the 2000 Act or specified in orders made by the *Secretary of State* under that section.

[2] Being, at the time of writing, the police, *services police*, Serious Organised Crime Agency, Scottish Crime and Drugs Agency, HM Revenue and Customs and Office of Fair Trading.

[3] See Chapter 2. It is assumed that intrusive surveillance will always result in the obtaining of *private information*.

it must be taken into account. *Public authorities* may also be required to justify, with regard to this code, the use or granting of *authorisations* in general or the failure to use or grant *authorisations* where appropriate.

1.7 Examples are included in this code to assist with the illustration and interpretation of certain provisions. Examples are not provisions of the code, but are included for guidance only. It is not possible for theoretical examples to replicate the level of detail to be found in real cases. Consequently, *authorising officers* should avoid allowing superficial similarities with the examples to determine their decisions and should not seek to justify their decisions solely by reference to the examples rather than to the law, including the provisions of this code.

SURVEILLANCE ACTIVITY TO WHICH THIS CODE APPLIES

1.8 Part II of the 2000 Act provides for the *authorisation* of covert surveillance by *public authorities* where that surveillance is likely to result in the obtaining of *private information* about a person.

1.9 Surveillance, for the purpose of the 2000 Act, includes monitoring, observing or listening to persons, their movements, conversations or other activities and communications. It may be conducted with or without the assistance of a surveillance device and includes the recording of any information obtained.[4]

1.10 Surveillance is covert if, and only if, it is carried out in a manner calculated to ensure that any persons who are subject to the surveillance are unaware that it is or may be taking place.[5]

1.11 Specifically, covert surveillance may be authorised under the 2000 Act if it is either intrusive or directed:

- Intrusive surveillance is covert surveillance that is carried out in relation to anything taking place on residential premises or in any private vehicle (and that involves the presence of an individual on the premises or in the vehicle or is carried out by a means of a surveillance device);[6]
- Directed surveillance is covert surveillance that is not intrusive but is carried out in relation to a specific investigation or operation in such a manner as is likely to result in the obtaining of *private information* about any person (other than by way of an immediate response to events or circumstances such that it is not reasonably practicable to seek *authorisation* under the 2000 Act).

1.12 Chapter 2 of this code provides a fuller description of directed and intrusive surveillance, along with definitions of terms, exceptions and examples.

BASIS FOR LAWFUL SURVEILLANCE ACTIVITY

1.13 The Human Rights Act 1998 gave effect in UK law to the rights set out in the European Convention on Human Rights (ECHR). Some of these rights are absolute, such as the prohibition on torture, while others are qualified, meaning that it is

---

[4] See section 48(2) of the 2000 Act.
[5] As defined in section 26(9)(a) of the 2000 Act.
[6] See Chapter 2 for full definition of residential premises and private vehicles, and note that the 2010 Order identifies a new category of surveillance to be treated as intrusive surveillance.

permissible for the state to interfere with those rights if certain conditions are satisfied. Amongst the qualified rights is a person's right to respect for their private and family life, home and correspondence, as provided for by Article 8 of the ECHR. It is Article 8 that is most likely to be engaged when public authorities seek to obtain private information about a person by means of covert surveillance. Article 6 of the ECHR, the right to a fair trial, is also relevant where a prosecution follows the use of covert techniques, particularly where the prosecution seek to protect the use of those techniques through public interest immunity procedures.

1.14 Part II of the 2000 Act provides a statutory framework under which covert surveillance activity can be authorised and conducted compatibly with Article 8. Where directed surveillance would not be likely to result in the obtaining of any *private information* about a person, no interference with Article 8 rights occurs and an *authorisation* under the 2000 Act is therefore not appropriate.

1.15 Similarly, an *authorisation* under the 2000 Act is not required if a *public authority* has another clear legal basis for conducting covert surveillance likely to result in the obtaining of *private information* about a person. For example the Police and Criminal Evidence Act 1984[7] provides a legal basis for the police covertly to record images of a suspect for the purposes of identification and obtaining certain evidence.

1.16 Chapter 2 of this code provides further guidance on what constitutes *private information* and examples of activity for which authorisations under Part II of the 2000 Act are or are not required.

RELEVANT PUBLIC AUTHORITIES

1.17 Only certain *public authorities* may apply for *authorisations* under the 2000, 1997 or 1994 Acts:

- Directed surveillance *applications* may only be made by those *public authorities* listed in or added to Part I and Part II of schedule 1 of the 2000 Act.
- Intrusive surveillance *applications* may only be made by those *public authorities* listed in or added to section 32(6) of the 2000 Act, or by those *public authorities* listed in or designated under section 41(1) of the 2000 Act.
- *Applications* to enter on, or interfere with, property or with wireless telegraphy may only be made (under Part III of the 1997 Act) by those *public authorities* listed in or added to section 93(5) of the 1997 Act; or (under section 5 of the 1994 Act) by the intelligence services.

SCOTLAND

1.18 Where all the conduct authorised is likely to take place in Scotland, *authorisations* should be granted under RIP(S)A, unless:

- the *authorisation* is to be granted or renewed (by any relevant *public authority*) for the purposes of national security or the economic well-being of the UK;
- the *authorisation* is being obtained by, or authorises conduct by or on behalf of, those *public authorities* listed in section 46(3) of the 2000 Act and the Regulation

---

[7] See also the Police & Criminal Evidence (Northern Ireland) Order 1989.

of Investigatory Powers (*Authorisations* Extending to Scotland) Order 2007; SI No 934); or,

- the *authorisation* authorises conduct that is surveillance by virtue of section 48(4) of the 2000 Act.

1.19 This code of practice is extended to Scotland in relation to *authorisations* granted under Part II of the 2000 Act which apply to Scotland. A separate code of practice applies in relation to *authorisations* granted under RIP(S)A.

INTERNATIONAL CONSIDERATIONS

1.20 *Authorisations* under the 2000 Act can be given for surveillance both inside and outside the UK. However, *authorisations* for actions outside the UK can usually only validate them for the purposes of UK law. Where action in another country is contemplated, the laws of the relevant country must also be considered.

1.21 *Public authorities* are therefore advised to seek *authorisations* under the 2000 Act for directed or intrusive surveillance operations outside the UK if the subject of investigation is a UK national or is likely to become the subject of criminal or civil proceedings in the UK, or if the operation is likely to affect a UK national or give rise to material likely to be used in evidence before a UK court.

1.22 *Authorisations* under the 2000 Act are appropriate for all directed and intrusive surveillance operations in overseas areas under the jurisdiction of the UK, such as UK Embassies, military bases and detention facilities.

1.23 Under the provisions of section 76A of the 2000 Act, as inserted by the Crime (International Co-Operation) Act 2003, foreign surveillance teams may operate in the UK subject to certain conditions. See Chapter 5 (*Authorisation* procedures for directed surveillance) for detail.

Chapter 2

Directed and intrusive surveillance definitions

2.1 This chapter provides further guidance on whether covert surveillance activity is directed surveillance or intrusive surveillance, or whether an *authorisation* for either activity would not be deemed necessary.

DIRECTED SURVEILLANCE

2.2 Surveillance is directed surveillance if the following are all true:

- it is covert, but not intrusive surveillance;
- it is conducted for the purposes of a specific investigation or operation;
- it is likely to result in the obtaining of *private information* about a person (whether or not one specifically identified for the purposes of the investigation or operation);
- it is conducted otherwise than by way of an immediate response to events or circumstances the nature of which is such that it would not be reasonably practicable for an *authorisation* under Part II of the 2000 Act to be sought.

2.3 Thus, the planned covert surveillance of a specific person, where not intrusive, would constitute directed surveillance if such surveillance is likely to result in the obtaining of *private information* about that, or any other person.

PRIVATE INFORMATION

2.4 The 2000 Act states that *private information* includes any information relating to a person's private or family life.[8] *Private information* should be taken generally to include any aspect of a person's private or personal relationship with others, including family [9] and professional or business relationships.

2.5 Whilst a person may have a reduced expectation of privacy when in a public place, covert surveillance of that person's activities in public may still result in the obtaining of *private information*. This is likely to be the case where that person has a reasonable expectation of privacy even though acting in public and where a record is being made by a *public authority* of that person's activities for future consideration or analysis.[10]

> **Example:** Two people holding a conversation on the street or in a bus may have a reasonable expectation of privacy over the contents of that conversation, even though they are associating in public. The contents of such a conversation should therefore still be considered as private information. A directed surveillance authorisation would therefore be appropriate for a public authority to record or listen to the conversation as part of a specific investigation or operation.

2.6 Private life considerations are particularly likely to arise if several records are to be analysed together in order to establish, for example, a pattern of behaviour, or if one or more pieces of information (whether or not available in the public domain) are covertly (or in some cases overtly) obtained for the purpose of making a permanent record about a person or for subsequent data processing to generate further information. In such circumstances, the totality of information gleaned may constitute *private information* even if individual records do not. Where such conduct includes surveillance, a directed surveillance *authorisation* may be considered appropriate.

> **Example:** Officers of a local authority wish to drive past a cafe for the purposes of obtaining a photograph of the exterior. Reconnaissance of this nature is not likely to require a directed surveillance authorisation as no private information about any person is likely to be obtained or recorded. However, if the authority wished to conduct a similar exercise, for example to establish a pattern of occupancy of the premises by any person, the accumulation of information is likely to result in the obtaining of private information about that person and a directed surveillance authorisation should be considered.

2.7 *Private information* may include personal data, such as names, telephone numbers and address details. Where such information is acquired by means of covert

---

[8] See section 26(10) of the 2000 Act.

[9] Family should be treated as extending beyond the formal relationships created by marriage or civil partnership.

[10] Note also that a person in police custody will have certain expectations of privacy.

surveillance of a person having a reasonable expectation of privacy, a directed surveillance *authorisation* is appropriate.[11]

Example: A surveillance officer intends to record a specific person providing their name and telephone number to a shop assistant, in order to confirm their identity, as part of a criminal investigation. Although the person has disclosed these details in a public place, there is nevertheless a reasonable expectation that the details are not being recorded separately for another purpose. A directed surveillance authorisation should therefore be sought.

SPECIFIC SITUATIONS REQUIRING DIRECTED SURVEILLANCE AUTHORISATIONS

2.8 The following specific situations may also constitute directed surveillance according to the 2000 Act:

- The use of surveillance devices designed or adapted for the purpose of providing information regarding the location of a vehicle alone does not necessarily constitute directed surveillance as they do not necessarily provide *private information* about any individual but sometimes only supply information about the location of that particular device at any one time. However, the use of that information, often coupled with other surveillance activity which may obtain *private information*, could interfere with Article 8 rights. A directed surveillance *authorisation* may therefore be appropriate.[12]
- surveillance consisting in the interception of a communication in the course of its transmission by means of a public postal service or telecommunication system where the communication is one sent or intended for a person who has consented to the interception of communications sent by or to him and where there is no interception *warrant*[13] authorising the interception.[14]

RECORDING OF TELEPHONE CONVERSATIONS

2.9 Subject to paragraph 2.8 above, the interception of communications sent by public post or by means of public telecommunications systems or private telecommunications is governed by Part I of the 2000 Act. Nothing in this code should be taken as granting dispensation from the requirements of that Part of the 2000 Act.

2.10 The recording or monitoring of one or both ends of a telephone conversation by a surveillance device as part of an authorised directed (or intrusive) surveillance operation will not constitute interception under Part I of the 2000 Act provided the process by which the product is obtained does not involve any modification of, or interference with, the telecommunications system or its operation. This will not constitute interception as sound waves obtained from the air are not in the course of transmission by

---

[11] The fact that a directed surveillance *authorisation* is available does not mean it is required. There may be other lawful means of obtaining personal data which do not involve directed surveillance.

[12] The use of such devices is also likely to require an *authorisation* for property interference under the 1994 or 1997 Act. See Chapter 7.

[13] i.e. under Part 1 Chapter 1 of the 2000 Act.

[14] See section 48(4) of the 2000 Act. The availability of a directed surveillance *authorisation* nevertheless does not preclude authorities from seeking an interception *warrant* under Part I of the 2000 Act in these circumstances.

means of a telecommunications system (which, in the case of a telephone conversation, should be taken to begin with the microphone and end with the speaker). Any such product can be treated as having been lawfully obtained.

Example: A property interference authorisation may be used to authorise the installation in a private car of an eavesdropping device with a microphone, together with an intrusive surveillance authorisation to record or monitor speech within that car. If one or both ends of a telephone conversation held in that car are recorded during the course of the operation, this will not constitute unlawful interception provided the device obtains the product from the sound waves in the vehicle and not by interference with, or modification of, any part of the telecommunications system.

Intrusive surveillance

2.11 Intrusive surveillance is covert surveillance that is carried out in relation to anything taking place on residential premises or in any private vehicle, and that involves the presence of an individual on the premises or in the vehicle or is carried out by a means of a surveillance device.

2.12 The definition of surveillance as intrusive relates to the location of the surveillance, and not any other consideration of the nature of the information that is expected to be obtained. In addition, surveillance under the ambit of the 2010 Order is to be treated as intrusive surveillance. Accordingly, it is not necessary to consider whether or not intrusive surveillance is likely to result in the obtaining of *private information*.

Residential premises

2.13 For the purposes of the 2000 Act, residential premises are considered to be so much of any premises as is for the time being occupied or used by any person, however temporarily, for residential purposes or otherwise as living accommodation. This specifically includes hotel or prison accommodation that is so occupied or used.[15] However, common areas (such as hotel dining areas) to which a person has access in connection with their use or occupation of accommodation are specifically excluded.[16]

2.14 The 2000 Act further states that the concept of premises should be taken to include any place whatsoever, including any vehicle or moveable structure, whether or not occupied as land.

2.15 Examples of residential premises would therefore include:

- a rented flat currently occupied for residential purposes;
- a prison cell (or police cell serving as temporary prison accommodation);
- a hotel bedroom or suite.

---

[15] See section 48(1) of the 2000 Act.
[16] See section 48(7) of the 2000 Act.

2.16 Examples of premises which would not be regarded as residential would include:

- a communal stairway in a block of flats (unless known to be used as a temporary place of abode by, for example, a homeless person);
- a prison canteen or police interview room;
- a hotel reception area or dining room;
- the front garden or driveway of premises readily visible to the public;
- residential premises occupied by a *public authority* for non-residential purposes, for example trading standards 'house of horrors' situations or undercover operational premises.

PRIVATE VEHICLES

2.17 A private vehicle is defined in the 2000 Act as any vehicle, including vessels, aircraft or hovercraft, which is used primarily for the private purposes of the person who owns it or a person otherwise having the right to use it. This would include, for example, a company car, owned by a leasing company and used for business and pleasure by the employee of a company.[17]

PLACES FOR LEGAL CONSULTATION

2.18 The 2010 Order provides that directed surveillance that is carried out in relation to anything taking place on so much of any premises specified in Article 3(2) of the Order as is, at any time during the surveillance, used for the purpose of legal consultations shall be treated for the purposes of Part II of the 2000 Act as intrusive surveillance. The premises identified in article 3(2) are:

(a) any place in which persons who are serving sentences of imprisonment or detention, remanded in custody or committed in custody for trial or sentence may be detained;

(b) any place in which persons may be detained under paragraph 16(1), (1A) or (2) of Schedule 2 or paragraph 2(2) or (3) of Schedule 3 to the Immigration Act 1971 or section 36(1) of the UK Border Act 2007;

(c) police stations;

(d) hospitals where high security psychiatric services are provided;

(e) the place of business of any professional legal adviser; and

(f) any place used for the sittings and business of any court, tribunal, inquest or inquiry.

FURTHER CONSIDERATIONS

2.19 Intrusive surveillance may take place by means of a person or device located in the residential premises or private vehicle or place for legal consultation under the 2010 Order. It may also take place by means of a device placed outside the premises or vehicle or place for legal consultation under the 2010 Order which consistently

---

[17] See section 48(1) and 48(7) of the 2000 Act.

provides information of the same quality and detail as might be expected to be obtained from a device inside.[18]

> **Example:** An observation post outside residential premises which provides a limited view compared to that which would be achievable from within the premises does not constitute intrusive surveillance. However, the use of a zoom lens, for example, which consistently achieves imagery of the same quality as that which would be visible from within the premises, would constitute intrusive surveillance.

2.20 The use of a device for the purpose of providing information about the location of any private vehicle is not considered to be intrusive surveillance.[19] Such use may, however, be authorised as directed surveillance, where the recording or use of the information would amount to the covert monitoring of the movements of the occupant(s) of that vehicle. A property interference *authorisation* may be appropriate for the covert installation or deployment of the device.

WHERE AUTHORISATION IS NOT REQUIRED

2.21 Some surveillance activity does not constitute intrusive or directed surveillance for the purposes of Part II of the 2000 Act and no directed or intrusive surveillance *authorisation* can be provided for such activity. Such activity includes:

- covert surveillance by way of an immediate response to events;
- covert surveillance as part of general observation activities;
- covert surveillance not relating to specified grounds;
- overt use of CCTV and ANPR systems;
- certain other specific situations.

2.22 Each situation is detailed and illustrated below.

IMMEDIATE RESPONSE

2.23 Covert surveillance that is likely to reveal *private information* about a person but is carried out by way of an immediate response to events such that it is not reasonably practicable to obtain an *authorisation* under the 2000 Act, would not require a directed surveillance *authorisation*. The 2000 Act is not intended to prevent law enforcement *officers* fulfilling their legislative functions. To this end section 26(2)(c) of the 2000 Act provides that surveillance is not directed surveillance when it is carried out by way of an immediate response to events or circumstances the nature of which is such that it is not reasonably practicable for an *authorisation* to be sought for the carrying out of the surveillance.

> **Example:** An authorisation under the 2000 Act would not be appropriate where police officers conceal themselves to observe suspicious persons that they come across in the course of a routine patrol.

---

[18] See section 26(5) of the 2000 Act.
[19] See section 26(4) of the 2000 Act.

GENERAL OBSERVATION ACTIVITIES

2.24 The general observation duties of many law enforcement *officers* and other *public authorities* do not require *authorisation* under the 2000 Act, whether covert or overt. Such general observation duties frequently form part of the legislative functions of *public authorities,* as opposed to the pre-planned surveillance of a specific person or group of people.

> **Example 1:** Plain clothes police officers on patrol to monitor a high street crime hot-spot or prevent and detect shoplifting would not require a directed surveillance authorisation. Their objective is merely to observe a location and, through reactive policing, to identify and arrest offenders committing crime. The activity may be part of a specific investigation but is general observational activity, rather than surveillance of individuals, and the obtaining of private information is unlikely. A directed surveillance authorisation need not be sought.

> **Example 2:** Local authority officers attend a car boot sale where it is suspected that counterfeit goods are being sold, but they are not carrying out surveillance of particular individuals and their intention is, through reactive policing, to identify and tackle offenders. Again this is part of the general duties of public authorities and the obtaining of private information is unlikely. A directed surveillance authorisation need not be sought.

> **Example 3:** Intelligence suggests that a local shopkeeper is openly selling alcohol to underage customers, without any questions being asked. A trained employee or person engaged by a public authority is deployed to act as a juvenile in order to make a purchase of alcohol. In these circumstances any relationship, if established at all, is likely to be so limited in regards to the requirements of the Act, that a public authority may conclude that a CHIS or a directed surveillance authorisation is unnecessary. However, if the test purchaser is wearing recording equipment but is not authorised as a CHIS, consideration should be given to granting a directed surveillance authorisation.

> **Example 4:** Surveillance officers intend to follow and observe Z covertly as part of a pre-planned operation to determine her suspected involvement in shoplifting. It is proposed to conduct covert surveillance of Z and record her activities as part of the investigation. In this case, private life considerations are likely to arise and the covert surveillance is pre-planned and not part of general observational duties or reactive policing. A directed surveillance authorisation should be sought.

NOT RELATING TO SPECIFIED GROUNDS OR CORE FUNCTIONS

2.25 An *authorisation* for directed or intrusive surveillance is only appropriate for the purposes of a specific investigation or operation, insofar as that investigation or operation relates to the grounds specified at section 28(3) of the 2000 Act. Covert surveillance for any other general purposes should be conducted under other legislation,if relevant, and an *authorisation* under Part II of the 2000 Act should not be sought.

2.26 The 'core functions' referred to by the Investigatory Powers Tribunal (*C v The Police and the Secretary of State for the Home Office –IPT/03/32/H dated 14 November 2006*) are the 'specific public functions', undertaken by a particular authority, in contrast to the 'ordinary functions' which are those undertaken by all authorities (e.g. employment issues, contractual arrangements etc). A *public authority* may only engage the 2000 Act when in performance of its 'core functions'. The disciplining of an employee is not a 'core function', although related criminal investigations may be. The protection of the 2000 Act may therefore be available in relation to associated criminal investigations so long as the activity is deemed to be necessary and proportionate.

> **Example:** A police officer is suspected by his employer of undertaking additional employment in breach of discipline regulations. The police force of which he is a member wishes to conduct covert surveillance of the officer outside the police work environment. Such activity, even if it is likely to result in the obtaining of private information, does not constitute directed surveillance for the purposes of the 2000 Act as it does not relate to the discharge of the police force's core functions. It relates instead to the carrying out of ordinary functions, such as employment, which are common to all public authorities. Activities of this nature are covered by the Data Protection Act 1998 and employment practices code.

> **Example 2:** A police officer claiming compensation for injuries allegedly sustained at work is suspected by his employer of fraudulently exaggerating the nature of those injuries. The police force of which he is a member wishes to conduct covert surveillance of the officer outside the work environment. Such activity may relate to the discharge of the police force's core functions as the police force may launch a criminal investigation. The proposed surveillance is likely to result in the obtaining of private information and, as the alleged misconduct amounts to the criminal offence of fraud, a directed surveillance authorisation may be appropriate.

CCTV AND ANPR (AUTOMATIC NUMBER PLATE RECOGNITION) CAMERAS

2.27 The use of overt CCTV cameras by *public authorities* does not normally require an *authorisation* under the 2000 Act. *Members* of the public will be aware that such systems are in use,[20] and their operation is covered by the Data Protection Act 1998 and the CCTV Code of Practice 2008, issued by the Information Commissioner's Office. Similarly, the overt use of ANPR systems to monitor traffic flows or detect motoring offences does not require an *authorisation* under the 2000 Act.

> **Example:** Overt surveillance equipment, such as town centre CCTV systems or ANPR, is used to gather information as part of a reactive operation (e.g. to identify individuals who have committed criminal damage after the event). Such use does not amount to covert surveillance as the equipment was overt and not subject to any covert targeting. Use in these circumstances would not require a directed surveillance authorisation.

---

[20] For example, by virtue of cameras or signage being clearly visible. See the CCTV Code of Practice 2008 for full guidance on establishing and operating overt CCTV systems.

2.28 However, where overt CCTV or ANPR cameras are used in a covert and pre-planned manner as part of a specific investigation or operation, for the surveillance of a specific person or group of people, a directed surveillance *authorisation* should be considered. Such covert surveillance is likely to result in the obtaining of *private information* about a person (namely, a record of their movements and activities) and therefore falls properly within the definition of directed surveillance. The use of the CCTV or ANPR system in these circumstances goes beyond their intended use for the general prevention or detection of crime and protection of the public.

> **Example:** A local police team receive information that an individual suspected of committing thefts from motor vehicles is known to be in a town centre area. A decision is taken to use the town centre CCTV system to conduct surveillance against that individual such that he remains unaware that there may be any specific interest in him. This targeted, covert use of the overt town centre CCTV system to monitor and/or record that individual's movements should be considered for authorisation as directed surveillance.

SPECIFIC SITUATIONS NOT REQUIRING DIRECTED SURVEILLANCE AUTHORISATION

2.29 The following specific activities also constitute neither directed nor intrusive surveillance:

- the use of a recording device by a covert human intelligence source in respect of whom an appropriate use or conduct *authorisation* has been granted permitting him to record any information obtained in his presence; [21]
- the recording, whether overt or covert, of an interview with a *member* of the public where it is made clear that the interview is entirely voluntary and that the interviewer is a *member* of a *public authority*. In such circumstances, whether the recording equipment is overt or covert, the *member* of the public knows that they are being interviewed by a *member* of a *public authority* and that information gleaned through the interview has passed into the possession of the *public authority* in question;
- the covert recording of suspected noise nuisance where the intention is only to record excessive noise levels from adjoining premises and the recording device is calibrated to record only excessive noise levels. In such circumstances the perpetrator would normally be regarded as having forfeited any claim to privacy and an *authorisation* may not be necessary;
- the use of apparatus outside any residential or other premises exclusively for the purpose of detecting the installation or use of a television receiver within those premises. The Regulation of Investigatory Powers (British Broadcasting Corporation) Order 2001 (SI No. 1057) permits the British Broadcasting Corporation to authorise the use of apparatus for this purpose under Part II of the 2000 Act, although such use constitutes neither directed nor intrusive surveillance; [22]
- entry on or interference with property or wireless telegraphy under section 5 of the 1994 Act or Part III of the 1997 Act (such activity may be conducted in support of surveillance, but is not in itself surveillance). [23]

---

[21] See section 48(3) of the 2000 Act.
[22] See section 26(6) of the 2000 Act.
[23] See section 48(3) of the 2000 Act.

Chapter 3

General rules on authorisations

OVERVIEW

3.1 An *authorisation* under Part II of the 2000 Act will, providing the statutory tests are met, provide a lawful basis for a *public authority* to carry out covert surveillance activity that is likely to result in the obtaining of *private information* about a person. Similarly, an *authorisation* under section 5 of the 1994 Act or Part III of the 1997 Act will provide lawful authority for *members* of the intelligence services, police, SOCA, SCDEA or HMRC to enter on, or interfere with, property or wireless telegraphy.

3.2 Responsibility for granting *authorisations* varies depending on the nature of the operation and the *public authority* involved. The relevant *public authorities* and *authorising officers* are detailed in the Regulation of Investigatory Powers (Directed Surveillance and Covert Human Intelligence Sources) Order 2010.

NECESSITY AND PROPORTIONALITY

3.3 The 2000 Act, 1997 Act and 1994 Act stipulate that the person granting an *authorisation* or *warrant* for directed or intrusive surveillance, or interference with property, must believe that the activities to be authorised are necessary on one or more statutory grounds.[24]

3.4 If the activities are deemed necessary on one of more of the statutory grounds, the person granting the *authorisation* or *warrant* must also believe that they are proportionate to what is sought to be achieved by carrying them out. This involves balancing the seriousness of the intrusion into the privacy of the subject of the operation (or any other person who may be affected) against the need for the activity in investigative and operational terms.

3.5 The *authorisation* will not be proportionate if it is excessive in the overall circumstances of the case. Each action authorised should bring an expected benefit to the investigation or operation and should not be disproportionate or arbitrary. The fact that a suspected offence may be serious will not alone render intrusive actions proportionate. Similarly, an offence may be so minor that any deployment of covert techniques would be disproportionate. No activity should be considered proportionate if the information which is sought could reasonably be obtained by other less intrusive means.

3.6 The following elements of proportionality should therefore be considered:

- balancing the size and scope of the proposed activity against the gravity and extent of the perceived crime or offence;
- explaining how and why the methods to be adopted will cause the least possible intrusion on the subject and others;

---

[24] These statutory grounds are laid out in sections 28(3) of the 2000 Act for directed surveillance; section 32(3) of the 2000 Act for intrusive surveillance; and section 93(2) of the 1997 Act and section 5 of the 1994 Act for property interference. They are detailed in Chapters 5, 6 and 7 for directed surveillance, intrusive surveillance and interference with property respectively.

- considering whether the activity is an appropriate use of the legislation and a reasonable way, having considered all reasonable alternatives, of obtaining the necessary result;
- evidencing, as far as reasonably practicable, what other methods had been considered and why they were not implemented.

3.7 It is important therefore that all those involved in undertaking directed or intrusive surveillance activities or interference with property under the 2000 Act, 1997 Act or 1994 Act are fully aware of the extent and limits of the *authorisation* or *warrant* in question.

Example 1: An individual is suspected of carrying out a series of criminal damage offences at a local shop, after a dispute with the owner. It is suggested that a period of directed surveillance should be conducted against him to record his movements and activities for the purposes of preventing or detecting crime. Although these are legitimate grounds on which directed surveillance may be conducted, it is unlikely that the resulting interference with privacy will be proportionate in the circumstances of the particular case. In particular, the obtaining of private information on the individual's daily routine is unlikely to be necessary or proportionate in order to investigate the activity of concern. Instead, other less intrusive means are likely to be available, such as overt observation of the location in question until such time as a crime may be committed.

Example 2: An individual is suspected of claiming a false address in order to abuse a school admission system operated by his local education authority. The local authority considers it necessary to investigate the individual for the purpose of preventing or detecting crime. Although these could be legitimate grounds for seeking a directed surveillance authorisation, if the individual's actions were capable of constituting a crime, such surveillance is unlikely to be necessary or proportionate to investigate the activity. Instead, it is likely that other less intrusive, and overt, means (such as unscheduled visits to the address in question) could be explored to obtain the required information.

Example 3: An individual is suspected of a relatively minor offence, such as littering, leaving waste out for collection a day early, or permitting dog-fouling in a public place without clearing up afterwards. It is suggested that covert surveillance should be conducted against her to record her movements and activities for the purposes of preventing or detecting crime, or preventing disorder. Although these could be legitimate grounds for seeking a directed surveillance authorisation, if the individual's actions were capable of constituting an offence or disorder, strong consideration should be given to the question of proportionality in the circumstances of this particular case and the nature of the surveillance to be conducted. In particular, the obtaining of private information on the individual's daily routine is unlikely to be necessary or proportionate in order to investigate the activity of concern. Instead, other less intrusive means are likely to be available, such as general observation of the location in question until such time as a crime may be committed. In addition, it is likely that such offences can be tackled using overt techniques.

COLLATERAL INTRUSION

3.8 Before authorising *applications* for directed or intrusive surveillance, the *authorising officer* should also take into account the risk of obtaining *private information* about persons who are not subjects of the surveillance or property interference activity (collateral intrusion).

3.9 Measures should be taken, wherever practicable, to avoid or minimise unnecessary intrusion into the privacy of those who are not the intended subjects of the surveillance activity. Where such collateral intrusion is unavoidable, the activities may still be authorised, provided this intrusion is considered proportionate to what is sought to be achieved. The same proportionality tests apply to the likelihood of collateral intrusion as to intrusion into the privacy of the intended subject of the surveillance.

3.10 All *applications* should therefore include an assessment of the risk of collateral intrusion and details of any measures taken to limit this, to enable the *authorising officer* fully to consider the proportionality of the proposed actions.

> **Example:** HMRC seeks to conduct directed surveillance against T on the grounds that this is necessary and proportionate for the collection of a tax. It is assessed that such surveillance will unavoidably result in the obtaining of some information about members of T's family, who are not the intended subjects of the surveillance. The authorising officer should consider the proportionality of this collateral intrusion, and whether sufficient measures are to be taken to limit it, when granting the authorisation. This may include not recording or retaining any material obtained through such collateral intrusion.

3.11 Where it is proposed to conduct surveillance activity or property interference specifically against individuals who are not suspected of direct or culpable involvement in the overall matter being investigated, interference with the privacy or property of such individuals should not be considered as collateral intrusion but rather as intended intrusion. Any such surveillance or property interference activity should be carefully considered against the necessity and proportionality criteria as described above (paragraphs 3.3-3.8).

> **Example:** A law enforcement agency seeks to conduct a covert surveillance operation to establish the whereabouts of N in the interests of preventing a serious crime. It is proposed to conduct directed surveillance against P, who is an associate of N but who is not assessed to be involved in the crime, in order to establish the location of N. In this situation, P will be the subject of the directed surveillance authorisation and the authorising officer should consider the necessity and proportionality of conducting directed surveillance against P, bearing in mind the availability of any other less intrusive means to identify N's whereabouts. It may be the case that directed surveillance of P will also result in obtaining information about P's family, which in this instance would represent collateral intrusion also to be considered by the authorising officer.

COMBINED AUTHORISATIONS

3.12 A single *authorisation* may combine:

- any number of *authorisations* under Part II of the 2000 Act;[25]
- an *authorisation* under Part II of the 2000 Act[26] and an *authorisation* under Part III of the 1997 Act;
- a *warrant* for intrusive surveillance under Part II of the 2000 Act;[27]
- and a *warrant* under section 5 of the 1994 Act.

3.13 For example, a single *authorisation* may combine *authorisations* for directed and intrusive surveillance. However, the provisions applicable for each of the *authorisations* must be considered separately by the appropriate *authorising officer*. Thus, a police superintendent could authorise the directed surveillance element but the intrusive surveillance element would need the separate *authorisation* of a chief constable and the approval of a Surveillance Commissioner, unless the case is urgent.

3.14 The above considerations do not preclude *public authorities* from obtaining separate *authorisations*

COLLABORATIVE WORKING

3.15 Any person granting or applying for an *authorisation* will also need to be aware of particular sensitivities in the local community where the surveillance is taking place and of any similar activities being undertaken by other *public authorities* which could impact on the employment of surveillance. It is therefore recommended that where an *authorising officer* from a *public authority* considers that conflicts might arise they should consult a senior *officer* within the police force area in which the investigation or operation is to take place.

3.16 In cases where one agency or force is acting on behalf of another, the tasking agency should normally obtain or provide the *authorisation* under Part II of the 2000 Act. For example, where surveillance is carried out by the police on behalf of HMRC, *authorisations* would usually be sought by HMRC and granted by the appropriate *authorising officer*. Where the operational support of other agencies (in this example, the police) is foreseen, this should be specified in the *authorisation*.

3.17 Where possible, *public authorities* should seek to avoid duplication of *authorisations* as part of a single investigation or operation. For example, where two agencies are conducting directed or intrusive surveillance as part of a joint operation, only one *authorisation* is required. Duplication of *authorisations* does not affect the lawfulness of the activities to be conducted, but may create an unnecessary administrative burden on authorities.

3.18 There are three further important considerations with regard to collaborative working:

3.19 SOCA and HMRC *applications* for directed or intrusive surveillance and property interference, and OFT *applications* for intrusive surveillance, must only be made by

---

[25] See section 43(2) of the 2000 Act.
[26] On the *application* of a *member* of a police force, SOCA, a customs *officer* or an *officer* of the OFT. See section 33(5) of the 2000 Act.
[27] On the *application* of a *member* of the intelligence services. See section 42(2) of the 2000 Act.

a *member* or *officer* of the same force or agency as the *authorising officer*, regardless of which force or agency is to conduct the activity.

3.20 Police *applications* for directed or intrusive surveillance and property interference must only be made by a *member* or *officer* of the same force as the *authorising officer*, unless the Chief *Officers* of the forces in question have made a collaboration agreement under either section 23 of the Police Act 1996, in the case of English and Welsh forces, or section 12 of the Police (Scotland) Act 1967, in the case of Scottish forces, and the collaboration agreement permits applicants and *authorising officers* to be from different forces.

3.21 *Authorisations* for intrusive surveillance relating to residential premises, and *authorisations* for property interference, may only authorise conduct where the premises or property in question are in the area of operation of the force or agency applying for the *authorisation*. This requirement does not apply where the Chief *Officers* of two or more police forces have made a collaboration agreement under either section 23 of the Police Act 1996, in the case of English and Welsh forces, or section 12 of the Police (Scotland) Act 1967, in the case of Scottish forces, and the collaboration agreement permits *authorising officers* to authorise conduct in relation to premises or property in the force areas of forces other than their own which are party to the agreement.

REVIEWING AUTHORISATIONS

3.22 Regular reviews of all *authorisations* should be undertaken to assess the need for the surveillance or property interference activity to continue. The results of a review should be retained for at least three years (see Chapter 8). Particular attention is drawn to the need to review *authorisations* frequently where the surveillance or property interference involves a high level of intrusion into private life or significant collateral intrusion, or *confidential information* is likely to be obtained.

3.23 In each case the frequency of reviews should be considered at the outset by the *authorising officer* or, for those subject to *authorisation* by the *Secretary of State*, the *member* or *officer* who made the *application* within the *public authority* concerned. This should be as frequently as is considered necessary and practicable.

3.24 In some cases it may be appropriate for an *authorising officer* to delegate the responsibility for conducting any reviews to a subordinate *officer*. The *authorising officer* is, however, usually best placed to assess whether the *authorisation* should continue or whether the criteria on which he based the original decision to grant an *authorisation* have changed sufficiently to cause the *authorisation* to be revoked. Support staff can do the necessary research and prepare the review process but the actual review is the responsibility of the original *authorising officer* and should, as a matter of good practice, be conducted by them or, failing that, by an *officer* who would be entitled to grant a new *authorisation* in the same terms.

3.25 Any proposed or unforeseen changes to the *nature* or extent of the surveillance operation that may result in the further or greater intrusion into the private life of any person should also be brought to the attention of the *authorising officer* by means of a review. The *authorising officer* should consider whether the proposed changes are proportionate (bearing in mind any extra intended intrusion into privacy or collateral intrusion), before approving or rejecting them. Any such changes must be highlighted at the next renewal if the *authorisation* is to be renewed.

3.26 Where a directed or intrusive surveillance *authorisation* provides for the surveillance of unidentified individuals whose identity is later established, the terms of the *authorisation* should be refined at a review to include the identity of these individuals. It would be appropriate to convene such a review specifically for this purpose. This process will not require a fresh *authorisation*, providing the scope of the original *authorisation* envisaged surveillance of such individuals. Such changes must be highlighted at the next renewal if the *authorisation* is to be renewed.

> **Example:** A directed surveillance authorisation is obtained by the police to authorise surveillance of "X and his associates" for the purposes of investigating their suspected involvement in a crime. X is seen meeting with A in a cafe and it is assessed that subsequent surveillance of A will assist the investigation. Surveillance of A may continue (he is an associate of X) but the directed surveillance authorisation should be amended at a review to include "X and his associates, including A".

GENERAL BEST PRACTICES

3.27 The following guidelines should be considered as best working practices by all *public authorities* with regard to all *applications* for *authorisations* covered by this code:

- *applications* should avoid any repetition of information;
- information contained in *applications* should be limited to that required by the relevant legislation;[28]
- where *authorisations* are granted orally under urgency procedures (see Chapters 5, 6 and 7 on *authorisation* procedures), a record detailing the actions authorised and the reasons why the urgency procedures were used should be recorded by the *applicant* and *authorising officer* as a priority. There is then no requirement subsequently to submit a full written *application*;
- an *application* should not require the sanction of any person in a *public authority* other than the *authorising officer*;
- where it is foreseen that other agencies will be involved in carrying out the surveillance, these agencies should be detailed in the *application*;
- *authorisations* should not generally be sought for activities already authorised following an *application* by the same or a different *public authority*.

3.28 Furthermore, it is considered good practice that within every relevant *public authority*, a senior responsible *officer* [29] should be responsible for:

- the integrity of the process in place within the *public authority* to authorise directed and intrusive surveillance and interference with property or wireless telegraphy;
- compliance with Part II of the 2000 Act, Part III of the 1997 Act and with this code;
- engagement with the Commissioners and inspectors when they conduct their inspections; and
- where necessary, overseeing the implementation of any post-inspection action plans recommended or approved by a Commissioner.

---

[28] As laid out in Chapters 5, 6 and 7 of this code.

[29] The senior responsible *officer* should be a person holding the office, rank or position of an *authorising officer* within the relevant *public authority*.

3.29 Within local authorities, the senior responsible officer should be a member of the corporate leadership team and should be responsible for ensuring that all *authorising officers* are of an appropriate standard in light of any recommendations in the inspection reports prepared by the Office of Surveillance Commissioners. Where an inspection report highlights concerns about the standards of *authorising officers*, this individual will be responsible for ensuring the concerns are addressed.

3.30 In addition, elected *members* of a local authority should review the authority's use of the 2000 Act and set the policy at least once a year. They should also consider internal reports on use of the 2000 Act on at least a quarterly basis to ensure that it is being used consistently with the local authority's policy and that the policy remains fit for purpose. They should not, however, be involved in making decisions on specific *authorisations*.

Chapter 4

Legally privileged and confidential information

Overview

4.1 The 2000 Act does not provide any special protection for '*confidential information*', although the 1997 Act makes special provision for certain categories of *confidential information*. Nevertheless, particular care should be taken in cases where the subject of the investigation or operation might reasonably expect a high degree of privacy, or where *confidential information* is involved. *Confidential information* consists of communications subject to *legal privilege*, communications between a *Member* of Parliament and another person on constituency matters, confidential personal information, or confidential journalistic material. So, for example, extra care should be taken where, through the use of surveillance, it is likely that knowledge will be acquired of communications between a minister of religion and an individual relating to the latter's spiritual welfare, or between a *Member* of Parliament and a constituent relating to constituency matters, or wherever matters of medical or journalistic confidentiality or *legal privilege* may be involved. References to a *Member* of Parliament include references to *Members* of both Houses of the UK Parliament, the European Parliament, the Scottish Parliament, the Welsh Assembly and the Northern Ireland Assembly.

4.2 *Authorisations* under the 1997 Act likely to result in the acquisition of knowledge of matters subject to *legal privilege*, confidential personal information or confidential journalistic material require (other than in urgent cases) the approval of a Surveillance Commissioner.

4.3 *Authorisations* for directed surveillance of legal consultations falling within the 2010 Order must comply with the enhanced *authorisation* regime described below. In cases where it is likely that knowledge of *confidential information* will be acquired, the use of covert surveillance is subject to a higher level of *authorisation* e.g. a Chief *Officer*. Annex A lists the *authorising officer* for each *public authority* permitted to authorise such surveillance.

4.4 Covert surveillance likely or intended to result in the acquisition of knowledge of matters subject to *legal privilege* may take place in circumstances covered by the 2010 Order, or in other circumstances. Similarly, property interference may be necessary in order to effect surveillance described in the 2010 Order, or in other circumstances where knowledge of matters subject to *legal privilege* is likely to be obtained.

4.5 The 2010 Order provides that directed surveillance that is carried out in relation to anything taking place on so much of any premises specified in article 3(2) of the Order as is, at any time during the surveillance, used for the purposes of 'legal consultations' shall be treated for the purposes of Part II of the 2000 Act as intrusive surveillance.

4.6 The 2010 Order defines 'legal consultation' for these purposes. It means:

(a) a consultation between a professional legal adviser and his client or any person representing his client, or
(b) a consultation between a professional legal adviser or his client or any such representative and a medical practitioner made in connection with or in contemplation of legal proceedings and for the purposes of such proceedings.

4.7 The definition of 'legal consultation' in the 2010 Order does not distinguish between legal consultations which are legally privileged, wholly or in part, and legal consultations which may be in furtherance of a criminal purpose are therefore not protected by *legal privilege*. Covert surveillance of all legal consultations covered by the 2010 Order (whether protected by *legal privilege* or not) is to be treated as intrusive surveillance.

4.8 *'Legal privilege'* is defined in section 98 of the 1997 Act. This definition should be used to determine how to handle material obtained through surveillance authorised under RIPA, including through surveillance which is treated as intrusive surveillance as a result of the 2010 Order. As discussed below, special safeguards apply to matters subject to *legal privilege*.

4.9 Under the definition in the 1997 Act, *legal privilege* does not apply to communications or items held, or oral communications made, with the intention of furthering a criminal purpose (whether the lawyer is acting unwittingly or culpably). Legally privileged communications or items will lose their protection for these other purposes if the professional legal adviser intends to hold or use them for a criminal purpose. But privilege is not lost if a professional legal adviser is properly advising a person who is suspected of having committed a criminal offence.

TESTS TO BE APPLIED WHEN AUTHORISING OR APPROVING COVERT SURVEILLANCE OR PROPERTY INTERFERENCE LIKELY OR INTENDED TO RESULT IN THE ACQUISITION OF KNOWLEDGE OF MATTERS SUBJECT TO LEGAL PRIVILEGE

4.10 All *applications* for covert surveillance or property interference that may result in the acquisition of knowledge of matters subject to *legal privilege* should state whether the covert surveillance or property interference is intended to obtain knowledge of matters subject to *legal privilege* as defined by section 98 of the 1997 Act.

4.11 If the covert surveillance or property interference is not intended to result in the acquisition of knowledge of matters subject to *legal privilege*, but it is likely that such knowledge will nevertheless be acquired during the operation, the *application* should identify all steps which will be taken to mitigate the risk of acquiring it. If the risk cannot be removed entirely, the *application* should explain what steps will be taken to ensure that any knowledge of matters subject to *legal privilege* which is obtained is not used in law enforcement investigations or criminal prosecutions.

4.12 Where covert surveillance or property interference is likely or intended to result in the acquisition of knowledge of matters subject to *legal privilege*, an *authorisation* shall only be granted or approved if the *authorising officer*, *Secretary of State* or approving Surveillance Commissioner, as appropriate, is satisfied that there are exceptional and compelling circumstances that make the *authorisation* necessary:

- Where the surveillance or property interference is not intended to result in the acquisition of knowledge of matters subject to *legal privilege*, such exceptional and compelling circumstances may arise in the interests of national security or the economic well-being of the UK, or for the purpose of preventing or detecting serious crime;
- Where the surveillance or property interference is intended to result in the acquisition of knowledge of matters subject to *legal privilege*, such circumstances will arise only in a very restricted range of cases, such as where there is a threat to life or limb, or to national security, and the surveillance or property interference is reasonably regarded as likely to yield intelligence necessary to counter the threat.

4.13 Further, in considering any *authorisation* for covert surveillance or property interference likely or intended to result in the acquisition of knowledge of matters subject to *legal privilege*, the *authorising officer*, *Secretary of State* or approving Surveillance Commissioner, as appropriate, must be satisfied that the proposed covert surveillance or property interference is proportionate to what is sought to be achieved. In relation to intrusive surveillance, including surveillance to be treated as intrusive as a result of the 2010 Order, section 32(4) will apply.

4.14 Directed surveillance likely to result in the acquisition of knowledge of matters subject to *legal privilege* may be authorised only by *authorising officers* entitled to grant *authorisations* in respect of *confidential information*. Intrusive surveillance, including surveillance which is treated as intrusive by virtue of the 2010 Order, or property interference likely to result in the acquisition of material subject to *legal privilege* may only be authorised by *authorising officers* entitled to grant intrusive surveillance or property interference *authorisations*.

4.15 Property interference likely to result in the acquisition of such material is subject to prior approval by a Surveillance Commissioner (unless the *Secretary of State* is the relevant *authorising officer* or the case is urgent). Intrusive surveillance, including surveillance which is treated as intrusive by virtue of the 2010 Order, is subject to prior approval by a Surveillance Commissioner (unless the *Secretary of State* is the relevant *authorising officer* or the case is urgent).

SURVEILLANCE UNDER THE 2010 ORDER

4.16 As noted above, the 2010 Order provides that directed surveillance that is carried out in relation to anything taking place on so much of any premises specified in article 3(2) of the Order as is, at any time during the surveillance, used for the purposes of 'legal consultations' shall be treated for the purposes of Part II of the 2000 Act as intrusive surveillance.

4.17 As a result of the 2010 Order, such surveillance cannot be undertaken without the prior approval of a Surveillance Commissioner (with the exception of urgent *authorisations* or *authorisations* granted by the *Secretary of State*).

4.18 The locations specified in the Order are:

(a) any place in which persons who are serving sentences of imprisonment or detention, remanded in custody or committed in custody for trial or sentence may be detained;

(b) any place in which persons may be detained under paragraph 16(1), (1A) or (2) of Schedule 2 or paragraph 2(2) or (3) of Schedule 3 to the Immigration Act 1971 or section 36(1) of the UK Border Act 2007;

(c) any place in which persons may be detained under Part VI of the Criminal Procedure (Scotland) Act 1995, the Mental Health (Care and Treatment) (Scotland) Act 2003 or the Mental Health Act 1983;

(d) police stations;

(e) the place of business of any professional legal adviser;

(f) any place used for the sittings and business of any court, tribunal, inquest or inquiry.

4.19 With the exception of urgent *applications* and *authorisations* granted by the *Secretary of State*, *authorisations* for surveillance which is to be treated as intrusive surveillance as a result of the 2010 Order shall not take effect until such time as:

(a) the *authorisation* has been approved by a Surveillance Commissioner; and

(b) written notice of the Commissioner's decision to approve the *authorisation* has been given to the *authorising officer*.

4.20 If an *authorisation* is to be granted by the *Secretary of State*, the provisions in Chapter 6 apply.

PROPERTY INTERFERENCE UNDER THE 1997 ACT LIKELY TO RESULT IN THE
ACQUISITION OF KNOWLEDGE OF MATTERS SUBJECT TO LEGAL PRIVILEGE

4.21 With the exception of urgent *authorisations*, where it is believed that the action authorised is likely to result in the acquisition of knowledge of matters subject to *legal privilege* an *authorisation* under the 1997 Act shall not take effect until such time as:

(a) the *authorisation* has been approved by a Surveillance Commissioner; and

(b) written notice of the Commissioner's decision to approve the *authorisation* has been given to the *authorising officer*.

THE USE AND HANDLING OF MATTERS SUBJECT TO LEGAL PRIVILEGE

4.22 Matters subject to legal privilege are particularly sensitive and surveillance which acquires such material may give rise to issues under Article 6 of the ECHR (right to a fair trial) as well as engaging Article 8.

4.23 Where public authorities deliberately acquire knowledge of matters subject to *legal privilege*, they may use that knowledge to counter the threat which led them to acquire it, but it will not be admissible in court. Public authorities should ensure that knowledge of matters subject to *legal privilege*, whether or not it is acquired deliberately, is kept separate from law enforcement investigations or criminal prosecutions.

4.24 In cases likely to result in the acquisition of knowledge of matters subject to *legal privilege*, the *authorising officer* or Surveillance Commissioner may require regular reporting so as to be able to decide whether the *authorisation* should continue. In those cases where legally privileged material has been acquired and retained, the matter should be reported to the *authorising officer* by means of a review and to the relevant Commissioner or Inspector during his next inspection (at which the material should be made available if requested).

4.25 A substantial proportion of the communications between a lawyer and his client(s) may be subject to *legal privilege*. Therefore, in any case where a lawyer is the subject of an investigation or operation, *authorising officers* should consider whether the special safeguards outlined in this chapter apply. Any material which has been retained from any such investigation or operation should be notified to the relevant Commissioner or Inspector during his next inspection and made available on request.

4.26 Where there is any doubt as to the handling and dissemination of knowledge of matters which may be subject to *legal privilege*, advice should be sought from a legal adviser within the relevant *public authority* before any further dissemination of the information takes place. Similar advice should also be sought where there is doubt over whether information is not subject to *legal privilege* due to the "in furtherance of a criminal purpose" exception. The retention of legally privileged material, or its dissemination to an outside body, should be accompanied by a clear warning that it is subject to *legal privilege*. It should be safeguarded by taking reasonable steps to ensure there is no possibility of it becoming available, or its contents becoming known, to any person whose possession of it might prejudice any criminal or civil proceedings to which the information relates. Any dissemination of legally privileged material to an outside body should be notified to the relevant Commissioner or Inspector during his next inspection.

CONFIDENTIAL INFORMATION

4.27 Special consideration must also be given to *authorisations* that involve confidential personal information, confidential constituent information and confidential journalistic material. Where such material has been acquired and retained, the matter should be reported to the relevant Commissioner or Inspector during his next inspection and the material be made available to him if requested.

4.28 Confidential personal information is information held in confidence relating to the physical or mental health or spiritual counselling of a person (whether living or dead) who can be identified from it.[30] Such information, which can include both oral and written communications, is held in confidence if it is held subject to an express or implied undertaking to hold it in confidence or it is subject to a restriction on disclosure or an obligation of confidentiality contained in existing legislation. Examples

---

[30] **Spiritual counselling** means conversations between a person and a religious authority acting in an official capacity, where the individual being counselled is seeking or the religious authority is imparting forgiveness, absolution or the resolution of conscience in accordance with their faith.

include consultations between a health professional and a patient, or information from a patient's medical records.

4.29 Confidential constituent information is information relating to communications between a *Member* of Parliament and a constituent in respect of constituency matters. Again, such information is held in confidence if it is held subject to an express or implied undertaking to hold it in confidence or it is subject to a restriction on disclosure or an obligation of confidentiality contained in existing legislation.

4.30 Confidential journalistic material includes material acquired or created for the purposes of journalism and held subject to an undertaking to hold it in confidence, as well as communications resulting in information being acquired for the purposes of journalism and held subject to such an undertaking.

4.31 Where there is any doubt as to the handling and dissemination of *confidential information*, advice should be sought from a legal adviser within the relevant *public authority* before any further dissemination of the material takes place.

Chapter 5

Authorisation procedures for directed surveillance

AUTHORISATION CRITERIA

5.1 Under section 28(3) of the 2000 Act an *authorisation* for directed surveillance may be granted by an *authorising officer* where he believes that the *authorisation* is necessary in the circumstances of the particular case on the grounds that it is:

(a) in the interests of national security;[31,32]
(b) for the purpose of preventing or detecting[33] crime or of preventing disorder;
(c) in the interests of the economic well-being of the UK;
(d) in the interests of public safety;
(e) for the purpose of protecting public health;[34]
(f) for the purpose of assessing or collecting any tax, duty, levy or other imposition, contribution or charge payable to a government department;[35] or

---

[31] One of the functions of the Security Service is the protection of national security and in particular the protection against threats from terrorism. An *authorising officer* in another *public authority* shall not issue a directed surveillance *authorisation* under Part II of the 2000 Act where the investigation or operation falls within the responsibilities of the Security Service, as set out above, except where the investigation or operation is to be carried out by a Special Branch or other police unit with formal counter-terrorism responsibilities (such as Counter Terrorism Units, Counter Terrorism Intelligence Units and Counter Terrorism Command) or where the Security Service has agreed that another *public authority* can carry out a directed surveillance investigation or operation which would fall within the responsibilities of the Security Service.

[32] HM Forces may also undertake operations in connection with a military threat to national security and other operations in connection with national security in support of the Security Service, the Police Service of Northern Ireland or other Civil Powers.

[33] Detecting crime is defined in section 81(5) of the 2000 Act and is applied to the 1997 Act by section 134 of that Act (as amended). Preventing or detecting crime goes beyond the prosecution of offenders and includes actions taken to avert, end or disrupt the commission of criminal offences.

[34] This could include investigations into infectious diseases, contaminated products or the illicit sale of pharmaceuticals.

[35] This could only be for a purpose which satisfies the criteria set out in Article 8(2) of the ECHR.

(g) for any other purpose prescribed by an order made by the *Secretary of State*.[36]

5.2 The *authorising officer* must also believe that the surveillance is proportionate to what it seeks to achieve (see 3.3–3.12).

RELEVANT PUBLIC AUTHORITIES

5.3 The *public authorities* entitled to authorise directed surveillance (including to acquire *confidential information*, with specified higher *authorisation*), are listed in Schedule 1 to the 2000 Act. The specific purposes for which each *public authority* may obtain a directed surveillance *authorisation* are laid out in the Regulation of Investigatory Powers (Directed Surveillance and Covert Human Intelligence Sources) Order 2010.

AUTHORISATION PROCEDURES

5.4 Responsibility for authorising the carrying out of directed surveillance rests with the *authorising officer* and requires the personal authority of the *authorising officer*. The Regulation of Investigatory Powers (Directed Surveillance and Covert Human Intelligence Sources) Order 2010 designates the *authorising officer* for each different *public authority* and the *officer*s entitled to act in urgent cases. Where an *authorisation* for directed surveillance is combined with a *Secretary of State authorisation* for intrusive surveillance, the combined *authorisation* must be issued by the *Secretary of State*.

5.5 An *authorising officer* must give *authorisations* in writing, except that in urgent cases they may be given orally by the *authorising officer* or in writing by the *officer* entitled to act in urgent cases. In such cases, a record that the *authorising officer* has expressly authorised the action should be recorded in writing by both the *authorising officer* and the applicant as soon as is reasonably practicable, together with the information detailed below.

5.6 A case is not normally to be regarded as urgent unless the time that would elapse before the *authorising officer* was available to grant the *authorisation* would, in the judgement of the person giving the *authorisation*, be likely to endanger life or jeopardise the investigation or operation for which the *authorisation* was being given. An *authorisation* is not to be regarded as urgent where the need for an *authorisation* has been neglected or the urgency is of the *authorising officer's* or a*pplicant's* own making.

5.7 *Authorising officers* should not normally be responsible for authorising operations in which they are directly involved, although it is recognised that this may sometimes be unavoidable, especially in the case of small organisations, or where it is necessary to act urgently or for security reasons. Where an *authorising officer* authorises such an investigation or operation the centrally retrievable record of *authorisations* (see Chapter 8) should highlight this and the attention of a Commissioner or Inspector should be invited to it during his next inspection.

INFORMATION TO BE PROVIDED IN APPLICATIONS FOR AUTHORISATION

5.8 A written *application* for a directed surveillance *authorisation* should describe any conduct to be authorised and the purpose of the investigation or operation. The *application* should also include:

---

[36] This could only be for a purpose which satisfies the criteria set out in Article 8(2) of the ECHR.

- the reasons why the *authorisation* is necessary in the particular case and on the grounds (e.g. for the purpose of preventing or detecting crime) listed in Section 28(3) of the 2000 Act;
- the nature of the surveillance;
- the identities, where known, of those to be the subject of the surveillance;
- a summary of the intelligence case and appropriate unique intelligence references where applicable;
- an explanation of the information which it is desired to obtain as a result of the surveillance;
- the details of any potential collateral intrusion and why the intrusion is justified;
- the details of any *confidential information* that is likely to be obtained as a consequence of the surveillance;
- the reasons why the surveillance is considered proportionate to what it seeks to achieve;
- the level of authority required (or recommended where that is different) for the surveillance; and,
- a subsequent record of whether *authorisation* was given or refused, by whom, and the time and date this happened.

5.9 In urgent cases, the above information may be supplied orally. In such cases the *authorising officer* and applicant, where applicable, should also record the following information in writing, as soon as is reasonably practicable (it is not necessary to record further detail):

- the identities of those subject to surveillance;
- the nature of the surveillance as defined at 1.9;
- the reasons why the *authorising officer* considered the case so urgent that an oral instead of a written *authorisation* was given; and,
- where the *officer* entitled to act in urgent cases has given written authority, the reasons why it was not reasonably practicable for the *application* to be considered by the *authorising officer* should also be recorded.

Duration of authorisations

5.10 A written *authorisation* granted by an *authorising officer* will cease to have *effect* (unless renewed or cancelled) *at the end of a period* of three months beginning with the time at which it took effect.

5.11 Urgent oral *authorisations* or written *authorisations* granted by a person who is entitled to act only in urgent cases will, unless renewed, cease to have effect after seventy-two hours, beginning with the time when the *authorisation* was granted.

Renewals

5.12 If, at any time before an *authorisation* for directed surveillance granted by a *member* of the intelligence services would cease to have effect, a *member* of the intelligence services who is entitled to grant such *authorisations* considers that it is necessary for the *authorisation* to continue on the grounds of national security or in the interests of the economic well-being of the UK, he may renew it for a further period of six months, beginning with the day on which it would have ceased to have effect but for the renewal.

227

5.13 If, at any time before any other directed surveillance *authorisation* would cease to have effect, the *authorising officer* considers it necessary for the *authorisation* to continue for the purpose for which it was given, he may renew it in writing for a further period of three months. Renewals may also be granted orally in urgent cases and last for a period of seventy-two hours. The renewal will take effect at the time at which the *authorisation* would have ceased to have effect but for the renewal.

5.14 An *application* for renewal should not be made until shortly before the *authorisation* period is drawing to an end. Any person who would be entitled to grant a new *authorisation* can renew an *authorisation*.

5.15 All *applications* for the renewal of a directed surveillance *authorisation* should record (at the time of *application*, or when reasonably practicable in the case of urgent cases approved orally):

- whether this is the first renewal or every occasion on which the *authorisation* has been renewed previously;
- any significant changes to the information in the initial *application*;
- the reasons why the *authorisation* for directed surveillance should continue;
- the content and value to the investigation or operation of the information so far obtained by the surveillance;
- the results of regular reviews of the investigation or operation.

5.16 *Authorisations* may be renewed more than once, if necessary and provided they continue to meet the criteria for *authorisation*. The details of any renewal should be centrally recorded (see Chapter 8).

CANCELLATIONS

5.17 During a review, the *authorising officer* who granted or last renewed the *authorisation* may amend specific aspects of the *authorisation*, for example, to cease surveillance against one of a number of named subjects or to discontinue the use of a particular tactic. They must cancel the *authorisation* if satisfied that the directed surveillance as a whole no longer meets the criteria upon which it was authorised. Where the original *authorising officer* is no longer available, this duty will fall on the person who has taken over the role of *authorising officer* or the person who is acting as *authorising officer* (see the Regulation of Investigatory Powers (Directed Surveillance and Covert Human Intelligence Sources) Order 2010).

5.18 As soon as the decision is taken that directed surveillance should be discontinued, the instruction must be given to those involved to stop all surveillance of the subject(s). The date the *authorisation* was cancelled should be centrally recorded and documentation of any instruction to cease surveillance should be retained (see Chapter 8). There is no requirement for any further details to be recorded when cancelling a directed surveillance *authorisation*. However effective practice suggests that a record should be retained detailing the product obtained from the surveillance and whether or not objectives were achieved.

FOREIGN SURVEILLANCE TEAMS OPERATING IN UK

5.19 The provisions of section 76A of the 2000 Act as inserted by the Crime (International Co-Operation) Act 2003 provide for foreign surveillance teams to operate in the UK, subject to the following procedures and conditions.

5.20 Where a foreign police or customs *officer*,[37] who is conducting directed or intrusive surveillance activity outside the UK,[38] needs to enter the UK for the purposes of continuing that surveillance, and where it is not reasonably practicable for a UK *officer*[39] to carry out the surveillance under the *authorisation* of Part II of the 2000 Act (or of RIP(S)A), the foreign *officer* must notify a person designated by the Director General of SOCA immediately after entry to the UK and shall request (if this has not been done already) that an *application* for a directed surveillance *authorisation* be made under Part II of the 2000 Act (or RIP(S)A 2000).

5.21 The foreign *officer* may then continue to conduct surveillance for a period of five hours beginning with the time when the *officer* enters the UK. The foreign *officer* may only carry out the surveillance, however, in places to which *members* of the public have or are permitted to have access, whether on payment or otherwise. The directed surveillance *authorisation*, if obtained, will then authorise the foreign *officers* to conduct such surveillance beyond the five hour period in accordance with the general provisions of the 2000 Act.

Chapter 6

Authorisation procedure for intrusive surveillance

GENERAL AUTHORISATION CRITERIA

6.1 An *authorisation* for intrusive surveillance may be granted by the *Secretary of State* – for *applications* by the intelligence services, the Ministry of Defence or HM Forces[40] – or by a *senior authorising officer* or designated deputy of the police, SOCA, HMRC or OFT, as listed in sections 32(6) and 34(6) of the 2000 Act.

6.2 In many cases, an investigation or operation using covert techniques may involve both intrusive surveillance and entry on, or interference with, property or with wireless telegraphy. In such cases, both activities may need *authorisation*. This can be done as a combined *authorisation* (see above, on combined *authorisations*).

6.3 Under section 32(2), (3) and (3A) of the 2000 Act the *Secretary of State* or the *senior authorising officer* or designated deputy may only authorise intrusive surveillance if they believe:

(a) that the *authorisation* is necessary in the circumstances of the particular case on the grounds that it is:
- in the interests of national security;[41]

---

[37] As defined in section 76(A)(10) of the 2000 Act.

[38] With the lawful authority of the country or territory in which it is being carried out and in respect of a suspected crime which falls within Article 40(7) of the Schengen Convention or which is a crime for the purposes of any other international agreement to which the UK is a party and which is specified for the purposes of section 76(A) of the 2000 Act in an order made by the *Secretary of State* with the consent of Scottish Ministers.

[39] Being a *member* of a police force, SOCA, HMRC or a police *member* of the Scottish Crime and Drug Enforcement Agency appointed in accordance with paragraph 7 of schedule 2 to the Police, Public Order and Criminal Justice (Scotland) Act 2006 (asp 10).

[40] Or any other *public authority* designated for this purpose under section 41(1) of the 2000 Act.

[41] A *senior authorising officer* or designated deputy of a law enforcement agency shall not issue an *authorisation* for intrusive surveillance where the investigation or operation is within the responsibilities

- for the purpose of preventing or detecting serious crime;[42]
- in the interests of the economic well-being of the UK; or
- (in the case of the OFT) for the purpose of preventing or detecting an offence under section 188 of the Enterprise Act 2002 (cartel offence); and

(b) that the surveillance is proportionate to what is sought to be achieved by carrying it out.

6.4 When deciding whether an *authorisation* is necessary and proportionate, it is important to consider whether the information which it is thought necessary to obtain by means of the intrusive surveillance could reasonably be obtained by other less intrusive means.

Authorisation procedures for the police, SOCA, HMRC and OFT – senior authorising officers and designated deputies

6.5 The *senior authorising officers* for these bodies are listed in section 32(6) of the 2000 Act. If the *senior authorising officer* is absent[43] then, under section 34(2) of the 2000 Act, an *authorisation* can be given by the designated deputy as provided for in section 12A of the Police Act 1996, section 5A of the Police (Scotland) Act 1967 and section 25 of the City of London Police Act 1839.

Urgent cases

6.6 The *senior authorising officer* or designated deputy should generally give *authorisations* in writing. However, in urgent cases, oral *authorisations* may be given by the *senior authorising officer* or designated deputy. In an urgent oral case, a statement that the *senior authorising officer* or designated deputy has expressly authorised the conduct should be recorded in writing by the applicant as soon as is reasonably practicable, together with the information detailed below.

6.7 In an urgent case, where it is not reasonably practicable having regard to the urgency of the case for either the *senior authorising officer* or the designated deputy to consider the *application*, an *authorisation* may be granted in writing by a person entitled to act only in urgent cases under section 34(4) of the 2000 Act.[44]

---

of one of the intelligence services and properly falls to be authorised by *warrant* issued by the *Secretary of State* under Part II of the 2000 Act or the 1994 Act.

[42] Serious crime is defined in section 81(2) and (3) as crime that comprises an offence for which a person who has attained the age of twenty-one and has no previous convictions could reasonably be expected to be sentenced to imprisonment for a term of three years or more, or which involves the use of violence, results in substantial financial gain or is conduct by a large number of persons in pursuit of a common purpose.

[43] The consideration of an authorisation by the senior authorising officer is only to be regarded as not reasonably practicable (within the meaning of section 34(2) of the 2000 Act) if he is on annual leave, is absent from his office and his home, or is for some reason not able within a reasonable time to obtain access to a secure telephone or fax machine. Pressure of work is not normally to be regarded as rendering it impracticable for a senior authorising officer to consider an application. Where a designated deputy gives an authorisation this should be made clear and the reason for the absence of the senior authorising officer given.

[44] Note that ACPO out-of-hours *officers* of assistant chief constable rank or above will be entitled to act for this purpose.

6.8 A case is not normally to be regarded as urgent unless the time that would elapse before the *authorising officer* was available to grant the *authorisation* would, in the judgement of the person giving the *authorisation*, be likely to endanger life or jeopardise the investigation or operation for which the *authorisation* was being given. An *authorisation* is not to be regarded as urgent where the need for an *authorisation* has been neglected or the urgency is of the *authorising officer's* or *applicant's* own making.

JURISDICTIONAL CONSIDERATIONS

6.9 A police or SOCA *authorisation* cannot be granted unless the *application* is made by a *member* of the same force or agency, unless, in the case of the police, a relevant collaboration agreement has been made (see above, on collaborative working). An HMRC or OFT *authorisation* cannot be granted unless the *application* is made by an *officer* of Revenue and Customs or OFT respectively.

6.10 Where the surveillance is carried out in relation to any residential premises, the *authorisation* cannot be granted unless the residential premises are in the same area of operation of the force or organisation, unless, in the case of the police, a relevant collaboration agreement has been made (see above, on collaborative working).

APPROVAL OF SURVEILLANCE COMMISSIONERS

6.11 Except in urgent cases a police, SOCA, HMRC or OFT *authorisation* granted for intrusive surveillance will not take effect until it has been approved by a Surveillance Commissioner and written notice of the Commissioner's decision has been given to the person who granted the *authorisation*. This means that the approval will not take effect until the notice has been received in the office of the person who granted the *authorisation* within the relevant force or organisation.

6.12 When the *authorisation* is urgent it will take effect from the time it is granted provided notice is given to the Surveillance Commissioner in accordance with section 35(3)(b) (see section 36(3) of the 2000 Act).

6.13 There may be cases that become urgent after approval has been sought but before a response has been received from a Surveillance Commissioner. In such a case, the *authorising officer* should notify the Surveillance Commissioner that the case is now urgent (pointing out that it has become urgent since the notification). In these cases, the *authorisation* will take effect immediately.

NOTIFICATIONS TO SURVEILLANCE COMMISSIONERS

6.14 Where a person grants, renews or cancels an *authorisation* for intrusive surveillance, he must, as soon as is reasonably practicable, give notice in writing to a Surveillance Commissioner, where relevant, in accordance with whatever arrangements have been made by the Chief Surveillance Commissioner.[45]

6.15 In urgent cases, the notification must specify the grounds on which the case is believed to be one of urgency. The urgency provisions should not be used routinely.

---

[45] The information to be included in the notification to the Surveillance Commissioner is set out in the Regulation of Investigatory Powers (Notification of *Authorisations* etc.) Order 2000; SI No: 2563.

If the Surveillance Commissioner is satisfied that there were no grounds for believing the case to be one of urgency, he has the power to quash the *authorisation*.

AUTHORISATION PROCEDURES FOR SECRETARY OF STATE AUTHORISATIONS

6.16 Intrusive surveillance by any of the intelligence services, the Ministry of Defence or HM Forces[46] requires the approval of a *Secretary of State*, unless these bodies are acting on behalf of another *public authority* that has obtained an *authorisation*.

6.17 Any *member* or official of the intelligence services, the Ministry of Defence and HM Forces can apply to the *Secretary of State* for an intrusive surveillance *authorisation*. *Applications* to the *Secretary of State* should specify those matters listed below.

6.18 Intelligence services *authorisations* must be made by issue of a *warrant*. Such *warrants* will generally be given in writing by the *Secretary of State*. In urgent cases, a *warrant* may be signed (but not renewed) by a senior official, with the express *authorisation* of the *Secretary of State*.

INFORMATION TO BE PROVIDED IN ALL APPLICATIONS FOR INTRUSIVE SURVEILLANCE

6.19 *Applications* should be in writing (unless urgent) and should describe the conduct to be authorised and the purpose of the investigation or operation. The *application* should specify:

- the reasons why the *authorisation* is necessary in the particular case and on the grounds (e.g. for the purpose of preventing or detecting serious crime) listed in section 32(3) of the 2000 Act;
- the nature of the surveillance;
- the residential premises or private vehicle in relation to which the surveillance will take place, where known;
- the identities, where known, of those to be the subject of the surveillance;
- an explanation of the information which it is desired to obtain as a result of the surveillance;
- details of any potential collateral intrusion and why the intrusion is justified;
- details of any *confidential information* that is likely to be obtained as a consequence of the surveillance;
- the reasons why the surveillance is considered proportionate to what it seeks to achieve;
- a record should be made of whether the *authorisation* was given or refused, by whom and the time and date at which this happened.

6.20 In urgent cases, the above information may be supplied orally. In such cases the applicant should also record the following information in writing, as soon as is reasonably practicable (it is not necessary to record further detail):

- the identities, where known, of those subject to surveillance;
- the nature and location of the surveillance;

---

[46] Or any other *public authority* designated for this purpose under section 41(1) of the 2000 Act, such as the Home Office on the *application* of a *member* of HM Prison Service (SI 1126; 2001).

- the reasons why the *authorising officer* or the *officer* entitled to act in urgent cases considered the case so urgent that an oral instead of a written *authorisation* was given; and/or
- the reasons why it was not reasonably practicable for the *application* to be considered by the *authorising officer*.

DURATION OF INTRUSIVE SURVEILLANCE AUTHORISATIONS – SECRETARY OF STATE WARRANTS FOR THE INTELLIGENCE SERVICES

6.21 A *warrant* issued by the *Secretary of State* will cease to have effect at the end of a period of six months beginning with the day on which it was issued. So an *authorisation* given at 09.00 on 12 February will expire on 11 August. (*Authorisations* (except those granted under urgency provisions) will cease at 23.59 on the last day.)

6.22 *Warrants* expressly authorised by a *Secretary of State*, but signed by a senior official under the urgency procedures, will cease to have effect at the end of the second working day following the day of issue of the *warrant* unless renewed by the *Secretary of State*.

DURATION OF INTRUSIVE SURVEILLANCE AUTHORISATIONS – ALL OTHER INTRUSIVE SURVEILLANCE AUTHORISATIONS

6.23 A written *authorisation* granted by a *Secretary of State*, a *senior authorising officer* or a designated deputy will cease to have effect (unless renewed) at the end of a period of three months, beginning with the day on which it took effect. So an *authorisation* given at 09.00 on 12 February will expire on 11 May. (*Authorisations* (except those lasting for 72 hours) will cease at 23.59 on the last day.)

6.24 Oral *authorisations* given in urgent cases by a *Secretary of State*, a *senior authorising officer* or designated deputy, and written *authorisations* given by those only entitled to act in urgent cases, will cease to have effect (unless renewed) at the end of the period of seventy-two hours beginning with the time when they took effect.

RENEWALS OF INTRUSIVE SURVEILLANCE AUTHORISATIONS – SECRETARY OF STATE AUTHORISATIONS

6.25 If at any time before an intelligence service *warrant* expires, the *Secretary of State* considers it necessary for the *warrant* to be renewed for the purpose for which it was issued, the *Secretary of State* may renew it in writing for a further period of six months, beginning with the day on which it would have ceased to have effect, but for the renewal.

6.26 If at any time before a *warrant* issued by a *Secretary of State* for any other *public authority* expires, the *Secretary of State* considers it necessary for the *warrant* to be renewed for the purpose for which it was issued, he may renew it in writing for a further period of three months, beginning with the day on which it would have ceased to have effect, but for the renewal.

RENEWALS OF INTRUSIVE SURVEILLANCE AUTHORISATIONS – ALL OTHER INTRUSIVE SURVEILLANCE AUTHORISATIONS

6.27 If, at any time before an *authorisation* expires, the *senior authorising officer* or, in his absence, the designated deputy considers that the *authorisation* should continue to have effect for the purpose for which it was issued, he may renew it in writing for a further period of three months.

6.28 As with the initial *authorisation*, the *senior authorising officer* must (unless it is a case to which the urgency procedure applies) seek the approval of a Surveillance Commissioner. The renewal will not take effect until the notice of the Surveillance Commissioner's approval has been received in the office of the person who granted the *authorisation* within the relevant force or organisation (but not before the day on which the *authorisation* would have otherwise ceased to have effect).

6.29 In urgent cases, a renewal can take effect immediately (provided this is not before the day on which the *authorisation* would have otherwise ceased to have effect). See sections 35 and 36 of the 2000 Act and the Regulation of Investigatory Powers (Notification of *Authorisations* etc.) Order 2000; SI No: 2563.

INFORMATION TO BE PROVIDED FOR ALL RENEWALS OF INTRUSIVE SURVEILLANCE AUTHORISATIONS

6.30 All *applications* for a renewal of an intrusive surveillance *authorisation* or *warrant* should record:

- whether this is the first renewal or every occasion on which the *warrant/authorisation* has been renewed previously;
- any significant changes to the information listed in paragraph 6.19;
- the reasons why it is necessary to continue with the intrusive surveillance;
- the content and value to the investigation or operation of the product so far obtained by the surveillance;
- the results of any reviews of the investigation or operation (see below).

6.31 *Authorisations* may be renewed more than once, if necessary, and details of the renewal should be centrally recorded (see Chapter 8).

CANCELLATIONS OF INTRUSIVE SURVEILLANCE ACTIVITY

6.32 The *senior authorising officer* who granted or last renewed the *authorisation* must cancel it, or the person who made the *application* to the *Secretary of State* must apply for its cancellation, if he is satisfied that the surveillance no longer meets the criteria upon which it was authorised. Where the *senior authorising officer* or person who made the *application* to the *Secretary of State* is no longer available, this duty will fall on the person who has taken over the role of *senior authorising officer* or taken over from the person who made the *application* to the *Secretary of State* or the person who is acting as the *senior authorising officer*.[47]

6.33 As soon as the decision is taken that intrusive surveillance should be discontinued, the instruction must be given to those involved to stop the intrusive surveillance.

---

[47] See the Regulation of Investigatory Powers (Cancellation of *Authorisations*) Order 2000; SI No: 2794.

The date the *authorisation* was cancelled should be centrally recorded and documentation of any instruction to cease surveillance should be retained (see Chapter 8). There is no requirement to record any further details. However, effective practice suggests that a record should be retained detailing the product obtained from the surveillance and whether or not objectives were achieved.

6.34 Following the cancellation of any intrusive surveillance *authorisation*, other than one granted by the *Secretary of State*, the Surveillance Commissioners must be notified of the cancellation.[48]

AUTHORISATIONS QUASHED BY A SURVEILLANCE COMMISSIONER

6.35 In cases where a police, SOCA, HMRC or OFT *authorisation* is quashed or cancelled by a Surveillance Commissioner, the *senior authorising officer* must immediately instruct those involved to stop carrying out the intrusive surveillance. Documentation of the date and time when such an instruction was given should be retained for at least three years (see Chapter 8).

Chapter 7

Authorisation procedures for property interference

GENERAL BASIS FOR LAWFUL ACTIVITY

7.1 *Authorisations* under section 5 of the 1994 Act or Part III of the 1997 Act should be sought wherever *members* of the intelligence services, the police, the *services police*, Serious and Organised Crime Agency (SOCA), Scottish Crime and Drug Enforcement Agency (SCDEA), HM Revenue and Customs (HMRC) or Office of Fair Trading (OFT), or persons acting on their behalf, conduct entry on, or interference with, property or with wireless telegraphy that would be otherwise unlawful.

7.2 For the purposes of this chapter, "property interference" shall be taken to include entry on, or interference with, property or with wireless telegraphy.

7.3 In many cases an operation using covert techniques may involve both directed or intrusive surveillance and property interference. This can be authorised as a combined *authorisation*, although the criteria for *authorisation* of each activity must be considered separately (see above, on combined *authorisations*).

> **Example:** The use of a surveillance device for providing information about the location of a vehicle may involve some physical interference with that vehicle as well as subsequent directed surveillance activity. Such an operation could be authorised by a combined authorisation for property interference (under Part III of the 1997 Act) and, where appropriate, directed surveillance (under the 2000 Act). In this case, the necessity and proportionality of the property interference element of the authorisation would need to be considered by the appropriate authorising officer separately to the necessity and proportionality of obtaining private information by means of the directed surveillance.

---

[48] This notification shall include the information specified in the Regulation of Investigatory Powers (Notification of *Authorisations* etc.) Order 2000; SI No: 2563.

7.4 A property interference *authorisation* is not required for entry (whether for the purpose of covert recording or for any other legitimate purpose) into areas open to the public in shops, bars, restaurants, hotel foyers, blocks of flats or any other premises to which, with the implied consent of the occupier, members of the public are afforded unqualified access. Nor is *authorisation* required for entry on any other land or premises at the invitation of the occupier. This is so whatever the purposes for which the premises are used. If consent for entry has been obtained by deception (e.g. requesting entry for a false purpose), however, an *authorisation* for property interference should be obtained.

INFORMED CONSENT

7.5 *Authorisations* under the 1994 Act and 1997 Act are not necessary where the *public authority* is acting with the informed consent of a person able to give permission in respect of the relevant property and actions. However, consideration should still be given to the need to obtain a directed or intrusive surveillance *authorisation* under Part II of the 2000 Act depending on the operation.

> **Example:** A vehicle is fitted with a security alarm to ensure the safety of an undercover officer. If the consent of the vehicle's owner is obtained to install this alarm, no authorisation under the 1997 Act is required. However, if the owner has not provided consent, an authorisation will be required to render lawful the property interference. The fact that the undercover officer is aware of the alarm installation is not relevant to the lawfulness of the property interference.

INCIDENTAL PROPERTY INTERFERENCE

7.6 The 2000 Act provides that no person shall be subject to any civil liability in respect of any conduct which is incidental to correctly authorised directed or intrusive surveillance activity and for which an *authorisation* or *warrant* is not capable of being granted or might not reasonably have been expected to have been sought under any existing legislation.[49] Thus a person shall not, for example, be subject to civil liability for trespass where that trespass is incidental to properly authorised directed or intrusive surveillance activity and where an *authorisation* under the 1994 Act or 1997 Act is available but might not reasonably have been expected to be sought (perhaps due to the unforeseeable nature or location of the activity).

7.7 Where an *authorisation* for the incidental conduct is not available (for example because the 1994 Act or 1997 Act do not apply to the *public authority* in question), the *public authority* shall not be subject to civil liability in relation to any incidental conduct, by virtue of section 27(2) of the 2000 Act. Where, however, a *public authority* is capable of obtaining an *authorisation* for the activity, it should seek one wherever it could be reasonably expected to do so.

> **Example:** Surveillance officers crossing an area of land covered by an authorisation under the 1997 Act are forced to temporarily and momentarily cross into neighbouring land to bypass an unforeseen obstruction, before returning to their authorised route.

---

[49] See section 27(2) of the Act.

SAMPLES

7.8 The acquisition of samples, such as DNA samples, fingerprints and footwear impressions, where there is no consequent loss of or damage to property does not of itself constitute unlawful property interference. However, wherever it is necessary to conduct otherwise unlawful property interference to access and obtain these samples, an *authorisation* under the 1994 or 1997 Act would be appropriate. An *authorisation* for directed or intrusive surveillance would not normally be relevant to any subsequent information, whether private or not, obtained as a result of the covert technique. Once a DNA sample, fingerprint or footwear impression has been obtained, any subsequent analysis of this information will not be surveillance as defined at section 48(2) of the 2000 Act. The appropriate lawful authority in these cases is likely to be the Data Protection Act.

> **Example 1:** Police wish to take fingerprints from a public telephone to identify a suspected criminal who is known recently to have used the telephone. The act of taking the fingerprints would not involve any unlawful property interference so no authorisation under the 1994 or 1997 Act is required. The subsequent recording and analysis of the information obtained to establish the individual's identity would not amount to surveillance and therefore would not require authorisation under the 2000 Act.

> **Example 2:** Police intend to acquire covertly a mobile telephone used by a suspected criminal, in order to take fingerprints. In this case, the acquisition of the telephone for the purposes of obtaining fingerprints could be authorised under the 1994 or 1997 Act where it would otherwise be unlawful.

AUTHORISATIONS FOR PROPERTY INTERFERENCE BY THE POLICE,
THE SERVICES POLICE, SOCA, SCDEA, HMRC AND OFT

7.9 Responsibility for these *authorisations* rests with the *authorising officer* as defined in section 93(5) of the 1997 Act, i.e. the chief constable or equivalent. *Authorisations* require the personal authority of the *authorising officer* (or his designated deputy) except in urgent situations, where it is not reasonably practicable for the *application* to be considered by such person. The person entitled to act in such cases is set out in section 94 of the 1997 Act.

7.10 Any person giving an *authorisation* for entry on or interference with property or with wireless telegraphy under section 93(2) of the 1997 Act must believe that:

- it is necessary for the action specified to be taken for the purpose of preventing or detecting serious crime;[50] and
- that the taking of the action is proportionate to what the action seeks to achieve.

---

[50] An *authorising officer* in a *public authority* other than the Security Service shall not issue an *authorisation* under Part III of the 1997 Act where the investigation or operation falls within the responsibilities of the Security Service. Where any doubt exists a *public authority* should confirm with the Security Service whether or not the investigation is judged to fall within Security Service responsibilities before seeking an *authorisation* under Part III of the 1997 Act. Where the *authorising officer* is the Chairman of the OFT, the only purpose falling within this definition is the purpose of preventing or detecting an offence under section 188 of the Enterprise Act 2002 (see section 93(2AA) of the 1997 Act).

237

7.11 The *authorising officer* must take into account whether what it is thought necessary to achieve by the authorised conduct could reasonably be achieved by other means.

COLLABORATIVE WORKING AND REGIONAL CONSIDERATIONS

7.12 *Authorisations* for the police, the *services police*, SOCA, SCDEA, HMRC and OFT may only be given by an *authorising officer* on *application* by a *member* or *officer* of the same force or agency unless, in the case of the police, a relevant collaboration agreement has been made which permits this rule to be varied.

7.13 *Authorisations* for the police, and SCDEA may only be given for property interference within the *authorising officer's* own area of operation unless, in the case of the police, a relevant collaboration agreement has been made which permits this rule to be varied. Unless a relevant collaboration agreement applies, an *authorising officer* may authorise property interference (excluding wireless telegraphy interference) outside the relevant area, solely for the purpose of maintaining (including replacing) or retrieving any device, apparatus or equipment the use of which within the relevant area has been authorised under the 1997 Act or 2000 Act. Unless a relevant collaboration agreement applies, an *authorisation* for maintenance or retrieval outside of the *authorising officer's* own area of operations can only be given for circumstances that do not require entry onto private land.

7.14 Any person granting or applying for an *authorisation* or *warrant* to enter on or interfere with property or with wireless telegraphy will also need to be aware of particular sensitivities in the local community where the entry or interference is taking place and of similar activities being undertaken by other *public authorities* which could impact on the deployment. In this regard, it is recommended that the *authorising officers* in the *services police*, SOCA, SCDEA, HMRC and OFT should consult a senior *officer* within the police force in which the investigation or operation takes place where the *authorising officer* considers that conflicts might arise. The Chief Constable of the Police Service of Northern Ireland should be informed of any surveillance operation undertaken by another law enforcement agency which involves its *officers* maintaining (including replacing) or retrieving equipment in Northern Ireland.

AUTHORISATION PROCEDURES

7.15 *Authorisations* will generally be given in writing by the *authorising officer*. However, in urgent cases, they may be given orally by the *authorising officer*. In such cases, a statement that the *authorising officer* has expressly authorised the action(s) should be recorded in writing by the applicant as soon as is reasonably practicable, together with that information detailed below.

7.16 If the *authorising officer* is absent then an *authorisation* can be given in writing or, in urgent cases, orally by the designated deputy as provided for in section 94(4) of the 1997 Act, section 12(A) of the Police Act 1996, section 5(A) of the Police (Scotland) Act 1967, section 25 of the City of London Police Act 1839 or section 93(5) of the 1997 Act (for SOCA).

7.17 Where, however, in an urgent case, it is not reasonably practicable for the *authorising officer* or designated deputy to consider an *application*, then written *authorisation* may be given by the following:

- in the case of the police, by an assistant chief constable (other than a designated deputy);[51]
- in the case of the Metropolitan Police and City of London Police, by a commander;
- in the case of MOD police or British Transport Police, by a deputy or assistant chief constable;
- in the case of the *services police*, by an assistant Provost Marshal (in the Royal Naval Police) or deputy Provost Marshal (in the Royal Military Police or Royal Air Force Police);
- in the case of SCDEA, by a chief constable, his designated deputy or assistant chief constable;
- in the case of SOCA a person designated by the Director General;
- in the case of HMRC, by a person designated by the Commissioners of Revenue and Customs;[52]
- in the case of the OFT, by an *officer* of the OFT designated for this purpose.

Information to be provided in applications

7.18 *Applications* to the *authorising officer* for the granting or renewal of an *authorisation* must be made in writing (unless urgent) by a police *officer*, Revenue and Customs *officer*, *SCDEA officer*, a *member* of SOCA or an *officer* of the OFT and should specify:

- the identity or identities, where known, of those who possess the property that is to be subject to the interference;
- sufficient information to identify the property which the entry or interference with will affect;
- the nature and extent of the proposed interference;
- the details of any collateral intrusion, including the identity of individuals and/or categories of people, where known, who are likely to be affected, and why the intrusion is justified;
- details of the offence suspected or committed;
- how the *authorisation* criteria (as set out above) have been met;
- any action which may be necessary to maintain any equipment, including replacing it;
- any action which may be necessary to retrieve any equipment;
- in case of a renewal, the results obtained so far, or a full explanation of the failure to obtain any results; and
- whether an *authorisation* was given or refused, by whom and the time and date on which this happened.

7.19 In urgent cases, the above information may be supplied orally. In such cases the *authorising officer* and the applicant should also record the following information

---

[51] ACPO out-of-hours *officers* of assistant chief constable rank or above will be entitled to act for this purpose.

[52] This will be an *officer* of the rank of assistant chief investigation *officer*.

in writing, as soon as is reasonably practicable (it is not necessary to record further detail):

- the identity or identities of those owning or using the property (where known);
- sufficient information to identify the property which will be affected;
- details of the offence suspected or committed;
- the reasons why the *authorising officer* or designated deputy considered the case so urgent that an oral instead of a written *authorisation* was given; and/or
- the reasons why (if relevant) it was not reasonably practicable for the *application* to be considered by the *authorising officer* or the designated deputy.

NOTIFICATIONS TO SURVEILLANCE COMMISSIONERS

7.20 Where a person gives, renews or cancels an *authorisation* in respect of entry on or interference with property or with wireless telegraphy, he must, as soon as is reasonably practicable, give notice of it in writing to a Surveillance Commissioner, where relevant, in accordance with arrangements made by the Chief Surveillance Commissioner. In urgent cases which would otherwise have required the approval of a Surveillance Commissioner, the notification must specify the grounds on which the case is believed to be one of urgency.

7.21 There may be cases which become urgent after approval has been sought but before a response has been received from a Surveillance Commissioner. In such a case, the *authorising officer* should notify the Surveillance Commissioner that the case is urgent (pointing out that it has become urgent since the previous notification). In these cases, the *authorisation* will take effect immediately.

7.22 Notifications to Surveillance Commissioners in relation to the granting, renewal and cancellation of *authorisations* in respect of entry on or interference with property should be in accordance with the requirements of the Police Act 1997 (Notifications of *Authorisations* etc) Order 1998; SI No. 3241.

CASES REQUIRING PRIOR APPROVAL OF A SURVEILLANCE COMMISSIONER

7.23 In certain cases, an *authorisation* for entry on or interference with property will not take effect until a Surveillance Commissioner has approved it and the notice of approval has been received in the office of the person who granted the *authorisation* within the relevant force or organisation (unless the urgency procedures are used). These are cases where the person giving the *authorisation* believes that:

- any of the property specified in the *authorisation*:
  - is used wholly or mainly as a dwelling or as a bedroom in a hotel; or
  - constitutes office premises;[53] or
- the action authorised is likely to result in any person acquiring knowledge of:
  - matters subject to legal privilege;
  - confidential personal information; or
  - confidential journalistic material.

---

[53] Office premises are defined as any building or part of a building whose sole or principal use is as an office or for office purposes (which means purposes of administration, clerical work, handling money and telephone or telegraph operation).

DURATION OF AUTHORISATIONS

7.24 Written *authorisations* in respect of entry on or interference with property or with wireless telegraphy given by *authorising officers* will cease to have effect at the end of a period of three months beginning with the day on which they took effect. So an *authorisation* given at 09.00 on 12 February will expire on 11 May. (*Authorisations* (except those lasting for 72 hours) will cease at 23.59 on the last day.)

7.25 In cases requiring prior approval by a Surveillance Commissioner, the duration of an *authorisation* is calculated from the time at which the person who gave the *authorisation* was notified that the Surveillance Commissioner had approved it. This can be done by presenting the *authorising officer* with the approval decision page to note in person or if the *authorising officer* is unavailable, sending the written notice by auditable electronic means. In cases not requiring prior approval, this means from the time the *authorisation* was granted.

7.26 Written *authorisations* given by the persons specified in 7.16 (section 94 of the 1997 Act) and oral *authorisations* given in urgent cases by:

- *authorising officers*
- or designated deputies

will cease at the end of the period of seventy-two hours beginning with the time when they took effect.

RENEWALS

7.27 If at any time before the time and day on which an *authorisation* expires the *authorising officer* or, in his absence, the designated deputy considers the *authorisation* should continue to have effect for the purpose for which it was issued, he may renew it in writing for a period of three months beginning with the day on which the *authorisation* would otherwise have ceased to have effect. *Authorisations* may be renewed more than once, if necessary, and details of the renewal should be centrally recorded (see Chapter 8).

7.28 Where relevant, the Commissioners must be notified of renewals of *authorisations*. The information to be included in the notification is set out in the Police Act 1997 (Notifications of *Authorisations* etc) Order 1998; SI No: 3241.

7.29 If, at the time of renewal, criteria exist which would cause an *authorisation* to require prior approval by a Surveillance Commissioner, then the approval of a Surveillance Commissioner must be sought before the renewal can take effect. The fact that the initial *authorisation* required the approval of a Commissioner before taking effect does not mean that its renewal will automatically require such approval. It will only do so if, at the time of the renewal, it falls into one of the categories requiring approval (and is not an urgent case).

CANCELLATIONS

7.30 The *senior authorising officer* who granted or last renewed the *authorisation* must cancel it if he is satisfied that the *authorisation* no longer meets the criteria upon which it was authorised. Where the *senior authorising officer* is no longer available, this duty will fall on the person who has taken over the role of *senior authorising officer* or the

241

person who is acting as the *senior authorising officer* (see the Regulation of Investigatory Powers (Cancellation of *Authorisations*) Order 2000; SI No: 2794).

7.31 Following the cancellation of the *authorisation*, the Surveillance Commissioners must be notified of the cancellation. The information to be included in the notification is set out in the Police Act 1997 (Notifications of *Authorisations* etc) Order 1998; SI No: 3421.

7.32 The Surveillance Commissioners have the power to cancel an *authorisation* if they are satisfied that, at any time after an *authorisation* was given or renewed, there were no reasonable grounds for believing that it should subsist. In such circumstances, a Surveillance Commissioner may order the destruction of records, in whole or in part, other than any that are required for pending criminal or civil proceedings.

RETRIEVAL OF EQUIPMENT

7.33 Because of the time it can take to remove equipment from a person's property it may also be necessary to renew an *authorisation* in order to complete the retrieval. The notification to Commissioners of such a renewal should state why the operation is being or has been stopped, why it has not been possible to remove the equipment and, where possible, a timescale for removal.

7.34 Where a Surveillance Commissioner quashes or cancels an *authorisation* or renewal, he will, if there are reasonable grounds for doing so, order that the *authorisation* remains effective for a specified period, to enable *officers* to retrieve anything left on the property by virtue of the *authorisation*. He can only do so if the *authorisation* or renewal makes provision for this. A decision by the Surveillance Commissioner not to give such an order can be the subject of an appeal to the Chief Surveillance Commissioner.

CEASING OF ENTRY ON OR INTERFERENCE WITH PROPERTY OR WITH WIRELESS TELEGRAPHY

7.35 Once an *authorisation* or renewal expires or is cancelled or quashed, the *authorising officer* must immediately give an instruction to cease all the actions authorised for the entry on or interference with property or with wireless telegraphy. The time and date when such an instruction was given should be centrally retrievable for at least three years (see Chapter 8).

AUTHORISATIONS FOR PROPERTY INTERFERENCE BY THE INTELLIGENCE SERVICES

7.36 An *application* for a *warrant* must be made by a *member* of the intelligence services for the taking of action in relation to that agency. In addition, the Security Service may make an *application* for a *warrant* to act on behalf of the Secret Intelligence Service (SIS) and the Government Communications Headquarters (GCHQ). SIS and GCHQ may not be granted a *warrant* for action in support of the prevention or detection of serious crime which relates to property in the British Isles.

7.37 The intelligence services should provide the same information as other agencies, as and where appropriate, when making *applications* for the grant or renewal of property *warrants*.

7.38 Before granting a *warrant*, the *Secretary of State* must:

- think it necessary for the action to be taken for the purpose of assisting the relevant agency in carrying out its functions;
- be satisfied that the taking of the action is proportionate to what the action seeks to achieve;
- take into account in deciding whether an *authorisation* is necessary and proportionate is whether the information which it is thought necessary to obtain by the conduct authorised by the *warrant* could reasonably be obtained by other means; and
- be satisfied that there are satisfactory arrangements in force under the 1994 Act or the 1989 Act in respect of disclosure of any material obtained by means of the *warrant*, and that material obtained will be subject to those arrangements.

Renewals of intelligence services warrants

7.39 A *warrant* shall, unless renewed, cease to have effect at the end of the period of six months beginning with the day on which it was issued (if the *warrant* was issued under the hand of the *Secretary of State*) or at the end of the period ending with the fifth working day following the day on which it was issued (in any other case).

7.40 If at any time before the day on which a *warrant* would cease to have effect the *Secretary of State* considers it necessary for the *warrant* to continue to have effect for the purpose for which it was issued, he may by an instrument under his hand renew it for a period of six months beginning with the day it would otherwise cease to have effect.

Cancellations of intelligence services warrants

7.41 The *Secretary of State* shall cancel a *warrant* if he is satisfied that the action authorised by it is no longer necessary.

7.42 The person who made the *application* to the *Secretary of State* must apply for its cancellation, if he is satisfied that the *warrant* no longer meets the criteria upon which it was authorised. Where the person who made the *application* to the *Secretary of State* is no longer available, this duty will fall on the person who has taken over from the person who made the *application* to the *Secretary of State* (see the Regulation of Investigatory Powers (Cancellation of *Authorisations*) Order 2000; SI No: 2794).

Retrieval of equipment by the intelligence services

7.43 Because of the time it can take to remove equipment from a person's property it may also be necessary to renew a property *warrant* in order to complete the retrieval. *Applications* to the *Secretary of State* for renewal should state why it is being or has been closed down, why it has not been possible to remove the equipment and any timescales for removal, where known.

Chapter 8

Keeping of records

CENTRALLY RETRIEVABLE RECORDS OF AUTHORISATIONS

Directed and intrusive surveillance authorisations

8.1 A record of the following information pertaining to all *authorisations* shall be centrally retrievable within each *public authority* for a period of at least three years from the ending of each *authorisation*. This information should be regularly updated whenever an *authorisation* is granted, renewed or cancelled and should be made available to the relevant Commissioner or an Inspector from the Office of Surveillance Commissioners upon request.

- the type of *authorisation*;
- the date the *authorisation* was given;
- name and rank/grade of the *authorising officer*;
- the unique reference number (URN) of the investigation or operation;
- the title of the investigation or operation, including a brief description and names of subjects, if known;
- whether the urgency provisions were used, and if so why;
- if the *authorisation* has been renewed, when it was renewed and who authorised the renewal, including the name and rank/grade of the *authorising officer*;
- whether the investigation or operation is likely to result in obtaining *confidential information* as defined in this code of practice;[54]
- whether the *authorisation* was granted by an individual directly involved in the investigation;[55]
- the date the *authorisation* was cancelled.

8.2 The following documentation should also be centrally retrievable for at least three years from the ending of each *authorisation*:

- a copy of the *application* and a copy of the *authorisation* together with any supplementary documentation and notification of the approval given by the *authorising officer*;
- a record of the period over which the surveillance has taken place;
- the frequency of reviews prescribed by the *authorising officer*;
- a record of the result of each review of the *authorisation*;
- a copy of any renewal of an *authorisation*, together with the supporting documentation submitted when the renewal was requested;
- the date and time when any instruction to cease surveillance was given;
- the date and time when any other instruction was given by the *authorising officer*.

PROPERTY INTERFERENCE AUTHORISATIONS

8.3 The following information relating to all *authorisations* for property interference should be centrally retrievable for at least three years:

- the time and date when an *authorisation* is given;

---

[54] See Chapter 4.
[55] See paragraph 5.7.

- whether an *authorisation* is in written or oral form;
- the time and date when it was notified to a Surveillance Commissioner, if applicable;
- the time and date when the Surveillance Commissioner notified his approval (where appropriate);
- every occasion when entry on or interference with property or with wireless telegraphy has occurred;
- the result of periodic reviews of the *authorisation*;
- the date of every renewal; and
- the time and date when any instruction was given by the *authorising officer* to cease the interference with property or with wireless telegraphy.

Chapter 9

Handling of material and use of material as evidence

USE OF MATERIAL AS EVIDENCE

9.1 Subject to the provisions in chapter 4 of this Code, material obtained through directed or intrusive surveillance, or entry on, or interference with, property or wireless telegraphy, may be used as evidence in criminal proceedings. The admissibility of evidence is governed primarily by the common law, the Civil Procedure Rules, section 78 of the Police and Criminal Evidence Act 1984[56] and the Human Rights Act 1998.

9.2 Any decisions by a Surveillance Commissioner in respect of granting prior approval for intrusive surveillance activity or entry on, or interference with, property or with wireless telegraphy, shall not be subject to appeal or be liable to be questioned in any court.[57]

RETENTION AND DESTRUCTION OF MATERIAL

9.3 Each *public authority* must ensure that arrangements are in place for the secure handling, storage and destruction of material obtained through the use of directed or intrusive surveillance or property interference. *Authorising officers*, through their relevant *Data Controller*, must ensure compliance with the appropriate data protection requirements under the Data Protection Act 1998 and any relevant codes of practice produced by individual authorities relating to the handling and storage of material.

9.4 Where the product of surveillance or interference with property or wireless telegraphy could be relevant to pending or future criminal or civil proceedings, it should be retained in accordance with established disclosure requirements[58] for a suitable further period, commensurate to any subsequent review.

9.5 There is nothing in the 2000 Act, 1994 Act or 1997 Act which prevents material obtained under directed or intrusive surveillance or property interference *authorisations* from being used to further other investigations.

---

[56] And section 76 of the Police & Criminal Evidence (Northern Ireland) Order 1989.
[57] See section 91(10) of the 1997 Act.
[58] For example, under the Criminal Procedure and Investigations Act 1996.

LAW ENFORCEMENT AGENCIES

9.6 In the cases of the law enforcement agencies, particular attention is drawn to the requirements of the code of practice issued under the Criminal Procedure and Investigations Act 1996. This requires that material which is obtained in the course of a criminal investigation and which may be relevant to the investigation must be recorded and retained.

THE INTELLIGENCE SERVICES, MOD AND HM FORCES

9.7 The heads of these agencies are responsible for ensuring that arrangements exist for securing that no information is stored by the authorities, except as necessary for the proper discharge of their functions. They are also responsible for arrangements to control onward disclosure. For the intelligence services, this is a statutory duty under the 1989 Act and the 1994 Act.

9.8 With regard to the service police forces (the Royal Navy Police, the Royal Military Police and the Royal Air Force Police), particular attention is drawn to the Criminal Procedure and Investigations Act 1996 (Code of Practice) (Armed Forces) Order 2008, which requires that the investigator retain all material obtained in a service investigation which may be relevant to the investigation.

Chapter 10

Oversight by Commissioners

10.1 The 1997 and 2000 Acts require the Chief Surveillance Commissioner to keep under review (with the assistance of the Surveillance Commissioners and Assistant Surveillance Commissioners) the performance of functions under Part III of the 1997 Act and Part II of the 2000 Act by the police (including the service police forces, the Ministry of Defence Police and the British Transport Police), SOCA, SCDEA, HMRC and the other *public authorities* listed in Schedule 1 of the 2000 Act and the Regulation of Investigatory Powers (Directed Surveillance and Covert Human Intelligence Sources) Order 2010 and, in Northern Ireland, officials of the Ministry of Defence and HM Forces.

10.2 The Intelligence Services Commissioner's remit is to provide independent oversight of the use of the powers contained within Part II of the 2000 Act and the 1994 Act by the Security Service, Secret Intelligence Service, GCHQ and the Ministry of Defence and HM Forces (excluding the service police forces, and in Northern Ireland officials of the Ministry of Defence and HM Forces).

10.3 This Code does not cover the exercise of any of the Commissioners' functions. It is the duty of any person who uses these powers to comply with any request made by a Commissioner to disclose or provide any information he requires for the purpose of enabling him to carry out his functions.

10.4 References in this Code to the performance of review functions by the Chief Surveillance Commissioner and other Commissioners apply also to Inspectors and other *members* of staff to whom such functions have been delegated.

Chapter 11

Complaints

11.1 The 2000 Act establishes an independent Tribunal. This Tribunal will be made up of senior *members* of the judiciary and the legal profession and is independent of the Government. The Tribunal has full powers to investigate and decide any case within its jurisdiction. This Code does not cover the exercise of the Tribunal's functions. Details of the relevant complaints procedure can be obtained from the following address:

Investigatory Powers Tribunal
PO Box 33220
London
SW1H 9ZQ
Tel: 020 7035 3711

Chapter 12

Glossary

Application A request made to an authorising officer to consider granting (or renewing) an authorisation for directed or intrusive surveillance (under the 2000 Act), or interference with property or wireless telegraphy (under the 1994 or 1997 Act). An application will be made by a member of a relevant public authority.

Authorisation An application which has received the approval of an authorising officer. Depending on the circumstances, an authorisation may comprise a written application that has been signed by the authorising officer, or an oral application that has been verbally approved by the authorising officer.

Authorising officer A person within a public authority who is entitled to grant authorisations under the 2000 or 1997 Acts or to apply to the Secretary of State for such warrants. Should be taken to include senior authorising officers.

Confidential information Confidential personal information (such as medical records or spiritual counselling), confidential journalistic material, confidential discussions between Members of Parliament and their constituents, or matters subject to legal privilege. See Chapter 4 for a full explanation.

Legal privilege Matters subject to legal privilege are defined in section 98 of the 1997 Act. This includes certain communications between professional legal advisers and their clients or persons representing the client.

Member An employee of an organisation, or a person seconded to that organisation (for example, under the terms of section 24 of the Police Act 1996).

Officer An officer of a police force, HMRC or the OFT, or a person seconded to one of these agencies as an officer.

Private information Any information relating to a person in relation to which that person has or may have a reasonable expectation of privacy. This includes information relating to a person's private, family or professional affairs. Private information includes information about any person, not just the subject(s) of an investigation.

Public authority Any public organisation, agency or police force (including the military police forces).

Secretary of State Any Secretary of State (in practice this will generally be the Home Secretary).

Senior authorising officer A person within a public authority who is entitled to grant intrusive surveillance authorisations under the 2000 Act or to apply to the Secretary of State for such warrants. See also Authorising officer.

Services police The Royal Naval Police, Royal
  Military Police or Royal Air Force Police.

Warrant A type of authorisation granted by a Secretary of
  State following an application for intrusive surveillance or
  property interference under the 1994, 1997 or 2000 Acts.

Annex A

Authorisation levels when knowledge of confidential information is likely to be acquired

Relevant public authority	Authorisation level
Police forces	
Any police force maintained under section 2 of the Police Act 1996 (police forces in England and Wales outside London)	Chief Constable
Any police force maintained under or by virtue of section 1 of the Police (Scotland) Act 1967	Chief Constable
The Metropolitan Police force	Assistant Commissioner
The City of London Police force	Commissioner
The Police Service of Northern Ireland	Deputy Chief Constable
The Ministry of Defence Police	Chief Constable
The Royal Navy Police	Provost Marshal
The Royal Military Police	Provost Marshal
The Royal Air Force Police	Provost Marshal
The Serious Organised Crime Agency	Deputy Director
The Serious Fraud Office	A Member of the Senior Civil Service or Head of Domain
The Intelligence Services:	
The Security Service (MI5)	Deputy Director General
The Secret Intelligence Service (MI6)	A Director of the Secret Intelligence Service
The Government Communications Headquarters (GCHQ)	A Director of GCHQ
HM Forces:	
The Royal Navy	Rear Admiral
The Army	Major General
The Royal Air Force	Air Vice-Marshal
The Commissioners for HM Revenue and Customs	Director Investigation, or Regional Heads of Investigation

The Department for Environment, Food and Rural Affairs:	
DEFRA Investigation Services	Head of DEFRA Investigation Services
Marine and Fisheries Agency	Head of DEFRA Prosecution Service
Centre for Environment, Fisheries & Aquaculture Science	Head of DEFRA Prosecution Service
The Department of Health:	
The Medicines & Healthcare Products Regulatory Agency	Chief Executive of the Medicines & Healthcare Products Regulatory Agency
The Home Office:	
The UK Border Agency	Strategic Director of the UK Border Agency, or (in his/her absence) Director of the UK Border Agency Intelligence Directorate
The Ministry of Justice	Chief Operating Officer in the National Offender Management Service
The Northern Ireland Office:	
The Northern Ireland Prison Service	Director or Deputy Director Operations in the Northern Ireland Prison Service
The Department of Business, Innovation and Skills:	The Director of Legal Services A
The Welsh Assembly Government	Head of Department for Health & Social Services, Head of Department for Health & Social Services Finance, Head of Rural Payments Division, Regional Director or equivalent grade in the Care & Social Services Inspectorate for Wales
Any county council or district council. In England, a London borough council, the Common Council of the City of London in its capacity as a local authority, the Council of the Isles of Scilly, and any county council or borough council in Wales	The Head of Paid Service, or (in his/her absence) the person acting as the Head of Paid Service
The Environment Agency	Chief Executive of the Environment Agency
The Financial Services Authority	Chairman of the Financial Services Authority
The Food Standards Agency	Head of Group, or Deputy Chief Executive or Chief Executive of the Food Standards Agency
The Health and Safety Executive	Director of Field Operations, or Director of Hazardous Installations Directorate, or Her Majesty's Chief Inspector of Nuclear Installations
NHS bodies in England and Wales:	
A Special Health Authority established under section 28 of the National Health Service Act 2006 or section 22 of the National Health Service (Wales) Act 2006	Managing Director of the NHS Counter Fraud and Security Management Services Division of the NHS Business Services Authority

The Royal Pharmaceutical Society of Great Britain	Deputy Registrar and Director of Regulation
The Department of Work and Pensions:	
Jobcentre Plus	Chief Executive of Jobcentre Plus
The Royal Mail Group Ltd, by virtue of being a Universal Service Provider within the meaning of the Postal Services Act 2000	Director of Security

Appendix B

Investigation of Protected Electronic Information

Code of Practice
Pursuant to section 71 of the Regulation of Investigatory Powers Act 2000

Chapter 1

Introduction

1.1 This code of practice relates to the powers and duties conferred or imposed under Part III of the Regulation of Investigatory Powers Act 2000 ('the Act'). It provides guidance to be followed when exercising powers under Part III of the Act ('Part III') to require disclosure of protected electronic information (electronic data) in an intelligible form or to acquire the means by which protected electronic information may be accessed or put in an intelligible form.

1.2 This code applies to the exercise and performance by any person (other than a judicial authority or a person holding judicial office) of the powers and duties conferred or imposed by or under Part III.

1.3 The code should be readily available, in written or electronic form, to members of any public authority involved in the investigation of protected electronic information and to persons upon whom any duty is imposed under Part III of the Act.

1.4 The Act provides that the code is admissible in evidence in criminal and civil proceedings. If any provision of the code appears relevant to a question before any court or tribunal hearing any such proceedings, or to the Tribunal established under the Act ('the Investigatory Powers Tribunal'), or to one of the Commissioners responsible for overseeing the powers conferred by the Act, it must be taken into account.

1.5 The exercise of powers and duties under Part III is kept under review by the Commissioners appointed under sections 57, 59 and 62 of the Act ('the Commissioners').

1.6 This code extends to the United Kingdom.

Chapter 2

Background

2.1 Information security technologies have allowed electronic commerce to flourish, enabling businesses and individuals to secure and protect their electronic data and to maintain the privacy of their electronic communications. Individuals going about their lawful business, both openly and privately, use these technologies every day.

2.2 Terrorists and criminals use the same technologies to protect their electronic data and the privacy of their electronic communications, to conceal evidence of their unlawful conduct and to evade detection or prosecution.

2.3 At its simplest the protection of electronic data is undertaken using a password which, if correct, gives access to the data in an intelligible form. More complex applications use cryptography both to protect access to the data and to put the data itself into a form that is unintelligible without the correct password or key.

2.4 Cryptographic technologies, which have been essential to the success of e-commerce and online businesses, have various uses:

Authentication – guaranteeing that the originator or recipient of data is the person they claim to be;

Availability – assurance that the systems responsible for delivering, storing and processing data are accessible when needed, by those who need them;

Confidentiality – protecting data to ensure that its contents cannot be read by anyone other than an intended recipient;

Integrity – guaranteeing that data has not been accidentally or deliberately corrupted;

Non-repudiation – preventing the denial of previous commitments or actions.

2.5 Primarily it is application of cryptography to the confidentiality of data which is exploited by terrorists and criminals to protect their data, whether it is stored data, on a disk or other storage device, or data being communicated from one to another or from one to many others. The measures in Part III are intended to ensure that the ability of public authorities to protect the public and the effectiveness of their other statutory powers are not undermined by the use of technologies to protect electronic information.

Chapter 3

Scope of the powers

3.1 Part III provides a statutory framework that enables public authorities to require protected electronic information which they have obtained lawfully or are likely to obtain lawfully to be put into an intelligible form; to acquire the means to gain access to protected information and to acquire the means to put protected information into an intelligible form.

3.2 The specific provisions are:

- power to require disclosure of protected information in an intelligible form (section 49);
- power to require disclosure of the means to access protected information (section 50(3)(c));
- power to require disclosure of the means of putting protected information into an intelligible form (section 50(3)(c)), and
- power to attach a secrecy provision to any disclosure requirement (section 54).

3.3 Failure to comply with a disclosure requirement or a secrecy requirement is a criminal offence.

3.4 Public authorities that use, or seek to use, the provisions in Part III will do so with the objective of securing necessary access to lawfully acquired protected information in an intelligible form, and, where necessary and proportionate to do so, to seek or to require assistance to do that.

3.5 In practice this means that investigators must take into account the legitimate needs of businesses and individuals to maintain the integrity of their information security management processes and will, wherever practical, require the disclosure, or seek assistance to secure the disclosure, of protected information in an intelligible form.

3.6 When exceptional circumstances do arise, access to protected information in an intelligible form may be achieved more readily by securing the application of an established process to the data rather than requiring the disclosure of key material and creating a bespoke decryption facility where the processing may, even then, be undertaken by a technically competent employee of a firm or business under supervision of the investigator. Processing data the way it would have been processed ordinarily, in so far as that is practical, will also reduce costs and minimise any potential collateral intrusion.

3.7 Requiring the disclosure of the means to access protected information or to put it into an intelligible form should be undertaken only where the investigator, or the person able to grant permission to impose that requirement, reasonably believes that assistance to make the protected information available in an intelligible form or in compliance with a requirement to disclose the protected information in an intelligible form is unlikely to be forthcoming or effective.

3.8 Consequently use of the power to require disclosure of key material can be expected to be used only where a person who is able to put the protected information into an intelligible form indicates or suggests that he will not exercise that ability either voluntarily or upon compulsion. In practice this means the power is more likely to be exercised in relation to individuals who are the subject of investigation and are responsible for protecting information which is believed to be evidence of unlawful conduct or relevant material to the investigation.

3.9 The National Technical Assistance Centre (NTAC),[1] which provides technical support to public authorities, particularly law enforcement agencies and the intelligence services, includes a facility for the complex processing of lawfully obtained protected electronic information.

3.10 NTAC is the lead national authority for all matters relating to the processing of protected information into intelligible form and to disclosure of key material. All public authorities should consult with NTAC at the earliest opportunity when considering the exercise of the powers in Part III. No public authority may serve any notice under section 49 of the Act or, when the authority considers it necessary, seek to obtain appropriate permission without the prior written approval of NTAC to do so. Such approval may be given in specific cases or it can be given to a public authority if NTAC assesses the authority is competent to exercise the powers in Part III.

3.11 In this way NTAC will support public authorities to ensure that the exercise of the powers in Part III is undertaken appropriately, expertly and with the highest regard for compliance with the requirements and principles of the Act and this code. The role of NTAC as a guardian and gatekeeper of the use of Part III will provide assurance to the Commissioners that the scope for inappropriate use of the powers is mitigated. Equally the Commissioners' oversight extends to NTAC itself.

PROTECTED INFORMATION

3.12 Protected information means any electronic data, which, without a key to the data cannot, or cannot readily: be accessed, or be put into an intelligible form.

---

[1] NTAC may be contacted at: ripaiii@ntac.gsi.gov.uk.

3.13 Section 49(1) of the Act describes various means by which protected information has come into, or may come into, the possession of any person within a public authority. This includes information that has been, or is likely to be:

Within the scope of section 49(1)(a) of the Act:

- acquired by exercising a statutory power to seize, detain, inspect;
- search for property or to interfere with documents or other property;
  - o for example, seized under a judicial search warrant under section 8 of the Police and Criminal Evidence Act 1984;
  - o for example, disclosed in compliance with a judicial production order under Schedule 1 of the Police and Criminal Evidence Act 1984;

Within the scope of section 49(1)(b) of the Act:

- acquired by the exercise of a statutory power to intercept communications, for example under a warrant issued personally or expressly authorised by the Secretary of State under Chapter I of Part I of the Act;

Within the scope of section 49(1)(c) of the Act:

- acquired by undertaking conduct authorised under section 22(3) of the Act (authorised conduct to obtain communications data);
- disclosed as a result of the giving of a notice under section 22(4) of the Act (notice requiring disclosure of communications data);
- acquired by undertaking conduct authorised under Part II of the Act (whether an authorisation for carrying out directed surveillance under section 28, for carrying out intrusive surveillance under section 32, or for the conduct or the use of a covert human intelligence source under section 29);

Within the scope of section 49(1)(d) of the Act:

- provided to, or disclosed to, a public authority in the exercise of any statutory duty whether or not the provision or disclosure of information was requested;

Within the scope of section 49(1)(e) of the Act:

- acquired lawfully by any of the intelligence services,[2] the police, Serious Organised Crime Agency (SOCA) or HM Revenue and Customs (HMRC) without using statutory powers, including information voluntarily disclosed to those authorities by a member of the public.

3.14 Section 49(1) provides by the words "has come in to the possession of any person .... or is likely to do so" that a public authority can seek permission to give a section 49 notice ('a notice') at the same time as seeking to exercise a statutory power to obtain the information or in anticipation of such action. This will occur in circumstances where there is an expectation that the information being sought is protected. For example an application for, and the issue of, a search warrant, production order or interception warrant may include reference to protected information likely to be seized, produced or intercepted.

---

[2] The Security Service, the Secret Intelligence Service and GCHQ.

3.15 A notice may be given where a person has appropriate permission[3] and reasonably believes that:

- a key[4] to the protected material is in possession of any person;[5]
- a disclosure requirement in respect of the protected information is necessary:
  - o in the interests of national security;[6]
  - o for the purpose of preventing or detecting crime;[7]
  - o in the interests of the economic well being of the United Kingdom,[8] or
  - o for the purpose of securing the effective exercise or proper performance by any public authority of any statutory power or statutory duty;
- the imposition of such a requirement is proportionate to what is sought to be achieved by its imposition; and
- that it is not reasonably practicable for the person with the appropriate permission to obtain possession of the protected information in an intelligible form without the giving of a notice.

PROTECTED INFORMATION IN AN INTELLIGIBLE FORM

3.16 In the Act and throughout this code references to protected information being 'intelligible' or 'put into an intelligible form' mean restoring the protected information to a condition it was in before being protected, whether by encryption or other process. This will be the condition in which the information or data was originally generated or processed before being protected or any condition it was in before being protected. In other words putting information into an intelligible form can include restoring it to a previously protected form to which further decryption or similar process needs to be applied to the information or data in order to comprehend it fully.

3.17 Information put into its original condition must remain in that condition for a period of time that is sufficient to meet the reasonable needs of the person to whom the disclosure is made. Information is not put into an intelligible form if it is put into its original condition, or restored to a previously protected form, only momentarily or for an unreasonably short period of time.

---

[3] See Section 9 of this code.

[4] Examples of the sorts of material that can constitute 'a key' are described in paragraph 3.18 to 3.21.

[5] Section 81(1) of Act defines 'person' to include any organisation and any association or combination of persons.

[6] One of the functions of the Security Service is the protection of national security and in particular the protection against threats from terrorism. Where a disclosure requirement is considered necessary in the interests of national security a person in another public authority should not give a notice under the Act where the operation or investigation falls within the responsibilities of the Security Service, as set out above, except where that person is a member of a Special Branch or the Metropolitan Police Counter Terrorism Command, or where the Security Service has agreed a notice may be given by a member of another public authority in relation to an operation or investigation which would fall within the responsibilities of the Security Service.

[7] Detecting crime includes establishing by whom, for what purpose, by what means and generally in what circumstances any crime was committed, the gathering of evidence for use in any legal proceedings and the apprehension of the person (or persons) by whom any crime was committed. See section 81(5) of the Act.

[8] Where, on the facts of the specific case, there is a connection with national security.

DESCRIPTION OF A KEY

3.18 A key to data means any key, code, password, algorithm or other data (including any proprietary software or cryptographic process) the use of which, by itself or with another key or keys:

- allows protected electronic data to be accessed, or
- facilitates putting protected electronic data into an intelligible form.

3.19 All manner of material can constitute a key. A key can be a plain language password or pass-phrase. It can include, for example, words, phrases or numbers written on any form of paper, plastic cards bearing numbers, electronic chips or magnetic strips and all forms of removable or fixed media for storing electronic data. It can include intangible material, for example, sounds or movements or comprise biometric data derived from, for example, fingerprint readers or iris scanners. Equally key material can be retained in the memory of an individual.

3.20 Ordinarily, for the purposes of this code and in the exercise of the powers contained in Part III, a key will be specific to protected information described in a corresponding notice.

3.21 Supporting information which takes the form of proprietary software that will render intelligible otherwise unintelligible data or more complex material such as algorithms for either or both encryption and decryption of data, comprising computer code (in written, source or executable form) or a functional description of the algorithm or code is unlikely to be a key that is unique to any specific protected electronic data but may, nonetheless, be a relevant key to such data. As such, any reference to a key or to key material can include supporting information.

3.22 Where supporting information is in the possession of a person, a notice for the disclosure of a key may require the disclosure of such supporting information.

3.23 A person from whom protected electronic data has been lawfully seized or otherwise acquired may not be in possession of supporting information that is the intellectual property or proprietary right of another person.

3.24 Reference to any key includes split-keys which, when used in combination, form a single key. Circumstances can arise where it is necessary to combine several split-keys before protected information can be made accessible or put into an intelligible form. This may require separate notices to be given to those persons holding the splitkeys (either all of them or sufficient number of them) to require them, acting together, to provide access to the protected information or disclose it in an intelligible form. Equally a notice may be served on a holder of a split-key who undertakes to seek the assistance of such other persons holding other parts of the key or holding any other part of the key in order to fulfil a requirement to provide access to the protected information or disclose it in an intelligible form.

ELECTRONIC SIGNATURE KEYS

3.25 Any key intended to be used for the purpose only of generating electronic signatures and which has not in fact been used for any other purpose can never be the subject of a disclosure requirement.[9]

---

[9] See Section 49(9) of the Act.

3.26 An electronic signature means anything in electronic form which is incorporated into or logically associated with any electronic communication or other electronic data, generated by the signatory or other source of the data, and which establishes the authenticity of the data, its integrity, or both by providing a link between the signatory or other source and the communication or data.

3.27 Where there are reasonable grounds to believe that a key used as an electronic signature has also been used for confidentiality purposes, that key may be required to be disclosed under the terms of the Act. Particular care must be taken when requiring the disclosure of a key that has been used as a signature key to ensure the key is used only for the purposes described in the disclosure notice.

Multi-use keys

3.28 Multi-use keys are keys used to protect more than one item of information, or have been used for signature purposes as well as for putting information into an intelligible form or for protecting all the communications sent to a person only some of which may be the subject of a disclosure notice. Particular care should be taken when a multi-use key is required to access protected information or to disclose it in an intelligible form. The notice must explain explicitly what is required and that it is proportionate to what is sought to be achieved.[10]

Session keys

3.29 Session keys are temporary keys used to encrypt or decrypt communications in a single 'session'. They are often ephemeral and usually unknown to their users. Even when they are not ephemeral a user may nonetheless have limited ability to generate, regenerate or recall them.

Possession of a key

3.30 Possession of a key by a person ('the person') can include circumstances where the key is in their own possession or in the possession of:

- an employee or other individual under their control, or
- a trusted third party or other service provider and the person has an immediate right of access to it or to have it transmitted or otherwise supplied to him.

3.31 Where the key is, or is contained in, anything which the person, an employee or other individual under their control is entitled, in exercise of any statutory power and without otherwise taking possession of it, to detain, inspect or search, that key is in the possession of the person. This means the key is, or is in, something to which the person or anyone under their control has lawful access.

3.32 Where more than one person is in possession of the key to protected information, and at least one of those is in possession of that key in his capacity as an officer or employee of a corporate body or firm and another is also an officer or employee of the body, or a partner of the firm (or is the corporate body or firm itself), a notice imposing a disclosure requirement shall not be given to any officer or employee of the body or employee of the firm who is in possession of the key unless that person is a senior

---

[10] See also paragraph 8.4.

officer of the body or a partner of the firm. In this context senior officer means a director, manager, secretary or other similar officer of the corporate body (and where the body is managed by its members a director means one of its members).

3.33 In practice this means notices should be served upon a person holding a position such as company secretary, legal director, chief information officer, information disclosure manager, law enforcement liaison manager, single point of contact or other post designated for the purpose of receiving notices served upon the company or firm.

3.34 Where it appears to a person giving a notice that there is no senior officer of the company, or partner of the firm, or a more senior employee to whom it would be reasonably practicable to give the notice, the notice shall be given to an officer or employee in possession of the key. This means an investigator giving a notice must always seek to give that notice to the most senior officer or employee in possession of the key whether or not any less senior officer or employee of the body, or employee of the firm, would be capable of complying with the disclosure notice.

3.35 The requirements for giving a notice to corporate bodies or firms do not apply where the special circumstances of the case mean that the purpose or purposes for which the notice is to be given would be defeated, in whole or in part, if the notice were required to be given to a senior officer of the company or a partner of the firm or a senior employee to whom it would otherwise be reasonably practicable to give the notice. This can include circumstances where a senior officer of the company or a partner of the firm is the subject of, or connected to, the investigation or operation.

NECESSITY AND PROPORTIONALITY

3.36 Exercise of the powers to require disclosure of protected information; disclosure of the means to access such information or to put it into an intelligible form may amount to interference with an individual's right to respect for their private and family life.

3.37 Such interference will be justifiable under Article 8 of the European Convention on Human Rights and in accordance with the Human Rights Act 1998 only if the conduct being required or taking place is both necessary and proportionate and in accordance with the law. The provisions in Part III are designed to meet the requirements that such activities are in accordance with law and to provide guidance to ensure that the activities are, in fact, both necessary and take place in a proportionate manner.

3.38 The person giving appropriate permission and, where different, the person with that permission must believe that the imposition of a disclosure requirement by a notice is necessary. They should consider whether other means to obtain the protected information in an intelligible form have failed, or would be bound to fail, for example that the person in possession of the key has not provided voluntarily the protected information in an intelligible form or would not do so.

3.39 He must also believe the imposition of that requirement to be proportionate to what is sought to be achieved by obtaining the disclosure of the protected information in an intelligible form or the disclosure of the means to gain access to the protected information or to put it in an intelligible form – that the disclosure requirement is no more than is required in the circumstances. This involves balancing the extent of the intrusiveness of the interference with an individual's right to respect for their private life against the benefit to the investigation or operation being undertaken by a relevant public authority in the public interest.

3.40 Consideration must also be given to any actual or potential infringement of the privacy of individuals who are not the subject of the investigation or operation, or to confidential business-client relationships where a disclosure requirement may be imposed upon a corporate body or firm. An application for appropriate permission to give a notice should draw attention to any circumstances which give rise to a meaningful degree of collateral intrusion.

3.41 Taking all these considerations into account in a particular case, an interference with the right to respect of individual privacy may still not be justified because the adverse impact on the privacy of an individual or group of individuals is too severe.

3.42 Any conduct that is excessive in the circumstances of both the interference and the aim of the investigation or operation, or is in any way arbitrary will not be proportionate.

Chapter 4

Rules on giving of notices

4.1 There are a number of statutory requirements that must be met before any disclosure requirement is imposed. Primarily only a person with appropriate permission may impose a disclosure requirement upon a person in respect of specific protected information. Schedule 2 to the Act defines persons able to grant appropriate permission, persons capable of having appropriate permission and describes the circumstances in which appropriate permission can be obtained.

Who may give notices?

4.2 Any public authority may, in the exercise of its functions, seek permission to serve a notice in relation to protected information that has already been obtained lawfully or in relation to protected information which is not yet in their lawful possession where they have a reasonable expectation of obtaining it.

Who may notices be served upon?

4.3 Section 49 notices may potentially be served on a wide variety of individuals, bodies or organisations. Individuals using products or services to protect data under their control, and businesses involved in producing or supplying such products or services, or using such technologies themselves could, conceivably, be in a position to disclose protected information in an intelligible form or to disclose a key required to put such information into an intelligible form.

4.4 Disclosure requirements are most likely to be imposed on individuals who have protected information directly relevant to an investigation or operation and are themselves a subject of, or are connected to, the investigation or operation. As a consequence of the way that information protection or cryptographic and other information technologies work, disclosure requirements may also be imposed on a person who has a relevant key to protected information by virtue of a personal or business relationship with an individual subject of, or connected to, an investigation or operation.

4.5 It is important in all circumstances where a notice is being contemplated that careful consideration is given by the person intending to seek appropriate permission or the person able to give that permission to whether a notice should be given, and if so, who should be given the notice. Where the imposition of a disclosure requirement upon a corporate body or firm is being considered, the person intending to seek appropriate permission must determine that body or firm would be able to comply with the proposed disclosure requirement and must determine which individual it should be served upon. That person may have a role for receiving legal notices and may have, or can call upon, the necessary technical expertise.

4.6 The imposition of a disclosure requirement upon a corporate body or firm without any prior consultation should be undertaken rarely and only in special circumstances. This is principally to be when there are reasonable grounds for believing that to do otherwise would prejudice an investigation or operation including where the corporate body or firm was suspected of complicity in unlawful conduct.

4.7 Prior consultation with a corporate body or firm must address the technical and practical implications for the business of a proposed disclosure requirement. This might include any unduly significant disruption to its business that would, or might, occur and any significant impact on the security of its operations that might expose it and its clients to risk or damages particularly when a requirement for disclosure of key material is being proposed. The business may require reasonable time to consider if it is technically able to meet the proposed requirement and, if so, to agree in what time the requirement can be met and, to the extent relevant, at what cost to the business.

4.8 Ordinarily a notice to a corporate body or firm should be served upon a central point of contact for legal or technical matters and should never be served upon an individual in a local office or branch without reference to that central point of contact.

APPLICATION FOR APPROPRIATE PERMISSION

4.9 Applications for appropriate permission must be made in writing or electronically to a person able to give appropriate permission, for example a judicial authority or a person holding judicial office. The person making the application will be a person involved in conducting an investigation or operation for a public authority. The applicant may be an individual who is seeking appropriate permission or is seeking the grant of appropriate permission on behalf of another person.

4.10 Persons able to give appropriate permission should not grant permission in relation to investigations or operations in which they are directly involved, although it is recognised that this may sometimes be unavoidable, especially in the case of small organisations or where it is necessary to act urgently or for security reasons.

4.11 Persons who grant, or who have, appropriate permission must have current working knowledge of human rights principles, specifically those of necessity and proportionality, and how they apply to the investigation of protected electronic data under Part III of the Act and this code.

4.12 Applications may be made orally in exceptional urgent circumstances[11] but a record of that application must be made in writing or electronically within one working day.

4.13 Applications – the original or a copy of which must be retained by the person with the appropriate permission – must:

- include the name (or designation)[12] and the office, rank or position held by the person making the application;
- where it is different from the applicant, include the name (or designation) and the office, rank or position held by the person for whom appropriate permission is being sought;
- include the operation name (if applicable) to which the application relates;
- specify the grounds on which the imposition of a disclosure requirement is necessary whether:
  - o in the interests of national security;
  - o for the purpose of preventing or detecting crime;
  - o in the interests of the economic well-being of the United Kingdom; or
  - o for the purpose of securing the effective exercise or proper performance by any public authority of any statutory power or statutory duty (and must identify that power or duty);
- describe the protected information which has been, or is likely to be, lawfully obtained;
- confirm the statutory power or other lawful means by which the protected information has been, or is likely to be, lawfully obtained;
- explain why it is reasonably believed that the person on whom it is intended to serve a section 49 notice has possession of a key or keys to the protected information described in the application;
- explain the scope of the disclosure requirement, why the imposition of that requirement is considered necessary and proportionate to what is sought to be achieved by its imposition;
- provide an assessment of the capability, technical or otherwise, of the person on whom it is intended to serve a notice to undertake the disclosure requirement;
- consider and, where appropriate, describe any meaningful collateral intrusion – the extent to which the privacy of any individual not under investigation may be infringed and why that intrusion is justified in the circumstances;
- explain why it is not reasonably practicable to acquire or obtain access to the protected information in an intelligible form by some other method without serving a section 49 notice;
- explain to whom the disclosure will be made, how the disclosed material will be handled, stored and safeguarded from unnecessary further disclosure; and
- identify and explain any urgency for which the proposed disclosure requirement is necessary.

---

[11] See paragraph 4.34.
[12] The use of a designation rather than a name will be appropriate only for persons in one of the Intelligence Services.

4.14 The decision to grant appropriate permission by a person able to do so shall be based upon information presented to them in an application. The grant of appropriate permission to any person must be in writing or, if not, in a manner that produces a record of it being granted.

4.15 The record of the grant of appropriate permission may take the form of a countersignature to the application, may be separate from that or be included in any warrant or order being given at the same time.

4.16 The exercise of appropriate permission by a person who has that permission by virtue of their rank or holding a designated office or position (in the police, SOCA, HMRC and members of HM forces) may be undertaken by them upon application from a person who would otherwise need to obtain appropriate permission. A record of the decision to exercise appropriate permission by a person who has that permission should be kept in the same way as if permission were being obtained from a person able to grant it.

Format of notices

4.17 The statutory requirements of the Act[13] mean that any notice imposing a disclosure requirement in respect of any protected information:

(a) must be given in writing or in a manner that produces a record which includes the date and time it was given;

(b) must describe the protected information to which the notice relates and, where known and where appropriate, identify any key to the protected information;

(c) must specify the grounds on which the notice is necessary including where appropriate the statutory power or duty within the meaning of section 49(2)(b)(ii) of the Act;

(d) must specify the office, rank or position of the individual giving the notice, and where appropriate and helpful to do so, their name (or designation);

(e) must specify the office, rank or position of the person who granted permission for the notice to be given and where appropriate, which will ordinarily be the name (or designation) of that person. If the person giving the notice does so without another persons' permission, the notice must set out why the person giving the notice is entitled to do so;

(f) must specify the time by which the notice is to be complied with, which must be reasonable in all the circumstances; and

(g) must set out clearly the extent of the disclosure required – whether a disclosure of the protected information in an intelligible form, or a disclosure of the means to either or both access the protected information and put it in an intelligible form – and must set out clearly how the disclosure is to be made.

4.18 A notice cannot require any person to make a disclosure to someone other than the person giving the notice, or such other person as is specified or identified in the notice where disclosure to another person is in accordance with the notice. For example,

---

[13] See section 49(4).

an investigator giving the notice may require disclosure to be made to a technical facility or to a named technician.

4.19 Section 49 notices must describe the form and manner in which the required disclosure of information is to be made (as described in paragraph 4.17 above). Notwithstanding this, it is best practice that the person giving the notice seeks, so far as possible, to agree with the person given the notice or with their professional legal adviser the manner in which the required disclosure should take place. The conditions under which compliance with the disclosure requirement takes place must be reasonable and practicable in all circumstances.

4.20 Notices should explain clearly that it is an offence to knowingly fail to make the required disclosure (section 53 of the Act) and, where a secrecy requirement is being imposed explain the 'tipping off' offence (section 54 of the Act).

4.21 Section 49 notices, including those which impose a secrecy requirement, should clarify that if the recipient has any doubt what they are required to do in response to the notice, they should contact a professional legal adviser.

AUTHENTICITY OF NOTICES

4.22 It is essential that any person who is given a notice is able to confirm its authenticity should they need to do so. Where such assurance is required the person given notice or their professional legal adviser should contact NTAC to seek confirmation that the notice is authentic and lawful. Doing so will not breach any secrecy requirement of the notice.

4.23 In practice the giving of a notice will be a stage in the progress of an investigation or operation and the person given the notice will usually have been involved earlier in that process, either as a consequence of their arrest or having been identified as being in possession of a key to the relevant information.

4.24 In addition to the statutory requirements all written notices must include a unique reference number, must identify the public authority and must provide the address of an office and a published contact telephone number using which the recipient of a notice may check its authenticity by speaking with the person who gave permission for the notice to be given or to another appropriate member of staff.

4.25 In exceptional urgent circumstances, the notice must always include contact details for the person who gave appropriate permission for the notice to be given.

4.26 Public authorities must provide a means for authenticating any notice they give at whatever time the notice is given. In addition, the person giving the notice should, when doing so in person, carry sufficient identification to confirm their office, rank or position and, if requested to do so, should produce that identification to the person being given the notice.

DESCRIPTION OF THE PROTECTED INFORMATION

4.27 Persons applying for appropriate permission must ensure that their application describes the protected information which has been, or is likely to be, lawfully obtained and in relation to which a disclosure requirement is sought to be imposed as precisely as possible. Where appropriate permission is granted or where a person has appropriate permission without another person's permission the consequent notice must similarly describe the protected information.

4.28 Any notice must be in sufficient detail to enable the person given notice to be clear about the protected information to which it relates and to enable identification of any, or all, keys (including any session key) which would enable the data to be put into an intelligible form. The information can be described by reference to file names, usernames, dates and times or by any other identifiers of data, storage media, software or hardware. Where a key to the protected information can be identified the identity of the key should be included in the notice.

4.29 In some cases, it may be appropriate in order to identify or to confirm the identification of the protected data to include in, attach to or accompany the notice some or all of the protected information or a copy of some or all of it.

4.30 In respect of protected information likely to be obtained it may not always be practicable to describe the information in the same detail or as precisely as information that has been obtained – although a fuller description may be provided subsequently in the form of a schedule to the original notice.

TIME TO COMPLY WITH A NOTICE

4.31 The time by which any notice has to be complied with must be reasonable and realistic in all the circumstances and must take into account the practical and technical requirements of undertaking the disclosure. It will vary depending on the type and extent of the disclosure required.

4.32 Any person given a notice or to be given a notice should be afforded a reasonable period of time to seek legal or technical advice before complying with it. Equally where appropriate to do so any person who will or may be given a notice should have time to take such advice before the notice is served.

4.33 Where appropriate the time period will be related to the duration of the underlying statutory power whereby the protected information has come into the possession of the public authority or is likely to do so.

4.34 In exceptional urgent circumstances it is possible that the time by which the notice is to be complied with must be curtailed. Examples of circumstances in which immediate compliance with a notice may be appropriate are:

- an immediate threat to life such that a person's life might be endangered if the period of time for compliance were not curtailed;
- an exceptionally urgent operational requirement where, within no more than 48 hours of the notice being given compliance with that notice will directly assist the prevention or detection of the commission of a serious crime[14] and the making of arrests or the seizure of illicit material, and where that operational opportunity will be lost if the period for compliance with the notice were not curtailed; or
- a credible and immediate threat to national security or a time critical or unique opportunity to secure, or prevent the loss of, information of vital importance to national security where that threat might be realised, or that opportunity lost, if the period for compliance with the notice were not curtailed.

---

[14] See Section 81(2) of the Act.

EXPLAINING THE NOTICE

4.35 The person giving the notice should take steps to explain, as far as is practicable and necessary (and to the extent such an explanation has not been offered before the notice is given), the contents of the notice and what is required to be done to comply with it. In particular the person giving the notice must be prepared to explain:

- on what grounds the disclosure requirement is being imposed;
- what is the relevant protected information;
- what is required to be disclosed, by when and to whom;
- any requirement to disclose a key (if appropriate) with clarification that the choice of which key to disclose is open to the recipient of the notice if that key, including any relevant session key, gives access to the information or puts it into an intelligible form;
- any secrecy provision (if appropriate);
- the consequences of not complying with the notice;
- that the person given the notice is entitled to seek legal advice about the effect of the notice and the provisions of the Act; and
- how the authenticity of the notice may be confirmed.

4.36 The person given notice must be provided with a copy of the notice which they may retain.

AMENDING A NOTICE

4.37 Amendment of a notice may be required and can only be undertaken in restricted circumstances which clarify or alleviate the imposition of the disclosure requirement. These are when:

- the protected information can be identified more precisely;
- the disclosure requirement can be specified more accurately;
- the time to comply with the notice can be extended;
- a secrecy requirement can be removed; or
- where the disclosure should be made to a person not specified in the original notice.

4.38 In these cases, the amendment to the notice must:

- be undertaken in writing to the person given the notice or, if not, in a manner that produces a record of the amendment which the person given the notice may retain;
- cross reference the original unique reference number;
- record the date and time of the amendment; and
- record the name or designation and the office, rank or position held by the person amending the notice (who shall be the person who gave the notice or a person who, in the same circumstances, could have given that notice).

4.39 Any amendments to a notice must reflect the considerations of necessity and proportionality upon which the original notice was given. This means the scope of a notice or the disclosure requirement it imposes can never be extended by any amendment nor can the time to comply be curtailed. In those circumstances a new notice must be given.

4.40 The grounds for which a notice is given can never be amended, nor can a secrecy requirement be imposed by amending a notice which did not contain such a requirement. Appropriate permission must be obtained to give a notice for a different purpose or to impose a secrecy requirement.

WITHDRAWAL OF A NOTICE

4.41 The person who had the appropriate permission to give the notice or the person who gave the notice shall withdraw it if, at any time after giving the notice and before any disclosure is made, it is no longer necessary for the person given notice to comply with it or the disclosure required by the notice is no longer proportionate to what was sought to be achieved.

4.42 Withdrawal of a notice must:

- be undertaken in writing to the person given the notice or, if not, in a manner that produces a record of the notice having been withdrawn and confirms that a disclosure is no longer required;
- identify, by reference to its unique reference number, the notice being withdrawn;
- record the date and, when appropriate to do so, the time when the notice was withdrawn; and
- record the name (or designation) and the office, rank or position held by the person withdrawing the notice.

CONTRIBUTIONS TO COSTS

4.43 Should any person or persons incur costs in complying with a notice an appropriate contribution towards those costs may be made by the public authority that has imposed the disclosure requirement or obtained appropriate permission to impose that requirement.

4.44 In practice, the issue of costs will be most relevant where a third party is assisting in an investigation or operation and should be dealt with in preliminary discussions between the public authority and the person to be given the notice or any person in a company or a firm who is responsible for assisting the execution of disclosure requirements imposed upon the company or firm. Such discussions should also address any costs that might be incurred preparatory to meeting a requirement which is then not imposed or is withdrawn.

CONFIRMATION OF COMPLIANCE WITH A NOTICE

4.45 Where a notice has been complied with, in full or as fully as practicable in all the circumstances, the person with appropriate permission for giving the notice or the person who gave the notice must provide written confirmation of that fact to the person given the notice and, where different, also to the person who has undertaken the disclosure.

4.46 Where a disclosure is required to be made other than to the person who gave the notice (for example to a technical facility or a named technician) the person to whom the disclosure is made must provide the person who gave the notice and the person making the disclosure with confirmation, in writing or in a manner that produces a record, that the notice has been, or appears to have been, complied with. Such confirmation must be provided as soon as is practicable.

Chapter 5

Rules on the effect of imposing disclosure requirements

DISCLOSURE OF PROTECTED INFORMATION IN AN INTELLIGIBLE FORM

5.1 The effect of giving a notice to a person who, at the time the notice is served, is in possession of both the protected information[15] and a means of obtaining access to the information and of disclosing it in intelligible form (using a key or keys) is that he:

- may use any key or keys in his possession to gain access to the information or to put it into an intelligible form, and
- is required to disclose the information described in the notice in an intelligible form, and
- is required to make that disclosure in accordance with the notice.

5.2 The person given notice to disclose the information in an intelligible form can nonetheless choose to disclose any key or keys giving access to the information in an intelligible form, together with any relevant details of the cryptographic or other process used to protect the information.

5.3 Voluntary disclosure of the key or keys providing access to the protected information in an intelligible form, to the person to whom disclosure of the intelligible information was required, and by the time that disclosure was required, will mean that the person given notice to disclose the information in an intelligible form shall have complied with the requirement imposed on him to do so.

5.4 Where a disclosure requirement is to be imposed upon a business or service provider in order to assist an investigation or operation, appropriate consideration must be given to minimising any actual or possible disruption to the business or service, or any actual or possible breach of confidence, inconvenience or unfairness to the customers of the business or users of the service.

Chapter 6

Special rules on the effect of imposing disclosure requirements

DISCLOSURE OF THE MEANS TO ACCESS PROTECTED INFORMATION OR
TO PUT IT INTO AN INTELLIGIBLE FORM

6.1 This section concerns the circumstances in which a notice can be complied with only by the disclosure of a key, in other words:

- requiring disclosure of the means to access protected information, or

---

[15] Possession of the protected information includes being provided with the protected information, or a copy of it, that has come into the possession of any person.

- requiring disclosure of the means to put protected information into an intelligible form.

6.2 No notice shall require the disclosure of a key unless the person granting permission for the notice to be given has directed that the disclosure requirement can only be complied with by disclosure of a key, or the person giving such a notice has appropriate permission to do so or has express permission for giving such a direction.

SPECIAL CIRCUMSTANCES REQUIRING DISCLOSURE OF A KEY

6.3 The Act imposes extra conditions upon requiring disclosure of a key, in addition to those for requiring the disclosure of protected information in an intelligible form.

6.4 No person able to do so shall give a direction that a disclosure requirement can be met only by disclosure of a key unless that person believes:

- that there are special circumstances of the case which mean that the purposes for which the disclosure notice is necessary would be defeated, in whole or in part, if a key was not required to be disclosed, and
- that the requirement for disclosure of a key is proportionate to what is sought to be achieved by preventing compliance with the disclosure requirement other than by disclosure of a key.

6.5 Matters to be considered in determining such proportionality include the extent and nature of any protected information (other than that to which the disclosure requirement relates) which is protected by the same key and any adverse effect that a disclosure requirement might have on a business carried on by the person on whom the requirement is imposed.

6.6 This means that the person giving a direction that a key is required to be disclosed must consider the actual or potential collateral intrusion that will or may arise from disclosure of the key and its application to specified protected information that has come into the possession of any person or is likely to do so or might do so.

6.7 Although the special circumstances for giving direction to require the disclosure of a key will vary with each case as will the proportionality of doing so, such a requirement may be appropriate where:

- trust is an issue – where there is doubt about the integrity of the person or organisation being asked to comply with a disclosure requirement, for example the person or organisation concerned is suspected of involvement in criminality or of protecting another person or persons involved in criminality;
- credibility is an issue – where a prior disclosure of protected information in an intelligible form, whether undertaken voluntarily or in supposed compliance with a notice, is demonstrably incomplete;
- timeliness is an issue – if a person or organisation has the key to protected information but cannot, for whatever reason and having been given the opportunity to do so, provide the information in an intelligible form in exceptional urgent circumstances;
- the content of the intelligible information is an issue – where the person required to make the disclosure or a person able to undertake the disclosure on their behalf might find the intelligible form of the material offensive, obscene or otherwise distressing or it is important in the interests of justice that they do not view or be reminded of the material;

271

- the key itself has evidential value – where there is reasonable belief that the key may provide evidence linking a person or persons to an offence or offences, for example where a person seeks to deny responsibility for protected information in their possession but a password or pass-phrase for the key is personal to the person being served the notice or is indicative of the material it protects. In practice it will be very rare for an investigator to reasonably believe there is a single key to the protected information which has evidential value or, less likely still, that all keys to the data have that value;
- practicality is an issue – where the key is divided into split-keys and it is not practicable or possible for the holders of the split-keys, or sufficient number of them, to act together to provide access to protected information or to disclose it in an intelligible form it may be necessary to require disclosure of one or more split-keys.

6.8 Particular care must be taken when considering the imposition of a requirement to disclose a key upon a provider of financial services in view of the crucial role that protected information has in the financial services sector. No such requirement should be imposed upon any company or firm authorised by the Financial Services Authority without prior notification to the Chief Executive of the Authority or a person designated by him for that purpose. The period of notification will be reasonable in all the circumstances of any instance.

6.9 Such notification to the Financial Services Authority will include sufficient detail to enable the Authority to understand why the requirement to disclose a key is sought to be imposed. The Authority shall consider whether the proposed disclosure requirement raises any concerns for or risks to its statutory objectives of maintaining market confidence, promoting public understanding of the financial system, the protection of consumers and the reduction of financial crime. If so, the Chief Executive of the Authority or the person designated by him will inform the applicant, or a senior official of the public authority, of those concerns or risks and the applicant must reconsider the proposed disclosure requirement taking account of those concerns or risks.

NOTICES REQUIRING DISCLOSURE OF A KEY

6.10 Where a direction has been given that a notice can be complied with only by disclosure of a key, the notice must explicitly state that the person on whom the notice is served may choose which key to disclose. The only requirement is that the key is capable of either or both obtaining access to the protected information or rendering it intelligible.

6.11 Where the person given notice is able to comply with a requirement to disclose a key without disclosing all of the keys in his possession and where there are different keys, or combinations of keys, that would enable compliance with the notice, the person given notice may choose which key or combination of keys to disclose.

6.12 Where a disclosure requirement is imposed on any person by a section 49 notice and:

- that person is not in possession of the information (either because they do not have the information, have not acquired the information or cannot be given possession);
- that person is incapable, without the use of a key that is not in his possession, of obtaining access to the information and of disclosing it in an intelligible form (or so disclosing it); or

- the notice states that it can only be complied with by the disclosure of a key to the information

the effect of imposing that disclosure requirement is that the person given the notice shall be required, in accordance with the notice imposing the requirement, to disclose any key to the protected information that is in his possession at a relevant time, that is the time when the notice is given or any subsequent time before the time by which the disclosure requirement has to be complied with.

6.13 Where a person has been given notice requiring that a key be disclosed, he may choose which key or keys to disclose together with any other requested relevant details of the cryptographic methods in use, including the relevant algorithm. The information given should be sufficient to allow the person giving the notice or the person to whom disclosure is required to be made to put the protected information described in the notice into intelligible form.

6.14 The recipient of a notice may disclose an alternative key such as a 'session key' if it enables the same access or functionality as any relevant longer term key would have enabled.

6.15 No person shall be required to disclose any key or keys other than those which are sufficient to enable the protected information described in the notice to be put into intelligible form – even if the person given notice to disclose a key is in possession of more than one key to that information. This also means that where a key is held within a multiple key store, for example among a number of keys on a smart card, necessary arrangements should be made to enable the person given notice to abstract the key and disclose it using alternative storage media.

6.16 Where a person is required by a section 49 notice to make a disclosure in respect of any protected information and that person:

- has had possession of the key to the protected information but no longer has possession of it;
- would have been required by the notice to disclose the key if it had continued to be in his possession; and
- when given the notice, or within the time by which the notice must be complied with, is in possession of any information that would facilitate the obtaining or discovery of the key or the putting of the protected information into an intelligible form;

the effect of the disclosure requirement is that he shall be required to disclose all such information to the person to whom he would have been required to disclose the protected information in an intelligible form or the key. In other words, to disclose anything they have that assists putting the protected information into an intelligible form.

Chapter 7

Keeping of records

7.1 Public authorities must retain copies of all written applications for permission to give a section 49 notice. Such applications must be available for scrutiny by the relevant independent Commissioner with a statutory oversight role.[16] Public authorities may be required to justify to the Commissioner the content of a particular application, or their general approach to, and handling of applications and giving of notices.

7.2 All public authorities must maintain a central record of all applications for appropriate permission to give notices, of approval given by NTAC, of the grant of appropriate permission, of the giving of all notices and of compliance with each notice. These records must be available for inspection by the relevant Commissioner and retained to allow the Investigatory Powers Tribunal, established under Part IV of the Act, to carry out its functions.[17]

7.3 Applications for permission to give notices, records of the giving of and compliance with notices, and information disclosed as a result of any notice, either directly or by using disclosed key material, which relate to any living identifiable individual are likely to constitute personal data and, therefore, can only be processed in accordance with the provisions of the Data Protection Act 1998.

7.4 This code of practice does not affect any other statutory obligations placed on public authorities to keep records under any other enactment. For example, where applicable in England and Wales, the relevant test given in the Criminal Procedure and Investigations Act 1996 as amended and the code of practice under that Act. This requires that material which is obtained in the course of an investigation and which may be relevant to the investigation must be recorded, retained and revealed to the prosecutor.

Chapter 8

Procedures for dealing with disclosed material

PROCEDURES FOR DEALING WITH DISCLOSED KEY MATERIAL

8.1 The Act clearly indicates[18] that it is the duty of every person[19] whose officers or employees include persons with duties that involve the giving of section 49 notices to ensure that arrangements are in force to safeguard keys and key material obtained by the imposition of disclosure requirements.

8.2 Such persons should ensure necessary arrangements are in force:

- that any disclosed key is used only for obtaining access to, or putting into intelligible form, protected information described in the notice as a result of which the key was disclosed (or could have been described in such a notice had the key not already been disclosed);

---

[16] See Section 11 of this code.

[17] The Tribunal will consider complaints made up to one year after the conduct to which the complaint relates and, where it is satisfied it is equitable to do so, may consider complaints made more than one year after the conduct to which the complaint relates. See section 67(5) of the Act.

[18] Section 55 of the Act.

[19] In particular the Secretary of State and every other Minister of the Crown in charge of a government department, every chief officer of police, the Director General of the Serious Organised Crime Agency and the Commissioners of Revenue and Customs.

- that the use of any disclosed key is reasonable with regard both to the uses to which the person with the key is entitled to put any protected information to which the key relates and to the other circumstances of the case (in other words only reasonable use may be made of any disclosed key);
- that the use of and retention of any disclosed key is proportionate to what is sought by its use or retention, and where any key is retained, its retention must be reviewed at appropriate intervals to confirm that the justification for its retention remains valid (otherwise it should be destroyed);
- that the number of persons to whom any disclosed key is made available and the number of copies made of the key, if any, are each limited to the minimum necessary for the purpose of putting the protected information in an intelligible form;
- that any disclosed key is stored, for as long as it is retained, in a secure manner. The appropriate level of security for any disclosed key should be proportionate to its intrinsic or financial value or to the sensitivity of the information protected by the key, and should at least correspond to its security before disclosure;
- that all physical key material no longer required to be retained is returned to the person who disclosed it;
- that all records of any disclosed key are destroyed permanently as soon as the key is no longer required for the purpose of enabling protected information to be put into an intelligible form.[20]

8.3 Such arrangements shall be recorded in writing setting out internal procedures for the disclosure, copying, storage and destruction of any disclosed key material, which minimise the availability of disclosed key material, and shall be agreed with the appropriate Commissioner.

8.4 Extra care and security should be afforded to a key (a 'multi-use key') that has been used to protect information in addition to the protected information in the possession of the public authority or likely to come into its possession. Even though a person given notice is able to choose which key to disclose, they may disclose a multi-use key. The person to whom disclosure is made should ensure that if a multi-use key is disclosed he is aware of that and can protect the key appropriately.

8.5 Key material must be stored in a *physically* secure way such that it cannot be accessed through any means other than physically. For example the use of a floppy disk or USB stick may be appropriate but a laptop would not as it could theoretically be accessed remotely.

8.6 Data should be secured behind an appropriate number of security zones using, where possible, different methods of security. For example material requiring the highest level of security should be stored in a combination safe, inside a locked store in an access controlled office which itself is within a 24 hour guarded building. Access to the data should not be possible by one person acting alone, requiring at least two people to have to conspire to unlawfully use any key. For example the combination to a safe in a locked store should not be known by a key holder of the store.

8.7 Where keys or copies of keys are made available to a person other than the person to whom the key was disclosed a full audit trail must be maintained and be available for inspection by the appropriate Commissioner.

---

[20] See paragraph 8.10.

8.8 The number of persons to whom the detail of any key or the fact of possession of a disclosed key is made available must be limited to the absolute minimum necessary to allow protected information to be made intelligible.

8.9 Neither the key, the detail of any key, nor the fact of possession of a key may be disclosed to any person unless that person's duties are such that he needs to know the information to carry out his duties. This obligation applies equally to disclosure to additional persons within an agency or public authority, to disclosure outside the agency or public authority and to any data processing facility.

8.10 Under normal circumstances where protected information is put into an intelligible form using a disclosed key, and that intelligible information is used in evidence or is disclosed in criminal proceedings, copies of the key will similarly be required for evidential or disclosure purposes (notwithstanding any necessary public interest immunity).

8.11 Where a requirement for disclosure of a key is necessary in relation to protected information obtained in exercise of a statutory power, that key will be handled with the due care and attention required for any sensitive or valuable evidential material. It shall be the duty of the person to whom the key is disclosed or the official in charge of any processing facility to afford it a higher level of security if that is necessary in the particular circumstances of the case and to protect the key material from unauthorised disclosure.

PROCEDURES FOR DEALING WITH DISCLOSED INTELLIGIBLE MATERIAL

8.12 Intelligible information which is disclosed in compliance with a notice should be handled with the same care and attention as other material that has been obtained by means of a statutory power to seize or otherwise require the production of documents or other property. Any loss or damage incurred by a relevant person (within the meaning in section 55(5) of the Act) arising from any failure to safeguard disclosed intelligible information may give rise to a civil action against the public authority or the person responsible for that failure.

DAMAGES

8.13 Should any person who has made a disclosure having been given a section 49 notice or whose own protected information or whose own key has been disclosed as a consequence of a notice incur any loss or damage in consequence of:

- any breach by a person on whom the duties to safeguard disclosed keys apply; or
- any contravention of the arrangements for those safeguards made by any person who is under the control of a person to whom section 55 of the Act applies;
- the injured person may take civil action in relation to such a breach or contravention against the person on whom the duties to safeguard disclosed keys apply.

8.14 Any court hearing such proceedings shall have regard to any opinion with respect to the matters to which the proceedings relate that is or has been given by a relevant Commissioner.

Chapter 9

Appropriate permission for the giving of notices

9.1 Any person using the powers in Part III, and specifically any person giving a section 49 notice, must have appropriate permission to do so. Circumstances in which appropriate permission may be granted or persons have the appropriate permission are described in Schedule 2 to the Act.

9.2 In general the permission to give a notice must be given by a person with at least the same level of authority as that required for the exercise of any power to obtain the protected information. With certain exceptions, the appropriate permission to give a notice should, so far as is practical, be given by the same person authorising, or who authorised, the use of any power to obtain the protected information.

9.3 No person can seek to obtain appropriate permission to give a notice without the approval of NTAC to do so. Persons able to grant appropriate permission for the giving of notices must ensure that the approval of NTAC has been obtained before granting appropriate permission.

9.4 Appropriate permission can never be given for a notice in respect of protected information that has been obtained unlawfully by a public authority.

<small>APPROPRIATE PERMISSION GRANTED BY A JUDICIAL AUTHORITY</small>

9.5 Public authorities may always seek appropriate permission for giving a section 49 notice from a judicial authority. Any member of a public authority will have appropriate permission if, and only if, written permission for giving the notice has been granted by:

- a Circuit judge, in England and Wales;
- a sheriff, in Scotland; or
- a county court judge, in Northern Ireland.

9.6 Where such a judicial authority has granted appropriate permission to give a section 49 notice, no further permission from any other person is required.

9.7 Where protected information has been obtained under statute but without a warrant (other than by the police, HMRC, SOCA or a member of HM forces) a person shall not have the appropriate permission, even where permission is granted by a judicial authority, unless:

- he is the person who exercised the statutory power to obtain the protected information (or is a person who could have exercised it); or
- he is the person to whom the protected information was provided or disclosed (or is a person to whom provision or disclosure of the information would have discharged the statutory duty); or
- he is or is likely to be such a person when the power is exercised or the protected information provided or disclosed.

<small>APPROPRIATE PERMISSION GRANTED BY A PERSON HOLDING JUDICIAL OFFICE</small>

9.8 Public authorities may obtain appropriate permission for giving a section 49 notice from persons holding judicial office where protected information is likely to be,

277

or has been, obtained under a warrant issued by such a person holding judicial office, that is to say:

- any judge of the Crown Court or of the High Court of Justice;
- any sheriff;
- any justice of the peace;
- any resident magistrate in Northern Ireland; or
- any person holding any such judicial office as entitles him to exercise the jurisdiction of a judge of the Crown Court or of a justice of the peace.

9.9 Appropriate permission may be given by the person who issues or issued the warrant or by a person holding judicial office who would have been entitled to issue the warrant. Such permission might be granted, for example, in relation to a search warrant or production order under the Police and Criminal Evidence Act 1984 as amended or the Drug Trafficking Act 1994 as amended.

9.10 Any person will have appropriate permission if:

- before protected information is obtained, the warrant contained explicit permission for giving section 49 notices in relation to protected information to be obtained under the warrant, or
- subsequent to the issue of the warrant, written permission is granted for giving section 49 notices in relation to protected information obtained under the warrant.

9.11 Only a person who was entitled to exercise the power conferred by the warrant or who is a person on whom the power conferred by the warrant was, or could have been, conferred may have appropriate permission to give a notice in relation to protected information obtained, or to be obtained, under a warrant issued by a person holding judicial office. In other words, a person only has appropriate permission if that person could execute, has executed or could have executed the warrant.

9.12 Where protected information is obtained under a statutory power without a warrant in the course of, or in connection with, the execution of a warrant containing appropriate permission, or where material unconnected with a search warrant is lawfully seized, for example under section 19 of the Police and Criminal Evidence Act 1984 ('PACE'), appropriate permission for giving a notice in respect of that additional information will be required.

APPROPRIATE PERMISSION GRANTED BY THE SECRETARY OF STATE

9.13 Where protected information is likely to be, or has been, obtained under a warrant issued by the Secretary of State (for example an interception warrant under section 8 of the Act, or a warrant for interference with wireless telegraphy, entry or interference with property under section 5 of the Intelligence Services Act 1994) appropriate permission for giving a section 49 notice in respect of that information may be obtained from the Secretary of State.

9.14 Only persons holding office under the Crown, the police, a member of staff of the SOCA or HMRC may have the appropriate permission in relation to protected information obtained, or to be obtained, under a warrant issued by the Secretary of State.

9.15 Such persons have appropriate permission if the warrant issued by the Secretary of State contains permission for giving section 49 notices in relation to protected information to be obtained under the warrant or, subsequent to the issue of the warrant, the Secretary of State grants written permission for giving section 49 notices in relation to protected information obtained under the warrant.

9.16 The Secretary of State may also grant written permission for giving section 49 notices where protected information has come, or is likely to come, into the possession of any of the intelligence services without a warrant or where protected information has been, or is likely to be, obtained lawfully by any of the intelligence services using a statutory power but without the exercise of a warrant[21] or where protected information is in the possession of any of the intelligence services, or is likely to come into their possession, for example material voluntarily disclosed or provided to any of the intelligence services.[22]

9.17 Where the Secretary of State's permission is sought he must grant the permission personally in writing or, in an urgent case, expressly authorise the grant of permission in which case a senior official may sign it.[23]

Appropriate permission granted by an authorising officer

9.18 Where protected information is likely to be, or has been, obtained in consequence of an authorisation under Part III of the Police Act 1997 (authorisation of otherwise unlawful action in respect of property) appropriate permission for giving a section 49 notice may be obtained from an authorising officer within the meaning of section 93 of the 1997 Act or, in urgent cases, section 94 of that Act.

9.19 Any person will have appropriate permission if, before protected information is obtained, the authorisation given under the 1997 Act contained permission for giving notices in relation to protected information to be obtained under the authorisation or, subsequent to the issue of the authorisation, written permission is granted for giving notices in relation to protected information obtained under the authorisation.

9.20 Only the police, SOCA and HM Revenue and Customs may have the appropriate permission in relation to protected information obtained, or to be obtained, under an authorisation under Part III of the Police Act 1997.

Appropriate permission granted by a person exercising a statutory function

9.21 The police, SOCA, HMRC and members of HM forces have appropriate permission, without requirement for permission to be granted by a judicial authority, in relation to protected information:

- that is likely to be, or has been, obtained by the exercise of a statutory power (and is not information obtained under a warrant issued by the Secretary of State or a person holding judicial office, or an authorisation under Part III of the Police Act 1997, or information obtained by the intelligence services), for example material obtained by the police under section 19 of PACE;
- that is likely to be provided or disclosed, or has been provided or disclosed, in pursuance of a statutory duty;

---

[21] See paragraph 3 of Schedule 2 to the Act.
[22] See paragraph 5(2) of Schedule 2 to the Act.
[23] See paragraph 8 of Schedule 2 to the Act.

- that is likely to come into possession of, or is in the possession of, the police, SOCA, HMRC or a member of HM forces under statute.

9.22 In these circumstances, if a section 49 notice is to require disclosure, such permission may be given in line with the general requirements relating to appropriate permission.

GENERAL REQUIREMENTS RELATING TO APPROPRIATE PERMISSION

9.23 Paragraph 6 of Schedule 2 to the Act sets out general requirements relating to persons having appropriate permission in the police, SOCA, HMRC or who are members of HM forces. A person has appropriate permission in relation to any protected information if he has possession of the protected information, or is likely to have possession of it, or is authorised to act on behalf of such a person.

9.24 Where protected information has come into the possession of the police by means of the exercise of powers conferred by section 44 of the Terrorism Act 2000 (power to stop and search), the appropriate permission to give a section 49 notice in relation to that information must be granted by an officer holding at least the rank of Assistant Chief Constable of a police force or the rank of Commander in the Metropolitan Police Service or the City of London Police.

9.25 Where protected information has come into the possession of the police, SOCA, HMRC or a member of HM forces, a person shall not have appropriate permission unless that person holds certain rank or designation:

- Police – Superintendent or above;
- SOCA – Director General or a member of staff of the SOCA of or above such level as the Director General may designate for this purpose;
- HMRC – the Commissioners for Revenue and Customs themselves or an officer of their department of or above such level as they may designate for this purpose;
- HM forces – Lieutenant Colonel or its equivalent or above.

APPROPRIATE ADDITIONAL PERMISSION FOR GIVING DIRECTIONS
FOR THE DISCLOSURE OF KEYS

9.26 Where a disclosure requirement can only be met by disclosure of a key, appropriate additional permission for giving such a direction is required in the following circumstances:

- for a direction by any constable (except a constable who is a member of the staff of the SOCA), and a member of Her Majesty's forces who is a member of the police, by or with the permission of a chief officer of police;
- for a direction by SOCA, by or with the permission of the Director General of the SOCA;
- for a direction by HMRC, by or with the permission of the Commissioners for Her Majesty's Revenue and Customs;
- for a direction by a member of Her Majesty's forces who is not a member of the police force, by or with the permission of, or above, the rank of Brigadier (or equivalent).

9.27 Any permission granted for giving a direction that a disclosure requirement can only be met by disclosure of a key must be given expressly in relation to the specific direction.

9.28 Any direction to disclose a key given by or with the permission of a chief officer of police, the Director General of the SOCA or the Commissioners for Her Majesty's Revenue and Customs must be notified to the Chief Surveillance Commissioner.

9.29 Any direction to disclose a key given by a member of Her Majesty's forces shall also be notified to the Chief Surveillance Commissioner except where the direction is given by a member of Her Majesty's forces who is not a member of a police force and is in connection with Her Majesty's forces other than those in Northern Ireland in which case notification must be given to the Intelligence Services Commissioner.

9.30 Notification to the appropriate Commissioner of any direction to disclose a key must be given in writing or electronically as soon as practicable and within no more than 5 working days of the direction being given. Failure to do so will constitute a breach of this code.

DURATION OF APPROPRIATE PERMISSION

9.31 Permission granted to any person to give a section 49 notice can cease to have effect.

9.32 All persons who grant permission for the giving of notices must attach an appropriate duration to all such permissions. Permission lasting for a lengthy period will always need careful ongoing consideration particularly with regard to whether in the specific circumstances the notice remains necessary and proportionate.

9.33 Permission, once granted, has effect – regardless of the cancellation, expiry or discharge of any warrant or authorisation in which that permission is contained or to which it relates – until such time, if any, as that permission:

- expires in accordance with the limitation on its duration that was contained in the terms of the permission, or
- is withdrawn by the person who granted the permission or by a person holding any office or other position that would have entitled that person to grant the permission.

Chapter 10

Offences

10.1 The Act provides for two criminal offences: failure to comply with a notice (Section 53) and making an unauthorised disclosure (tipping-off) (Section 54).

FAILURE TO COMPLY WITH A NOTICE

10.2 Where a person given a section 49 notice knowingly fails to make the disclosure required they commit an offence. If the disclosure required is necessary in the interests of national security they may be convicted on indictment to a maximum of 5 years imprisonment[24] or in any other case 2 years. On summary conviction they may be

---

[24] Section 53 as amended by Section 15, Terrorism Act 2006.

liable to a maximum six-month term of imprisonment or a fine not exceeding the statutory maximum or both.

10.3 In proceedings against any person for failing to comply with a notice, if it is shown beyond a reasonable doubt that he was in possession of a key to the protected information at any time before the notice was given, that person shall be considered to be in possession of that key at all subsequent times unless it is shown that the key was not in his possession after the giving of the notice and before the time that he was required to disclose it.

10.4 If the person fails to raise some doubt as to whether he had the key when the notice was given or before any subsequent time by which he was required to make the disclosure, that person shall be taken to have continued to be in possession of that key.

10.5 A person shall be taken to have shown they were not in possession of a key to protected information at a particular time if sufficient evidence of that fact is adduced to raise an issue with respect to their not having had possession of the key. The prosecutor has to prove the contrary beyond reasonable doubt.

10.6 It is a defence for a person to show it was not reasonably practicable to make the disclosure required within the time limit given in the notice, for example for purely technical reasons, but that the disclosure was made as soon afterwards as was reasonably practicable.

10.7 A person shall have failed to comply with a notice where a disclosure is made and it is shown beyond a reasonable doubt that the disclosure made is not in compliance with the notice given, for example the information put into intelligible form is demonstrably partial, incomplete or information other than the protected information described in the notice.

TIPPING OFF

10.8 Section 49 notices may contain a provision requiring the person to whom the notice is given and every other person who is permitted to or who necessarily becomes aware of it or of its contents to keep secret the giving of the notice, its contents and the things done to comply with it. The inclusion of a secrecy requirement in a notice requires the consent of the person granting permission for the notice to be given or for the person giving the notice to have that permission.

10.9 This secrecy requirement is designed to preserve – but only where necessary – the covert nature of an investigation and to deter deliberate and intentional behaviour designed to frustrate statutory procedures and assist others to evade detection.

10.10 The circumstances in which a secrecy requirement may be imposed are restricted in section 54 of the Act. There are two conditions;

- the first condition is that the protected information has come, or is likely to come, into the possession of the police, SOCA, HMRC or the intelligence services;
- the second condition is that the means by which the information was obtained needs to be kept secret in order to maintain the effectiveness of an investigation or operation or of investigative techniques generally, or in the interests of the safety or well-being of any person.

10.11 Public authorities other than those specified in section 54 may not include a secrecy requirement in their disclosure notices.

10.12 In imposing any secrecy requirement it is enough for any person giving consent for that requirement or giving a notice including such a requirement to have considered that there is a particular person from whom it is reasonable to withhold the information.

10.13 Where a secrecy requirement is imposed, the notice must make this clear and the person given notice and any other person who needs to know about the notice should be made aware explicitly of that requirement. The notice should also inform the recipient that he may nonetheless approach a professional legal adviser for advice about the effect of the provisions of Part III of the Act and that he may revoke any key that is disclosed provided the underlying reason for its revocation is not disclosed.

10.14 The tipping-off offence is committed by a person who makes a disclosure to any other person of anything that he is required by the section 49 notice to keep secret.

10.15 A notice containing a secrecy requirement can never be imposed upon a vulnerable person or a child.

AUTOMATIC TIPPING OFF

10.16 For security purposes, certain software has been designed to give an automatic warning when a key has been disclosed or has ceased to be secure. This can conflict with a secrecy requirement, although the person seeking permission to give the notice should, so far as is practicable, establish whether the intended recipient of the notice uses such software and if so what reasonable steps they can take to prevent or defer such disclosure.

10.17 Where a disclosure occurs contrary to a secrecy requirement it is a defence for a person to show that the disclosure was automatic and effected entirely by software designed to indicate that a key to protected information has ceased to be secure and they could not reasonably have prevented that taking place, whether after being given the notice or becoming aware of it or its contents.

10.18 It is also a defence for a person to show that the disclosure was made by or to a professional legal adviser as part of giving advice to a client of his about the effect of the provisions of Part III of the Act and that the person to whom or by whom the disclosure was made was the client or a representative of the client; or where a disclosure was made by a legal adviser in connection with any proceedings before a court or tribunal.

10.19 If a disclosure is made by or to a professional legal adviser with a view to furthering any criminal purpose that disclosure shall not be a defence in proceedings for a Section 54 offence.

AUTHORISED DISCLOSURE

10.20 It is not the intention of the Act to penalise individuals within organisations who, for example, have been given a notice imposing a secrecy requirement but need the assistance of another colleague in order to comply with the notice. That other person must be made aware of the secrecy requirement. Should proceedings be brought for an unlawful disclosure in respect of the notice it is a defence for a person other than the person to whom the notice was given to show that he neither knew nor had reason to suspect the notice contained a secrecy requirement.

10.21 In section 54(9) the Act provides a statutory defence to unauthorised disclosure where the disclosure was made to a relevant Commissioner or was authorised by a Commissioner; by the terms of the notice; by, or on behalf of, the person who gave the notice or by, or on behalf of, a person in lawful possession of the protected information to which the notice relates.

Chapter 11

Oversight

11.1 The Act provides for Commissioners whose remit is to provide independent oversight of the exercise and performance of the powers and duties contained in Part III – except where those powers and duties are being exercised by a judicial authority.

11.2 There are three independent Commissioners with relevant oversight responsibilities:

- **the Interception of Communications Commissioner** who keeps under review:
  - o the exercise and performance by the Secretary of State of the powers and duties conferred or imposed on him by or under Part III, particularly the grant of appropriate permission for the giving of a section 49 notice in relation to information obtained under Part I (intercepted material and other related communications data), and
  - o the adequacy of the arrangements for complying with the safeguards in section 55 in relation to key material for protected information obtained under Part I.
- **the Intelligence Services Commissioner** who keeps under review (so far as they are not required to be kept under review by the Interception of Communications Commissioner):
  - o the exercise and performance by the Secretary of State of the powers and duties conferred or imposed on him by Part III particularly the grant of appropriate permission for the giving of a section 49 notice in connection with, or in relation to, the activities of the intelligence services and the activities (other than activities in Northern Ireland) of the Ministry of Defence ('MOD') and members of HM forces;
  - o the exercise and performance by members of the intelligence services of the powers and duties conferred or imposed on them by or under Part III;
  - o the exercise and performance, in places other than Northern Ireland, by officials of the MOD and members of HM forces of the powers and duties conferred or imposed on such officials or members of HM forces by or under Part III; and
  - o the adequacy of the arrangements for complying with the safeguards in section 55 in relation to members of the intelligence services and, in connection with any of their activities in places other than Northern Ireland, in relation to officials of the MOD and members of HM forces.

- **the Chief Surveillance Commissioner** who keeps under review, so far as they are not kept under review by the other Commissioners:

  o the exercise and performance, by any person (other than a judicial authority or a person holding judicial office) of the powers and duties conferred or imposed, otherwise than with the permission of a judicial authority or a person holding judicial office, by or under Part III, and

  o the adequacy of the arrangements for complying with the safeguards in section 55 by those persons whose conduct is subject to review by the Chief Surveillance Commissioner.

11.3 This code does not cover the exercise of the Commissioners' functions. It is the duty of any person who uses the powers conferred by Part III, or on whom duties are conferred, to comply with any request made by a Commissioner to provide any information he requires for the purposes of enabling him to discharge his functions.

11.4 Should any Commissioner establish that an individual has been adversely affected by any wilful or reckless failure by any person within a public authority exercising or complying with the powers and duties under Part III of the Act he shall, subject to safeguarding national security, inform the affected individual of the existence of the Tribunal and its role. The Commissioner should disclose sufficient information to the affected individual to enable him to effectively engage the Tribunal.

Chapter 12

Complaints

12.1 The Act established an independent Tribunal ('the Investigatory Powers Tribunal'). The Tribunal is made up of senior members of the judiciary and the legal profession and is independent of the Government. The Tribunal has full powers to investigate and decide any case within its jurisdiction, which includes the giving of a notice under section 49 or any disclosure or use of a key to protected information.

12.2 This code does not cover the exercise of the Tribunal's functions. Details of the relevant complaints procedures can be obtained from the following address:

The Investigatory Powers Tribunal,
PO Box 33220
London
SW1H 9ZQ
Tel: 020 7035 3711

Appendix C

Acquisition and Disclosure of Communications Data

Code of Practice
Pursuant to section 71 of the Regulation of
Investigatory Powers Act 2000

1.1 This code of practice relates to the powers and duties conferred or imposed under Chapter II of Part I of the Regulation of Investigatory Powers Act 2000 ('the Act'). It provides guidance on the procedures to be followed when acquisition of communications data takes place under those provisions.

1.2 This code applies to relevant public authorities within the meaning of the Act: those listed in section 25 or specified in orders made by the Secretary of State under section 25.[1]

1.3 Relevant public authorities for the purposes of Chapter II of Part I of the Act ('Chapter II') should not:

- use other statutory powers to obtain communications data from a postal or telecommunications operator unless that power provides explicitly for obtaining communications data,[2] or is conferred by a warrant or order issued by the Secretary of State or a person holding judicial office, or
- require, or invite, any postal or telecommunications operator to disclose communications data by exercising any exemption to the principle of non-disclosure of communications data under the Data Protection Act 1998 ('the DPA').

Chapter 1

Introduction

1.4 This code should be readily available to members of a relevant public authority involved in the acquisition of communications data and the exercise of powers to do so under the Act, and to communications service operators involved in the disclosure of communications data to public authorities under duties imposed by the Act.[3]

1.5 Throughout this code an operator who provides a postal or telecommunications service is described as a communications service provider ('CSP'). The meaning of telecommunications service is defined in the Act[4] and extends to CSPs providing such services where the system for doing so is wholly or partly in the United Kingdom or elsewhere. This includes, for example, a CSP providing a telecommunications system to persons in the United Kingdom where communications data relating to that system is either, or both, processed and stored outside the United Kingdom.

---

[1] See paragraph 2.10.

[2] For example, the power available to Ofcom under section 128 of the Communications Act 2003 to assess whether companies are or have been misusing an electronic communications network or electronic communications service. The purpose for which those assessments are undertaken falls outside the scope of section 22(2) of the Act. See also paragraph 3.23.

[3] See section 22(6) of the Act.

[4] Sections 2(1) and 81(1) of the Act defines 'telecommunications service' to mean any service that consists in the provision of access to, and of facilities for making use of, any telecommunication system (whether or not one provided by the person providing the service); and defines 'telecommunications system' to mean any system (including the apparatus comprised in it) which exists (whether wholly or partly in the United Kingdom or elsewhere) for the purpose of facilitating the transmission of communications by any means involving the use of electrical or electro-magnetic energy.

1.6 The Act provides that the code is admissible in evidence in criminal and civil proceedings. If any provision of the code appears relevant to a question before any court or tribunal hearing any such proceedings, or to the Tribunal established under the Act,[5] or to one of the Commissioners responsible for overseeing the powers conferred by the Act, it must be taken into account.

1.7 The exercise of powers and duties under Chapter II is kept under review by the Interception of Communications Commissioner ('the Commissioner') appointed under section 57 of the Act and by his inspectors who work from the Interception of Communications Commissioner's Office (IOCCO).

1.8 This code **does not** relate to the interception of communications nor to the acquisition or disclosure of the contents of communications. The Code of Practice on Interception of Communications issued pursuant to Section 71 of the Act provides guidance on procedures to be followed in relation to the interception of communications.[6]

1.9 Communications data that is obtained directly as a consequence of the execution of an interception warrant ('related communications data'[7]) is intercept product.

1.10 Any related communications data, and any other specific communications data ('other related data') derived directly from it, must be treated in accordance with the restrictions on the use of intercepted material and related communications data.[8]

1.11 Related communications data may be used as a basis for the acquisition of other related data for intelligence purposes[9] only, if there is sufficient intercept product or non-intercept material available to a designated person to allow that person to consider the necessity and proportionality of acquiring the other related data. The application to the designated person[10] and the resultant data acquired should be treated as product of the interception.

1.12 Related communications data may be used as a basis for the acquisition of other related data for use in legal proceedings provided that the related communications data does not identify itself as intercept product and there is sufficient non-intercept material available to the designated person to allow that person to consider the necessity and proportionality of acquiring the other related data. In practice it will be rare to achieve this. Consequently, it is best practice when undertaking the acquisition of other related data for use in legal proceedings that the provenance of such data is from a source other than conduct authorised by an interception warrant.

1.13 This code extends to the United Kingdom.[11]

---

[5] See paragraphs 9.1 and 9.2.

[6] ISBN 0-11 -341 281-9.

[7] Section 20 of the Act defines 'related communications data' in relation to a communication intercepted in the course of its transmission, by means of a postal service or telecommunications system, to mean so much of any communications data (within the meaning of Chapter II of Part I of the Act) as: (a) is obtained by, or in connection with, the interception; and (b) relates to the communication or to the sender or recipient, or intended recipient, of the communication.

[8] See sections 15, 17, 18 and 19 of the Act.

[9] Section 81(5) of the Act qualifies the reference to preventing or detecting serious crime in section 5(3) – grounds for the issue of an interception warrant – to exclude gathering of evidence for use in any legal proceedings.

[10] See paragraph 3.7

[11] This code and the provisions of Chapter II of Part I of the Act do not extend to the Crown Dependencies and British Overseas Territories.

Chapter 2

General extent of powers

SCOPE OF POWERS, NECESSITY AND PROPORTIONALITY

2.1 The acquisition of communications data under the Act will be a justifiable interference with an individual's human rights under Article 8 of the European Convention on Human Rights only if the conduct being authorised or required to take place is both necessary and proportionate and in accordance with law.

2.2 The Act stipulates that conduct to be authorised or required must be necessary for one or more of the purposes set out in section 22(2) of the Act:[12]

- in the interests of national security;[13]
- for the purpose of preventing or detecting crime[14] or of preventing disorder; in the interests of the economic well-being of the United Kingdom;[15]
- in the interests of public safety;
- for the purpose of protecting public health;
- for the purpose of assessing or collecting any tax, duty, levy or other imposition, contribution or charge payable to a government department;
- for the purpose, in an emergency, of preventing death or injury or any damage to a person's physical or mental health, or of mitigating any injury or damage to a person's physical or mental health;
- to assist investigations into alleged miscarriages of justice;[16]
- for the purpose of assisting in identifying any person who has died otherwise than as a result of crime or who is unable to identify himself because of a physical or mental condition, other than one resulting from crime (such as a natural disaster or an accident);[17] and

---

[12] The Act permits the Secretary of State to add further purposes by means of an Order subject to the affirmative resolution procedure in Parliament.

[13] One of the functions of the Security Service is the protection of national security and in particular the protection against threats from terrorism. These functions extend throughout the United Kingdom. A designated person in another public authority should not grant an authorisation or give a notice under the Act where the operation or investigation falls within the responsibilities of the Security Service, as set out above, except where the conduct is to be undertaken by a Special Branch, by the Metropolitan Police Counter Terrorism Command, or where the Security Service has agreed that another public authority can acquire communications data in relation to an operation or investigation which would fall within the responsibilities of the Security Service.

[14] Detecting crime includes establishing by whom, for what purpose, by what means and generally in what circumstances any crime was committed, the gathering of evidence for use in any legal proceedings and the apprehension of the person (or persons) by whom any crime was committed. See section 81(5) of the Act. Where an investigation relates to an allegation of criminal conduct by a member of a public authority, that public authority (or another public authority appointed to investigate the complaint) may use their powers under Chapter II to obtain communications data for the purpose of preventing and detecting the alleged or suspected crime where the investigating officer intends the matter to be subject of a prosecution within a criminal court. Should it be determined there are insufficient grounds to continue the investigation or insufficient evidence to initiate a prosecution within a criminal court, it will, with immediate effect, no longer be appropriate to obtain communications data under the Act.

[15] See paragraph 2.11.

[16] See article 2 (a), SI 2006/1878.

[17] See article 2 (b) (i), SI 2006/1878.

- in relation a person who has died or is unable to identify himself, for the purpose of obtaining information about the next of kin or other connected persons of such a person or about the reason for his death or condition.[18]

2.3 The purposes for which some public authorities may seek to acquire communications data are restricted by order.[19] The designated person may only consider necessity on grounds open to his or her public authority and only in relation to matters that are the statutory or administrative function of their respective public authority.

2.4 There is a further restriction upon the acquisition of communications data:

- in the interests of public safety;
- for the purpose of protecting public health;
- for the purpose of assessing or collecting any tax, duty, levy or other imposition, contribution or charge payable to a government department.

Only communications data within the meaning of section 21(4)(c) of the Act may be acquired for these purposes and only by those public authorities permitted by order to acquire communications data for one or more of those purposes.[20]

2.5 The designated person must believe that the conduct required by any authorisation or notice is necessary. He or she must also believe that conduct to be proportionate to what is sought to be achieved by obtaining the specified communication data – that the conduct is no more than is required in the circumstances. This involves balancing the extent of the intrusiveness of the interference with an individual's right of respect for their private life against a specific benefit to the investigation or operation being undertaken by a relevant public authority in the public interest.

2.6 Consideration must also be given to any actual or potential infringement of the privacy of individuals who are not the subject of the investigation or operation. An application for the acquisition of communications data should draw attention to any circumstances which give rise to a meaningful degree of collateral intrusion.

2.7 Taking all these considerations into account in a particular case, an interference with the right to respect of individual privacy may still not be justified because the adverse impact on the privacy of an individual or group of individuals is too severe.

2.8 Any conduct that is excessive in the circumstances of both the interference and the aim of the investigation or operation, or is in any way arbitrary will not be proportionate.

2.9 Exercise of the powers in the Act to acquire communications data is restricted to designated persons in relevant public authorities. A designated person is someone holding a prescribed office, rank or position within a relevant public authority that has been designated for the purpose of acquiring communications data by order.[21]

2.10 The relevant public authorities for Chapter II are set out in section 25(1). They are:

- a police force (as defined in section 81(1) of the Act);[22]

---

[18] See article 2 (b) (ii) SI 2006/1878.

[19] See article 6, SI 2003/3172.

[20] See article 7, SI 2003/3172.

[21] See articles 2 and 4, SI 2003/3172. By virtue of article 5 of the order all more senior personnel to the designated office, rank or position are also allowed to grant authorisations or give notices.

[22] Each police force is a separate relevant public authority which has implications for the separation of roles in the acquisition of data under the Act.

- the Serious Organised Crime Agency;[23]
- HM Revenue and Customs;[24]
- the Security Service;
- the Secret Intelligence Service;
- the Government Communications Headquarters.

These and additional relevant public authorities are listed in schedules to the Regulation of Investigatory Powers (Communications Data) Order 2003[25] and the Regulation of Investigatory Powers (Communications Data) (Amendment) Order 2005,[26] the Regulation of Investigatory Powers (Communications Data) (Additional Functions and Amendment) Order 2006 [27] and any similar future orders made under section 25 of the Act.

2.11 Where acquisition of communications data is necessary in the interests of the economic well-being of the United Kingdom, a designated person must take into account whether the economic well-being of the United Kingdom is, on the facts of the specific case, directly related to State security. The term 'State security', which is used in Directive 2002/58/EC (concerning the processing of personal data and the protection of privacy in the electronic communications sector), should be interpreted in the same way as the term 'national security' which is used elsewhere in the Act and this code.

COMMUNICATIONS DATA

2.12 The code covers any conduct relating to the exercise of powers and duties under Chapter II of Part I of the Act to acquire or disclose communications data. Communications data is defined in section 21(4) of the Act.

2.13 The term 'communications data' embraces the 'who', 'when' and 'where' of a communication but not the content, not what was said or written. It includes the manner in which, and by what method, a person or machine communicates with another person or machine. It excludes what they say or what data they pass on within a communication including text, audio and video (with the exception of traffic data to establish another communication such as that created from the use of calling cards, redirection services, or in the commission of 'dial through' fraud and other crimes where data is passed on to activate communications equipment in order to obtain communications services fraudulently).

2.14 Communications data is generated, held or obtained in the provision, delivery and maintenance of communications services, those being postal services[28] or telecommunications services.[29]

---

[23] References in the Act to the National Criminal Intelligence Service and the National Crime Squad have been amended by the Serious Organised Crime and Police Act 2005.

[24] References in the Act to HM Customs and Excise and Inland Revenue have been amended by the Commissioners for Revenue and Customs Act 2005.

[25] SI 2003/3172 *www.opsi.gov.uk/si/si2003/20033172.htm*.

[26] SI 2005/1083 *www.opsi.gov.uk/si/si2005/20051083.htm*.

[27] SI 2006/1878 *www.opsi.gov.uk/si/si2006/20061878.htm*.

[28] Sections 2(1) and 81(1) of the Act define 'postal service' to mean any service which consists in the collection, sorting, conveyance, distribution and delivery (whether in the United Kingdom or elsewhere) of postal items and is offered or provided as a service the main purpose of which, or one of the main purposes of which, is to transmit postal items from place to place.

[29] See footnote 4 Chapter 2.

2.15 Communications service providers may therefore include those persons who provide services where customers, guests or members of the public are provided with access to communications services that are ancillary to the provision of another service, for example in hotels, restaurants, libraries and airport lounges.

2.16 In circumstances where it is impractical for the data to be acquired from or disclosed by the service provider, or there are security implications in doing so, the data may be sought from the communications service provider which provides the communications service offered by such hotels, restaurants, libraries and airport lounges. Equally circumstances may necessitate the acquisition of further communications data for example, where a hotel is in possession of data identifying specific telephone calls originating from a particular guest room.

2.17 Consultation with the public authority's Single Point of Contact (SPoC)[30] will determine the most appropriate plan for acquiring data where the provision of a communication service engages a number of providers.

2.18 Any conduct to determine the communications service provider that holds, or may hold, specific communications data is not conduct to which the provisions of Chapter II apply. This includes, for example, establishing from information available to the public or, where necessary, from a service provider which provider makes available a specific service, such as a particular telephone number or an internet protocol address.

TRAFFIC DATA

2.19 The Act defines certain communications data as 'traffic data' in sections 21(4)(a) and 21(6) of the Act. This is data that is or has been comprised in or attached to a communication for the purpose of transmitting the communication and which 'in relation to any communication':

- identifies, or appears to identify, any person, equipment[31] or location to or from which a communication is or may be transmitted;
- identifies or selects, or appears to identify or select, transmission equipment;
- comprises signals that activate equipment used, wholly or partially, for the transmission of any communication (such as data generated in the use of carrier pre-select or redirect communication services or data generated in the commission of, what is known as, 'dial through' fraud);
- identifies data as data comprised in or attached to a communication. This includes data which is found at the beginning of each packet in a packet switched network that indicates which communications data attaches to which communication.

2.20 Traffic data includes data identifying a computer file or a computer program to which access has been obtained, or which has been run, by means of the communication – but only to the extent that the file or program is identified by reference to the apparatus in which the file or program is stored. In relation to internet communications, this means traffic data stops at the apparatus within which files or programs are stored, so that traffic data may identify a server or domain name (web site) but not a web page.

---

[30] See paragraph 3.15.
[31] In this code equipment has the same meaning as 'apparatus', which is defined in section 81(1) of the Act to mean 'any equipment, machinery, device, wire or cable'.

2.21 Examples of traffic data, within the definition in section 21(6), include:

- information tracing the origin or destination of a communication that is, or has been, in transmission (including incoming call records);
- information identifying the location of equipment when a communication is, has been or may be made or received (such as the location of a mobile phone);
- information identifying the sender or recipient (including copy recipients) of a communication from data comprised in or attached to the communication;
- routing information identifying equipment through which a communication is or has been transmitted (for example, dynamic IP address allocation, file transfer logs and e-mail headers – to the extent that content of a communication, such as the subject line of an e-mail, is not disclosed);
- web browsing information to the extent that only a host machine, server, domain name or IP address is disclosed;
- anything, such as addresses or markings, written on the outside of a postal item (such as a letter, packet or parcel) that is in transmission and which shows the item's postal routing;
- record of correspondence checks comprising details of traffic data from postal items in transmission to a specific address; and
- online tracking of communications (including postal items and parcels).

2.22 Any message written on the outside of a postal item, which is in transmission, may be content (depending on the author of the message) and fall within the scope of the provisions for interception of communications. For example, a message written by the sender will be content but a message written by a postal worker concerning the delivery of the postal item will not. All information on the outside of a postal item concerning its postal routing, for example the address of the recipient, the sender and the post-mark, is traffic data within section 21(4)(a) of the Act.

SERVICE USE INFORMATION

2.23 Data relating to the use made by any person of a postal or telecommunications service, or any part of it, is widely known as 'service use information' and falls within section 21(4)(b) of the Act.

2.24 Service use information is, or can be, routinely made available by a CSP to the person who uses or subscribes to the service to show the use of a service or services and to account for service charges over a given period of time. Examples of data within the definition at section 21(4)(b) include:

- itemised telephone call records (numbers called);[32]
- itemised records of connections to internet services;
- itemised timing and duration of service usage (calls and/or connections);
- information about amounts of data downloaded and/or uploaded;
- information about the use made of services which the user is allocated or has sub-scribed to (or may have subscribed to) including conference calling, call messaging, call waiting and call barring telecommunications services;
- information about the use of forwarding/redirection services;

---

[32] Itemised bills can include an indication of the cost for receiving communications, for example calls and messages received by a mobile telephone that has been 'roaming' on another network.

- information about selection of preferential numbers or discount calls;
- records of postal items, such as records of registered post, recorded or special delivery postal items, records of parcel consignment, delivery and collection.

SUBSCRIBER INFORMATION

2.25 The third type of communication data, widely known as 'subscriber information', is set out in section 21(4)(c) of the Act. This relates to information held or obtained by a CSP about persons[33] to whom the CSP provides or has provided a communications service. Those persons will include people who are subscribers to a communications service without necessarily using that service and persons who use a communications service without necessarily subscribing to it.

2.26 Examples of data within the definition at section 21(4)(c) include:

- 'subscriber checks' (also known as 'reverse look ups') such as "who is the subscriber of phone number 012 345 6789?", "who is the account holder of e-mail account example@example.co.uk?" or
- "who is entitled to post to web space *www.example.co.uk?*";
- information about the subscriber to a PO Box number or a Postage Paid Impression used on bulk mailings;
- information about the provision to a subscriber or account holder of forwarding/redirection services, including delivery and forwarding addresses;
- subscribers or account holders' account information, including names and addresses for installation, and billing including payment method(s), details of payments;
- information about the connection, disconnection and reconnection of services to which the subscriber or account holder is allocated or has subscribed to (or may have subscribed to) including
- conference calling, call messaging, call waiting and call barring telecommunications services;
- information about apparatus used by, or made available to, the subscriber or account holder, including the manufacturer, model, serial numbers and apparatus codes;[34]
- information provided by a subscriber or account holder to a CSP, such as demographic information or sign-up data (to the extent that information, such as a password, giving access to the content of any stored communications is **not** disclosed save where the requirement for such information is necessary in the interests of national security[35]).

2.27 It can be appropriate to undertake the acquisition of subscriber information before obtaining related traffic data or service use information to confirm information within the investigation or operation.

---

[33] Section 81(1) of the Act defines 'person' to include any organisation and any association or combination of persons.

[34] This includes PUK (Personal Unlocking Key) codes for mobile phones. These are initially set by the handset manufacturer and are required to be disclosed in circumstances where a locked handset has been lawfully seized as evidence in criminal investigations or proceedings.

[35] Information which provides access to the content of any stored communications may only be used for that purpose with necessary lawful authority.

2.28 Where there is sufficient provenance of information within the investigation or operation to justify an application to obtain traffic data or service use information in the first instance this may be undertaken. For example, in circumstances where:

- a victim reports receiving nuisance or threatening telephone calls or messages;
- a person who is subject of an investigation or operation is identified from high-grade intelligence to be using a specific communication service;
- a victim, a witness or a person who is subject of an investigation or operation has used a public payphone;[36]
- a person who is subject of an investigation or operation is identified during a time critical investigation (such as a kidnap) or from detailed analysis of data available to the investigator to be using a specific communication service;
- a mobile telephone is lawfully seized and communications data is requested relating to either or both the device or its SIM card(s);
- a witness presents certain facts and there is a need to corroborate or research the veracity of those, such as to confirm the time of an incident they have witnessed, or
- an investigation of the allocation of IP addresses is needed to determine relevant subscriber information.

2.29 Where the acquisition of the subscriber information is required to assist an investigation or operation or for evidential purposes, that requirement can be included on an application for traffic data or service use information.

Chapter 3

General rules on the granting of the authorizations and giving of notices

3.1 Acquisition of communications data under the Act involves four roles within a relevant public authority:

- the applicant
- the designated person
- the single point of contact
- the senior responsible officer.

3.2 The Act provides two alternative means for acquiring communications data, by way of:

- an authorisation under section 22(3), or
- a notice under section 22(4).

THE APPLICANT

3.3 The applicant is a person involved in conducting an investigation or operation for a relevant public authority who makes an application in writing or electronically for the acquisition of communications data. The applicant completes an application

---

[36] The telephone number and address of a public payphone is normally displayed beside it to assist persons making emergency calls to give their location to the emergency operator.

form, setting out for consideration by the designated person, the necessity and pro-portionality of a specific requirement for acquiring communications data.

3.4 Applications may be made orally in exceptional circumstances,[37] but a record of that application must be made in writing or electronically as soon as possible.

3.5 Applications[38] – the original or a copy of which must be retained by the SPoC within the public authority – must:

- include the name (or designation[39]) and the office, rank or position held by the person making the application;
- include a unique reference number;
- include the operation name (if applicable) to which the application relates;
- specify the purpose for which the data is required, by reference to a statutory purpose under 22(2) of the Act;
- describe the communications data required, specifying, where relevant, any historic or future date(s) and, where appropriate, time period(s);
- explain why the acquisition of that data is considered necessary and proportionate to what is sought to be achieved by acquiring it;
- consider and, where appropriate, describe any meaningful collateral intrusion – the extent to which the privacy of any individual not under investigation may be infringed and why that intrusion is justified in the circumstances, and identify and explain the time scale within which the data is required.[40]

3.6 The application should record subsequently whether it was approved or not by a designated person, and by whom and when that decision was made. If approved, the application form should, to the extent necessary, be cross-referenced to any authorisation granted[41] or notice given.

THE DESIGNATED PERSON

3.7 The designated person is a person holding a prescribed office in a relevant public authority who considers the application and records his considerations at the time

---

[37] See paragraph 3.56.

[38] Public authorities should ensure their application processes are efficient and do not impose unnecessary bureaucracy on their operational staff which goes beyond the requirements of the Act and this code. To assist public authorities the Home Office publishes specimen forms.

[39] The use of a designation rather than a name will be appropriate only for applicants in one of the security and intelligence agencies.

[40] The Data Communications Group (DCG) which comprises representatives of CSPs, UK law enforcement and other public authorities to manage the strategic relationship between public authorities and the communications industry has adopted a grading scheme to indicate the appropriate timeliness of the response to requirements for disclosure of communications data. There are three grades:

- Grade 1 – an immediate threat to life;
- Grade 2 – an exceptionally urgent operational requirement for the prevention or detection of seri-ous crime or a credible and immediate threat to national security;
- Grade 3 – matters that are routine but, where appropriate, will include specific or time critical issues such as bail dates, court dates, or where persons are in custody or where a specific line of investiga-tion into a serious crime and early disclosure by the CSP will directly assist in the prevention or detection of that crime. The emphasis within Grade 1 and 2 is the urgent provision of the communi-cations data will have an immediate and positive impact on the investigation or operation.

[41] Cross-referencing will be unnecessary in circumstances where the grant of an authorisation is recorded in the same document as the relevant application.

(or as soon as is reasonably practicable) in writing or electronically. If the designated person believes it is necessary and proportionate in the specific circumstances, an authorisation is granted or a notice is given.

3.8 Individuals who undertake the role of a designated person must have current working knowledge of human rights principles, specifically those of necessity and proportionality, and how they apply to the acquisition of communications data under Chapter II and this code.

3.9 Designated persons must ensure that they grant authorisations or give notices only for purposes and only in respect of types of communications data that a designated person of their office, rank or position in the relevant public authority may grant or give.

3.10 The designated person shall assess the necessity for any conduct to acquire or obtain communications data taking account of any advice provided by the single point of contact (SPoC).

3.11 Designated persons should not be responsible for granting authorisations or giving notices in relation to investigations or operations in which they are directly involved, although it is recognised that this may sometimes be unavoidable, especially in the case of small organisations or where it is necessary to act urgently or for security reasons. Where a designated person is directly involved in the investigation or operation their involvement and their justification for undertaking the role of the designated person must be explicit in their recorded considerations.

3.12 Particular care must be taken by designated persons when considering any application to obtain communications data to identify equipment (such as a mobile telephone) at or within a location or locations and at or between times on a given date or dates where the identity of the equipment is unknown.[42] Unless the application is based on information that the equipment was used or was likely to have been used in a particular location or locations at a particular time or times it will, in practice, be rare that any conduct to obtain communications data will be proportionate or the collateral intrusion justified.

3.13 In situations where there is an immediate threat to life (for example a person threatening to take their own or someone else's life or where threats are made to a victim in a kidnap) some CSPs will undertake to bespoke their systems beyond the requirements of their normal business practice to be able to assist the police in preserving life. The use of such bespoke systems must be proportionate, and any collateral intrusion justified, to the specific circumstances of any investigation or operation.

3.14 Where there is no immediate threat to life in an investigation or operation, any conduct to obtain communications data using any other bespoke systems (for example, those used to trace malicious and nuisance communications) must be reliant upon both the co-operation and technical capability of the CSP to provide such assistance outside of its normal business practice.

---

[42] DCG is able to offer additional advice to SPoCs where investigations or operations in their public authority are considering the acquisition of such data.

THE SINGLE POINT OF CONTACT

3.15 The single point of contact (SPoC) is either an accredited individual or a group of accredited individuals trained to facilitate lawful acquisition of communications data and effective co-operation between a public authority and CSPs. To become accredited an individual must complete a course of training appropriate for the role of a SPoC and have been issued a SPoC Personal Identification Number (PIN). Details of all accredited individuals are available to CSPs for authentication purposes.

3.16 An accredited SPoC promotes efficiency and good practice in ensuring only practical and lawful requirements for communications data are undertaken. This encourages the public authority to regulate itself. The SPoC provides objective judgement and advice to both the applicant and the designated person. In this way the SPoC provides a 'guardian and gatekeeper' function ensuring that public authorities act in an informed and lawful manner.

3.17 The SPoC[43] should be in a position to:

- engage proactively with applicants to develop strategies to obtain communications data and use it effectively in support of operations or investigations;
- assess whether the acquisition of specific communications data from a CSP is reasonably practical or whether the specific data required is inextricably linked to other data;[44]
- advise applicants on the most appropriate methodology for acquisition of data where the data sought engages a number of CSPs;
- advise applicants and designated persons on the interpretation of the Act, particularly whether an authorisation or notice is appropriate;
- provide assurance to designated persons that authorisations and notices are lawful under the Act and free from errors;
- provide assurance to CSPs that authorisations and notices are authentic and lawful;
- assess whether communications data disclosed by a CSP in response to a notice fulfils the requirement of the notice;
- assess whether communications data obtained by means of an authorisation fulfils the requirement of the authorisation;
- assess any cost and resource implications to both the public authority and the CSP of data requirements.

3.18 Public authorities unable to call upon the services of an accredited SPoC should not undertake the acquisition of communications data. In circumstances where a CSP is approached by a person who cannot be authenticated as an accredited individual and who seeks to obtain data under the provisions of the Act, the CSP may refuse to comply with any apparent requirement for disclosure of data until confirmation of the person's accreditation and PIN is obtained from the Home Office.

3.19 The SPoC may be an individual who is also a designated person. The SPoC may be an individual who is also an applicant. The same person should never be an

---

[43] Advice and consideration given by the SPoC in respect of any application may be recorded in the same document as the application and/or authorisation.

[44] In the event that the required data is inextricably linked to, or inseparable from, other traffic data or service use data the designated person must take that into account in their consideration of necessity, proportionality and collateral intrusion.

applicant, a designated person and a SPoC. Equally the same person should never be both the applicant and the designated person.

3.20 Where a public authority seeks to obtain communications data using provisions providing explicitly for the obtaining of communications data (other than Chapter II of Part I of the Act) or using statutory powers conferred by a warrant or order issued by the Secretary of State or a person holding judicial office, the SPoC should be engaged in the process of obtaining the data to ensure effective cooperation between the public authority and the CSP.

3.21 Similarly, where a public authority seeks lawful access to the content of a stored communication held by a CSP or to data held by a CSP that is neither communications data or the content of a communication, the SPoC should be engaged to liaise with the CSP[45] (for example to obtain access to a deceased's voicemail).

The senior responsible officer

3.22 Within every relevant public authority a senior responsible officer[46] must be responsible for:

- the integrity of the process in place within the public authority to acquire communications data;
- compliance with Chapter II of Part I of the Act and with this code;
- oversight of the reporting of errors to IOCCO and the identification of both the cause(s) of errors and the implementation of processes to minimise repetition of errors;
- engagement with the IOCCO inspectors when they conduct their inspections, and where necessary, oversee the implementation of post-inspection action plans approved by the Commissioner.

Authorisations

3.23 An authorisation provides for persons within a public authority to engage in specific conduct, relating to a postal service or telecommunications system, to obtain communications data.

3.24 Any designated person in a public authority may only authorise persons working in the same public authority to engage in specific conduct. This will normally be the public authority's SPoC.

3.25 The decision of a designated person whether to grant an authorisation shall be based upon information presented to them in an application.

3.26 An authorisation may be appropriate where:

- a CSP is not capable of obtaining or disclosing the communications data;[47]
- there is an agreement in place between a public authority and a CSP relating to appropriate mechanisms for disclosure of communications data; or

---

[45] Sections 1(5)(c), 2(7), 2(8), 3(1) and 3(2) of the Act explain how stored communications may be in the course of their transmission and may be lawfully intercepted without a warrant.

[46] The senior responsible officer should be a person holding the office, rank or position of a designated person within the public authority who may authorise communications falling within section 21(4)(a) and/or 21(4)(b).

[47] Where possible, this assessment will be based upon information provided by the CSP.

- a designated person considers there is a requirement to identify a person to whom a service is provided but a CSP has yet to be conclusively determined as the holder of the communications data.

3.27 An authorisation is not served upon a CSP, although there may be circumstances where a CSP may require or may be given an assurance that conduct being, or to be, undertaken is lawful. That assurance may be given by disclosing details of the authorisation or the authorisation itself.

3.28 An authorisation[48] – the original or a copy of which must be retained by the SPoC within the public authority – must:

- be granted in writing or, if not, in a manner that produces a record of it having been granted;
- describe the conduct which is authorised and describe the communications data to be acquired by that conduct specifying, where relevant, any historic or future date(s) and, where appropriate, time period(s);
- specify the purpose for which the conduct is authorised, by reference to a statutory purpose under section 22(2) of the Act;
- specify the office, rank or position held by the designated person granting the authorisation. The designated person should also record their name (or designation) on any authorisation they grant, and record the date and, when appropriate to do so, the time[49] when the authorisation was granted by the designated person.

3.29 SPoCs should be mindful when drafting authorisations within the meaning of section 23(1) of the Act to ensure the description of the required data corresponds with the way in which the CSP processes, retains and retrieves its data for lawful disclosure. CSPs cannot necessarily or reasonably edit or bespoke their systems to take account of every possible variation of what may be specified in authorisations.

3.30 Requirements to identify a person to whom a service is, or has been, provided – for example telephone number subscriber checks – account for the vast majority of disclosures under the Act. As a consequence of these requirements, some CSPs permit the lawful acquisition of this data by SPoCs, subject to security and audit controls. Where a SPoC has been authorised to engage in conduct to obtain details of a person to whom a service has been provided and concludes that data is held by a CSP from which it cannot be acquired directly, the SPoC may provide the CSP with details of the authorisation granted by the designated person in order to seek disclosure of the required data.[50]

3.31 At the time of giving a notice or granting an authorisation to obtain specific traffic data or service use data, a designated person may also authorise, to the extent necessary and proportionate at that time, the consequential acquisition of specific subscriber information relating to the traffic data or service use data to be obtained.

---

[48] Where the grant of an authorisation is recorded separately from the relevant application they should be cross-referenced to each other.

[49] Recording of the time an authorisation is granted (or a notice is given) will be appropriate in urgent and time critical circumstances.

[50] Where details of an authorisation are provided to a CSP in writing, electronically or orally those details must additionally specify the manner in which the data should be disclosed and, where appropriate, provide an indication of any urgency or time within which the data need to be obtained.

This is relevant where there is a necessary and proportionate requirement to identify with whom a person has been in communication, for example:

- to identify with whom a victim was in contact, within a specified period, prior to their murder;
- to identify to whom the target of an investigation or operation was observed to make several calls from a public pay phone;
- to identify a person making unlawful and unwarranted demands (as in the case of kidnap, extortion and blackmail demands and threats of violence); and
- where a victim or a witness has identified a specific communication or communications and corroboration of facts may reveal a potential offender or other witness.

3.32 It is the duty of the senior responsible officer to ensure that the designated person, applicant or other person makes available to the SPoC such information as the senior responsible officer thinks necessary to ensure the integrity of any requirements for the acquisition of subscriber information to be obtained directly upon the acquisition or disclosure of any traffic data or service use data, and their compliance with Chapter II and with this code.[51]

NOTICES

3.33 Giving of a notice is appropriate where a CSP is able to retrieve or obtain specific data, and to disclose that data, unless the grant of an authorisation is more appropriate. A notice may require a CSP to obtain any communications data, if that data is not already in its possession.

3.34 The decision of a designated person whether to give a notice shall be based upon information presented to them in an application.

3.35 The 'giving of a notice' means the point at which a designated person determines that a notice should be given to a CSP. In practice, subsequent to the designated person giving that notice it is served upon a CSP whether in writing or, in an emergency, orally.

3.36 The notice should contain enough information to allow the CSP to comply with the requirements of the notice.

3.37 A notice – the original or a copy of which must be retained by the SPoC within the public authority – must:

- be given in writing[52] or, if not, in a manner that produces a record, within the public authority, of its having been given;
- include a unique reference number and also identify the public authority;[53]

---

[51] Ordinarily the applicant or other person within the investigation or operation will prepare a schedule of data, for example telephone numbers, to enable the SPoC to undertake the acquisition of subscriber information. The schedule will include details of the person who prepared it, cross reference it to the relevant notice or authorisation and specify the traffic data or service use information from which the data are derived.

[52] The preparation and format of a notice must take into account that when served on a CSP by the use of a facsimile machine or other means the notice remains legible.

[53] This can be a code or an abbreviation. It could be that part of a public authority's name which appears in its e-mail address. For police services it will be appropriate to use the Police National Computer (PNC) force coding.

- specify the purpose for which the notice has been given, by reference to a statutory purpose under 22(2) of the Act;
- describe the communications data to be obtained or disclosed under the notice specifying, where relevant, any historic or future date(s) and, where appropriate, time period(s);
- include an explanation that compliance with the notice is a requirement of the Act;
- specify the office, rank or position held by the designated person giving the notice. The name (or designation) of the designated person giving the notice should also be recorded;
- specify the manner in which the data should be disclosed. The notice should contain sufficient information including the contact details of the SPoC to enable a CSP to confirm the notice is authentic and lawful;
- record the date and, when appropriate to do so, the time when the notice was given by the designated person, and where appropriate, the notice should provide an indication of any urgency or time within which the CSP is requested to comply with the requirements of the notice.[54]

3.38 A notice must not place a CSP under a duty to do anything which is not reasonably practicable for the CSP to do.[55] SPoCs should be mindful when drafting notices to ensure the description of the required data corresponds with the ways in which the CSP processes, retains and retrieves its data for lawful disclosure. CSPs cannot necessarily or reasonably edit or bespoke their systems to take account of every possible variation of what may be specified in notices.

3.39 In giving notice a designated person may only require a CSP to disclose the communications data to the designated person or to a specified person working within the same public authority. This will normally be the public authority's SPoC.

3.40 Ordinarily the CSP should disclose, in writing or electronically, the communications data to which a notice relates not later than the end of the period of ten working days from the date the notice is served upon the CSP.

3.41 Where the designated person determines, if necessary upon the advice of the SPoC, that there are specific circumstances which mean that if a notice were given the CSP could not comply within ten working days the designated person shall indicate such longer period as the notice may specify up to a period of one month from the date notice is given.[56]

DURATION OF AUTHORISATIONS AND NOTICES

3.42 Relevant to all authorisations and notices is the date upon which authorisation is granted or notice given. From that date, when the authorisation or notice becomes

---

[54] See footnote 40.

[55] See Section 22(7) of the Act.

[56] Where a CSP required to disclose communications data is unable ordinarily to comply within 10 working days, a senior officer of the CSP should seek an interim service level agreement with the Home Office.

valid, it has a validity of a maximum of one month.[57] This means the conduct authorised should have been commenced or the notice served within that month.

3.43 All authorisations and notices should refer to the acquisition or disclosure of data relating to a specific date or period.[58] Any period should be clearly indicated in the authorisation or notice. The start date and end date should be given, and where a precise start and end time are relevant these must be specified.[59] Where the data to be acquired or disclosed is specified as 'current', the relevant date should be taken to be the date on which the authorisation was granted or the notice given by the designated person. There can be circumstances when the relevant date or period cannot be specified other than 'the last transaction' or 'the most recent use of the service'.

3.44 Where an authorisation or a notice relates to the acquisition or obtaining of specific data that will or may be generated in the future, the future period is restricted to no more than one month from the date upon which the authorisation was granted or the notice given.

3.45 Designated persons should give particular consideration to any periods of days or shorter periods of time for which they may approve for the acquisition or disclosure of historic or future data. They should specify the shortest period in which the objective for which the data is sought can be achieved. To do otherwise will impact on the proportionality of the authorisation or notice and impose an unnecessary burden upon a CSP given such notice.

RENEWAL OF AUTHORISATIONS AND NOTICES

3.46 Any valid authorisation or a notice may be renewed for a period of up to one month by the grant of a further authorisation or the giving of a further notice. A renewed authorisation or notice takes effect upon the expiry of the authorisation or notice it is renewing.

3.47 Renewal may be appropriate where there is a continuing requirement to acquire or obtain data that will or may be generated in the future. The reasoning for seeking renewal should be set out by an applicant in an addendum to the application upon which the authorisation or notice being renewed was granted or given.

3.48 Where a designated person is granting a further authorisation or giving a further notice to renew an earlier authorisation or notice,[60] the designated person should:

- have considered the reasons why it is necessary and proportionate to continue with the acquisition of the data being generated, and
- record the date and, when appropriate to do so, the time when the authorisation or notice is renewed.

---

[57] Throughout this Code, a month means a period of time extending from a date in one calendar month to the date one day before the corresponding or nearest date in the following month. For example, a month beginning on 7 June ends on 6 July, a month beginning on 30 January ends on 28 February or 29 February in a leap year.

[58] For example, details of traffic data or service use on a specific date or for a specific period or the details of a subscriber on a specific date or for a specific period.

[59] In the case of Internet Protocol data, any timings should include an explicit indication of which time zone applies to those timings.

[60] This can include an authorisation or notice that has been renewed previously.

3.49 A designated person who has given notice to a CSP under section 22(4) of the Act shall cancel the notice if, at any time after giving the notice,[61] it is no longer necessary for the CSP to comply with the notice or the conduct required by the notice is no longer proportionate to what was sought to be achieved.

3.50 Reporting the cancellation of a notice to a CSP shall be undertaken by the designated person directly or, on that person's behalf, by the public authority's SPoC. Where human rights considerations are such that a notice should be cancelled with immediate effect the designated person or the SPoC will notify the CSP.[62]

3.51 Cancellation of a notice reported to a CSP must:

- be undertaken in writing or, if not, in a manner that produces a record of the notice having been cancelled;
- identify, by reference to its unique reference number, the notice being cancelled; and
- record the date and, when appropriate to do so, the time when the notice was cancelled.

3.52 In cases where the SPoC has initiated the cancellation of a notice and reported the cancellation to the CSP, the designated person must confirm the decision in writing for the SPoC or, if not, in a manner that produces a record of the notice having been cancelled by the designated person. Where the designated person who gave the notice to the CSP is no longer available, this duty should fall on a person who has temporarily or permanently taken over the role of the designated person.

3.53 Similarly where a designated person considers an authorisation[63] should cease to have effect, because the conduct authorised becomes unnecessary or no longer proportionate to what was sought to be achieved, the authorisation must be withdrawn. It may be the case that it is the SPoC who is first aware that the authorisation is no longer necessary or proportionate and may cease the authorised conduct, and then inform the designated person who granted the authorisation.

3.54 Withdrawal of an authorisation should:

- be undertaken in writing or, if not, in a manner that produces a record of it having been withdrawn;
- identify, by reference to its unique reference number, the authorisation being withdrawn;
- record the date and, when appropriate to do so, the time when the authorisation was cancelled; and
- record the name and the office, rank or position held by the designated person informed of the withdrawal of the authorisation.

---

[61] This can include a renewed notice.

[62] If the notice being cancelled relates to an urgent operational situation that has been resolved, or has changed, it may be appropriate for the senior officer dealing with the situation, on the ground or in a control room, to notify the CSP that the notice is cancelled where that person has the earliest opportunity to do so.

[63] This can include a renewed authorisation.

3.55 When it is appropriate to do so a CSP should be advised of the withdrawal of an authorisation, for example where details of an authorisation have been disclosed to a CSP.

URGENT ORAL GIVING OF NOTICE OR GRANT OF AUTHORISATION

3.56 In exceptionally urgent circumstances,[64] application for the giving of a notice or the grant of an authorisation may be made by an applicant, approved by a designated person and either notice given to a CSP or an authorisation granted orally. Circumstances in which an oral notice or authorisation may be appropriate are:

- an immediate threat to life such that a person's life might be endangered if the application procedure were undertaken in writing from the outset;
- an exceptionally urgent operational requirement where, within no more than 48 hours of the notice being given or the authorisation being granted orally, the acquisition of communications data will directly assist the prevention or detection of the commission of a serious crime[65] and the making of arrests or the seizure of illicit material, and where that operational opportunity will be lost if the application procedure is undertaken in writing from the outset; or
- a credible and immediate threat to national security or a time critical and unique opportunity to secure, or prevent the loss of, information of vital importance to national security where that threat might be realised, or that opportunity lost, if the application procedure were undertaken in writing from the outset.

3.57 The use of urgent oral process must be justified for each application within an investigation or operation. The fact that any part of an investigation or operation is undertaken urgently must not be taken to mean that all requirements to obtain communications data in connection with that investigation or operation be undertaken using the urgent oral process.

3.58 When, in a matter of urgency, a designated person decides, having consulted the SPoC, that the oral giving of a notice or grant of an authorisation is appropriate that notice should be given or the authorised conduct undertaken as soon as practicable after the making of that decision.

3.59 Particular care must be given to the use of the urgent oral process. When notice or authorisation is given orally, the SPoC when relaying service of the oral notice or authorisation to the CSP must make a note of the time, provide a unique reference number for the notice, provide the name (or designation) of the designated person and the name and contact details of the SPoC and, if required by the CSP, their PIN. Where telephone numbers (or other identifiers) are being relayed, the relevant number must be read twice and repeated back by the CSP to confirm the correct details have been taken.

---

[64] There is a general undertaking by CSPs to respond outside of normal office hours where there is an immediate threat to life.

[65] See section 81(2) of the Act.

3.60 Written notice[66] must be given to the CSP retrospectively within one working day[67] of the oral notice being given. Failure to do so will constitute an error which may be reported to the Commissioner by the CSP and must be recorded by the public authority.

3.61 After the period of urgency,[68] a written process must be completed demonstrating the consideration given to the circumstances and the decisions taken. The applicant or the SPoC shall collate details or copies of control room or other operational logs which provide contemporaneous records of the consideration given to the acquisition of data, decision(s) made by the designated person and the actions taken in respect of the decision(s).

3.62 In all cases where urgent oral notice is given or authorisation granted an explanation of why the urgent process was undertaken must be recorded.

Chapter 4

Making contributions towards the costs incurred by communications service providers

4.1 The Act[69] recognises that CSPs incur costs in complying with notices to disclose communications data, and allows for arrangements for making appropriate payments to them to facilitate the timely disclosure of communications data. In this code 'timely disclosure' means that ordinarily a CSP should disclose data within ten working days of being required to do so. Similar arrangements are appropriate where a CSP incurs costs in making provision for the acquisition of communications data upon the grant of an authorisation under the Act.

4.2 Significant public funding is made available to CSPs to ensure that they can provide, outside of their normal business practices, an effective and efficient response to public authorities' necessary, proportionate and lawful requirements for the disclosure and acquisition of communications data in support of their investigations and operations to protect the public and to bring to justice those who commit crime.

4.3 It is legitimate for a CSP to seek contributions towards its costs which may include an element providing funding of those general business overheads required in order to comply with notices or to provide for the acquisition and timely disclosure of communications data. This is especially relevant for CSPs which employ staff specifically to manage compliance with the requirements made under the Act, supported by bespoke information systems. Contributions can also be appropriate towards costs incurred by a CSP which needs to update its systems to maintain, or make more efficient, its disclosure process or where the provision of new services will require investment in

---

[66] Likewise where details of an authorisation are provided to a CSP orally in a matter of urgency, they should be confirmed in writing within one working day.

[67] Working day means any day other than a Saturday, a Sunday, Christmas Day, Good Friday or a day which is a bank holiday under the Banking and Financial Dealings Act 1971 in that part of the United Kingdom where the relevant public authority is located.

[68] In some instances where life is at risk, for example in kidnap investigations, the period of urgency may be prolonged.

[69] Section 24 of the Act.

technology in order to comply with requirements for the disclosure and acquisition of communications data relating to the use made of such services.

4.4 Any CSPs seeking to recover appropriate contributions towards its costs should make available to the Home Office such information or assurance as the Home Office requires to provide assurance that proposed cost recovery charges represent an appropriate contribution to the costs incurred by the CSP.

Chapter 5

Special rules on the granting of authorisations and giving of notices in specific matters of public interest

SUDDEN DEATHS, SERIOUS INJURIES AND VULNERABLE PERSONS

5.1 There are circumstances when the police undertake enquiries in relation to specific matters of public interest where the disclosure of communications data may be necessary and proportionate. Article 2(b) of the Regulation of Investigatory Powers (Communications Data) (Additional Functions and Amendment) Order 2006 specified additional purposes for which the acquisition and disclosure of communications data may be necessary. These purposes assist the police in carrying out its functions. For example:

- identifying any person who has died or who is unable to identify himself, because of a physical or mental condition, other than as a resulting from crime (such as a natural disaster or an accident);
- obtaining information about the reason for a person's death or condition;
- locating and notifying next of kin following a sudden or unexpected death;
- locating and notifying next of kin of a seriously injured person;
- locating and notifying the next of kin or responsible adult of a child or other vulnerable person where there is a concern for the child's or the vulnerable person's welfare.

5.2 Often a telephone, telephone number or other communications details may be the only information available to identify a person or to identify their next of kin or a person responsible for their welfare.

5.3 Equally communications data can help establish the facts relevant to a person's death or serious injury, where no crime has occurred. For example, where the police undertake an investigation to assist Her Majesty's Coroner, communications data can indicate the activity of a deceased person prior to their death, such as in a fatal accident, or identify a person who may assist the Coroner to establish the facts of a person's death.

5.4 Under the Act communications data may also be obtained and disclosed in serious and urgent welfare cases where it is necessary within the meaning of section 22(2)(g) and the conduct authorised or required is proportionate to what is sought to be achieved by obtaining the data.

PUBLIC EMERGENCY CALL SERVICE (999/112 CALLS)

5.5 Certain CSPs have obligations under the Communications Act 2003[70] in respect of emergency calls made to 999 and 112 emergency numbers. They must ensure that any service user can access the emergency authorities by using the emergency numbers and, to the extent technically feasible, make caller location information available to the emergency authorities for all 999/112 calls.

5.6 Caller location information, which provides the geographic position of the equipment being used by the person making the emergency call, facilitates a fast response in emergency situations where the caller is unable to give their position (for example because the caller does not know, is panicking or is incapacitated).

5.7 Handling of an emergency call involves four phases:

- connection of the caller to the Emergency Operator using the 999/112 number;
- selection by the Emergency Operator of the required Emergency Authority Control Room (Police, Fire, Ambulance or Coastguard)('the emergency service');
- connection of the caller to the Emergency Authority Control Room;
- listening by the Emergency Operator to ensure the caller is connected to the correct emergency service and to provide further assistance to the caller or the emergency service when required.[71]

5.8 Best practice dictates that the emergency operator will disclose location information to the emergency service during the initial call hand-over. In many cases this will be done automatically by the call handling system.

5.9 In automated cases, data relating to the emergency call is automatically displayed at the relevant emergency service, the instant a call is routed from the Emergency Operator. This data is available to the emergency service throughout the duration of the emergency call, but disappears once the call has ended unless retained by the emergency service.

5.10 The Privacy and Electronic Communications (EC Directive) Regulations 2003 ('the Privacy Regulations')[72] allows telephone users the choice whether or not their telephone number is displayed or can be accessed by the recipient of a call they make. However when an emergency call using 999 or 112 is made, the option to withhold the number making the call is not available. Instead the calling line identity and location data (fixed or mobile) are automatically disclosed to the emergency services in order to facilitate a rapid response to the emergency call.

DROPPED 999/112 CALLS (AND CIRCUMSTANCES WHERE DATA MAY BE
ACQUIRED OR DISCLOSED OUTSIDE THE PROVISIONS OF THE ACT)

5.11 To enable the provision of emergency assistance in response to emergency calls which are 'dropped' or incomplete, the emergency service can call upon an Emergency

---

[70] General Conditions of Entitlement set by Ofcom under section 45 of the 2003 Act.

[71] This can also include silent emergency calls where the call is connected but the caller, for whatever reason, is unable to speak to the emergency operator or the emergency service.

[72] SI 2003/2426 *www.legislation.hmso.gov.uk/si/si2003/20032426.htm*. Regulation 10 concerns prevention of calling line identification in relation to outgoing calls.

309

Operator or relevant service provider to disclose data about the maker[73] of an emergency call within the emergency period (within one hour of the termination of the emergency call) outside the provisions of the Act.

5.12 This is necessary in situations where the Emergency Operator may become aware of the premature termination of an emergency call. There are a number of reasons for these 'dropped' or incomplete emergency calls, which cannot be reconnected. For example:

- there is a fault on the line;
- the emergency service requests to be reconnected where the caller was incapacitated or unable to maintain the call and reconnection is tried and fails;
- the emergency service considers that safety of the person making the call may be put at risk if the Emergency Operator seeks to reconnect the call, particularly in cases where a crime is in progress, for example domestic violence or a robbery;
- the Emergency Operator diagnoses a problem with the call or the strength of a mobile phone signal.

5.13 If an emergency call is disconnected prematurely for any reason, technical or otherwise, and the Emergency Operator is aware or is made aware of this, then the Emergency Operator can elect to represent the data disclosed when the call was put to the emergency service initially. This voluntary disclosure would fall outside the scope of the Act.

5.14 The Emergency Operator can anticipate the needs of the emergency service and represent the information disclosed automatically to the emergency service without prompting.

5.15 The Emergency Operator can choose to represent the data, whether prompted or unprompted, only for the period of time that the data is held specifically as emergency call data. This period is not normally longer than one hour from the termination of the emergency call.

5.16 There are circumstances where the Emergency Operator cannot automatically present the emergency service with communications data about the maker of an emergency call. For example, because the emergency service does not have equipment to receive the data automatically or the data is held by a third party service provider and not readily available to the Emergency Operator. In those circumstances, and in order to provide an effective emergency service, the Emergency Operator may disclose the data it has orally.

5.17 When disclosure of data about the maker of an emergency call is required during the emergency period, the emergency service controller must provide a unique reference number for the emergency call and provide the name of the authorising officer and sufficient detail to link the disclosure to the originator of the request. Where telephone numbers (or other identifiers) are being relayed, the relevant number must be read twice and repeated back by the CSP to confirm the correct details have been taken.

5.18 If the emergency call is clearly a hoax there is no emergency. Where an emergency service concludes that an emergency call is a hoax and the reason for acquiring

---

[73] In practice this means sufficient detail disclosed to identify the origin of the call and, if appropriate, to enable the deployment of an emergency service to the scene of an emergency.

data in relation to that call is to detect the crime of making a hoax call – and **not** to provide an emergency service – then the application process under the Act must be undertaken.

5.19 Should an emergency service require communications data relating to the making of any emergency call after the expiry of the emergency period of one hour from the termination of the call, that data must be acquired or obtained under the provisions of the Act.

5.20 Where communications data about a third party (other than the maker of an emergency call) is required to deal effectively with an emergency call, the emergency service may make an urgent oral application for the data.

MALICIOUS AND NUISANCE COMMUNICATIONS

5.21 Many CSPs offer services to their customers to deal with complaints concerning malicious and nuisance communications.[74] Although these services vary all CSPs believe that such calls can be very distressing for their customers and that every effort should be made to resolve such situations as efficiently and effectively as possible.

5.22 The victim of malicious or nuisance communications may, in the first instance, bring it to the attention of their CSP or report it to the police.

5.23 When contacted directly by a customer the CSP may consider the circumstances of the complaint are such that the customer will be advised to report the matter without delay to the police for investigation.

5.24 Additionally the CSP can offer practical advice on how to deal with nuisance communications and may, for example, arrange a change of telephone number. The advice given by the CSP may indicate that the circumstances could constitute a criminal offence. The CSP may choose to disclose data to its customer relating to the source of the malicious or nuisance communications, but must ensure that the disclosure complies with the provisions of both the DPA and the Privacy Regulations.

5.25 Upon receipt of a complaint a CSP may retrieve and retain relevant specific data that, if appropriate, can be disclosed to the police later. If the complainant wishes the matter to be investigated, it is essential for the CSP and the police[75] to liaise with one another to ensure the lawful disclosure of data to enable any offence to be effectively investigated.

5.26 Where the complainant reports a matter to the police that has been previously raised with the CSP, any data already collated by the CSP may be disclosed to the police SPoC under the provisions of the DPA or the Privacy Regulations.[76] Subsequent police investigation may require the acquisition or disclosure of additional communications data from the complainant's CSP or other CSPs under the provisions of the Act.

5.27 Whether the initial complaint is reported to the CSP or directly to the police careful consideration should be given to whether the occurrence of malicious or nuisance communications are, or may be, related to other incidents or events. Specifically this

---

[74] The Association of Chief Police Officers has produced guidelines on 'Dealing with Malicious and Nuisance Communications'. See *www.acpo.police.uk/policies.asp.*

[75] Ordinarily this will be overseen and coordinated by the police force's SPoC.

[76] Regulation 15 concerns tracing of malicious or nuisance calls.

could be where the complainant is a victim of another crime or is a witness or a member of a trial jury in ongoing or forthcoming criminal proceedings.

Chapter 6

Keeping of records

RECORDS TO BE KEPT BY A RELEVANT PUBLIC AUTHORITY

6.1 Applications, authorisations copies of notices, and records of the withdrawal of authorisations and the cancellation of notices, must be retained by the relevant public authority in written or electronic form, and physically attached or cross-referenced where they are associated with each other. The public authority should also keep a record of the date and, when appropriate to do so, the time when each notice or authorisation is given or granted, renewed or cancelled. Records kept by the public authority must be held centrally by the SPoC or in accordance with arrangements previously agreed with the Commissioner.

6.2 These records must be available for inspection by the Commissioner and retained to allow the Investigatory Powers Tribunal, established under Part IV of the Act, to carry out its functions.[77]

6.3 Where the records contain, or relate to, material obtained directly as a consequence of the execution of an interception warrant those records must be treated in accordance with the safeguards which the Secretary of State has approved in conformity with the duty imposed upon him by the Act.[78]

6.4 This code does not affect any other statutory obligations placed on public authorities to keep records under any other enactment. For example, where applicable in England and Wales, the relevant test given in the Criminal Procedure and Investigations Act 1996 ('the CPIA') as amended and the code of practice under that Act. This requires that material which is obtained in the course of an investigation and which may be relevant to the investigation must be recorded, retained and revealed to the prosecutor.

6.5 Each relevant public authority must also keep a record of the following items:

- number of applications submitted to a designated person for a decision to obtain communications data which were rejected after due consideration;
- number of notices requiring disclosure of communications data within the meaning of each subsection of section 21(4) of the Act or any combinations of data;
- number of authorisations for conduct to acquire communications data within the meaning of each subsection of section 21(4) of the Act or any combinations of data;
- number of times an urgent notice is given orally, or an urgent authorisation granted orally, requiring disclosure of communications data within the meaning of each subsection of section 21(4) of the Act or any combinations of data.

---

[77] The Tribunal will consider complaints made up to one year after the conduct to which the complaint relates and, where it is satisfied it is equitable to do so, may consider complaints made more than one year after the conduct to which the complaint relates. See section 67(5) of the Act.

[78] Under section 15 of the Act and the statutory code of practice on Interception of Communications.

6.6 This record must be sent in written or electronic form to the Commissioner as determined by him. Where appropriate, guidance on format or timing may be issued by or sought from IOCCO.

RECORDS TO BE KEPT BY A COMMUNICATIONS SERVICE PROVIDER

6.7 To assist the Commissioner carry out his statutory function in relation to Chapter II, CSPs should maintain a record of the disclosures it has made or been required to make. This record should be available to the Commissioner and his inspectors to enable comparative scrutiny of the records kept by public authorities. Guidance on the maintenance of records by CSPs may be issued by or sought from IOCCO.

6.8 The records to be kept by a CSP, in respect of each notice or authorisation, should include:

- the name of the public authority;
- the URN of the notice or authorisation;
- the date the notice was served upon the CSP, the authorisation disclosed to the CSP;
- a description of any communications data required where no disclosure took place or could have taken place; and
- the date when the communications data was made available to the public authority or, where secure systems are provided by the CSP, the date when the acquisition and disclosure of communications data was undertaken.

ERRORS

6.9 Proper application of the Act and thorough procedures for operating its provisions, including the careful preparation and checking of applications, notices and authorisations, should reduce the scope for making errors whether by public authorities or by CSPs.

6.10 An error can only occur after a designated person:

- has granted an authorisation and the acquisition of data has been initiated, or
- has given notice and the notice has been served on a CSP in writing, electronically or orally.

6.11 Any failure by a public authority to apply correctly the process of acquiring or obtaining communications data set out in this code will increase the likelihood of an error occurring.

6.12 Where any error occurs, in the grant of an authorisation, the giving of a notice or as a consequence of any authorised conduct or any conduct undertaken to comply with a notice, a record should be kept.

6.13 Where communications data is acquired or disclosed wrongly a report must be made to the Commissioner ('reportable error'). Such errors can have very significant consequences on an affected individual's rights with details of their private communications being disclosed to a public authority and, in extreme circumstances, being wrongly detained or wrongly accused of a crime as a result of that error.

6.14 In cases where an error has occurred but is identified by the public authority or the CSP without data being acquired or disclosed wrongly, a record will be maintained by the public authority of such occurrences ('recordable error'). These records must be available for inspection by the Commissioner.

6.15 This section of the code cannot provide an exhaustive list of possible causes of reportable or recordable errors. Examples can include:

Reportable errors

- an authorisation or notice made for a purpose, or for a type of data, which the relevant public authority cannot call upon, or seek, under the Act;
- human error, such as incorrect transposition of information from an application to an authorisation or notice disclosure of the wrong data by a CSP when complying with a notice;
- acquisition of the wrong data by a public authority when engaging in conduct specified in an authorisation;

Recordable errors

- a notice given which is impossible for a CSP to comply with and an attempt to impose the requirement has been undertaken by the public authority;
- failure to review information already held, for example unnecessarily seeking the acquisition or disclosure of data already acquired or obtained for the same investigation or operation,[79] or data for which the requirement to acquire or obtain it is known to be no longer valid;
- failure to serve written notice (or where appropriate an authorisation) upon a CSP within one working day of urgent oral notice being given or an urgent oral authorisation granted.

6.16 Reporting and recording of errors will draw attention to those aspects of the process of acquisition and disclosure of communications data that require further improvement to eliminate errors and the risk of undue interference with any individual's rights.

6.17 When a reportable error has been made the public authority which made the error, or established that the error had been made, must establish the facts and report the error to the authority's senior responsible officer and then to the IOCCO, in written or electronic form, within no more than five working days of the error being discovered. All errors should be reported as they arise. If the report relates to an error made by a CSP the public authority should also inform the CSP of the report in written or electronic form. This will enable the CSP to investigate the cause or causes of the reported error.

6.18 The report sent to the IOCCO by a public authority in relation to a reportable error must include details of the error, identified by the public authority's unique reference number of the relevant authorisation or notice, explain how the error occurred, indicate whether any unintended collateral intrusion has taken place and provide an indication of what steps have been, or will be, taken to ensure that a similar error does

---

[79] In this context seeking the disclosure of communications data unnecessarily means any failure to collate or record information already obtained which results in repeatedly obtaining the same data within the same investigation or operation. This does not restrict a relevant public authority undertaking the acquisition of communications data where necessary and proportionate, for example to extend the time frame of communications data already obtained, which may include elements of data previously obtained, or as a consequence of new evidence.

not recur. When a public authority reports an error made by a CSP, the report must include details of the error and indicate whether the CSP has been informed or not (in which case the public authority must explain why the CSP has not been informed of the report).

6.19 Where a CSP discloses communications data in error it must report each error to the IOCCO within no more than five working days of the error being discovered. It is appropriate for a person holding a suitably senior position within a CSP to do so, identifying the error by reference to the public authority's unique reference number and providing an indication of what steps have been, or will be, taken to ensure that a similar error does not recur. Errors by service providers could include responding to a notice by disclosing incorrect data or by disclosing the required data to the wrong public authority.

6.20 The records kept by a public authority accounting for recordable errors must include details of the error, explain how the error occurred and provide an indication of what steps have been, or will be, taken to ensure that a similar error does not reoccur. The authority's senior responsible officer must undertake a regular review of the recording of such errors.

6.21 Where material is disclosed by a CSP in error which has no connection or relevance to any investigation or operation undertaken by the public authority receiving it, that material and any copy of it should be destroyed as soon as the report to the Commissioner has been made.

6.22 Communications identifiers can be readily transferred, or 'ported', between CSPs. When a correctly completed authorisation or notice results in a CSP indicating to a public authority that, for example, a telephone number has been 'ported' to another CSP that authorisation or notice will not constitute an error – unless the fact of the porting was already known to the public authority.

EXCESS DATA

6.23 Where authorised conduct by a public authority results in the acquisition of excess data, or its disclosure by a CSP in order to comply with the requirement of a notice, all the data acquired or disclosed should be retained by the public authority.

6.24 Where a public authority is bound by the CPIA and its code of practice, there will be a requirement to record and retain data which is relevant to a criminal investigation, even if that data was disclosed or acquired beyond the scope of a valid notice or authorisation. If a criminal investigation results in proceedings being instituted all material that may be relevant must be retained at least until the accused is acquitted or convicted or the prosecutor decides not to proceed.

6.25 If having reviewed the excess data it is intended to make use of the excess data in the course of the investigation or operation, an applicant must set out the reason(s) for needing to use that material in an addendum to the application upon which the authorisation or notice was originally granted or given. The designated person will then consider the reason(s) and review all the data and consider whether it is necessary and proportionate for the excess data to be used in the investigation or operation.

Chapter 7

Data protection safeguards

7.1 Communications data acquired or obtained under the provisions of the Act, and all copies, extracts and summaries of it, must be handled and stored securely. In addition, the requirements of the Data Protection Act 1998 ('the DPA')[80] and its data protection principles must be adhered to.

7.2 Communications data ('related communications data') that is obtained directly as a consequence of the execution of an interception warrant must be treated in accordance with the safeguards which the Secretary of State has approved in conformity with the duty imposed upon him by the Act.

Disclosure of communications data and subject access rights

7.3 This section of the code provides guidance on the relationship between disclosure of communications data under the Act and the provisions for subject access requests under the DPA, and the balance between CSPs obligations to comply with a notice to disclose data and individuals' right of access under section 7 of the DPA to personal data held about them.

7.4 There is no provision in the Act preventing CSPs from informing individuals about whom they have been required by notice to disclose communications data in response to a Subject Access Request made under section 7 of the DPA. However a CSP may exercise certain exemptions to the right of subject access under Part IV of the DPA.

7.5 Section 28 provides that data are always exempt from section 7 where such an exemption is required for the purposes of safeguarding national security.

7.6 Section 29 provides that personal data processed for the purposes of the prevention and detection of crime; the apprehension or prosecution of offenders, or the assessment or collection of any tax or duty or other imposition of a similar nature are exempt from section 7 to the extent to which the application of the provisions for rights of data subjects would be likely to prejudice any of those matters.

7.7 The exercise of the exemption to subject access rights possible under section 29 does not automatically apply to notices given under the Act. In the event that a CSP receives a subject access request where the fact of a disclosure under the Act might itself be disclosed the CSP concerned must carefully consider whether in the particular case disclosure of the fact of the notice would be likely to prejudice the prevention or detection of crime.

7.8 Where a CSP is uncertain whether disclosure of the fact of a notice would be likely to prejudice an investigation or operation, it should approach the SPoC of the public authority which gave the notice – and do so in good time to respond to the subject access request. The SPoC can make enquiries within the public authority to determine whether disclosure of the fact of the notice would likely be prejudicial to the matters in section 29.[81]

---

[80] Guidance is available from *www.dca.gov.uk/foi/datprot.htm* or *www.informationcommissioner.gov.uk*.

[81] The SPoC must provide a response which will enable the CSP to comply with its obligations to respond to the subject access request within 40 days.

7.9 Where a CSP withholds a piece of information in reliance on the exemption in section 28 or 29 of the DPA, it is not obliged to inform an individual that any information has been withheld. It can simply leave out that piece of information and make no reference to it when responding to the individual who has made the subject access request.

7.10 CSPs should keep a record of the steps they have taken in determining whether disclosure of the fact of a notice would prejudice the apprehension or detection of offenders. This might be useful in the event of the data controller having to respond to enquiries made subsequently by the Information Commissioner, the courts and, in the event of prejudice, the police.

Acquisition of communication data on behalf of overseas authorities

7.11 Whilst the majority of public authorities which obtain communications data under the Act have no need to disclose that data to any authority outside the United Kingdom, there can be occasions when it is necessary, appropriate and lawful to do so in matters of international co-operation.

7.12 There are two methods by which communications data, whether obtained under the Act or not, can be acquired and disclosed to overseas public authorities:[82]

- Judicial co-operation
- Non-judicial co-operation.

Neither method compels United Kingdom public authorities to disclose data to overseas authorities. Data can only be disclosed when a United Kingdom public authority is satisfied that it is in the public interest to do so and all relevant conditions imposed by domestic legislation have been fulfilled.

Judicial co-operation

7.13 If the United Kingdom receives a formal request from an overseas court or other prosecuting authority that appears to have a function of making requests for legal assistance, the Secretary of State (in Scotland the Lord Advocate) will consider the request under the Crime (International Co-operation) Act 2003. In order to assist he must be satisfied that the request is made in connection with criminal proceedings or a criminal investigation being carried on outside the United Kingdom.

7.14 If such a request is accepted, that request will be passed to a nominated court in the United Kingdom. That court may make an order requiring a CSP to disclose the relevant information to the court for onward transmission to the overseas authority.

Non-judicial co-operation

7.15 Public authorities in the United Kingdom can receive direct requests for assistance from their counterparts in other countries. These can include requests for the acquisition and disclosure of communications data for the purpose of preventing or detecting crime. On receipt of such a request the United Kingdom public authority

---

[82] This includes public authorities within the Crown Dependencies and the British Overseas Territories.

may consider seeking the acquisition or disclosure of the requested data under the provisions of Chapter II of Part I of the Act.

7.16 The United Kingdom public authority must be satisfied that the request complies with United Kingdom obligations under human rights legislation. The necessity and proportionality of each case must be considered before the authority processes the authorisation or notice.

DISCLOSURE OF COMMUNICATIONS DATA TO OVERSEAS AUTHORITIES

7.17 Where a United Kingdom public authority is considering the acquisition of communications data on behalf of an overseas authority and transferring the data to that authority it must consider whether the data will be adequately protected outside the United Kingdom and what safeguards may be needed to ensure that.[83] Such safeguards might include attaching conditions to the processing, storage and destruction of the data.

7.18 If the proposed transfer of data is to an authority within the European Union that authority will be bound by the European Data Protection Directive (95/46/EC) and its national data protection legislation. Any data disclosed will be protected there without need for additional safeguards.

7.19 If the proposed transfer is to an authority outside of the European Union and the European Economic Area (Iceland, Liechtenstein and Norway) then it must not be disclosed unless the overseas authority can ensure an adequate level of data protection. The European Commission has determined that certain countries, including Canada and Switzerland, have laws providing an adequate level of protection where data can be transferred without need for further safeguards.

7.20 In all other circumstances the United Kingdom public authority must decide in each case, before transferring any data overseas, whether the data will be adequately protected there. If necessary the Information Commissioner can give guidance.

7.21 The DPA recognises that it will not always be possible to ensure adequate data protection in countries outside of the European Union and the European Economic Area, and there are exemptions to the principle, for example if the transfer of data is necessary for reasons of 'substantial public interest'.[84] There may be circumstances when it is necessary, for example in the interests of national security, for communications data to be disclosed to a third party country, even though that country does not have adequate safeguards in place to protect the data. That is a decision that can only be taken by the public authority holding the data on a case by case basis.

---

[83] The eighth data protection principle is: 'Personal data shall not be transferred to a country or territory outside the European Economic Area unless that country or territory ensures an adequate level of protection for the rights and freedoms of data subjects in relation to the processing of personal data.' (Paragraph 8, Schedule 1, DPA 1998)

[84] Paragraph 4, Schedule 4, DPA 1998.

Chapter 8

Oversight

8.1 The Act provides for an Interception of Communications Commissioner ('the Commissioner') whose remit is to provide independent oversight of the exercise and performance of the powers and duties contained under Chapter II of Part I of the Act. The Commissioner is supported by his inspectors who work from the Interception of Communications Commissioner's Office (IOCCO).

8.2 This code does not cover the exercise of the Commissioner's functions. It is the duty of any person who uses the powers conferred by Chapter II, or on whom duties are conferred, to comply with any request made by the Commissioner to provide any information he requires for the purposes of enabling him to discharge his functions.

8.3 Should the Commissioner establish that an individual has been adversely affected by any wilful or reckless failure by any person within a relevant public authority exercising or complying with the powers and duties under the Act in relation to the acquisition or disclosure of communications data, he shall, subject to safeguarding national security, inform the affected individual of the existence of the Tribunal and its role. The Commissioner should disclose sufficient information to the affected individual to enable him or her to effectively engage the Tribunal.

8.4 Reports made by the Commissioner concerning the inspection of public authorities and their exercise and performance of powers under Chapter II may be made available by the Commissioner to the Home Office to promulgate good practice and help identify training requirements within public authorities and CSPs.

8.5 Subject to the approval of the Commissioner public authorities may publish their inspection reports, in full or in summary, to demonstrate both the oversight to which they are subject and their compliance with Chapter II of the Act and this code. Approval should be sought on a case by case basis at least 10 working days prior to intended publication, stating whether the report is to be published in full, and if not stating which parts are to be published or how it is to be summarised.

Chapter 9

Complaints

9.1 The Act established an independent Tribunal ('the Investigatory Powers Tribunal'). The Tribunal is made up of senior members of the judiciary and the legal profession and is independent of the Government. The Tribunal has full powers to investigate and decide any case within its jurisdiction which includes the acquisition and disclosure of communications data under the Act.

9.2 This code does not cover the exercise of the Tribunal's functions. Details of the relevant complaints procedure can be obtained from the following address:

The Investigatory Powers Tribunal
PO Box 33220
London
SW1H 9ZQ
Tel : 020 7035 3711

Appendix D

Interception of Communications

Code of Practice
Pursuant to section 71 of the Regulation of
Investigatory Powers Act 2000

Authors' note: the version of the code reproduced here is the latest available and at the time of writing this third edition (December 2011) is the version published online on the Home Office website. Readers are advised that this version is in need of revision and updating, a process which the Home Office has indicated to the authors (in correspondence dated 5th December 2011) is underway.

1.1 This code of practice relates to the powers and duties conferred or imposed under Chapter I of Part I of the Regulation of Investigatory Powers Act 2000 ("the Act"). It provides guidance on the procedures that must be followed before interception of communications can take place under those provisions. It is primarily intended for use by those public authorities listed in section 6(2) of the Act. It will also prove useful to postal and telecommunication operators and other interested bodies to acquaint themselves with the procedures to be followed by those public authorities.

1.2 The Act provides that all codes of practice relating to the Act are admissible as evidence in criminal and civil proceedings. If any provision of this code appears relevant before any court or tribunal considering any such proceedings, or to the Tribunal established under the Act, or to one of the Commissioners responsible for overseeing the powers conferred by the Act, it must be taken into account.

Chapter 1

General

2.1 There area limited number of persons by whom, or on behalf of whom, applications for interception warrants may be made. These persons are:

- The Director-General of the Security Service.
- The Chief of the Secret Intelligence Service.
- The Director of GCHQ.
- The Director-General of the National Criminal Intelligence Service *[N.B. The current text of the Code notwithstanding, this designation has changed in the statute to the Director General of the Serious Organised Crime Agency following the incorporation of NCIS within SOCA. In due course this role will be undertaken by the National Crime Authority when it becomes operational.]*
- The Commissioner of the Police of the Metropolis (the Metropolitan Police Special Branch handle interception on behalf of Special Branches in England and Wales).
- The Chief Constable of the Police Service of Northern Ireland.
- The Chief Constable of any police force maintained under or by virtue of section 1 of the Police (Scotland) Act 1967.
- The Commissioners of Customs and Excise *[N.B. The current text of the Code notwithstanding, this designation has changed in the statute to the Commissioners of Revenue and Customs.]*
- The Chief of Defence Intelligence.
- A person who, for the purposes of any international mutual assistance agreement, is the competent authority of a country or territory outside the United Kingdom.
- Any application made on behalf of one of the above must be made by a person holding office under the Crown.

Chapter 2

General rules on interception with a warrant

2.2 All interception warrants are issued by the Secretary of State.[1] Even where the urgency procedure is followed, the Secretary of State personally authorises the warrant, although it is signed by a senior official.

2.3 Before issuing an interception warrant, the Secretary of State must believe that what the action seeks to achieve is necessary for one of the following section 5(3) purposes:

- in the interests of national security;
- for the purpose of preventing or detecting serious crime; or
- for the purpose of safeguarding the economic well-being of the UK,

and that the conduct authorised by the warrant is proportionate to what is sought to be achieved by that conduct.

NECESSITY AND PROPORTIONALITY

2.4 Obtaining a warrant under the Act will only ensure that the interception authorised is a justifiable interference with an individual's rights under Article 8 of the European Convention of Human Rights (the right to privacy) if it is necessary and proportionate for the interception to take place. The Act recognises this by first requiring that the Secretary of State believes that the authorisation is necessary on one or more of the statutory grounds set out in section 5(3) of the Act. This requires him to believe that it is necessary to undertake the interception which is to be authorised for a particular purpose falling within the relevant statutory ground.

2.5 Then, if the interception is necessary, the Secretary of State must also believe that it is proportionate to what is sought to be achieved by carrying it out. This involves balancing the intrusiveness of the interference, against the need for it in operational terms. Interception of communications will not be proportionate if it is excessive in the circumstances of the case or if the information which is sought could reasonably be obtained by other means. Further, all interception should be carefully managed to meet the objective in question and must not be arbitrary or unfair.

IMPLEMENTATION OF WARRANTS

2.6 After a warrant has been issued it will be forwarded to the person to whom it is addressed, in practice the intercepting agency which submitted the application. The Act (section 11) then permits the intercepting agency to carry out the interception, or to require the assistance of other persons in giving effect to the warrant. Warrants cannot be served on those outside the jurisdiction of the UK.

---

[1] Interception of communications will not be proportionate if it is excessive in the circumstances of the case or if the information which is sought could Interception warrants may be issued on "serious crime" grounds by Scottish Ministers, by virtue of arrangements under the Scotland Act 1998. In this Code references to the "Secretary of State" should be read as including Scottish Ministers where appropriate. The functions of the Scottish Ministers also cover renewal and cancellation arrangements.

323

PROVISION OF REASONABLE ASSISTANCE

2.7 Any postal or telecommunications operator (referred to as communications service providers) in the United Kingdom may be required to provide assistance in giving effect to an interception. The Act places a requirement on postal and telecommunications operators to take all such steps for giving effect to the warrant as are notified to them (section 11(4) of the Act). But the steps which may be required are limited to those which it is reasonably practicable to take (section 11(5)). What is reasonably practicable should be agreed after consultation between the postal or telecommunications operator and the Government. If no agreement can be reached it will be for the Secretary of State to decide whether to press forward with civil proceedings. Criminal proceedings may also be instituted by or with the consent of the Director of Public Prosecutions.

2.8 Where the intercepting agency requires the assistance of a communications service provider in order to implement a warrant, they should provide the following to the communications service provider:

- A copy of the warrant instrument signed and dated by the Secretary of State (or in an urgent case, by a senior official);
- The relevant schedule for that service provider setting out the numbers, addresses or other factors identifying the communications to be intercepted;
- A covering document from the intercepting agency requiring the assistance of the communications service provider and specifying any other details regarding the means of interception and delivery as may be necessary. Contact details with respect to the intercepting agency will either be provided in this covering document or will be available in the handbook provided to all postal and telecommunications operators who maintain an intercept capability.

PROVISION OF INTERCEPT CAPABILITY

2.9 Whilst all persons who provide a postal or telecommunications service are obliged to provide assistance in giving effect to an interception, persons who provide a public postal or telecommunications service, or plan to do so, may also be required to provide a reasonable intercept capability. The obligations the Secretary of State considers reasonable to impose on such persons to ensure they have such a capability will be set out in an order made by the Secretary of State and approved by Parliament. The Secretary of State may then serve a notice upon a communications service provider setting out the steps they must take to ensure they can meet these obligations. A notice will not be served without consultation over the content of the notice between the Government and the service provider having previously taken place. When served with such a notice, a communications service provider, if he feels it unreasonable, will be able to refer that notice to the Technical Advisory Board (TAB) on the reasonableness of the technical requirements and capabilities that are being sought. Details of how to submit a notice to the TAB will be provided either before or at the time the notice is served.

2.10 Any communications service provider obliged to maintain a reasonable intercept capability will be provided with a handbook which will contain the basic information they require to respond to requests for reasonable assistance for the interception of communications.

2.11 All interception warrants are valid for an initial period of three months. Upon renewal, warrants issued on serious crime grounds are valid for a further period of three months. Warrants renewed on national security/ economic well-being grounds are valid for a further period of six months. Urgent authorisations are valid for five working days following the date of issue unless renewed by the Secretary of State.

2.12 Where modifications take place, the warrant expiry date remains unchanged. However, where the modification takes place under the urgency provisions, the modification instrument expires after five working days following the date of issue unless renewed following the routine procedure.

2.13 Where a change in circumstance prior to the set expiry date leads the intercepting agency to consider it no longer necessary or practicable for the warrant to be in force, it should be cancelled with immediate effect.

2.14 Section 2(7) of the Act defines a communication in the course of its transmission as also encompassing any time when the communication is being stored on the communication system in such a way as to enable the intended recipient to have access to it. This means that a warrant can be used to obtain both communications that are in the process of transmission and those that are being stored on the transmission system.

2.15 Stored communications may also be accessed by means other than a warrant. If a communication has been stored on a communication system it may be obtained with lawful authority by means of an existing statutory power such as a production order (under the Police and Criminal Evidence Act 1984) or a search warrant.

Chapter 3

Special rules on interception with a warrant

3.1 Consideration should be given to any infringement of the privacy of individuals who are not the subject of the intended interception, especially where communications relating to religious, medical, journalistic or legally privileged material may be involved. An application for an interception warrant should draw attention to any circumstances which give rise to an unusual degree of collateral infringement of privacy, and this will be taken into account by the Secretary of State when considering a warrant application. Should an interception operation reach the point where individuals other than the subject of the authorisation are identified as directly relevant to the operation, consideration should be given to applying for separate warrants covering those individuals.

CONFIDENTIAL INFORMATION

3.2 Particular consideration should also be given in cases where the subject of the interception might reasonably assume a high degree of privacy, or where confidential information is involved. Confidential information consists of matters subject to legal privilege, confidential personal information or confidential journalistic material (see paragraphs 3.9–3.11). For example, extra consideration should be given where interception might involve communications between a minister of religion and an individual relating to the latter's spiritual welfare, or where matters of medical or journalistic confidentiality or legal privilege may be involved.

COMMUNICATIONS SUBJECT TO LEGAL PRIVILEGE

3.3 Section 98 of the Police Act 1997 describes those matters that are subject to legal privilege in England and Wales. In relation to Scotland, those matters subject to legal privilege contained in section 33 of the Criminal Law (Consolidation) (Scotland) Act 1995 should be adopted. With regard to Northern Ireland, Article 12 of the Police and Criminal Evidence (Northern Ireland) Order 1989 should be referred to.

3.4 Legal privilege does not apply to communications made with the intention of furthering a criminal purpose (whether the lawyer is acting unwittingly or culpably). Legally privileged communications will lose their protection if there are grounds to believe, for example, that the professional legal advisor is intending to hold or use the information for a criminal purpose. But privilege is not lost if a professional legal advisor is properly advising a person who is suspected of having committed a criminal offence. The concept of legal privilege applies to the provision of professional legal advice by any individual, agency or organisation qualified to do so.

3.5 The Act does not provide any special protection for legally privileged communications. Nevertheless, intercepting such communications is particularly sensitive and is therefore subject to additional safeguards under this Code. The guidance set out below may in part depend on whether matters subject to legal privilege have been obtained intentionally or incidentally to some other material which has been sought.

3.6 In general, any application for a warrant which is likely to result in the interception of legally privileged communications should include, in addition to the reasons why it is considered necessary for the interception to take place, an assessment of how likely it is that communications which are subject to legal privilege will be intercepted. In addition, it should state whether the purpose (or one of the purposes) of the interception is to obtain privileged communications. This assessment will be taken into account by the Secretary of State in deciding whether an interception is necessary under section 5(3) of the Act and whether it is proportionate. In such circumstances, the Secretary of State will be able to impose additional conditions such as regular reporting arrangements so as to be able to exercise his discretion on whether a warrant should continue to be authorised. In those cases where communications which include legally privileged communications have been intercepted and retained, the matter should be reported to the Interception of Communications Commissioner during his inspections and the material be made available to him if requested.

3.7 Where a lawyer is the subject of an interception, it is possible that a substantial proportion of the communications which will be intercepted will be between the lawyer and his client(s) and will be subject to legal privilege. Any case where a lawyer is the subject of an investigation should be notified to the Interception of Communications Commissioner during his inspections and any material which has been retained should be made available to him if requested.

3.8 In addition to safeguards governing the handling and retention of intercept material as provided for in section 15 of the Act, caseworkers who examine intercepted communications should be alert to any intercept material which may be subject to legal privilege. Where there is doubt as to whether the communications are subject to legal privilege, advice should be sought from a legal adviser within the intercepting agency. Similar advice should also be sought where there is doubt over whether communications are not subject to legal privilege due to the "in furtherance of a criminal purpose" exception.

COMMUNICATIONS INVOLVING CONFIDENTIAL PERSONAL INFORMATION AND CONFIDENTIAL JOURNALISTIC MATERIAL

3.9 Similar consideration to that given to legally privileged communications must also be given to the interception of communications that involve confidential personal information and confidential journalistic material. Confidential personal information is information held in confidence concerning an individual (whether living or dead) who can be identified from it, and the material in question relates to his physical or mental health or to spiritual counselling. Such information can include both oral and written communications. Such information as described above is held in confidence if it is held subject to an express or implied undertaking to hold it in confidence or it is subject to a restriction on disclosure or an obligation of confidentiality contained in existing legislation. For example, confidential personal information might include consultations between a health professional and a patient, or information from a patient's medical records.

3.10 Spiritual counselling is defined as conversations between an individual and a Minister of Religion acting in his official capacity, and where the individual being counselled is seeking or the Minister is imparting forgiveness, absolution or the resolution of conscience with the authority of the Divine Being(s) of their faith.

3.11 Confidential journalistic material includes material acquired or created for the purposes of journalism and held subject to an undertaking to hold it in confidence, as well as communications resulting in information being acquired for the purposes of journalism and held subject to such an undertaking.

Chapter 4

Interception warrants (section 8(1))

4.1 This section applies to the interception of communications by means of a warrant complying with section 8(1) of the Act. This type of warrant may be issued in respect of the interception of communications carried on any postal service or telecommunications system as defined in section 2(1) of the Act (including a private telecommunications system). Responsibility for the issuing of interception warrants rests with the Secretary of State.

APPLICATION FOR A SECTION 8(1) WARRANT

4.2 An application for a warrant is made to the Secretary of State. Interception warrants, when issued, are addressed to the person who submitted the application. This person may then serve a copy upon any person who may be able to provide assistance in giving effect to that warrant. Each application, a copy of which must be retained by the applicant, should contain the following information:

- Background to the operation in question.
- Person or premises to which the application relates (and how the person or premises feature in the operation).
- Description of the communications to be intercepted, details of the communications service provider(s) and an assessment of the feasibility of the interception operation where this is relevant.[2]
- Description of the conduct to be authorised as considered necessary in order to carry out the interception,[3] where appropriate.
- An explanation of why the interception is considered to be necessary under the provisions of section 5(3).
- A consideration of why the conduct to be authorised by the warrant is proportionate to what is sought to be achieved by that conduct.
- A consideration of any unusual degree of collateral intrusion and why that intrusion is justified in the circumstances. In particular, where the communications in question might affect religious, medical or journalistic confidentiality or legal privilege, this must be specified in the application.
- Where an application is urgent, supporting justification should be provided.
- An assurance that all material intercepted will be handled in accordance with the safeguards required by section 15 of the Act.

AUTHORISATION OF A SECTION 8(1) WARRANT

4.3 Before issuing a warrant under section 8(1), the Secretary of State must believe the warrant is necessary [4]

- in the interests of national security;
- for the purpose of preventing or detecting serious crime; or
- for the purpose of safeguarding the economic well-being of the United Kingdom.

4.4 In exercising his power to issue an interception warrant for the purpose of safeguarding the economic well-being of the United Kingdom (as provided for by section 5(3)(c) of the Act), the Secretary of State will consider whether the economic well-being of the United Kingdom which is to be safeguarded is, on the facts of each case, directly related to state security. The term "state security", which is used in Directive 97/66/EC (concerning the processing of personal data and the protection of privacy in the telecommunications sector), should be interpreted in the same way as the term "national security" which is used elsewhere in the Act and this Code. The Secretary of State will not issue a warrant on section 5(3)(c) grounds if this direct link between the

---

[2] This assessment is normally based upon information provided by the relevant communication service provider.

[3] This conduct may include the interception of other communications (section 5(6)(a)).

[4] A single warrant can be justified on more than one of the grounds listed.

economic well-being of the United Kingdom and state security is not established. Any application for a warrant on section 5(3)(c) grounds should therefore explain how, in the applicant's view, the economic well-being of the United Kingdom which is to be safeguarded is directly related to state security on the facts of the case.

4.5 The Secretary of State must also consider that the conduct authorised by the warrant is proportionate to what it seeks to achieve (section 5(2)(b)). In considering necessity and proportionality, the Secretary of State must take into account whether the information sought could reasonably be obtained by other means (section 5(4)).

Urgent authorisation of a Section 8(1) Warrant

4.6 The Act makes provision (section 7(l)(b)) for cases in which an interception warrant is required urgently, yet the Secretary of State is not available to sign the warrant. In these cases the Secretary of State will still personally authorise the interception but the warrant is signed by a senior official, following discussion of the case between officials and the Secretary of State. The Act restricts issue of warrants in this way to urgent cases where the Secretary of State has himself expressly authorised the issue of the warrant (section 7(2)(a)), and requires the warrant to contain a statement to that effect (section 7(4)(a)). A warrant issued under the urgency procedure lasts for five working days following the day of issue unless renewed by the Secretary of State, in which case it expires after 3 months in the case of serious crime or 6 months in the case of national security or economic well-being in the same way as other non-urgent section 8(l) warrants. An urgent case is one in which interception authorisation is required within a twenty four hour period.

Format of a Section 8(1) Warrant

4.7 Each warrant comprises two sections, a warrant instrument signed by the Secretary of State listing the subject of the interception or set of premises, a copy of which each communications service provider will receive, and a schedule or set of schedules listing the communications to be intercepted. Only the schedule relevant to the communications that can be intercepted by the specified communications service provider will be provided to that service provider.

4.8 The warrant instrument should include:

- The name or description of the interception subject or of a set of premises in relation to which the interception is to take place.
- A warrant reference number.
- The persons who may subsequently modify the scheduled part of the warrant in an urgent case (if authorised in accordance with section 10(8) of the Act).

4.9 The scheduled part of the warrant will comprise one or more schedules. Each schedule should contain:

- The name of the communication service provider, or the other person who is to take action.
- A warrant reference number.
- A means of identifying the communications to be intercepted.[5]

---

[5] This may include addresses, numbers, apparatus or other factors, or combination of factors, that are to be used for identifying communications (section 8(2) of the Act).

MODIFICATION OF SECTION 8(1) WARRANT

4.10 Interception warrants may be modified under the provisions of section 10 of the Act. The unscheduled part of a warrant may only be modified by the Secretary of State or, in an urgent case, by a senior official[6] with the express authorisation of the Secretary of State. In these cases, a statement of that fact must be endorsed on the modifying instrument, and the modification ceases to have effect after five working days following the day of issue unless it is renewed by the Secretary of State. The modification will then expire upon the expiry date of the warrant.

4.11 Scheduled parts of a warrant may be modified by the Secretary of State, or by a senior official acting upon his behalf. A modification to the scheduled part of the warrant may include the addition of a new schedule relating to a communication service provider on whom a copy of the warrant has not been previously served. Modifications made in this way expire at the same time as the warrant expires. There also exists a duty to modify a warrant by deleting a communication identifier if it is no longer relevant. When a modification is sought to delete a number or other communication identifier, the relevant communications service provider must be advised and interception suspended before the modification instrument is signed.

4.12 In an urgent case, and where the warrant specifically authorises it, scheduled parts of a warrant may be modified by the person to whom the warrant is addressed (the person who submitted the application) or a subordinate (where the subordinate is identified in the warrant). Modifications of this kind are valid for five working days following the day of issue unless the modification instrument is endorsed by a senior official acting on behalf of the Secretary of State. Where the modification is endorsed in this way, the modification expires upon the expiry date of the warrant.

RENEWAL OF A SECTION 8(1) WARRANT

4.13 The Secretary of State may renew a warrant at any point before its expiry date. Applications for renewals must be made to the Secretary of State and should contain an update of the matters outlined in paragraph 4.2 above. In particular, the applicant should give an assessment of the value of interception to the operation to date and explain why he considers that interception continues to be necessary for one or more of the purposes in section 5(3).

4.14 Where the Secretary of State is satisfied that the interception continues to meet the requirements of the Act he may renew the warrant. Where the warrant is issued on serious crime grounds, the renewed warrant is valid for a further three months. Where it is issued on national security/economic well-being grounds, the renewed warrant is valid for six months. These dates run from the date of signature on the renewal instrument.

4.15 A copy of the warrant renewal instrument will be forwarded by the intercepting agency to all relevant communications service providers on whom a copy of the original warrant instrument and a schedule have been served, providing they are still

---

[6] Neither the senior official to whom the warrant is addressed, nor any of his subordinates may modify the scheduled parts of the warrant, except in an urgent case where the warrant contains an expressly a uthorised provision to this effect.

actively assisting. A warrant renewal instrument will include the reference number of the warrant and description of the person or premises described in the warrant.

4.16 The Secretary of State is under a duty to cancel an interception warrant if, at any time before its expiry date, he is satisfied that the warrant is no longer necessary on grounds falling within section 5(3) of the Act. Intercepting agencies will therefore need to keep their warrants under continuous review. In practice, cancellation instruments will be signed by a senior official on his behalf.

4.17 The cancellation instrument should be addressed to the person to whom the warrant was issued (the intercepting agency) and should include the reference number of the warrant and the description of the person or premises specified in the warrant. A copy of the cancellation instrument should be sent to those communications service providers who have held a copy of the warrant instrument and accompanying schedule during the preceding twelve months.

RECORDS

4.18 The oversight regime allows the Interception of Communications Commissioner to inspect the warrant application upon which the Secretary of State based his decision, and the applicant may be required to justify the content. Each intercepting agency should keep the following to be made available for scrutiny by the Commissioner as he may require:

- all applications made for warrants complying with section 8(l) and applications made for the renewal of such warrants;
- all warrants, and renewals and copies of schedule modifications (if any);
- where any application is refused, the grounds for refusal as given by the Secretary of State;
- the dates on which interception is started and stopped.

4.19 Records shall also be kept of the arrangements by which the requirements of section 15(2) (minimisation of copying and destruction of intercepted material) and section 15(3) (destruction of intercepted material) are to be met. For further details see section on "Safeguards".

4.20 The term "intercepted material" is used throughout to embrace copies, extracts or summaries made from the intercepted material as well as the intercept material itself.

Chapter 5

Interception warrants (section 8(4))

5.1 This section applies to the interception of external communications by means of a warrant complying with section 8(4) of the Act. External communications are defined by the Act to be those which are sent or received outside the British Isles. They include those which are both sent and received outside the British Isles, whether or not they pass through the British Isles in course of their transit. They do not include communications both sent and received in the British Isles, even if they pass outside the British Isles en route. Responsibility for the issuing of such interception warrants rests with the Secretary of State.

Application for a Section 8(4) Warrant

5.2 An application for a warrant is made to the Secretary of State. Interception warrants, when issued, are addressed to the person who submitted the application. This person may then serve a copy upon any person who may be able to provide assistance in giving effect to that warrant. Each application, a copy of which must be retained by the applicant, should contain the following information:

- Background to the operation in question.
- Description of the communications to be intercepted, details of the communications service provider(s) and an assessment of the feasibility of the operation where this is relevant.[7]
- Description of the conduct to be authorised, which must be restricted to the interception of external communications, or to conduct necessary [8] in order to intercept those external communications, where appropriate.
- The certificate that will regulate examination of intercepted material.
- An explanation of why the interception is considered to be necessary for one or more of the section 5(3) purposes.
- A consideration of why the conduct to be authorised by the warrant is proportionate to what is sought to be achieved by that conduct.
- A consideration of any unusual degree of collateral intrusion, and why that intrusion is justified in the circumstances. In particular, where the communications in question might affect religious, medical or journalistic confidentiality or legal privilege, this must be specified in the application.
- Where an application is urgent, supporting justification should be provided.
- An assurance that intercepted material will be read, looked at or listened to only so far as it is certified, and it meets the conditions of sections 16(2)–16(6) of the Act.
- An assurance that all material intercepted will be handled in accordance with the safeguards required by sections 15 and 16 of the Act.

Authorisation of a Section 8(4) Warrant

5.3 Before issuing a warrant under section 8(4), the Secretary of State must believe that the warrant is necessary;[9]

- in the interests of national security;
- for the purpose of preventing or detecting serious crime; or
- for the purpose of safeguarding the economic well-being of the United Kingdom.

5.4 In exercising his power to issue an interception warrant for the purpose of safeguarding the economic well-being of the United Kingdom (as provided for by section 5(3)(c) of the Act), the Secretary of State will consider whether the economic

---

[7] This assessment is normally based upon information provided by the relevant communications service provider.

[8] This conduct may include the interception of other communications (section 5(6)(a)).

[9] A single warrant can be justified on more than one of the grounds listed.

well-being of the United Kingdom which is to be safeguarded is, on the facts of each case, directly related to state security. The term "state security", which is used in Directive 97/66/EC (concerning the processing of personal data and the protection of privacy in the telecommunications sector), should be interpreted in the same way as the term "national security" which is used elsewhere in the Act and this Code. The Secretary of State will not issue a warrant on section 5(3)(c) grounds if this direct link between the economic well-being of the United Kingdom and state security is not established. Any application for a warrant on section 5(3)(c) grounds should therefore explain how, in the applicant's view, the economic well-being of the United Kingdom which is to be safeguarded is directly related to state security on the facts of the case.

5.5 The Secretary of State must also consider that the conduct authorised by the warrant is proportionate to what it seeks to achieve (section 5(2)(b)). In considering necessity and proportionality, the Secretary of State must take into account whether the information sought could reasonably be obtained by other means (section 5(4)).

5.6 When the Secretary of State issues a warrant of this kind, it must be accompanied by a certificate in which the Secretary of State certifies that he considers examination of the intercepted material to be necessary for one or more of the section 5(3) purposes. The Secretary of State has a duty to ensure that arrangements are in force for securing that only that material which has been certified as necessary for examination for a section 5(3) purpose, and which meets the conditions set out in section 16(2) to section 16(6) is, in fact, read, looked at or listened to. The Interception of Communications Commissioner is under a duty to review the adequacy of those arrangements.

URGENT AUTHORISATION OF A SECTION 8(4) WARRANT

5.7 The Act makes provision (section 7(l)(b)) for cases in which an interception warrant is required urgently, yet the Secretary of State is not available to sign the warrant. In these cases the Secretary of State will still personally authorise the interception but the warrant is signed by a senior official, following discussion of the case between officials and the Secretary of State. The Act restricts issue of warrants in this way to urgent cases where the Secretary of State has himself expressly authorised the issue of the warrant (section 7(2)(a)), and requires the warrant to contain a statement to that effect (section 7(4)(a)).

5.8 A warrant issued under the urgency procedure lasts for five working days following the day of issue unless renewed by the Secretary of State, in which case it expires after 3 months in the case of serious crime or 6 months in the case of national security or economic well-being in the same way as other section 8(4) warrants.

FORMAT OF A SECTION 8(4) WARRANT

5.9 Each warrant is addressed to the person who submitted the application. This person may then serve a copy upon such providers of communications services as he believes will be able to assist in implementing the interception. Communications service providers will not receive a copy of the certificate. The warrant should include the following:

- A description of the communications to be intercepted.
- The warrant reference number.

- The persons who may subsequently modify the scheduled part of the warrant in an urgent case (if authorised in accordance with section 10(8) of the Act).

MODIFICATION OF A SECTION 8(4) WARRANT

5.10 Interception warrants maybe modified under the provisions of section 10 of the Act. The warrant may only be modified by the Secretary of State or, in an urgent case, by a senior official with the express authorisation of the Secretary of State. In these cases a statement of that fact must be endorsed on the modifying instrument, and the modification ceases to have effect after five working days following the day of issue unless it is endorsed by the Secretary of State.

5.11 The certificate must be modified by the Secretary of State, save in an urgent case where a certificate may be modified under the hand of a senior official provided that the official holds a position in respect of which he is expressly authorised by provisions contained in the certificate to modify the certificate on the Secretary of State's behalf, or the Secretary of State has himself expressly authorised the modification and a statement of that fact is endorsed on the modifying instrument. Again the modification shall cease to have effect after five working days following the day of issue unless it is endorsed by the Secretary of State.

RENEWAL OF A SECTION 8(4) WARRANT

5.12 The Secretary of State may renew a warrant at any point before its expiry date. Applications for renewals are made to the Secretary of State and contain an update of the matters outlined in paragraph 5.2 above. In particular, the applicant must give an assessment of the value of interception to the operation to date and explain why he considers that interception continues to be necessary for one or more of purposes in section 5(3).

5.13 Where the Secretary of State is satisfied that the interception continues to meet the requirements of the Act he may renew the warrant. Where the warrant is issued on serious crime grounds, the renewed warrant is valid for a further three months. Where it is issued on national security/economic well-being grounds the renewed warrant is valid for six months. These dates run from the date of signature on the renewal instrument.

5.14 In those circumstances where the assistance of communications service providers has been sought, a copy of the warrant renewal instrument will be forwarded by the intercepting agency to all those on whom a copy of the original warrant instrument has been served, providing they are still actively assisting. A warrant renewal instrument will include the reference number of the warrant and description of the communications to be intercepted.

WARRANT CANCELLATION

5.15 The Secretary of State shall cancel an interception warrant if, at any time before its expiry date, he is satisfied that the warrant is no longer necessary on grounds falling within Section 5(3) of the Act. In practice, cancellation instruments will be signed by a senior official on his behalf.

5.16 The cancellation instrument will be addressed to the person to whom the warrant was issued (the intercepting agency). A copy of the cancellation instrument should be sent to those communications service providers, if any, who have given effect to the warrant during the preceding twelve months.

RECORDS

5.17 The oversight regime allows the Interception of Communications Commissioner to inspect the warrant application upon which the Secretary of State based his decision, and the applicant may be required to justify the content. Each intercepting agency should keep, so to be made available for scrutiny by the Interception of Communications Commissioner, the following:

- all applications made for warrants complying with section 8(4), and applications made for the renewal of such warrants;
- all warrants and certificates, and copies of renewal and modification instruments (if any);
- where any application is refused, the grounds for refusal as given by the Secretary of State;
- the dates on which interception is started and stopped.

Records shall also be kept of the arrangements in force for securing that only material which has been certified for examination for a purpose under section 5(3) and which meets the conditions set out in section 16(2)–16(6) of the Act in accordance with section 15 of the Act. Records shall be kept of the arrangements by which the requirements of section 15(2) (minimisation of copying and distribution of intercepted material) and section 15(3) (destruction of intercepted material) are to be met. For further details see section on "Safeguards".

Chapter 6

Safeguards

6.1 All material (including related communications data) intercepted under the authority of a warrant complying with section 8(1) or section 8(4) of the Act must be handled in accordance with safeguards which the Secretary of State has approved in conformity with the duty imposed upon him by the Act. These safeguards are made available to the Interception of Communications Commissioner, and they must meet the requirements of section 15 of the Act which are set out below. In addition, the safeguards in section 16 of the Act apply to warrants complying with section 8(4). Any breach of these safeguards must be reported to the Interception of Communications Commissioner.

6.2 Section 15 of the Act requires that disclosure, copying and retention of intercept material be limited to the minimum necessary for the authorised purposes. The authorised purposes defined in section 15(4) of the Act include:

- if the material continues to be, or is likely to become, necessary for any of the purposes set out in section 5(3) – namely, in the interests of national security, for the purpose of preventing or detecting serious crime, for the purpose of safeguarding the economic well-being of the United Kingdom;

- if the material is necessary for facilitating the carrying out of the functions of the Secretary of State under Chapter I of Part I of the Act;
- if the material is necessary for facilitating the carrying out of any functions of the Interception of Communications Commissioner or the Tribunal;
- if the material is necessary to ensure that a person conducting a criminal prosecution has the information he needs to determine what is required of him by his duty to secure the fairness of the prosecution;
- if the material is necessary for the performance of any duty imposed by the Public Record Acts.

6.3 Section 16 provides for additional safeguards in relation to material gathered under section 8(4) warrants, requiring that the safeguards:

- ensure that intercepted material is read, looked at or listened to by any person only to the extent that the material is certified;
- regulate the use of selection factors that refer to individuals known to be for the time being in the British Isles.

The Secretary of State must ensure that the safeguards are in force before any interception under warrants complying with section 8(4) can begin. The Interception of Communications Commissioner is under a duty to review the adequacy of the safeguards.

DISSEMINATION OF INTERCEPTED MATERIAL

6.4 The number of persons to whom any of the material is disclosed, and the extent of disclosure, must be limited to the minimum that is necessary for the authorised purposes set out in section 15(4) of the Act. This obligation applies equally to disclosure to additional persons within an agency, and to disclosure outside the agency. It is enforced by prohibiting disclosure to persons who do not hold the required security clearance, and also by the need-to-know principle: intercepted material must not be disclosed to any person unless that person's duties, which must relate to one of the authorised purposes, are such that he needs to know about the material to carry out those duties. In the same way only so much of the material may be disclosed as the recipient needs; for example if a summary of the material will suffice, no more than that should be disclosed.

6.5 The obligations apply not just to the original interceptor, but also to anyone to whom the material is subsequently disclosed. In some cases this will be achieved by requiring the latter to obtain the originator's permission before disclosing the material further. In others, explicit safeguards are applied to secondary recipients.

COPYING

6.6 Intercepted material may only be copied to the extent necessary for the authorised purposes set out in section 15(4) of the Act. Copies include not only direct copies of the whole of the material, but also extracts and summaries which identify themselves as the product of an interception, and any record referring to an interception which is a record of the identities of the persons to or by whom the intercepted material was sent. The restrictions are implemented by requiring special treatment of such copies, extracts and summaries that are made by recording their making, distribution and destruction.

STORAGE

6.7 Intercepted material, and all copies, extracts and summaries of it, must be handled and stored securely, so as to minimise the risk of loss or theft. It must be held so as to be inaccessible to persons without the required level of security clearance. This requirement to store intercept product securely applies to all those who are responsible for the handling of this material, including communications service providers. The details of what such a requirement will mean in practice for communications service providers will be set out in the discussions they will be having with the Government before a Section 12 Notice is served (see paragraph 2.9).

DESTRUCTION

6.8 Intercepted material, and all copies, extracts and summaries which can be identified as the product of an interception, must be securely destroyed as soon as it is no longer needed for any of the authorised purposes. If such material is retained, it should be reviewed at appropriate intervals to confirm that the justification for its retention is still valid under section 15(3) of the Act.

PERSONNEL SECURITY

6.9 Each intercepting agency maintains a distribution list of persons who may have access to intercepted material or need to see any reporting in relation to it. All such persons must be appropriately vetted. Any person no longer needing access to perform his duties should be removed from any such list. Where it is necessary for an officer of one agency to disclose material to another, it is the former's responsibility to ensure that the recipient has the necessary clearance.

Chapter 7

Disclosure to ensure fairness in criminal proceedings

7.1 Section 15(3) of the Act states the general rule that intercepted material must be destroyed as soon as its retention is no longer necessary for a purpose authorised under the Act. Section 15(4) specifies the authorised purposes for which retention is necessary.

7.2 This part of the Code applies to the handling of intercepted material in the context of criminal proceedings where the material has been retained for one of the purposes authorised in section 15(4) of the Act. For those who would ordinarily have had responsibility under the Criminal Procedure and Investigations Act 1996 to provide disclosure in criminal proceedings, this includes those rare situations where destruction of intercepted material has not taken place in accordance with section 15(3) and where that material is still in existence after the commencement of a criminal prosecution, retention having been considered necessary to ensure that a person conducting a criminal prosecution has the information he needs to discharge his duty of ensuring its fairness (section 15(4)(d)).

EXCLUSION OF MATTERS FROM LEGAL PROCEEDINGS

7.3 The general rule is that neither the possibility of interception nor intercepted material itself plays any part in legal proceedings. This rule is set out in section 17 of the Act, which excludes evidence, questioning, assertion or disclosure in legal proceedings likely to reveal the existence (or the absence) of a warrant issued under this Act (or the Interception of Communications Act 1985). This rule means that the intercepted material cannot be used either by the prosecution or the defence. This preserves "equality of arms" which is a requirement under Article 6 of the European Convention on Human Rights.

7.4 Section 18 contains a number of tightly-drawn exceptions to this rule. This part of the Code deals only with the exception in subsections (7) to (11).

DISCLOSURE TO A PROSECUTOR

7.5 Section 18(7)(a) provides that intercepted material obtained by means of a warrant and which continues to be available, may, for a strictly limited purpose, be disclosed to a person conducting a criminal prosecution.

7.6 This may only be done for the purpose of enabling the prosecutor to determine what is required of him by his duty to secure the fairness of the prosecution. The prosecutor may not use intercepted material to which he is given access under section 18(7)(a) to mount a cross-examination, or to do anything other than ensure the fairness of the proceedings.

7.7 The exception does not mean that intercepted material should be retained against a remote possibility that it might be relevant to future proceedings. The normal expectation is, still, for the intercepted material to be destroyed in accordance with the general safeguards provided by section 15. The exceptions only come into play if such material has, in fact, been retained for an authorised purpose. Because the authorised purpose given in section 5(3)(b) (*"for the purpose of preventing or detecting serious crime"*) does not extend to gathering evidence for the purpose of a prosecution, material intercepted for this purpose may not have survived to the prosecution stage, as it will have been destroyed in accordance with the section 15(3) safeguards. There is, in these circumstances, no need to consider disclosure to a prosecutor if, in fact, no intercepted material remains in existence.

7.8 Be that as it may, section 18(7)(a) recognises the duty on prosecutors, acknowledged by common law, to review all available material to make sure that the prosecution is not proceeding unfairly. "Available material" will only ever include intercepted material at this stage if the conscious decision has been made to retain it for an authorised purpose.

7.9 If intercepted material does continue to be available at the prosecution stage, once this information has come to the attention of the holder of this material the prosecutor should be informed that a warrant has been issued under section 5 and that material of possible relevance to the case has been intercepted.

7.10 Having had access to the material, the prosecutor may conclude that the material affects the fairness of the proceedings. In these circumstances, he will decide how the prosecution, if it proceeds, should be presented.

DISCLOSURE TO A JUDGE

7.11 Section 18(7)(b) recognises that there may be cases where the prosecutor, having seen intercepted material under subsection (7)(a), will need to consult the trial judge. Accordingly, it provides for the judge to be given access to intercepted material, where there are exceptional circumstances making that disclosure essential in the interests of justice.

7.12 This access will be achieved by the prosecutor inviting the judge to make an order for disclosure to him alone, under this subsection. This is an exceptional procedure; normally, the prosecutor's functions under subsection (7)(a) will not fall to be reviewed by the judge. To comply with section 17(l), any consideration given to, or exercise of, this power must be carried out without notice to the defence. The purpose of this power is to ensure that the trial is conducted fairly.

7.13 The judge may, having considered the intercepted material disclosed to him, direct the prosecution to make an admission of fact. The admission will be abstracted from the interception; but, in accordance with the requirements of section 17(l), it must not reveal the fact of interception. This is likely to be a very unusual step. The Act only allows it where the judge considers it essential in the interests of justice.

7.14 Nothing in these provisions allows intercepted material, or the fact of interception, to be disclosed to the defence.

Chapter 8

Oversight

8.1 The Act provides for an Interception of Communications Commissioner whose remit is to provide independent oversight of the use of the powers contained within the warranted interception regime under Chapter I of Part I of the Act.

8.2 This Code does not cover the exercise of the Commissioner's functions. However, it will be the duty of any person who uses the above powers to comply with any request made, by the Commissioner to provide any information as he requires for the purpose of enabling him to discharge his functions.

Chapter 9

Complaints

9.1 The Act establishes an independent Tribunal. This Tribunal will be made up of senior members of the judiciary and the legal profession and is independent of the Government. The Tribunal has full powers to investigate and decide any case within its jurisdiction.

9.2 This code does not cover the exercise of the Tribunal's functions. Details of the relevant complaints procedure can be obtained from the following address:

The Investigatory Powers Tribunal
PO Box 33220
London
SWIH 9ZQ
Tel: 0207 273 4514

Chapter 10

Interception without a warrant

10.1 Section 1(5) of the Act permits interception without a warrant in the following circumstances:

- where it is authorised by or under sections 3 or 4 of the Act (see below);
- where it is in exercise, in relation to any stored communication, of some other statutory power exercised for the purpose of obtaining information or of taking possession of any document or other property, for example, the obtaining of a production order under Schedule 1 to the Police and Criminal Evidence Act 1984 for stored data to be produced.

Interception in accordance with a warrant under section 5 of the Act is dealt with under parts 2, 3, 4 and 5 of this Code.

10.2 For lawful interception which takes place without a warrant, pursuant to sections 3 or 4 of the Act or pursuant to some other statutory power, there is no prohibition in the Act on the evidential use of any material that is obtained as a result. The matter may still, however, be regulated by the exclusionary rules of evidence to be found in the common law, section 78 of the Police and Criminal Evidence Act 1984, and/or pursuant to the Human Rights Act 1998.

INTERCEPTION WITH THE CONSENT OF BOTH PARTIES

10.3 Section 3(l) of the Act authorises the interception of a communication if both the person sending the communication and the intended recipient(s) have consented to its interception, or where the person conducting the interception has reasonable grounds for believing that all parties have consented to the interception.

INTERCEPTION WITH THE CONSENT OF ONE PARTY

10.4 Section 3(2) of the Act authorises the interception of a communication if either the sender or intended recipient of the communication has consented to its interception, and directed surveillance by means of that interception has been authorised under Part II of the Act. Further details can be found in chapter 4 of the Covert Surveillance Code of Practice and in chapter 2 of the Covert Human Intelligence Sources Code of Practice.

Interception for the Purposes of a Communication Service Provider

10.5 Section 3(3) of the Act permits a communication service provider or a person acting upon their behalf to carry out interception for purposes connected with the operation of that service or for purposes connected with the enforcement of any enactment relating to the use of the communication service.

Lawful Business Practice

10.6 Section 4(2) of the Act enables the Secretary of State to make regulations setting out those circumstances where it is lawful to intercept communications for the purpose of carrying on a business. These regulations apply equally to public authorities. These Lawful Business Practice Regulations can be found on the following Department of Trade and Industry website: www.dti.gov.uk/cii/regulation.html.

Appendix E

Covert Human Intelligence Sources

Code of Practice
Pursuant to section 71 of the Regulation of Investigatory Powers Act 2000

Chapter 1

Introduction

DEFINITIONS

1.1. In this code the:

- "1989 Act" means the Security Service Act 1989;
- "1994 Act" means the Intelligence Services Act 1994;
- "1997 Act" means the Police Act 1997;
- "2000 Act" means the Regulation of Investigatory Powers Act 2000;
- "RIP(S)A" means the Regulation of Investigatory Powers (Scotland) Act 2000;
- "2010 Order" means the Regulation of Investigatory Powers (Covert Human Intelligence Sources: Matters Subject to Legal Privilege) Order 2010.

BACKGROUND

1.2. This code of practice provides guidance on the authorisation of the use or conduct of covert human intelligence sources ("CHIS") by public authorities under Part II of the 2000 Act.

1.3. This code is issued pursuant to Section 71 of the 2000 Act, which stipulates that the Secretary of State shall issue one or more codes of practice in relation to the powers and duties in Parts I to III of the 2000 Act, section 5 of the 1994 Act and Part III of the 1997 Act. This code replaces the previous code of practice issued in 2002.

1.4. This code is publicly available and should be readily accessible by members of any relevant public authority seeking to use the 2000 Act to authorise the use or conduct of CHIS.[1]

EFFECT OF CODE

1.5. The 2000 Act provides that all codes of practice relating to the 2000 Act are admissible as evidence in criminal and civil proceedings. If any provision of this code appears relevant to any court or tribunal considering any such proceedings, or to the Investigatory Powers Tribunal established under the 2000 Act, or to one of the Commissioners responsible for overseeing the powers conferred by the 2000 Act, it must be taken into account. Public authorities may also be required to justify, with regard to this code, the use or granting of authorisations in general or the failure to use or grant authorisations where appropriate.

1.6. Examples are included in this code to assist with the illustration and interpretation of certain provisions. Examples are not provisions of the code, but are included for guidance only. It is not possible for theoretical examples to replicate the level of detail to be found in real cases. Consequently, authorising officers should avoid allowing superficial similarities with the examples to determine their decisions and

---

[1] Being those listed in or added to Part I of schedule 1 of the 2000 Act.

should not seek to justify their decisions solely by reference to the examples rather than to the law, including the provisions of this code.

SCOPE OF COVERT HUMAN INTELLIGENCE SOURCE ACTIVITY
TO WHICH THIS CODE APPLIES

1.7. Part II of the 2000 Act provides for the authorisation of the use or conduct of CHIS. The definitions of these terms are laid out in section 26 of the 2000 Act and Chapter 2 of this code.

1.8. Not all human sources of information will fall within these definitions and an authorisation under the 2000 Act will therefore not always be appropriate.

1.9. Neither Part II of the 2000 Act nor this code of practice is intended to affect the existing practices and procedures surrounding criminal participation of CHIS.

Chapter 2

Covert human intelligence sources: definitions and examples

DEFINITION OF A COVERT HUMAN INTELLIGENCE SOURCE (CHIS)

2.1. Under the 2000 Act, a person is a CHIS if:

a) he establishes or maintains a personal or other relationship with a person for the covert purpose of facilitating the doing of anything falling within paragraph b) or c);

b) he covertly uses such a relationship to obtain information or to provide access to any information to another person; or

c) he covertly discloses information obtained by the use of such a relationship or as a consequence of the existence of such a relationship.[2]

2.2. A relationship is established or maintained for a covert purpose if and only if it is conducted in a manner that is calculated to ensure that one of the parties to the relationship is unaware of the purpose.[3]

2.3. A relationship is used covertly, and information obtained is disclosed covertly, if and only if the relationship is used or the information is disclosed in a manner that is calculated to ensure that one of the parties to the relationship is unaware of the use or disclosure in question.[4]

SCOPE OF "USE" OR "CONDUCT" AUTHORISATIONS

2.4. Subject to the procedures outlined in Chapter 3 of this Code, an authorisation may be obtained under Part II of the 2000 Act for the use or conduct of CHIS.

2.5. The use of a CHIS involves any action on behalf of a public authority to induce, ask or assist a person to engage in the conduct of a CHIS, or to obtain information by

---

[2] See section 26(8) of the 2000 Act.
[3] See section 26(9)(b) of the 2000 Act for a full definition.
[4] See section 26(9)(c) of the 2000 Act for a full definition.

means of the conduct of a CHIS.[5] In general, therefore, an authorisation for use of a CHIS will be necessary to authorise steps taken by a public authority in relation to a CHIS.

2.6. The conduct of a CHIS is any conduct of a CHIS which falls within paragraph 2.1 above or is incidental to anything falling within that paragraph. In other words, an authorisation for conduct will authorise steps taken by the CHIS on behalf, or at the request, of a public authority.[6]

2.7. Most CHIS authorisations will be for both use and conduct. This is because public authorities usually take action in connection with the CHIS, such as tasking the CHIS to undertake covert action, and because the CHIS will be expected to take action in relation to the public authority, such as responding to particular tasking.

2.8. Care should be taken to ensure that the CHIS is clear on what is/is not authorised at any given time and that all the CHIS's activities are properly risk assessed. Care should also be taken to ensure that relevant applications, reviews, renewals and cancellations are correctly performed. A CHIS may in certain circumstances be the subject of different use or conduct authorisations obtained by one or more public authorities. Such authorisations should not conflict.

CIRCUMSTANCES IN WHICH IT WOULD BE APPROPRIATE TO
AUTHORISE THE USE OR CONDUCT OF A CHIS

2.9. Public authorities are not required by the 2000 Act to seek or obtain an authorisation just because one is available (see section 80 of the 2000 Act). The use or conduct of a CHIS, however, can be a particularly intrusive and high risk covert technique, requiring dedicated and sufficient resources, oversight and management. This will include ensuring that all use or conduct is:

- necessary and proportionate to the intelligence dividend that it seeks to achieve;
- in compliance with relevant Articles of the European Convention on Human Rights, particularly Articles 6 and 8.

2.10. Unlike directed surveillance, which relates specifically to private information, authorisations for the use or conduct of a CHIS do not relate specifically to private information, but to the covert manipulation of a relationship to gain any information. ECHR case law makes it clear that Article 8 includes the right to establish and develop relationships. Accordingly, any manipulation of a relationship by a public authority (e.g. one party having a covert purpose on behalf of a public authority) is likely to engage Article 8, regardless of whether or not the public authority intends to acquire private information.

2.11. It is therefore strongly recommended that a public authority consider an authorisation whenever the use or conduct of a CHIS is likely to engage an individual's rights under Article 8, whether this is through obtaining information, particularly private information, or simply through the covert manipulation of a relationship.

---

[5] See section 26(7)(b) of the 2000 Act.
[6] See section 26(7)(a) of the 2000 Act.

2.12. The word "establishes" when applied to a relationship means "set up". It does not require, as "maintains" does, endurance over any particular period. Consequently, a relationship of seller and buyer may be deemed to exist between a shopkeeper and a customer even if only a single transaction takes place. Repetition is not always necessary to give rise to a relationship, but whether or not a relationship exists depends on all the circumstances including the length of time of the contact between seller and buyer and the nature of any covert activity.

Example 1: Intelligence suggests that a local shopkeeper is openly selling alcohol to underage customers, without any questions being asked. A juvenile is engaged and trained by a public authority and then deployed in order to make a purchase of alcohol. In these circumstances any relationship, if established at all, is likely to be so limited in regards to the requirements of the 2000 Act that a public authority may conclude that a CHIS authorisation is unnecessary. However, if the test purchaser is wearing recording equipment but is not authorised as a CHIS, consideration should be given to granting a directed surveillance authorisation.

Example 2: In similar circumstances, intelligence suggests that a shopkeeper will sell alcohol to juveniles from a room at the back of the shop, providing he has first got to know and trust them. As a consequence the public authority decides to deploy its operative on a number of occasions, to befriend the shopkeeper and gain his trust, in order to purchase alcohol. In these circumstances a relationship has been established and maintained for a covert purpose and therefore a CHIS authorisation should be obtained.

HUMAN SOURCE ACTIVITY FALLING OUTSIDE CHIS DEFINITION

2.13. Not all human source activity will meet the definition of a CHIS. For example, a source may be a public volunteer who discloses information out of professional or statutory duty, or has been tasked to obtain information other than by way of a relationship.

PUBLIC VOLUNTEERS

2.14. In many cases involving human sources, a relationship will not have been established or maintained for a covert purpose. Many sources merely volunteer or provide information that is within their personal knowledge, without being induced, asked, or tasked by a public authority. This means that the source is not a CHIS for the purposes of the 2000 Act and no authorisation under the 2000 Act is required.[7]

Example 1: A member of the public volunteers a piece of information to a member of a public authority regarding something he has witnessed in his neighbourhood. The member of the public would not be regarded as a CHIS. He is not passing information as a result of a relationship which has been established or maintained for a covert purpose.

---

[7] See Chapter 2 of this code for further guidance on types of source activity to which authorisations under Part II of the 2000 Act may or may not apply.

Example 2: A caller to a confidential hotline (such as Crimestoppers, the Customs Hotline, the Anti-Terrorist Hotline, or the Security Service Public Telephone Number) reveals that he knows of criminal or terrorist activity. Even if the caller is involved in the activities on which he is reporting, the caller would not be considered a CHIS as the information is not being disclosed on the basis of a relationship which was established or maintained for that covert purpose. However, should the caller be asked to maintain his relationship with those involved and to continue to supply information, an authorisation for the use or conduct of a CHIS may be appropriate.

PROFESSIONAL OR STATUTORY DUTY

2.15. Certain individuals will be required to provide information to public authorities or designated bodies out of professional or statutory duty. For example, employees within organisations regulated by the money laundering provisions of the Proceeds of Crime Act 2002 will be required to comply with the Money Laundering Regulations 2003 and report suspicious transactions. Similarly, financial officials, accountants or company administrators may have a duty to provide information that they have obtained by virtue of their position to the Serious Fraud Office.

2.16. Any such regulatory or professional disclosures should not result in these individuals meeting the definition of a CHIS, as the business or professional relationships from which the information derives will not have been established or maintained for the covert purpose of disclosing such information.

2.17. Furthermore, this reporting is undertaken "in accordance with the law" and any action likely to interfere with an individual's privacy, will not engage a person's human rights by virtue of Article 8(2) ECHR.

2.18. This statutory or professional duty, however, would not extend to the situation where a person is asked to provide information which they acquire as a result of an existing professional or business relationship with the subject but that person is under no obligation to pass it on. For example, a travel agent who is asked by the police to find out when a regular client next intends to fly to a particular destination is not under an obligation to pass this information on. In these circumstances a CHIS authorisation may be appropriate.

TASKING NOT INVOLVING RELATIONSHIPS

2.19. Tasking a person to obtain information covertly may result in authorisation under Part II of the 2000 Act being appropriate. However, this will not be true in all circumstances. For example, where the tasking given to a person does not require that person to establish or maintain a relationship for the purpose of obtaining, providing access to or disclosing the information sought or where the information is already within the personal knowledge of the individual, that person will not be a CHIS.

Example: A member of the public is asked by a member of a public authority to maintain a record of all vehicles arriving and leaving a specific location or to record the details of visitors to a neighbouring house. A relationship has not been established or maintained in order to gather the information and a CHIS authorisation is therefore not available. Other authorisations under the Act, for example, directed surveillance may need to be considered where there is an interference with the Art 8 rights of an individual.

IDENTIFYING WHEN A HUMAN SOURCE BECOMES A CHIS

2.20. Individuals or members of organisations (e.g. travel agents, housing associations and taxi companies) who, because of their work or role have access to personal information, may voluntarily provide information to the police on a repeated basis and need to be managed appropriately. Public authorities must keep such human sources under constant review to ensure that they are managed with an appropriate level of sensitivity and confidentiality, and to establish whether, at any given stage, they should be authorised as a CHIS.

2.21. Determining the status of an individual or organisation is a matter of judgement by the public authority. Public authorities should avoid inducing individuals to engage in the conduct of a CHIS either expressly or implicitly without obtaining a CHIS authorisation.

Example: Mr Y volunteers information to a member of a public authority about a work colleague out of civic duty. Mr Y is not a CHIS at this stage as he has not established or maintained (or been asked to establish or maintain) a relationship with his colleague for the covert purpose of obtaining and disclosing information. However, Mr Y is subsequently contacted by the public authority and is asked if he would ascertain certain specific information about his colleague. At this point, it is likely that Mr Y's relationship with a colleague is being maintained and used for the covert purpose of providing that information. A CHIS authorisation would therefore be appropriate to authorise interference with the Article 8 right to respect for private and family life of Mr Y's work colleague.

2.22. However, the tasking of a person should not be used as the sole benchmark in seeking a CHIS authorisation. It is the activity of the CHIS in exploiting a relationship for a covert purpose which is ultimately authorised by the 2000 Act, whether or not that CHIS is asked to do so by a public authority. It is possible therefore that a person will become engaged in the conduct of a CHIS without a public authority inducing, asking or assisting the person to engage in that conduct.

Chapter 3

General rules on authorisations

AUTHORISING OFFICER

3.1. Responsibility for giving the authorisation will depend on which public authority is responsible for the CHIS. For the purposes of this and future chapters, the person in a public authority responsible for granting an authorisation will be referred to as the "authorising officer". The relevant public authorities and authorising officers are listed in the Regulation of Investigatory Powers (Directed Surveillance and Covert Human Intelligence Sources) Order 2010.

NECESSITY AND PROPORTIONALITY

3.2. The 2000 Act stipulates that the authorising officer must believe that an authorisation for the use or conduct of a CHIS is necessary in the circumstances of the particular case for one or more of the statutory grounds listed in section 29(3) of the 2000 Act.

3.3. If the use or conduct of the CHIS is deemed necessary, on one or more of the statutory grounds, the person granting the authorisation must also believe that it is proportionate to what is sought to be achieved by carrying it out. This involves balancing the seriousness of the intrusion into the private or family life of the subject of the operation (or any other person who may be affected) against the need for the activity in investigative and operational terms.

3.4. The authorisation will not be proportionate if it is excessive in the overall circumstances of the case. Each action authorised should bring an expected benefit to the investigation or operation and should not be disproportionate or arbitrary. The fact that a suspected offence may be serious will not alone render the use or conduct of a CHIS proportionate. Similarly, an offence may be so minor that any deployment of a CHIS would be disproportionate. No activity should be considered proportionate if the information which is sought could reasonably be obtained by other less intrusive means.

3.5. The following elements of proportionality should therefore be considered:

- balancing the size and scope of the proposed activity against the gravity and extent of the perceived crime or offence;
- explaining how and why the methods to be adopted will cause the least possible intrusion on the subject and others;
- considering whether the activity is an appropriate use of the legislation and a reasonable way, having considered all reasonable alternatives, of obtaining the necessary result;
- evidencing, as far as reasonably practicable, what other methods had been considered and why they were not implemented.

EXTENT OF AUTHORISATIONS

3.6. An authorisation under Part II of the 2000 Act for the use or conduct of a CHIS will provide lawful authority for any such activity that:

- involves the use or conduct of a CHIS as is specified or described in the authorisation;
- is carried out by or in relation to the person to whose actions as a CHIS the authorisation relates; and
- is carried out for the purposes of, or in connection with, the investigation or operation so described.[8]

---

[8] See section 29(4) of the 2000 Act.

3.7. In the above context, it is important that the CHIS is fully aware of the extent and limits of any conduct authorised and that those involved in the use of a CHIS are fully aware of the extent and limits of the authorisation in question.

COLLATERAL INTRUSION

3.8. Before authorising the use or conduct of a source, the authorising officer should take into account the risk of interference with the private and family life of persons who are not the intended subjects of the CHIS activity (collateral intrusion).

3.9. Measures should be taken, wherever practicable, to avoid or minimize interference with the private and family life of those who are not the intended subjects of the CHIS activity. Where such collateral intrusion is unavoidable, the activities may still be authorised providing this collateral intrusion is considered proportionate to the aims of the intended intrusion. Any collateral intrusion should be kept to the minimum necessary to achieve the objective of the operation.

3.10. All applications should therefore include an assessment of the risk of any collateral intrusion, and details of any measures taken to limit this, to enable the authorising officer fully to consider the proportionality of the proposed use or conduct of a CHIS.

3.11. Where CHIS activity is deliberately proposed against individuals who are not suspected of direct or culpable involvement in the matter being investigated, interference with the private and family life of such individuals should not be considered as collateral intrusion but rather as intended intrusion. Any such interference should be carefully considered against the necessity and proportionality criteria as described above.

Example 1: An undercover operative is deployed to obtain information about the activities of a suspected criminal gang under CHIS authorisation. It is assessed that the operative will in the course of this deployment obtain private information about some individuals who are not involved in criminal activities and are of no interest to the investigation. The authorising officer should consider the proportionality of this collateral intrusion, and whether sufficient measures are to be taken to limit it, when granting the authorisation.

Example 2: The police seek to establish the whereabouts of Mr W in the interests of national security. In order to do so, an undercover operative is deployed to seek to obtain this information from Mr P, an associate of Mr W who is not of direct security interest. An application for a CHIS authorisation is made to authorise the deployment. The authorising officer will need to consider the necessity and proportionality of the operation against Mr P and Mr W, who will be the direct subjects of the intrusion. The authorising officer will also need to consider the proportionality of any collateral intrusion that will arise if there is any additional interference with the private and family life of other individuals of no interest to the investigation.

3.12. Where possible, the authorising officer who grants an authorisation should be responsible for considering subsequent renewals of that authorisation and any related security and welfare issues.

3.13. The authorising officer will stipulate the frequency of formal reviews and the controller (see paragraph 6.9 below) should maintain an audit of case work sufficient to ensure that the use or conduct of the CHIS remains within the parameters of the extant authorisation. This will not prevent additional reviews being conducted by the authorising officer in response to changing circumstances such as described below.

3.14. Where the nature or extent of intrusion into the private or family life of any person becomes greater than that anticipated in the original authorisation, the authorising officer should immediately review the authorisation and reconsider the proportionality of the operation. This should be highlighted at the next renewal.

3.15. Where a CHIS authorisation provides for interference with the private and family life of initially unidentified individuals whose identity is later established, a new authorisation is not required provided the scope of the original authorisation envisaged interference with the private and family life of such individuals.

Example: An authorisation is obtained by the police to authorise a CHIS to use her relationship with "Mr X and his close associates" for the covert purpose of providing information relating to their suspected involvement in a crime. Mr X introduces the CHIS to Mr A, a close associate of Mr X. It is assessed that obtaining more information on Mr A will assist the investigation. The CHIS may use her relationship with Mr A to obtain such information but the review of the authorisation should specify any interference with the private and family life of "Mr X and his associates, including Mr A" and that such an interference is in accordance with the original authorisation.

3.16. Any proposed changes to the nature of the CHIS operation (i.e. the activities involved) should immediately be brought to the attention of the authorising officer. The authorising officer should consider whether the proposed changes are within the scope of the existing authorisation and whether they are proportionate (bearing in mind any extra interference with private or family life or collateral intrusion), before approving or rejecting them. Any such changes should be highlighted at the next renewal.

LOCAL CONSIDERATIONS AND COMMUNITY IMPACT ASSESSMENTS

3.17. Any person granting or applying for an authorisation will also need to be aware of any particular sensitivities in the local community where the CHIS is being used and of similar activities being undertaken by other public authorities which could have an impact on the deployment of the CHIS. Consideration should also be given to any adverse impact on community confidence or safety that may result from the use or conduct of a CHIS or use of information obtained from that CHIS.

3.18. It is therefore recommended that where an authorising officer from a public authority considers that conflicts might arise they should, where possible, consult a senior officer within the police force area in which the CHIS is deployed. All public authorities, where possible, should consider consulting with other relevant public authorities to gauge community impact.

COMBINED AUTHORISATIONS

3.19. A single authorisation may combine two or more different authorisations under Part II of the 2000 Act.[9] For example, a single authorisation may combine authorisations for intrusive surveillance and the conduct of a CHIS. In such cases the provisions applicable to each of the authorisations must be considered separately by the appropriate authorising officer. Thus, a police superintendent, or above, can authorise the conduct of a CHIS but an authorisation for intrusive surveillance by the police needs the separate authorisation of a chief constable (and the prior approval of a Surveillance Commissioner, except in cases of urgency).

3.20. Where an authorisation for the use or conduct of a CHIS is combined with a Secretary of State authorisation for intrusive surveillance, the combined authorisation must be issued by the Secretary of State.

3.21. The above considerations do not preclude public authorities from obtaining separate authorisations.

OPERATIONS INVOLVING MULTIPLE CHIS

3.22. A single authorisation under Part II of the 2000 Act may be used to authorise more than one CHIS. However, this is only likely to be appropriate for operations involving the conduct of several undercover operatives acting as CHISs in situations where the activities to be authorised, the subjects of the operation, the interference with private and family life, the likely collateral intrusion and the environmental or operational risk assessments are the same for each officer.

COVERT SURVEILLANCE OF A POTENTIAL CHIS

3.23. It may be necessary to deploy covert surveillance against a potential CHIS, other than those acting in the capacity of an undercover operative, as part of the process of assessing their suitability for recruitment, or in planning how best to make the approach to them. Covert surveillance in such circumstances may or may not be necessary on one of the statutory grounds on which directed surveillance authorisations can be granted, depending on the facts of the case. Whether or not a directed surveillance authorisation is available, any such surveillance must be justifiable under Article 8(2) of the ECHR.

USE OF COVERT HUMAN INTELLIGENCE SOURCE WITH TECHNICAL EQUIPMENT

3.24. A CHIS wearing or carrying a surveillance device does not need a separate intrusive or directed surveillance authorisation, provided the device will only be used in the presence of the CHIS. However, if a surveillance device is to be used other than in the presence of the CHIS, an intrusive or directed surveillance authorisation should be obtained where appropriate, together with an authorisation for interference with

---

[9] See section 43(2) of the 2000 Act.

property, if applicable. See the Covert Surveillance and Property Interference Code of Practice.

3.25. A CHIS, whether or not wearing or carrying a surveillance device, in residential premises or a private vehicle, does not require additional authorisation to record any activity taking place inside those premises or that vehicle which takes place in his presence. This also applies to the recording of telephone conversations or other forms of communication, other than by interception, which takes place in the source's presence. Authorisation for the use or conduct of that source may be obtained in the usual way.

OVERSIGHT OF USE OF COVERT HUMAN INTELLIGENCE
SOURCES BY LOCAL AUTHORITIES

3.26. Elected members of a local authority should review the authority's use of the 2000 Act and set the policy at least once a year. They should also consider internal reports on use of the 2000 Act on at least a quarterly basis to ensure that it is being used consistently with the local authority's policy and that the policy remains fit for purpose. They should not, however, be involved in making decisions on specific authorisations.

Chapter 4

Special considerations for authorisations

LEGALLY PRIVILEGED MATERIAL AND OTHER CONFIDENTIAL INFORMATION

4.1. The 2000 Act does not provide any special protection for "confidential information". Nevertheless, particular care should be taken in cases where the subject of the intrusion might reasonably expect a high degree of privacy, or where confidential information is involved. Confidential information consists of matters subject to legal privilege, confidential personal information, confidential constituent information or confidential journalistic material. So, for example, extra care should be taken where, through the use or conduct of a CHIS, it would be possible to acquire knowledge of discussions between a minister of religion and an individual relating to the latter's spiritual welfare, or between a Member of Parliament and a constituent relating to private constituency matters, or wherever matters of medical or journalistic confidentiality or legal privilege may be involved. References to a Member of Parliament include references to Members of both Houses of the UK Parliament, the European Parliament, the Scottish Parliament, the Welsh Assembly and the Northern Ireland Assembly.

4.2. In cases where through the use or conduct of a CHIS it is likely that knowledge of legally privileged material or other confidential information will be acquired, the deployment of the CHIS is subject to a higher level of authorisation. The Regulation of Investigatory Powers (Directed Surveillance and Covert Human Intelligence Sources) Order 2010 lists the authorising officer for each public authority permitted to authorise such use or conduct of a CHIS.

4.3. Section 98 of the 1997 Act defines those matters that are subject to legal privilege. Under this definition, legal privilege does not apply to communications or items held, or oral communications made, with the intention of furthering a criminal purpose (whether the lawyer is acting unwittingly or culpably). Legally privileged communications will lose their protection if the professional legal adviser is intending to hold or use them for a criminal purpose. But privilege is not lost if a professional legal adviser is properly advising a person who is suspected of having committed a criminal offence.

4.4. Public authorities may obtain knowledge of matters subject to legal privilege via CHIS in three scenarios: first, where the public authority responsible for the CHIS deliberately authorised the use or conduct of the CHIS in order to obtain knowledge of matters subject to legal privilege; second, where the CHIS obtains knowledge of matters subject to legal privilege through conduct incidental (within the meaning of section 26(7)(a)) to his conduct as a CHIS; and, third, where a CHIS obtains knowledge of matters subject to legal privilege where his conduct cannot properly be regarded as incidental to his conduct as a CHIS. Separate guidance is relevant to each scenario.

AUTHORISATIONS FOR THE USE OR CONDUCT OF A CHIS TO OBTAIN,
PROVIDE ACCESS TO OR DISCLOSE KNOWLEDGE OF
MATTERS SUBJECT TO LEGAL PRIVILEGE

4.5. If a public authority seeks to grant or renew an authorisation for the use or conduct of a CHIS in order to obtain, provide access to or disclose knowledge of matters subject to legal privilege, the 2010 Order will apply. The 2010 Order creates an enhanced regime of prior approval for such authorisations. The 2010 Order provides that before an authorising officer grants or renews an authorisation to which the Order applies, he must give notice to the relevant approving officer. The relevant approving officer will be the Secretary of State in the case of a member of the intelligence services, an official of the Ministry of Defence, an individual holding an office, rank or position in Her Majesty's Prison Service or the Northern Ireland Prison Service. In all other cases, the relevant approving officer will be an ordinary Surveillance Commissioner. The authorising officer is prohibited from granting or renewing an authorisation to which the 2010 Order applies until he has received confirmation in writing that the approving officer has approved the application. If the approving officer does not approve the application, the authorising officer may still grant an authorisation in respect of the use or conduct of the CHIS in question, but may not authorise the use or conduct of the CHIS to obtain, provide access to or disclose knowledge of matters subject to legal privilege.

4.6. Approving officers may only approve, and authorising officers may only authorise, the use or conduct of a CHIS to acquire knowledge of matters subject to legal privilege if they are satisfied that there are exceptional and compelling circumstances that make the authorisation necessary. Such circumstances will arise only in a very restricted range of cases, such as where there is a threat to life or limb, or to national security, and the use or conduct of a CHIS to acquire knowledge of matters subject to legal privilege is reasonably regarded as likely to yield intelligence necessary to counter the threat.

CIRCUMSTANCES IN WHICH THE OBTAINING OF KNOWLEDGE OF MATTERS
SUBJECT TO LEGAL PRIVILEGE BY A CHIS OR PUBLIC AUTHORITY IS INCIDENTAL
TO THE CONDUCT AUTHORISED IN THE AUTHORISATION

4.7. The reactive nature of the work of a CHIS, and the need for a CHIS to maintain cover, may make it necessary for a CHIS to engage in conduct which was not envisaged at the time the authorisation was granted, but which is incidental to that conduct. Such incidental conduct is regarded as properly authorised by virtue of sections 26(7)(a), 27 and 29(4) of the 2000 Act, even though it was not specified in the initial authorisation.

4.8. This is likely to occur only in exceptional circumstances, such as where the obtaining of such knowledge is necessary to protect life and limb, including in relation to the CHIS, or national security, in circumstances that were not envisaged at the time the authorisation was granted.

4.9. If any of these situations arise, the public authority should draw it to the attention of the relevant Commissioner or Inspector during his next inspection (at which the material should be made available if requested). In addition, the public authority in question should ensure that any knowledge of matters subject to legal privilege obtained through conduct incidental to the use or conduct of a CHIS specified in the authorisation is not used in law enforcement investigations or criminal prosecutions.

4.10. If it becomes apparent that it will be necessary for the CHIS to continue to obtain, provide access to or disclose knowledge of matters subject to legal privilege, the initial authorisation should be replaced by an authorisation that has been subject to the prior approval procedure set out in the 2010 Order at the earliest reasonable opportunity.

UNINTENTIONAL OBTAINING OF KNOWLEDGE OF MATTERS SUBJECT
TO LEGAL PRIVILEGE BY A CHIS

4.11. Public authorities should make every effort to avoid their CHIS unintentionally obtaining, providing access to or disclosing knowledge of matters subject to legal privilege. If a public authority assesses that a CHIS may be exposed to such knowledge unintentionally, the public authority should task the CHIS in such a way that this possibility is reduced as far as possible. When debriefing the CHIS, the public authority should make every effort to ensure that any knowledge of matters subject to legal privilege which the CHIS may have obtained is not disclosed to the public authority, unless there are exceptional and compelling circumstances that make such disclosure necessary. If, despite these steps, knowledge of matters subject to legal privilege is unintentionally disclosed to the public authority, the public authority in question should ensure that it is not used in law enforcement investigations or criminal prosecutions. Any unintentional obtaining of knowledge of matters subject to legal privilege by a public authority, together with a description of all steps taken in relation to that material, should be drawn to the attention of the relevant Commissioner or Inspector during his next inspection (at which the material should be made available if requested).

THE USE AND HANDLING OF MATERIAL SUBJECT TO LEGAL PRIVILEGE

4.12. Legally privileged information is particularly sensitive and any use or conduct of a CHIS which obtains, provides access to or discloses such material may give rise to issues under Article 6 of the ECHR (right to a fair trial) as well as engaging Article 8.

4.13. Where public authorities deliberately obtain knowledge of matters subject to legal privilege via the conduct of a CHIS, they may use it to counter the threat which led them to obtain it; but not for other purposes. In particular, public authorities should ensure that knowledge of matters subject to legal privilege is kept separate from law enforcement investigations or criminal prosecutions.

4.14. In cases likely to result in the obtaining by a public authority of knowledge of matters subject to legal privilege, the authorising officer or Surveillance Commissioner may require regular reporting so as to be able to decide whether the authorisation should continue. In those cases where knowledge of matters subject to legal privilege has been obtained and retained, the matter should be reported to the authorising officer by means of a review and to the relevant Commissioner or Inspector during his next inspection (at which the material should be made available if requested).

4.15. A substantial proportion of the communications between a lawyer and his client(s) may be subject to legal privilege. Therefore, in any case where a lawyer is the subject of an investigation or operation, authorising officers should consider whether the special safeguards outlined in this chapter apply. Any material which has been retained from any such investigation or operation should be notified to the relevant Commissioner or Inspector during his next inspection and made available on request.

4.16. Where there is any doubt as to the handling and dissemination of information which may be subject to legal privilege, advice should be sought from a legal adviser within the relevant public authority before any further dissemination of the material takes place. Similar advice should also be sought where there is doubt over whether information is not subject to legal privilege due to the "in furtherance of a criminal purpose" exception. The retention of legally privileged information, or its dissemination to an outside body, should be accompanied by a clear warning that it is subject to legal privilege. It should be safeguarded by taking reasonable steps to ensure there is no possibility of it becoming available, or its contents becoming known, to any person whose possession of it might prejudice any criminal or civil proceedings to which the information relates. Any dissemination of legally privileged material to an outside body should be notified to the relevant Commissioner or Inspector during his next inspection.

CONFIDENTIAL INFORMATION

4.17. Similar consideration must also be given to authorisations for use or conduct that are likely to result in the obtaining of confidential personal information, confidential constituent information and confidential journalistic material. Where such material has been acquired and retained, the matter should be reported to the relevant Commissioner or Inspector during his next inspection and the material be made available to him if requested.

4.18. Confidential personal information is information held in confidence relating to the physical or mental health or spiritual counselling of a person (whether living or dead) who can be identified from it.[10] Such information, which can include both oral and written communications, is held in confidence if it is held subject to an express or implied undertaking to hold it in confidence or it is subject to a restriction on disclosure or an obligation of confidentiality contained in existing legislation. Examples might include consultations between a health professional and a patient, or information from a patient's medical records.

4.19. Confidential constituent information is information held in confidence in relation to communications between a Member of Parliament and a constituent in respect of constituency matters. Again, such information is held in confidence if it is held subject to an express or implied undertaking to hold it in confidence or it is subject to a restriction on disclosure or an obligation of confidentiality contained in existing legislation.

4.20. Confidential journalistic material includes material acquired or created for the purposes of journalism and held subject to an undertaking to hold it in confidence, as well as communications resulting in information being acquired for the purposes of journalism and held subject to such an undertaking.

4.21. Where there is any doubt as to the handling and dissemination of confidential information, advice should be sought from a legal adviser, who is independent from the investigation, within the relevant public authority before any further dissemination of the material takes place. Any dissemination of confidential material to an outside body should be notified to the relevant Commissioner or Inspector during his next inspection.

Vulnerable individuals

4.22. A vulnerable individual is a person who is or may be in need of community care services by reason of mental or other disability, age or illness and who is or may be unable to take care of himself, or unable to protect himself against significant harm or exploitation. Any individual of this description should only be authorised to act as a CHIS in the most exceptional circumstances. In these cases, Annex A lists the authorising officer for each public authority permitted to authorise the use of a vulnerable individual as a CHIS.

Juvenile sources

4.23. Special safeguards also apply to the use or conduct of juveniles, that is, those under 18 years old, as sources. On no occasion should the use or conduct of a CHIS under 16 years of age be authorised to give information against his parents or any person who has parental responsibility for him. In other cases, authorisations should not be granted unless the special provisions contained within The Regulation of Investigatory Powers (Juveniles) Order 2000; SI No. 2793 are satisfied. Authorisations for juvenile sources should be granted by those listed in the attached table at Annex A.

---

[10] **Spiritual counselling** means conversations between a person and a religious authority acting in an official capacity, where the individual being counselled is seeking or the religious authority is imparting forgiveness, absolution or the resolution of conscience in accordance with their faith.

The duration of such an authorisation is one month from the time of grant or renewal (instead of twelve months). For the purpose of these rules, the age test is applied at the time of the grant or renewal of the authorisation.

SCOTLAND

4.24. Where all the conduct authorised is likely to take place in Scotland, authorisations should be granted under RIP(S)A, unless:

- the authorisation is being obtained by those public authorities listed in section 46(3) of the 2000 Act and the Regulation of Investigatory Powers (Authorisations Extending to Scotland) Order 2000; SI No. 2418;
- the authorisation is to be granted or renewed (by any relevant public authority) for the purposes of national security or the economic well-being of the UK; or
- the authorisation authorises conduct that is surveillance by virtue of section 48(4) of the 2000 Act.

4.25. This code of practice is extended to Scotland in relation to authorisations granted under Part II of the 2000 Act which apply to Scotland. A separate code of practice applies in relation to authorisations granted under RIP(S)A.

INTERNATIONAL

4.26. Authorisations under the 2000 Act can be given for the use or conduct of CHIS both inside and outside the UK. However, authorisations for actions outside the UK can usually only validate them for the purposes of UK law.

4.27. Public authorities are therefore advised to seek authorisations where available under the 2000 Act for any overseas operations where the subject of investigation is a UK national or is likely to become the subject of criminal or civil proceedings in the UK, or if the operation is likely to affect a UK national or give rise to material likely to be used in evidence before a UK court.

4.28. Public authorities must have in place internal systems to manage any overseas CHIS deployments and it is recognised practice for UK law enforcement agencies to follow the authorisation and management regime under the 2000 Act, even where such deployments are only intended to impact locally and are therefore authorised under domestic law. However, public authorities should take care to monitor such deployments to identify where civil or criminal proceedings may become a prospect in the UK and ensure that, where appropriate, an authorisation under Part II of the 2000 Act is sought if this becomes the case.

4.29. The Human Rights Act 1998 applies to all activity taking place within the UK. This should be taken to include overseas territories and facilities which are within the jurisdiction of the UK. Authorisations under the 2000 Act may therefore be appropriate for overseas covert operations occurring in UK Embassies, military bases, detention facilities, etc., in order to comply with rights to privacy under Article 8 of the ECHR.[11]

---

[11] See *R v Al Skeini* June 2007. If conduct is to take place overseas the ACPO Covert Investigation (Legislation and Guidance) Steering Group may be able to offer additional advice.

4.30. Members of foreign law enforcement or other agencies or a CHIS of those agencies may be authorised under the 2000 Act in the UK in support of domestic and international investigations.

Chapter 5

Authorisation procedures for covert human intelligence sources

AUTHORISATION CRITERIA

5.1. Under section 29(3) of the 2000 Act an authorisation for the use or conduct of a CHIS may be granted by the authorising officer where he believes that the authorisation is necessary:

- in the interests of national security;[12]
- for the purpose of preventing or detecting[13] crime or of preventing disorder;
- in the interests of the economic well-being of the UK;
- in the interests of public safety;
- for the purpose of protecting public health;[14]
- for the purpose of assessing or collecting any tax, duty, levy or other imposition, contribution or charge payable to a government department; or
- for any other purpose prescribed in an order made by the Secretary of State.[15]

5.2. The authorising officer must also believe that the authorised use or conduct of a CHIS is proportionate to what is sought to be achieved by that use or conduct.

RELEVANT PUBLIC AUTHORITIES

5.3. The public authorities entitled to authorise the use or conduct of a CHIS, together with the specific purposes for which each public authority may authorise the use or conduct of a CHIS, are laid out in Schedule 1 of the 2000 Act and the Regulation of Investigatory Powers (Directed Surveillance and Covert Human Intelligence Sources) Order 2010.

---

[12] One of the functions of the Security Service is the protection of national security and in particular the protection against threats from terrorism. These functions extend throughout the UK. An authorising officer in another public authority should not issue an authorisation under Part II of the 2000 Act where the operation or investigation falls within the responsibilities of the Security Service, as set out above, except where it is to be carried out by a Special Branch, Counter Terrorist Unit or where the Security Service has agreed that another public authority can authorise the use or conduct of a CHIS which would normally fall within the responsibilities of the Security Service. HM Forces may also undertake operations in connection with national security in support of the Security Service or other Civil Powers.

[13] Detecting crime is defined in section 81(5) of the 2000 Act. Preventing and detecting crime goes beyond the prosecution of offenders and includes actions taken to avert, end or disrupt the commission of criminal offences.

[14] This could include investigations into infectious diseases, contaminated products or the illicit sale of pharmaceuticals.

[15] This could only be for a purpose which satisfies the criteria set out in Article 8(2) of the ECHR.

AUTHORISATION PROCEDURES

5.4. Responsibility for authorising the use or conduct of a CHIS rests with the authorising officer and all authorisations require the personal authority of the authorising officer. The Regulation of Investigatory Powers (Directed Surveillance and Covert Human Intelligence Sources) Order 2010 designates the authorising officer for each different public authority and the officers entitled to act only in urgent cases. In certain circumstances the Secretary of State will be the authorising officer (see section 30(2) of the 2000 Act).

5.5. The authorising officer must give authorisations in writing, except in urgent cases, where they may be given orally. In such cases, a statement that the authorising officer has expressly authorised the action should be recorded in writing by the applicant (or the person with whom the authorising officer spoke) as a priority. This statement need not contain the full detail of the application, which should however subsequently be recorded in writing when reasonably practicable (generally the next working day).

5.6. Other officers entitled to act in urgent cases may only give authorisation in writing e.g. written authorisation for directed surveillance given by an Inspector.

5.7. A case is not normally to be regarded as urgent unless the time that would elapse before the authorising officer was available to grant the authorisation would, in the judgement of the person giving the authorisation, be likely to endanger life or jeopardise the operation or investigation for which the authorisation was being given. An authorisation is not to be regarded as urgent where the need for an authorisation has been neglected or the urgency is of the applicant's or authorising officer's own making.

5.8. Authorising officers should not be responsible for authorising their own activities, e.g. those in which they, themselves, are to act as the CHIS or as the handler of the CHIS. Furthermore, authorising officers should, where possible, be independent of the investigation. However, it is recognised that this is not always possible, especially in the cases of small organisations, or where it is necessary to act urgently or for security reasons. Where an authorising officer authorises his own activity the central record of authorisations should highlight this and the attention of a Commissioner or Inspector should be invited to it during his next inspection.

5.9. Authorising officers within the SCDEA and SOCA may only grant authorisations on application by a member of (including those formally seconded to) their own force or agency. The same rules apply to authorising officers within police forces, unless relevant Chief Officers have made collaboration agreements under section 23 of the Police Act 1996 or section 12 of the Police (Scotland) Act 1967 which permit authorising officers to grant authorisations on application from members of other forces. Authorising officers within HMRC may only grant authorisations on application by an officer of Revenue and Customs.

INFORMATION TO BE PROVIDED IN APPLICATIONS FOR AUTHORISATION

5.10. An application for authorisation for the use or conduct of a CHIS should be in writing and record:

- the reasons why the authorisation is necessary in the particular case and on the grounds listed in section 29(3) of the 2000 Act (e.g. for the purpose of preventing or detecting crime);

- the purpose for which the CHIS will be tasked or deployed (e.g. in relation to drug supply, stolen property, a series of racially motivated crimes etc.);
- where a specific investigation or operation is involved, the nature of that investigation or operation;
- the nature of what the CHIS conduct will be;
- the details of any potential collateral intrusion and why the intrusion is justified;
- the details of any confidential information that is likely to be obtained as a consequence of the authorisation;
- the reasons why the authorisation is considered proportionate to what it seeks to achieve;
- the level of authorisation required (or recommended, where that is different); and
- a subsequent record of whether authorisation was given or refused, by whom and the time and date.

5.11. Additionally, in urgent cases, the authorisation should record (as the case may be):

- the reasons why the authorising officer considered the case so urgent that an oral instead of a written authorisation was given; or
- the reasons why the officer entitled to act in urgent cases considered the case so urgent and why it was not reasonably practicable for the application to be considered by the authorising officer.

5.12. Where the authorisation is oral, the detail referred to above should be recorded in writing by the applicant when reasonably practicable (generally the next working day).

Duration of authorisations

5.13. A written authorisation will, unless renewed, cease to have effect at the end of a period of twelve months beginning with the day on which it took effect, except in the case of a juvenile CHIS.

5.14. Urgent oral authorisations or authorisations granted or renewed by a person who is entitled to act only in urgent cases will, unless renewed, cease to have effect after seventy-two hours, beginning with the time when the authorisation was granted.

Reviews

5.15. Regular reviews of authorisations should be undertaken by the authorising officer to assess whether it remains necessary and proportionate to use a CHIS and whether the authorisation remains justified. The review should include the use made of the CHIS during the period authorised, the tasks given to the CHIS and the information obtained from the CHIS. The results of a review should be retained for at least three years (see chapter 7). Particular attention is drawn to the need to review authorisations frequently where the use of a CHIS provides access to confidential information or involves significant collateral intrusion.

5.16. In each case the authorising officer within each public authority should determine how often a review should take place. This should be as frequently as is considered necessary and practicable, but should not prevent reviews being conducted in response to changing circumstances.

RENEWALS

5.17. Before an authorising officer renews an authorisation, he must be satisfied that a review has been carried out of the use of a CHIS, as outlined above, and that the results of the review have been considered.

5.18. If, before an authorisation would cease to have effect, the authorising officer considers it necessary for the authorisation to continue for the purpose for which it was given, he may renew it in writing for a further period of twelve months. Renewals may also be granted orally in urgent cases and last for a period of seventy-two hours.

5.19. A renewal takes effect at the time at which the authorisation would have ceased to have effect but for the renewal. An application for renewal should therefore not be made until shortly before the authorisation period is drawing to an end.

5.20. Any person who would be entitled to grant a new authorisation can renew an authorisation. However, where possible the authorising officer who granted the original authorisation should consider the renewal.

5.21. Authorisations may be renewed more than once, if necessary, provided they continue to meet the criteria for authorisation. Documentation of the renewal should be retained for at least three years (see Chapter 7).

5.22. All applications for the renewal of an authorisation should record:

- whether this is the first renewal or every occasion on which the authorisation has been renewed previously;
- any significant changes to the information in the initial application;
- the reasons why it is necessary for the authorisation to continue;
- the use made of the CHIS in the period since the grant or, as the case may be, latest renewal of the authorisation;
- the tasks given to the CHIS during that period and the information obtained from the use or conduct of the CHIS; and
- the results of regular reviews of the use of the CHIS.

CANCELLATIONS

5.23. The authorising officer who granted or renewed the authorisation must cancel it if he is satisfied that the use or conduct of the CHIS no longer satisfies the criteria for authorisation or that arrangements for the CHIS's case no longer satisfy the requirements described in section 29 of the 2000 Act. Where the authorising officer is no longer available, this duty will fall on the person who has taken over the role of authorising officer or the person who is acting as authorising officer.

5.24. Where necessary, the safety and welfare of the CHIS should continue to be taken into account after the authorisation has been cancelled.

Chapter 6

Management of covert human intelligence sources

TASKING

6.1. Tasking is the assignment given to the CHIS by the persons defined at section 29(5)(a) and (b) of the 2000 Act, asking him to obtain, provide access to or disclose information. Authorisation for the use or conduct of a CHIS will be appropriate prior to any tasking where such tasking involves the CHIS establishing or maintaining a personal or other relationship for a covert purpose.

6.2. Authorisations should not be drawn so narrowly that a separate authorisation is required each time the CHIS is tasked. Rather, an authorisation might cover, in broad terms, the nature of the source's task. If the nature of the task changes significantly, then a new authorisation may need to be sought.

6.3. It is difficult to predict exactly what might occur each time a meeting with a CHIS takes place, or the CHIS meets the subject of an investigation. There may be occasions when unforeseen action or undertakings occur. When this happens, the occurrence must be recorded as soon as practicable after the event and if the existing authorisation is insufficient it should either be updated at a review (for minor amendments only) or it should be cancelled and a new authorisation should be obtained before any further such action is carried out.

6.4. Similarly, where it is intended to task a CHIS in a significantly greater or different way than previously identified, the persons defined at section 29(5)(a) or (b) of the 2000 Act must refer the proposed tasking to the authorising officer, who should consider whether the existing authorisation is sufficient or needs to be replaced. This should be done in advance of any tasking and the details of such referrals must be recorded. Efforts should be made to minimise the number of authorisations per CHIS to the minimum necessary in order to avoid generating excessive paperwork.

HANDLERS AND CONTROLLERS

6.5. Public authorities should ensure that arrangements are in place for the proper oversight and management of CHIS, including appointing individual officers as defined in section 29(5)(a) and (b) of the 2000 Act for each CHIS.

6.6. Oversight and management arrangements for undercover operatives, while following the principles of the Act, will differ, in order to reflect the specific role of such individuals as members of public authorities.

6.7. The person referred to in section 29(5)(a) of the 2000 Act (the "handler") will have day to day responsibility for:

- dealing with the CHIS on behalf of the authority concerned;
- directing the day to day activities of the CHIS;
- recording the information supplied by the CHIS; and monitoring the CHIS's security and welfare.

6.8. The handler of a CHIS will usually be of a rank or position below that of the authorising officer.

6.9. The person referred to in section 29(5)(b) of the 2000 Act (the "controller") will normally be responsible for the management and supervision of the "handler" and general oversight of the use of the CHIS.

JOINT WORKING

6.10. In cases where the authorisation is for the use or conduct of a CHIS whose activities benefit more than a single public authority, responsibilities for the management and oversight of that CHIS may be taken up by one authority or can be split between the authorities. The controller and handler of a CHIS need not be from the same public authority.

6.11. There are many cases where the activities of a CHIS may provide benefit to more than a single public authority. Such cases may include:

- The prevention or detection of criminal matters affecting a national or regional area, for example where the CHIS provides information relating to cross boundary or international drug trafficking;
- The prevention or detection of criminal matters affecting crime and disorder, requiring joint agency operational activity, for example where a CHIS provides information relating to environmental health issues and offences of criminal damage, in a joint police/local authority anti-social behaviour operation on a housing estate;
- Matters of national security, for example where the CHIS provides information relating to terrorist activity and associated criminal offences for the benefit of the police and the Security Service.

6.12. In such situations, however, the public authorities involved must lay out in writing their agreed oversight arrangements.

6.13. Management responsibility for CHIS, and relevant roles, may also be divided between different police forces where the Chief Officers of the forces concerned have made a collaboration agreement under section 23 of the Police Act 1996 or section 12 of the Police (Scotland) Act 1967, and the collaboration agreement provides for this to happen.

SECURITY AND WELFARE

6.14. Any public authority deploying a CHIS should take into account the safety and welfare of that CHIS when carrying out actions in relation to an authorisation or tasking, and the foreseeable consequences to others of that tasking. Before authorising the use or conduct of a CHIS, the authorising officer should ensure that a risk assessment is carried out to determine the risk to the CHIS of any tasking and the likely consequences should the role of the CHIS become known. The ongoing security and welfare of the CHIS, after the cancellation of the authorisation, should also be considered at the outset. Also, consideration should be given to the management of any requirement to disclose information tending to reveal the existence or identity of a CHIS to, or in, court.

6.15. The CHIS handler is responsible for bringing to the attention of the CHIS controller any concerns about the personal circumstances of the CHIS, insofar as they might affect:

- the validity of the risk assessment;

- the conduct of the CHIS; and
- the safety and welfare of the CHIS.

6.16. Where appropriate, concerns about such matters must be considered by the authorising officer, and a decision taken on whether or not to allow the authorisation to continue.

Chapter 7

Keeping of records

CENTRALLY RETRIEVABLE RECORD OF AUTHORISATIONS

7.1. A centrally retrievable record of all authorisations should be held by each public authority. These records need only contain the name, code name, or unique identifying reference of the CHIS, the date the authorisation was granted, renewed or cancelled and an indication as to whether the activities were self-authorised. These records should be updated whenever an authorisation is granted, renewed or cancelled and should be made available to the relevant Commissioner or an Inspector from the Office of Surveillance Commissioners upon request. These records should be retained for a period of at least three years from the ending of the authorisations to which they relate.

7.2. While retaining such records for the time stipulated, public authorities must take into consideration the duty of care to the CHIS, the likelihood of future criminal or civil proceedings relating to information supplied by the CHIS or activities undertaken, and specific rules relating to data retention, review and deletion under the Data Protection Act and, where applicable, the Code of Practice on the Management of Police Information.

INDIVIDUAL RECORDS OF AUTHORISATION AND USE OF CHIS

7.3. Detailed records must be kept of the authorisation and use made of a CHIS. Section 29(5) of the 2000 Act provides that an authorising officer must not grant an authorisation for the use or conduct of a CHIS unless he believes that there are arrangements in place for ensuring that there is at all times a person with the responsibility for maintaining a record of the use made of the CHIS. The Regulation of Investigatory Powers (Source Records) Regulations 2000; SI No: 2725 details the particulars that must be included in these records.

7.4. Public authorities are encouraged to consider maintaining such records also for human sources who do not meet the definition of a CHIS. This may assist authorities to monitor the status of a human source and identify whether that source becomes a CHIS.

FURTHER DOCUMENTATION

7.5. In addition, records or copies of the following, as appropriate, should be kept by the relevant authority for at least three years:

- a copy of the authorisation together with any supplementary documentation and notification of the approval given by the authorising officer;

- a copy of any renewal of an authorisation, together with the supporting documentation submitted when the renewal was requested;
- the reason why the person renewing an authorisation considered it necessary to do so;
- any authorisation which was granted or renewed orally (in an urgent case) and the reason why the case was considered urgent;
- any risk assessment made in relation to the CHIS;
- the circumstances in which tasks were given to the CHIS;
- the value of the CHIS to the investigating authority;
- a record of the results of any reviews of the authorisation;
- the reasons, if any, for not renewing an authorisation;
- the reasons for cancelling an authorisation; and
- the date and time when any instruction was given by the authorising officer that the conduct or use of a CHIS must cease.

7.6. The records kept by public authorities should be maintained in such a way as to preserve the confidentiality, or prevent disclosure of the identity of the CHIS, and the information provided by that CHIS.

Chapter 8

Handling of material

RETENTION AND DESTRUCTION OF MATERIAL

8.1. Each public authority must ensure that arrangements are in place for the secure handling, storage and destruction of material obtained through the use or conduct of a CHIS. Authorising officers must ensure compliance with the appropriate data protection requirements under the Data Protection Act 1998 and any relevant codes of practice produced by individual authorities relating to the handling and storage of material.

8.2. Where the product of the use or conduct of a CHIS could be relevant to pending or future criminal or civil proceedings, it should be retained in accordance with applicable disclosure requirements.

8.3. Subject to the provisions in Chapter 4 above, there is nothing in the 2000 Act or this Code of Practice which prevents material obtained from authorisations for the use or conduct of a CHIS for a particular purpose from being used to further other purposes.

LAW ENFORCEMENT AGENCIES

8.4. In the cases of the law enforcement agencies, particular attention is drawn to the requirements of the code of practice issued under the Criminal Procedure and Investigations Act 1996. This requires that material which is obtained in the course of a criminal investigation and which may be relevant to the investigation must be recorded and retained.

The intelligence services, MOD and HM Forces

8.5. The heads of these agencies are responsible for ensuring that arrangements exist to make sure that no information is stored by the authorities, except as necessary for the proper discharge of their functions. They are also responsible for arrangements to control onward disclosure. For the intelligence services, this is a statutory duty under the 1989 Act and the 1994 Act.

8.6. With regard to the service police forces (the Royal Navy Police, the Royal Military Police and the Royal Air Force Police), particular attention is drawn to the Criminal Procedure and Investigations Act 1996 (Code of Practice) (Armed Forces) Order 2008, which requires that the investigator retain all material obtained in a service investigation which may be relevant to the investigation.

Use of material as evidence

8.7. Subject to the provisions in Chapter 4 above, material obtained from a CHIS may be used as evidence in criminal proceedings.[16] The admissibility of evidence is governed by the common law, the Civil Procedure Rules, section 78 of the Police and Criminal Evidence Act 1984[17] and the Human Rights Act 1998. Whilst this code does not affect the application of those rules, obtaining appropriate authorisations should help ensure the admissibility of evidence derived from CHIS.

8.8. Product obtained by a CHIS is subject to the ordinary rules for retention and disclosure of material under the Criminal Procedure and Investigations Act 1996, where those rules apply to the law enforcement body in question.

8.9. There are also well-established legal procedures under public interest immunity provisions that can be applied when seeking to protect the identity of a source from disclosure in such circumstances.

Chapter 9

Senior responsible officers and oversight by Commissioners

The senior responsible officer

9.1. Within every relevant public authority a senior responsible officer must be responsible for:

- the integrity of the process in place within the public authority for the management of CHIS;
- compliance with Part II of the Act and with this code;
- oversight of the reporting of errors to the relevant oversight Commissioner and the identification of both the cause(s) of errors and the implementation of processes to minimise repetition of errors;

---

[16] Whether these proceedings are brought by the public authority that obtained the authorisation or by another public authority (subject to handling arrangements agreed between the authorities).

[17] And section 76 of the Police & Criminal Evidence (Northern Ireland) Order 1989.

- engagement with the OSC inspectors when they conduct their inspections, where applicable; and
- where necessary, oversight of the implementation of post inspection action plans approved by the relevant oversight Commissioner.

9.2. Within local authorities, the senior responsible officer should be a member of the corporate leadership team and should be responsible for ensuring that all authorising officers are of an appropriate standard in light of any recommendations in the inspection reports prepared by the Office of Surveillance Commissioners. Where an inspection report highlights concerns about the standards of authorising officers, this individual will be responsible for ensuring the concerns are addressed.

OVERSIGHT BY COMMISSIONERS

9.3. The 2000 Act requires the Chief Surveillance Commissioner to keep under review (with the assistance of the Surveillance Commissioners and Assistant Surveillance Commissioners) the performance of functions under Part III of the 1997 Act and Part II of the 2000 Act by the police (including the service police forces, the Ministry of Defence Police and the British Transport Police), SOCA, SCDEA, HMRC and the other public authorities listed in Schedule 1 of the 2000 Act and the Regulation of Investigatory Powers (Directed Surveillance and Covert Human Intelligence Sources) Order 2010, and in Northern Ireland officials of the Ministry of Defence and HM Forces.

9.4. The Intelligence Services Commissioner's remit is to provide independent oversight of the use of Part II of the 2000 Act and the 1994 Act by the Security Service, Secret Intelligence Service, GCHQ and the Ministry of Defence and HM Forces (excluding the service police forces, and in Northern Ireland officials of the Ministry of Defence and HM Forces).

9.5. This code does not cover the exercise of any of the Commissioners' functions. It is the duty of any person who uses Part II of RIPA to comply with any request made by a Commissioner to disclose or provide any information he requires for the purpose of enabling him to carry out his functions.

9.6. References in this code to the performance of review functions by the Chief Surveillance Commissioner and other Commissioners apply also to Inspectors and other members of staff to whom such functions have been delegated.

9.7. Reports made by the Commissioners concerning the inspection of public authorities and their exercise and performance of powers under Part II may be made available by the Commissioners to the Home Office to promulgate good practice and help identify training requirements within public authorities.

9.8. Subject to the approval of the relevant Commissioner public authorities may publish their inspection reports, in full or in summary, to demonstrate both the oversight to which they are subject and their compliance with Part II of the Act and this code. Approval should be sought on a case by case basis at least 10 working days prior to intended publication, stating whether the report is to be published in full, and if not stating which parts are to be published or how it is to be summarised.

Chapter 10

Complaints

10.1. The 2000 Act establishes an independent Tribunal. This Tribunal will be made up of senior members of the judiciary and the legal profession and is independent of the Government. The Tribunal has full powers to investigate and decide any case within its jurisdiction. This code does not cover the exercise of the Tribunal's functions. Details of the relevant complaints procedure can be obtained from the following address:

Investigatory Powers Tribunal
PO Box 33220
London
SWIH 9ZQ
Tel: 020 7035 3711

Annex A

Authorisation levels when knowledge of confidential information is likely to be acquired or when a vulnerable individual or juvenile is to be used as a source.

Relevant Public Authority	Authorisation level for when knowledge of Confidential Information is likely to be acquired	Authorisation level for when a vulnerable individual or a juvenile is to be used as a source
Police forces		
Any police force maintained under section 2 of the Police Act 1996 (police forces in England and Wales outside London)	Chief Constable	Assistant Chief Constable
Any police force maintained under or by virtue of section 1 of the Police (Scotland) Act 1967	Chief Constable	Assistant Chief Constable
The Metropolitan Police force	Assistant Commissioner	Commander
The City of London Police force	Assistant Commissioner	Commander
The Police Service of Northern Ireland	Deputy Chief Constable	Assistant Chief Constable
The Ministry of Defence Police	Chief Constable	Assistant Chief Constable
The Royal Navy Police	Provost Marshal	Provost Marshal
The Royal Military Police	Provost Marshal	Provost Marshal
The Royal Air Force Police	Provost Marshal	Provost Marshal
SOCA	Deputy Director	Deputy Director

The SFO	A Member of the Senior Civil Service or Head of Domain	A Member of the Senior Civil Service or Head of Domain
The Intelligence Services		
The Security Service (MI5)	Deputy Director General	Deputy Director General
The Secret Intelligence Service (MI6)	A Director of the Secret Intelligence Service	A member of the Secret Intelligence Service not below the equivalent rank to that of a Grade 5 in the Home Civil Service
The Government Communications Headquarters	A Director of GCHQ	A Director of GCHQ
HM Forces		
The Royal Navy	Rear Admiral	Rear Admiral
The Army	Major General	Major General
The Royal Air Force	Air Vice-Marshal	Air Vice-Marshal
The Commissioners for HM Revenue and Customs	Director of Investigation, or Regional Heads of Investigation	Grade 7 (Intelligence)
The Department for Environment, Food and Rural Affairs:		
DEFRA Investigation Services	Head of DEFRA Investigation Services	Head of DEFRA Investigation Services
Marine and Fisheries Agency	Head of DEFRA Prosecution Service	
Centre for Environment, Fisheries & Aquaculture Science	Head of DEFRA Prosecution Service	Head of DEFRA Prosecution Service
The Department of Health:		
The Medicines & Healthcare Products Regulatory Agency	Chief Executive	Head of Division for Inspection and Enforcement
The Home Office:		
The UK Border Agency	Strategic Director of the UK Border Agency, or (in his/her absence) Director of the UK Border Agency Intelligence Directorate	Strategic Director of the UK Border Agency
The Ministry of Justice	Chief Operating Officer in the National Offender Management Service	A member of the Senior Civil Service in the National Offender Management Service not below the equivalent rank of a Grade 5 in the Home Civil Service

The Northern Ireland Office:		
The Northern Ireland Prison Service	Director or Deputy Director Operations in the Northern Ireland Prison Service	Director or Deputy Director Operations in the Northern Ireland Prison Service
The Department of Business, Innovation and Skills:	The Director of Legal Services A	The Director of Legal Services A
The Welsh Assembly Government	Head of Department for Health & Social Services, Head of Department for Health & Social Services Finance, Head of Rural Payments Division, Regional Director or equivalent grade in the Care & Social Services Inspectorate for Wales	Head of Department for Health & Social Services, Head of Department for Health & Social Services Finance, Head of Rural Payments Division, Regional Director or equivalent grade in the Care & Social Services Inspectorate for Wales
Any county council or district council in England, a London borough council, the Common Council of the City of London in its capacity as a local authority, the Council of the Isles of Scilly, and any county council or borough council in Wales	The Head of Paid Service, or (in his absence) the person acting as the Head of Paid Service	The Head of Paid Service, or (in his absence) the person acting as the Head of Paid Service
The Environment Agency	Chief Executive of the Environment Agency	Executive Manager in the Environment Agency
The Financial Services Authority	Chairman of the Financial Services Authority	Chairman of the Financial Services Authority
The Food Standards Agency	Head of Group, or Deputy Chief Executive or Chief Executive of the Food Standards Agency	Head of Group, or Deputy Chief Executive or Chief Executive of the Food Standards Agency
The Gambling Commission		Chief Executive
The Health and Safety Executive	Director of Field Operations, or Director of Hazardous Installations Directorate, or Her Majesty's Chief Inspector of Nuclear Installations	Director of Field Operations, or Director of Hazardous Installations Directorate, or Her Majesty's Chief Inspector of Nuclear Installations

Index